Published by

Swami Sarvabhutananda
Secretary
Ramakrishna Mission Institute of Culture
Gol Park, Kolkata-700 029, India

First published in 1991
Third reprint : June 2009

Price : Rupees one hundred and sixty only

ISBN 81-87332-43-3

Printed at

Pelican Press
85 B. B. Ganguly Street
Kolkata 700012

SOCIAL PHILOSOPHY OF SWAMI VIVEKANANDA

Santwana Dasgupta

THE RAMAKRISHNA MISSION
INSTITUTE OF CULTURE
GOL PARK, KOLKATA 700 029

Dedicated to the sacred memories of

Srimat Swami Abhayanandaji Maharaj
Srimat Swami Omkaranandaji Maharaj
Srimat Swami Vimuktanandaji Maharaj
Srimat Swami Vasudevanandaji Maharaj
of the Ramakrishna Mission;
Professor Benoy Kumar Sarkar,
renowned economist and sociologist;
Sri Manada Shankar Dasgupta (my father),
biographer of Sri Ramakrishna, Swami Vivekananda,
and Holy Mother Sri Sarada Devi

—all of whom inspired me to discover
Vivekananda for myself.

FOREWORD

Miss Santwana Dasgupta has closely studied Swami Vivekananda's thoughts on sociology and has also written profusely on the subject. On her retirement from teaching as Head of the Department of Economics at Bethune College, Calcutta, she has spent the last two years or so studying the subject more intensely. As the readers will see, she is now convinced more than ever that the social model advocated by Swami Vivekananda is by far the best. She analyses other better known models and points out where they err. The point she tries to make is that the problem of man is basically spiritual and it is at that level that man has to undergo a revolutionary change. This does not preclude social and economic changes. They are welcome, but they do not go far enough. Something drastic is needed. This is where Vedanta comes in. It is only Vedanta that gives man his total emancipation. Anything short of that does not satisfy him.

One may or may not agree with Miss Dasgupta's contentions, but that she makes a good point no one will dispute. The book deserves serious notice not from sociologists alone but from all thoughtful persons.

January 12, 1991 — Swami Lokeswarananda

The Ramakrishna Mission
Institute of Culture
Gol Park, Calcutta 700 029

PUBLISHER'S NOTE

Like many of her classmates, the young Santwana Dasgupta (1922-1999) was deeply stirred by Professor Benoy Kumar Sarkar's revolutionary ideas about Swami Vivekananda, presented with his great erudition and elocution. But unlike her classmates, Santwana, who was then a postgraduate student, could not readily accept her respected teacher's conclusion that Vivekananda's socialism was not scientific and that he was a romantic socialist. What began as embers flared into a conflagration as she proceeded with her comprehensive study of Vivekananda's social, political, economic, historical, and cultural ideas. By the time she retired as the Head of the Department of Economics at Bethune College, Kolkata, she firmly believed that Swamiji had given us 'a comprehensive social philosophy of everlasting value, built on the strong foundations of Vedanta'. Her lifelong research bore fruit with her magnum opus entitled *Vivekananda, the Prophet of Human Emancipation*, published in 1991.

The first edition was well received by scholars and serious readers and was quickly out of print. Her sister Smt. Vijaya Dasgupta, publisher of the volume, then approached us to republish it. We welcomed her proposal. However, we have chosen a new title for the volume, *Social Philosophy of Swami Vivekananda*, befitting the subject matter that has been dealt with so ardently by Professor Dasgupta.

The book is as relevant now—if not more so—than when it was first published. I believe the great Swami's vibrant and thought-provoking ideas will have an impact on all serious readers, particularly young men and women.

October 3, 2005 Swami Prabhananda

Contents

'*Unselfishness is God.* One may live on a throne, in a golden palace, and be perfectly unselfish; and then he is in God. Another may live in a hut and wear rags, and have nothing in the world; yet, if he is selfish, he is intensely merged in the world.'

PREFACE

I

As a young student at the school level I was first introduced to the Ramakrishna-Vivekananda literature by my parents, both of whom were direct disciples of the Holy Mother Sri Sarada Devi. And when I was a post-graduate student at the Calcutta University during the early forties, I had the very good fortune of having Professor Benoy Kumar Sarkar, the renowned Indian economist and sociologist, as my teacher. He made Swami Vivekananda and his revolutionary spirit and the revolutionary import of his fiery message for future social transformation, living in his class lectures with his exceptional capacity of erudition and elocution.

One day my father drew my attention to two most remarkable lectures of Swami Vivekananda, viz., 'Vedanta and Privilege' and 'Privilege' (*Complete Works of Swami Vivekananda*, Vol. I), which contained the essence of Vivekananda's Social Philosophy. I was deeply impressed and henceforth drawn to read intensively Vivekananda's writings in which I found a new world of illuminating ideas and I was excitingly absorbed in it.

But on another day my teacher, Professor Sarkar, knocked me out of my world of exciting absorption and mental delight when he stated in his class that 'Vivekananda was the father of socialism in India but his socialism was not scientific, he was a romantic socialist.' I could not agree with my learned professor since whenever I studied Vivekananda, what struck me most was the wonderful rationality and scientific character of his thought. I protested but when my revered teacher demanded supporting arguments, I could not supply them with my the then very limited knowledge of Vivekananda, modern science and scientific socialism. I was very unhappy, restless and did not know what to do, losing completely my mental peace for days and months together.

Then one day, after a year or two, when my student days were over, at a public meeting, which both of us went to attend,

Professor Sarkar introduced me to a little brochure with the heading 'The Social Philosophy of Swami Vivekananda' and its author Sri Trilochan Das, one of his former students. A glance through the brochure made it clear that it was a repetition of the views of Dr Sarkar, viz., that Vivekananda was a romanic and not a scientific socialist. I decided at once to carry on investigations myself to find out whether Vivekananda's social philosophy had a scientific basis or not.

Now, Professor Sarkar loved to see his students disagreeing with him and making independent investigations and establishing independent views. No doubt such a teacher is rarely to be found. He wanted me to make independent enquiries and discover Vivekananda for myself and not to repeat his opinions merely. Thus Professor Sarkar led me to the path of carrying on life-long researches on Vivekananda and be blessed by the exhilarating experience of being merged in the ocean of the wonderful thoughts of the great prophet and master-mind all my life. With a sense of deep respect and indebtedness I remember my departed teacher today.

Towards the late forties my first article on Vivekananda entiled 'Vivekananda Sāmyavād' was published in the Bengali journal *Taruṇer Swapna* at the initiative of its editor Smt. Malavika Dutta. My next article on social changes was published in *Udbodhan* by Swami Shraddhananda, the then editor of the paper. Towards the end of the fifties my articles on 'Vivekanander Samājtantravād' was serially published in *Udbodhan*, the Bengali organ of the Ramakrishna Order. And when Vivekananda Centenary Celebration was near at hand, I was persuaded by Swami Niramayananda, the then editor of *Udbodhan*, to get the whole thing published in the form of a book. And Sri Suresh Das, of General Printers and Publishers, offering to publish it, the book came out in 1963 with a new title —*Vivekanander Samāj-Darśan*.

On January 1, 1964, Swami Sambuddhanandaji, Secretary, Vivekananda Centenary Committee, persuaded me to read a paper on 'Vedanta and the Social Philosophy of Swami Vivekananda' at the day's session of the weak-long Parliament of Religions, that were being held in Calcutta at the time to observe the birth centenary of Swami Vivekananda. The paper was highly appreciated and was later on published in the *Parliament of Religions 1963-64* by the Centenary Committee.

In 1969 I was invited to contribute to an anthology named *Bases of Indian Culture* by the Swami Abhedananda Centenary Committee, Ramakrishna Vedanta Math, Calcutta, and my contribution to it was published under the title 'Socio-Religious Views of Swami Vivekananda'. In 1976 The Ramakrishna Mission Institute of Culture published an anthology (in Bengali) of research-oriented papers on Swami Vivekananda under the title *Chintānāyak Vivekananda* in which I contributed an article entitled 'Vivekananda Samājdarśane Rāṣtranaitik O Arthanaitik Chintā' at the request of the Institute. In 1979 I was invited by the same Institute to contribute another article on 'The Political and Economic Ideas of Swami Vivekananda' for its proposed publication on the history of the Indian Renaissance which I readily wrote and submitted. The book is yet to be publised. In November 1981 I was invited by the Institute to deliver two lectures under the Kashi-Saudamini endowment lecture scheme on 'The Humanism of Swami Vivekananda'. These lectures were published serially in the *Bulletin* of the Ramakrishna Mission Institute of Culture in 1982 in its January to April issues.

Now, all these efforts spread over more than four decades, have gradually resulted in the development of the present book. In 1987 I was granted a research fellowship by the Ramakrishna Mission Institute of Culture to enable me to complete my book which was then more than half-way through.

II

When my first series of articles appeared in *Udbodhan*, there was practically no work on the social philosophy or social ideas of Swami Vivekananda besides Professor Sarkar's own brochure on 'The Might of Man in the Social Philosophy of Ramakrishna-Vivekananda' and a few more stray remarks from him here and there, the brochure of Sri Trilochan Das, and a small book *Vivekananda Samājtantravād* by Swami Sundarananda. None of these, however, is a systematic study of the comprehensive social philosophy of the great prophet, philosopher and apostle of activism. Hence I had to do all the laborious pioneering work which was not an easy task in view of the fact that Vivekananda's thoughts were scattered all over the 8 volumes of his *Complete Works*. To collect them without leaving out any of the important thought on the matter, to arrange them in proper order, interpreting them to find out the connecting links, was really a stupendous task demanding high degree of tenacity, courage, sincerity, capacity of understanding and concentration lasting over the years. These and such other sterling qualities of head and heart I hardly had in me. I carried on, however, being motivated by the sheer joy of discovering Vivekananda. All the time I was aware that I was not to impose any of my own ideas or prejudices while interpreting Vivekananda. This made the task more difficult and a real fiery ordeal. And when I saw my first publication in print (in Bengali (1963), I was very happy that I could accomplish it. Long afterwards, in 1987, I was awarded the Nivedita Prize by the Howrah Ramakrishna-Vivekananda Ashrama, financed by the Ananda Bazar Patrika Ltd., for doing this pioneering work.

Two outstanding scholars also have made very important contributions to the field. They are Dr Rabindra Kumar DasGupta in his brochure on 'The Revolutionary Ideas of Swami Vivekananda' and in his lectures published in the *Bulletin* of the Ramakrishna Mission Institute of Culture under the title 'Vedanta Socialism of Swami Vivekananda', and Professor Sankari Prasad Basu in his monumental work *Vivekananda O Samakālīn Bhāratvarṣa*, divided into seven volumes. These two outstanding scholars, of course, have recognized in their works my humble contribution to the field.

E. P. Chelishev of Soviet Rusia in an article on 'The Great Indian Humanist, Democrat and Patriot' in the *Vivekananda Centenary Memorial Volume* has made a very illuminating study on the subject. Of course, of greatest help to any research worker is the most outstanding work of rare scholarship by Marie Louise Burke—*Swami Vivekananda in the West—New Discoveries* in six volumes. It is a source book which has been of immense help to me in my journey towards discovering Vivekananda's social philosophy. I express my indebtedness to all these outstanding scholars.

In spite of the fact that large number of books on the subject have come out during all these years, there is still scope for adding some more since Vivekananda is a very vast subject, almost an inexhaustible mine of golden thoughts. My present book prepared bit by bit over the years is in no respect a repetition of what have been already stated. Besides, my approach is quite different. I do not think that Swamiji has given a few stray thoughts on social reform. I firmly believe that he has given us a comprehensive social philosophy of everlasting value built on the strong foundation of Vedanta. I have made an attempt to present this comprehensive social philosophy of Swami Vivekananda in my humble study.

III

The book is divided into eight parts.

Part I is devoted to the study of the background philosophy of Vedanta as interpreted by Vivekananda with its revolutionary significance for society. The great significance of the convergence of Science and Vedanta for society has also been dealt with in this section. To avoid misinterpretation scientists' views have been given in their own languages as far as practicable. In this part the revolutionary concepts of 'man' and 'religion' as conceived by Vivekananda have also been dealt with.

Part II deals with the historical ideas of Vivekananda, giving in detail the main trends of his investigations and his startling findings. Many are not aware of the depth of his historical investigations. An attempt has been made here to give an idea about it.

His most original sociological ideas—concept of society—its functions and laws of social evolution have been dealt with in part III. It has been pointed out that his concepts of 'involution' and 'immanent change' have revolutionized the theory of social evolution.

Part IV deals with his most original and revolutionary political concepts, the concepts of 'State', 'Government', 'Liberty', 'Equality', 'Rights', 'Revolution', 'Democracy', 'Socialism', 'Nationalism', and 'Internationalism'. It has been shown that socialism has been integrated with democracy, individual liberty and bedrocked on the 'Universal-Science-Religion' by Swami Vivekananda. The changes in the concept of socialism that are taking place to-day have made it free from the moorings of Leninism and Stalinism and even of Marxism to a considerable extent. It has been shown here that the concept is now much more akin to Vivekananda's concept.

Part V deals with his economic ideas. Little is known today about the fact that Vivekananda, a man of religion, had very good knowledge of economics, both theoretical and practical. It has been shown also that he was in fact one of the most notable thinker of the nineteenth century India in the field, making important contributions towards solving India's problem of poverty and under-development and his ideas on development bear similarities with the ideas of some of the modern development economists. It has been shown that he was the only nineteenth century Indian thinker who had a clear understanding of the world background of Indian economic maladies, viz., of capitalism, imperialism and colonialism and he was the lone person in India at the time to raise his voice against colonial exploitation and against imperialism as such.

Recently, the two major socialist countries Russia and China, are taking a good deal of interest in the wholesome thoughts of Ramakrishna and Vivekananda. They have even hailed them as the 'prophets of human emancipation, of peace and amity'. An assessment of their views and studies have been attempted in Part VI.

Part VII deals with Vivekananda's illuminating ideas on the emancipation of the women and the people. An assessment of the constructive activities of the Ramakrishna Mission, founded by him in 1897, towards fulfilling his mission, has also been attempted in this part. Of course, the growing volume of the book to an alarming proportion has prevented me from doing it more fully. It contains a chapter on Vivekananda's illuminating thoughts on education under the caption 'Education as an instrument of Social Revolution' and another on 'Vivekananda's contributions to the socio-economic and cultural transformations in India'. These chapters are a sort of summarization of the previous chapters relating to the topic.

Part VIII contains an epilogue with the conclusions :

(1) that his ideas are epoch-making and are silently working to build up the 'City of Mankind';

(2) that his ideas shall for ever be a source of inspiration to the dispossessed, oppressed and the disinherited for the redemption of their birth-rights;

(3) and that he is truly the prophet of human emancipation who has worked untiringly all his life to secure emancipation of the humanity from every kind of fetters put by nature, by society, by other institutions, by blind faith,dogmas and doctrines;

(4) that his gospel is the gospel of *śakti*, of manliness, of dynamism which would sustain mankind eternally through the struggles towards emancipation and liberation.

IV

I do not know how to express my indebtedness and gratitude to Swami Lokeswaranandaji Maharaj, the Secretary of the Ramakrishna Mission Institute of Culture, who constantly encouraged me and inspired me with a word of appreciation whenever I met him in the early days of my Vivekananda studies when my first articles appeared in *Udbodhan*. He was at the time building up the wonderful educational complex at Narendrapur near Calcutta. Actually he made me to carry on my investigations and write major portions of the book by asking me to write for *Chintānāyak Vivekananda* and for the proposed History of Indian Renaissance. And when I approached him for a research fellowship of the Institute in 1987 he very kindly granted it readily. But for this assistance and financial support, the library facilities, etc., that go with the fellowship, it would never have been possible for me, a retired person, to complete the book, which had by this time grown in volume, and get it published in these days of high and continuously escalating cost.Though these days he is very busy with the activities of the Ramakrishna-Vivekananda Movement and moving about all over the world, he has very kindly written the foreward. I convey my deepest respect to him.

I had the blessings also and words of appreciation from personalities like Swami Gambhiranandaji, the late President of the Ramakrishna Order, Swami Omkaranandaji, a late Vice-

President, Swami Sambuddhanandaji, Swami Vijayanandaji, Swami Niramayanandaji, Swami Nityaswarupanandaji, Swami Ranganathanandaji and many other monks. Among the nuns of the Sarada Math, Pravrajika Muktipranaji, General Secretary of Sri Sarada Math and the Ramakrishna Sarada Mission, encouraged me to carry on my endeavours. I convey my deepest respect to all of them. Some of these personalities have now left their mortal frames and no longer they would come to encourage me with their words of appreciation. I remember them all with reverence today and convey my deep gratitude to others. Words of appreciation from erudite scholars like Dr Bimanbehari Mazumdar, Professor Nirmal Kumar Bhattacharya, who have also left their mortal frames, and from Dr Rabindra Kumar DasGupta, Professor Sankari Prasad Basu, Dr Pranab Ranjan Ghose and many others have been a constant source of inspiration to me.

I convey my deep respect and gratitude to Swami Atmasthanandaji Maharaj, Assistant Secretary, Ramakrishna Math and Mission, who supplied me with some reports and journals and souvenirs containing informations and appraisals of the activities of the Ramakrishna Mission, which helped me to write the evaluative chapter on the activities of the Ramakrishna Mission.

I convey my respect and thanks to Swami Balabhadranandaji of the Ramakrishna Mission Institute of Culture who very kindly assisted me with such practical affairs as dealing with the press, the paper dealer and such other matters which I personally am incapable of dealing with. Without this help it would never have been possible for me—a person with little knowledge of the printing and the publishing world—to get my book published. In this matter I got also a good deal of assistance from Sri Shyamal Dutta of the Institute office. I convey him my sincere thanks.

Last but not least, to mention some members of my family whose unstinted cooperation made this work possible. My neice Sm. Parna Ghose, read some portions of the manuscript and made valuable suggestions. My sister Sm. Bijaya Dasgupta, kept me free during all these years from the burden of domestic responsibilities, taking the entire burden on her lone shoulders. I remember also friends and other relatives, whose names are not mentioned here, but who have very kindly borne patiently with me when I was disinterested in domestic and other affairs and encouraged me to carry on with my work.

V

Finally, the views expressed here are exclusively mine and no one else is responsible for them. I regret also the blemishes, which are plenty in the book. I failed to cope with the tremendous task of researching, writing and editing the type-script and correcting all the proof sheets running into thousands of pages almost single-handedly with my failing health, advancing age and very poor eye-sight. And there were other pressures so common in the case of a woman belonging to the middle-class in our society, pressures which often kept me away from my work and caused lapses in my concentration. Certain external factors, also beyond my control, proved too much to get the work done blemishfree, e.g., the inordinate delaying of printing due to unprecedented load-shedding and for sundry other reasons known to those who are acquainted with the ways of the printing press nowadays. I regret that I failed to make my work, the fruit of my life-long study and hard labour, error-free and without blemishes. Of course, I have faith in that section of the reading public who are serious about the contents and are not deterred by other short-comings of an work like this. It is they who have encouraged and sustained me so long through their appreciation when parts of this book were published in the form of independent articles and as papers read at seminars, etc. If the book is of any help to anyone who seeks to understand Vivekananda and his revolutionary message better, I shall consider myself amply rewarded. One thing must be remembered by all that people the world over are becoming more and more conscious everyday about the wonderful revolutionary message of Ramakrishna-Vivekananda, the prophets of human emancipation in the modern era.

Santwana Dasgupta

16 February 1991
Golf Green, Calcutta

Part - I

The Background : Vedanta and Science

CHAPTER 1

Genesis

I

NINETEENTH CENTURY RENAISSANCE AND RAMAKRISHNA-VIVEKANANDA :

According to its literal meaning, the term 'renaissance' means 'to be reborn', 'springing up anew'.[1] In this sense, in the nineteenth century India was reborn in Ramakrishna, who was, as aptly pointed out by Romain Rolland, 'the consummation of two thousand years of spiritual life of three hundred million people'.[2] Re-birth, in the case of a nation does not, however, necessarily mean repetition of the past only or revival of the old, as it is also 'springing up anew'. The seed is a product of the past, but the sappling is a new one. And it is evident in the life of Swami Vivekananda, the great disciple of Ramakrishna, how India, five thousand years or more old, emerged anew in the nineteenth century. Actually, in Swami Vivekananda the nineteenth century Indian renaissance found its culmination. He represented the time-spirit and his dynamic philosophy promised to fulfil the aspirations of the renascent nation as well as that of the humanity as a whole, ushering in a new era of radiant hope, peace, prosperity and progress.

II

THE SETTING : INDIAN

In the nineteenth century when Swami Vivekananda was born (1863) everything in this country was in the melting pot.

---

1. *Pocket Oxford Dictionary* (fourth edition), p. 686.
2. Romain Rolland—*Life of Ramakrishna* (fifth edition), Advaita Ashrama, p. 14.

The British rule, over a century old at the time, was instrumental in bringing this ancient land into contact with the technologically and materially advanced West. The consequence was a serious cultural confusion. The conflict of ideologies was at its zenith. Religion or Science? Reason or Faith? Theism or Atheism? Polytheism or Monism? Secularism or Spirituality? Economic Prosperity or Asceticism? Ancient or Modern values? Which way to turn? Which one to choose? The vexed people hardly knew the answer. Exponents of each of these conflicting ideals put forward equally formidable arguments in favour of their own pet theories.

In spite of the seemingly chaos on the surface, a new spirit was lurking somewhere underneath, a new awakening was coming, a new awareness of national identity, of the greatness of the national ideals, was emerging. New thought currents generated reform movements seeking to eradicate the social evils and superstitions which like a cancerous growth was eating up the vitality of the nation. The reformers were enamoured by the western social pattern and hence they tried to recast our society after the western model. They considered the British rule in India a blessing. But all these moves could not put an end to the turmoil, it rather accentuated it since the protagonists of the status quo sought to idealize every social institution that was considered an evil and every prejudice that was sought to be eradicated. Similarly, the reformers erred in holding religion of the land responsible for all the social evils that prevailed at the time. And the reformists and the anti-reformists were equal in strength.

On the political front, battles and strifes were the order of the day as the native princes were overthrown one by one by the British and there was no peace and security for the masses. In the turmoil on the political front they were the worst-sufferers. On the economic front there were burning problems, consequences of the colonial exploitative economic policies of the imperialistic rulers. Under the patronage of the rulers the competition from the technologically advanced West shocked the very foundation of the age-old economic system of this country based on flourishing urban handicrafts and isolated village communities. The results were devastating famines, decline of the handicrafts, mass movements of population from the urban to the rural areas, leading to increased pressure of population on land and decline of agricultural productivity, accentuating in its turn spreading of poverty all over the land. In spite of the efforts of some benevolent Christian missionaries and philanthropists to spread English education in this country, this was the time chosen by their other compatriots to buy the soul of India and impose Christianity on the land. India revolted under this pressure and there broke out mutiny, mass uprising, agrarian revolt—turmoils of every possible variety even in the remotest corner of the country. Thus India was caught in the currents and cross-currents of devastating tempests on every front—social, economic, political, cultural and religious. Obviously, this was one of the most critical periods in her long and chequered history.

Naren (as Swami Vivekananda was called at the time), then a young boy only, was caught in the tempests of the day and felt involved in every burning question since he had a very sensitive mind and his heart bled to find a solution. Even as a boy in his teens Naren had a rare intellect, 'the fire of genius burnt in his eyes', and above all there was a born seeker of Truth in him. He devoured western philosophy, history, science, sociology and political economy and grew all the more restless since the answer he sought was not to be found therein. The western intellectualism of the time which emerged after the European revolutions of 1789-1830 was bourgeois intellectualism, wedded to secularism and mechanistic and deterministic science. This hollow intellectualism failed to satisfy the deeper spiritual urges of young Naren. Herein lies the deficiency of this intellectualism—it cannot satisfy the deeper urges of the human spirit since it totally ignores the human spirit. At last a chance meeting with Ramakrishna brought him face to face with what he had been seeking for, viz., a bold and a direct and a sensible assertion of the Ultimate Truth.

Ramakrishna was apparently ignorant of the burning questions of the day, having emerged from the womb of India's past. He had hardly any formal education, being born in a poor Brahmin family, dependent on agriculture, in a distant village in the district of Hooghly in West Bengal, India in 1836. He was brought up in the traditional way in his rural home. But when he was engaged as a priest in the Kālī Temple of Dakshineshwar near Calcutta, he had the opportunity to learn by listening to various Sanskrit scholars and spiritually advanced persons, monks and nuns of various denominations, who used to flock to the place for pilgrimage. For twelve long years he rigorously practised religion strictly, according to the various schools of Hinduism and even according to Islam and Christianity, under the guidance of enlightened persons and every time he had the same realization of fathomless God. At last he was convinced that all the religions of the world were equally true, they all converged on the same goal. And he had the direct perception of the Vedantic truth that every living being is Brahman, that '*Jīva* is Shiva' as he expressed it.

In a beautifully composed poem poet Tagore has thrown light on Ramakrishna's spiritual realizations. The poem runs as follows :

> 'Diverse courses of worship
> from varied springs of fulfilment
> have mingled in your meditation.
> The manifold revelation of the joy of the Infinite
> has given form to a shrine of unity in your life
> where from far and near arrive salutations
> to which I join my own.'[3]

The poem has beautifully brought out in full the significance of Ramakrishna's life. In him has been formed a shrine of unity wherein diverse courses of worship have mingled. And it is quite apparent that all the conflicting ideals are unified in this shrine of unity.

All this was revealed to Vivekananda, as is clear from his following significant statement about Ramakrishna : 'The time was ripe for one to be born, who in one body would have the intellect of Śaṅkara and the wonderfully expansive heart of Chaitanya; one who would see in every sect the same spirit working, the same God; one who would see God in every being, one whose heart would weep for the poor, for the weak, for the downtrodden, for every one in this world, inside India or outside

---

3. *Prabuddha Bhārata*, February 1936.

India, and at the same time whose grand brilliant intellect would conceive of such noble thoughts as would harmonize all conflicting sects, not only in India but outside India, and bring a marvellous harmony. ... The time was ripe, it was necessary that such a man should be born . . . and I had the good fortune to sit at his feet. ... He came, the living spirit of the Upanishads, the accomplishment of Indian sages, the sage for the present day . . . the harmony... . '[4] And when Vivekananda received from his Master the fiery message—'*Jīva* is Shiva', emerging from his Advaita realization, 'that everything in this universe is Brahman', he saw a new light. He had the genius to realize that this was a message which could revolutionize the world. Yet, he was to see more, learn more, have more experiences of life, for realizing the full significance of this fiery message for society.

He gathered these experiences after he had completed his spiritual training under Ramakrishna, after he had realized that 'God is in various forms in this world' and that 'loving service to mankind is the true worship of God'. After the passing away of his Master, he was overtaken by an unfathomable restlessness of spirit and he set forth, mostly on the soles of his feet, to traverse through the length and breadth of this vast subcontinent and was engulfed by the ocean of mass-life. While covering mile after mile through the vast countryside, he mingled his life with those of the peasants in the field, the cobblers at their jobs, the artisans in their cottages, petty traders in the marts and markets, the tribals living in the forests and hills, and shared their oppressions, privations and miseries. In the course of his pilgrimage throughout India he stopped also at the newly growing industrial cities, where the new proletariat class was just emerging, and saw with his own eyes their pitiable conditions. He realized that the common people living on the fruits of their labour were exploited and persecuted by the upper class elites, the *zamindar*s, the priests, and the imperialist foreign rulers. He saw also how these common men and women were great in their simple life of labour with sparks of divinity in them. The problems and misery of these living men and women engulfed him and he carried 'a soul of

4. Lectures on the 'Sages of India' quoted by Romain Rolland : *Life of Vivekananda*, fourth impression (Advaita Ashrama), p. 284.

fire' for the rest of his life. He stated often, 'My aim is not Ramakrishna, nor Vedanta, but the masses.'

As pointed out earlier, India was at this time passing through perhaps the worst crisis in her economic history—the period of those devastating famines which took place in one or other part of the country almost every year beginning from 1770, the year of the great Bengal famine when people died in millions, up to 1900, as a result of which not only millions and millions died out of starvation, but millions turned paupers. These famines were the direct result of the new land revenue arrangements and overall economic policy of the British which upset the established system of production and distribution leading to the decline of both agriculture and industries.

Vivekananda visited the native princes and tried to make them conscious of the appalling conditions of the poor masses and of the misrule of the foreigners. Very soon he was totally disillusioned of the upper class 'who were more dead than alive'. He gave up all hope of the upper class playing any vital role in the regeneration of India. He realized by this time that the landed aristocracy along with the priestly class were equally responsible with the foreign rulers for the ruthless exploitation of the masses, their degradation and their appalling poverty and ignorance. For two long years during his Indian itinerary he was as if in a 'seething cauldron', knowing no peace of mind. He literally cried in agony—'A country where millions of people live on flowers of Mahua plant and a million or two of Sadhus and a hundred million or so of Brahmins suck the blood out of these poor people, without even the least efforts for their amelioration—is that a country or hell?'[5]

This direct contact with the masses led him to realize also the inherent unity of the people of India in spite of their endless varieties. As stated by Romain Rolland—'From North to South, the ancient land of India was full of gods, yet the unbroken chain of their countless arms formed only one God. . . . He realized it also in communion with the living of all castes and all outside castes.'[6] At last when his long itinerary ended at Kanyakumari in

5. *Letters of Swami Vivekananda*—third edition, Advaita Ashrama, p. 91.
6. Romain Rolland—*Life of Vivekananda*, p. 22.

1893, he had himself become the living embodiment of 'the conscience of India', its unity and destiny, and the world was to witness all this in him very soon. He was to attend the Parliament of Religions at Chicago in September 1893 at the behest of his own inward urge, for by this time he came to realize unconsciously that he had a mission for the West just as he had a mission for the East. He proclaimed it in Hyderabad publicly and when arrangements for his departure were being made he declared that he was going 'on behalf of the people and the poor'.[7]

On his way to the West he visited China and he saw with his own eyes how the masses in that great country with a glorious past civilization was crushing under the tyranny of feudalism and foreign imperialism and his heart bled for them. On his way westward he paid a visit also to Japan, which was making a headway in the path of economic prosperity and he wished India could also do the same.

III

THE SETTING : WESTERN

When finally he arrived at Chicago to champion the cause of the oppressed people, the poor, in his unfortunate motherland, he had no idea that the West was also waiting for his arrival. The West was spiritually starved amidst its spectacular achievements in the field of science, technology and economic prosperity. He realized that if India needed science and technology for her economic development, the West needed spiritual sustenance for happiness and peace. Advancement of knowledge in the field of science had posed a serious challenge to the long-cherished religious doctrines and dogmas resulting in the loss of faith in religion among the elites. This and other intriguing problems of a material civilization, which had firmly established itself in the West, demanded a solution. Taking up the challenge Vivekananda preached that 'Religion is not in dogmas, or in doctrines' but 'the realization of spirit as spirit',[8] that 'all sciences are but

7. ibid., pp. 29-30.

8. *C. W.*, I, p. 469.

manifestations of religion'[9], and that 'Art, science, and religion are but three different ways of expressing a single truth.'[10]

He found also that if the East was groaning under the tyranny of the priests, the West was groaning under the tyranny of the Shylocks. He felt that the West was sitting on a volcano and the eruption could take place any moment.[11] He saw clearly that the political slogans—'Democracy', 'Rights', 'Liberty' and 'Equality' —were mere meaningless high-sounding words, 'mere void full of poisonous gas'. And he showed how Vedanta could serve as the broad base for building up a lasting unity between varieties of peoples, races, cultures, religions and ideologies and that only it could make a communistic society lasting.[12] He emphasized that 'The one essential attitude for all people was the affirmation of their substantive divinity, not as a background philosophy or theory but as a living, immediately relevant fact.'[13] This was exactly the message that was needed—the savants and the thinkers felt so.

IV

THE INDIAN MISSION

Meanwhile, he did not forget the long suffering masses of India and his motherland. His fiery letters written from America to his Indian followers are full of his plans and directives for the regeneration of the country and her masses. Returning to India in 1897 he formulated a comprehensive programme of mass education, of economic regeneration for amelioration of poverty and a 'root and branch reform' of society. It was a plan for 'a revolution through social service'.

He founded the Ramakrishna Mission on May 1, 1897 to carry on the two-fold mission of regenerating India and working for the harmony, peace and prosperity of mankind as a whole and for that matter providing for the spiritual sustenance of the people in the West. And for this purpose, spreading of the Vedantic

---

9. ibid., II, p. 116.
10. ibid., I, p. xvi.
11. ibid., III, p. 277.
12. ibid., V, pp. 212-13.
13. Marie Louise Burke—*Swami Vivekananda In America: His Second Visit To The West* (first edition), Advaita Ashrama, p. 628.

ideas, as illustrated in the life of Ramakrishna, was also to be taken up. The methods of action of the newly formed body was to include also training men so as to make them competent to teach such knowledge of sciences that were conducive to the material and spiritual welfare of the masses; and promoting and encouraging arts and industries.[14] He wrote on July 9, 1897 'the movement is begun. It will never stop', and sometime later 'only one idea was burning in my brain— to start the machine for elevating the Indian masses and that I have succeeded in doing it.'[15]

His Call of Unity and the National Awakening : Earlier on his return from the West, he traversed once again throughout the length and breadth of India, from Kanyakumari to Kashmir, giving his call of unity to the people. And as stated by Romain Rolland, it was a call of 'unity of every Indian man and woman (and world unity as well); of all the powers of the spirit, dream and action, reason, love and work, unity of hundred races of India with their hundred different tongues and hundred thousand gods—springing from the same religious centre, the core of present and future reconstruction. Unity of hundred sects of Hinduism, unity within the vast ocean of all religious thought and all rivers past and present, Western and Eastern. . . .'[16] India rang with his voice and this call brought forth a new awakening in India based on its cultural distinctiveness inherited from the past and a new aspiration to vindicate its prestige as a free nation. The nationalist spirit was charged with dynamism and the freedom movement still a dream of a few chosen strong men was ushered in with full force to rock the citadel of foreign power. And thousands rushed to sacrifice their lives at the altar of the freedom of the motherland.

V

THE ROLE OF RAMMOHAN, RAMAKRISHNA AND VIVEKANANDA IN THE NATIONAL AWAKENING

This was a different type of national awakening that was ushered in by Vivekananda—different in character and import

14. Romain Rolland—*Life of Vivekananda*, pp. 122-23.
15. ibid., p. 135.
16. ibid., p. 289.

from the earlier awakening that was brought by Rammohan. It is true that Rammohan stopped the rot in the national life and its downhill rush towards degradation that characterized the period when he was born. It is also true that his advent marked the line of demarcation between the dark middle age and the modern era of 'enlightenment' as he was instrumental in bringing the 'enlightenment' by opting for English education and by adopting a rational-critical attitude in matters religious and social. But as it has been very importantly pointed out by Romain Rolland that Rammohan's 'Universal Religion' fell short of true universalism since he failed to recognize religious realities in the form of polytheism professed by world's two-third population scattered all over the world.[17]

Again, Rammohan's social reform measures never sought to touch the basic problems of our masses, viz., poverty, ignorance and illiteracy. To be brief, Rammohan had no programme of mass education or mass uplift whatsoever. Although his great contribution towards abolishing the abhorrent 'Satī' rites would be remembered eternally by a grateful nation, it cannot be overlooked that he did not utter a single word against the exploitation of the masses by the landed aristocracy. Nor did he raise his voice against British imperialism. His arguments justifying European settlement in India so that our society could be remoulded after the western pattern did never appeal to the nation. Our nation, having a rich heritage to be proud of and a glorious past history of achievements in the fields both temporal and spiritual, refused to subscribe to the idea of foreign domination in their social life.[18]

Romain Rolland, evaluating Rammohan's role in our national awakening rightly observes, '. . . and herein lies the difference between the awakening of Ramakrishna-Vivekananda and of Rammohan and Brahmo Samaj—in these days India refuses allegiance to the imperious civilization of the West, she defended her own ideas, she has stepped into her age-long heritage with the firm intention not to sacrifice any part of it.'[19] Thus it is clear that

17. Romain Rolland—*Life of Ramakrishna*, p. 104.
18. B. N. Ganguly—*Indian Economic Thought*, Tata McGrow-Hill, 1977, p. 50.
19. Romain Rolland—*Life of Vivekananda*, p. 289.

Rammohan's programme of reforms failed to fulfil the aspirations of the awakened nation. This new awakening was brought by Vivekananda who declared, 'India had a glorious past, but its future is to be still more glorious', and that 'India would be the central force in the incoming new era.' The sociological studies of Pitirim Sorokin and the historical investigations of Arnold Toynbee support this view to a large extent since they were convinced that the next era will be the era of predominance of the East.[20]

VI

THE WORLD MISSION

Vivekananda's second visit to the West completely disillusioned him of the glamorous materialistic prosperity of the West and its apparent democracy, as this time 'the brutal face of Imperialism of the West' was fully unveiled to him and he was 'full of rapacious hatred'.[21] During his two visits to the West he mixed not only with the elites and the wealthy but also with the labourers, artisans and farmers and felt their pulse.[22] He studied carefully the labour-capital strifes that were mounting at the time in the West and just emerging in India. He noticed the emergence of the socialistic movements which he hailed but was aware of their deficiencies unmistakably. He met the social revolutionaries of the West and scrutinized their methods, viz., the political method and violent revolutions and all that, which he found wanting as instruments of social welfare. And he had the courage and the genius to offer to the suffering world an alternative to the political method, which he discovered in Indian history. His study of Indian history revealed to him that in India politics was never an active agent of social change. All social changes in India came in the trail of spiritual upheavals.

---

20. P. A. Sorokin—'Three Major Trends of Our Time'—*Vedanta and the West,* No. 127— 'Introduction to Sri Ramakrishna and His Unique Message' by Swami Ghanananda.
21. Romain Rolland—*Life of Vivekananda*, p. 150.
22. Marie Louise Burke—*Swami Vivekananda In America—New Discoveries* (second edition), Advaita Ashrama, p. 664.

He saw also with his deep historical insight that the coming age was to be the 'Age of Man' (meaning the age of the common man) when the toiling masses would come to attain supremacy in society. He discovered in Vedanta—more precisely in its doctrine of the 'divinity of man' received from his great master, Ramakrishna through his message '*Jīva* is Shiva', —a philosophy for revolutionising society, for the redemption of the rights of the common man—the toiling masses. Vedanta was, however, remoulded by him to convert it into a revolutionary weapon for the vindication of the rights of man as man.

This is to be particularly noted here that Vivekananda has shown the common grounds of science and Vedanta. And therefore his social philosophy, which is based on Vedanta, can be claimed a scientific philosophy. We will see more about it in a subsequent chapter.

VII

THE MASTER-MIND

Swami Vivekananda is generally known today as a great religious leader. If we leave out Ramakrishna, his illustrious guru, he was undoubtedly the greatest figure in the field of religion and spirituality in the modern epoch. In truth, he was the only 'Man of God' in the experience of the modern West, to whom Christ was then merely a legendary figure. Marie Louise Burke observes in a revealing statement about him—'Never before had the people of America seen one in whom spiritual truths had been fully realized.'[23] Sister Nivedita, the celebrated western disciple of Vivekananda, sounding the same note said—'In him I found the heir to the spiritual discoveries and religious struggles of innumerable teachers and saints in the past of India and the world.'[24] Ela Wheeler Wilcox, the famous American journalist and poet, added in the same strain—'I believe him to be the incarnation of some great spirit—perhaps Buddha, perhaps Christ.'[25] William Earnest Hocking, a well-known and influential

23. M. L. Burke—*New Discoveries* (third edition).
24. Sister Nivedita—*The Master As I Saw Him* (1977), p. 80.
25. M. L. Burke—*New Discoveries*, Vol. I, Part I (third edition), p. 44.

philosopher, wrote in his *Recollections of Swami Vivekananda*—'What I could feel and understand was that this man was speaking from what he knew, not from what he had been told. He was well aware of the books; but he was more immediately aware of his own experience . . . and what he said would have to be taken into account in any final world-view.'[26]

From all these evidences it is clear that Vivekananda was one of the greatest religious leaders of all time like Buddha, like Christ. But this was not the entire truth about him. He was at the same time one of the greatest intellectuals and learned men of all time. How learned he was is evident from the following remarks of some outstanding personalities of different periods. Professor Dr John Henry Wright, Professor, Harvard University, himself an outstanding scholar, observed—'This young man of thirty is more learned than all our professors put together.'[27] Reverend Dr Mills said about him—'. . . a man of gigantic intellect indeed to whom the greatest of our professors were mere children.'[28] Speaking about Vivekananda's outstanding book *Rāja-Yoga*, Tolstoy, the Russian savant, remarked—'. . . so far humanity had frequently gone backwards from this true and lofty and clear concept of the principles of life and never surpassed it.'[29]

Swamiji's vast knowledge was not confined to religious texts, scriptures and philosophies only, he had complete command over the natural and social sciences as well. Evidences on this point are not lacking. While recapitulating his first impression of Vivekananda's lectures, Eric Hammond, an English admirer, writes—'Swamiji soon showed that he was equally versed in history and political economy.'[30] Madam Ema Calve, the world-famous singer and a very talented lady of her own time, observes in her reminiscences—'Science, philosophy and history had no secrets from him.'[31] At the end of the first volume of her

---

26. *Reminiscences of Swami Vivekananda* (third edition), Advaita Ashrama, p. 118.
27. M. L. Burke—*New Discoveries* (third edition), Part I, p. 20.
28. M. L. Burke—*Swami Vivekananda : His Second Visit To The West* (first edition), p. 298.
29. *Vishva-Vivek* (Bengali), p. 135.
30. *Reminiscences of Swami Vivekananda* (first edition), Advaita Ashrama, p. 298.
31. ibid., p. 268.

outstanding work on Vivekananda, Marie Louise Burke observes—'He understood and studied the modern civilization with the combined insight of a sociologist, psychologist, historian, philosopher and a mystic.'[32] That Swamiji had a good grasp of even a secular subject like economics, is evident from the fact that before he became famous at the Parliament of Religions he lectured at a meeting of the distinguished economists of the American Social Science Association on purely an economic topic, viz., the 'Use of Silver in India'. A newspaper report in going to comment on Vivekananda's talk wrote—'He is interested in social science and is an interesting and intelligent speaker.'[33] The fact is that he was not only interested in social science but was a master of it. He read August Comte, Herbert Spencer, James Mill, John Stuart Mill and a lot of other social scientists, while he was still a student. At the age of eighteen only he was in correspondence with Spencer in the course of which he is said to have disputed one of Spencer's theories. It is further stated by his biographers that Spencer was much impressed by the originality and rationality of young Naren's viewpoint.

It may also be noted here that Vivekananda's vast knowledge was not what is called mere 'book-learning'. He was of course a voracious reader all his life. Wherever he went, whatever the condition under which he had been living at any moment, even when he had been going through his hurricane tour over the different continents, he always found time to read something every day. The books he read were on all possible subjects—sometimes a French book on music, sometimes rare commentaries on Vedanta or Sanskrit grammar, sometimes on scientific discoveries and so on and so forth. In Belgaon in 1892 during the days of his Indian itinerary, Sri Haripada Mitra, a forest officer, was astonished to hear him quoting pages from a secular book like *Pickwick Papers*.[34] M. L. Burke quotes a lady who states—'At one dinner party at Detroit a gentleman asked Kananda [Vivekananda] what books he would advise him to read on chemistry, whereupon the Hindu monk responded with a long list of English works on this science, which one would expect an American to know more

32. M. L. Burke—*New Discoveries* (first edition), Advaita Ashrama, p. 596.
33. ibid., p. 45.
34. *Reminiscences*—(1983), p. 29.

about than a Hindu. Another gentleman followed by a request as to books on astronomy, to which Kananda obligingly answered with equally good list of English astronomical works.'[35] Instances need not be multiplied. Anyone who is interested can go through the references he used, a list of which has been given at the end of the Bengali version of his *Complete Works*. And anyone who undertakes the trouble can get a glimpse of his vast study—it is so vast that one cannot help getting astounded.

Nevertheless, reading was not the only instrument of knowledge to him. He availed all the direct instruments. Throwing light on the matter Sister Nivedita writes—'Museums, universities, institutions, local history, found in him an eager student.'[36] M. L. Burke also points out in a revealing statement—'He acquired greatest familiarity with the institutions of the country, religious, political and social. Nor was this familiarity acquired through contacts with intellectuals alone, . . . he spoke also with the labourers and farmers, his fingers were, as it were, on the pulse of the nation.'[37] Thus it is evident that Swami Vivekananda had direct knowledge of the working of the various social systems of the world and firsthand knowledge about mass-life all over the world.

VIII

SOURCES OF VIVEKANANDA'S SOCIAL PHILOSOPHY

As a man with a vision of the Truth, a powerful intellect, a vast study and a direct knowledge of the various social systems of the world and above all with direct knowledge of mass-life, his knowledge of the social phenomenon—its evolutionary process, its past, present and future phases of development—was complete. It must not also be forgotten that he was not a mere theoretician, but a man with the true revolutionary spirit, having a dream of a 'root and branch reform' of the world. He had also a workable scheme of his own for giving it a desirable mould. To be precise, Vivekananda had a social philosophy of his own. However anachronistic it may sound, it is an undeniable fact that

35. *New Discoveries* (third edition), p. 365.
36. *The Master As I Saw Him*, p. 221.
37. *New Discoveries*, p. 596.

the contribution of this man of religion to the field of social philosophy and to actual social transformation is no less outstanding than his contribution to the field of religion and spirituality. And it may be noted here that his social philosophy has sprung from his religious experiences and is based on Vedanta, the crown of all Indian philosophies. It may also be emphasised here that he spoke of a value-based social philosophy, his social philosophy having both a light-bearing and a fruit-bearing import. It means that his aim in elaborating his social philosophy was to give the society a desirable mould. His aim was not mere knowledge for knowledge's sake.

Of course, he had no time in his brief span of life to write down his thesis on social philosophy in the form of a complete treatise. He never had that intention also, his mission of life being something higher and nobler. He was born to usher in a new world order for which the whole world was waiting. His social thoughts are for that matter scattered all over his *Complete Works*. But that does not mean that these thoughts are just so many stray and casual thoughts. When they are collected together and arranged properly they take the shape of a complete system of thought, unique in its originality and unassailable in its logic.

The outstanding characteristics of this social philosophy are : (a) It is deeply rooted in history; (b) it is thoroughly scientific, not only because it is in complete agreement with modern science but also because it seeks to present a determinate theory of social evolution; (c) it provides a solution to the most pressing problem of the day, viz.—(i) the securing of the human rights by the dispossessed; (ii) securing of world peace and amity among nations, and (iii) securing of, finally, spiritual elevation of man.

In building up his social philosophy Vivekananda has utilized (1) Vedanta philosophy, (2) modern sciences, (3) materials provided by history, (4) materials gathered from the direct study of mass-life.

In the chapters following we would be attempting to have a glimpse into this social philosophy, presented by a master-mind and by one who has been described by the Russian scholar E. P. Chelishev as 'the prophet of human emancipation, of equality and human progress'.

CHAPTER 2

Vedanta : Its Revolutionary Significance

ADVAITA VEDANTA AS LIVING TRUTH

Vivekananda's social philosophy has its foundation on the ancient philosophy of Advaita Vedanta, the crown of Indian philosophical thought. And he breathed a new life into the scholastic and abstruse philosophy associated with the name of Śaṅkara to make it 'living and poetic'. He could do it since he made his stand on the direct spiritual experiences of Ramakrishna and of himself. There was identification of One and the Many—of Brahman and *Jīva*, and Brahman and the Universe, composed of different objects, in their realization. They realized or directly experienced that there was no other reality but Brahman, One and all pervading and the manifold objects we call nature was nothing but the same Brahman only. Ramakrishna explained this with the help of an illustration from life—just as sugar dolls made of the same material differ in form only, the Brahman appears as many in the universe. Thus the Vedantic doctrines *Tattvamasi* (Thou art that) and *Sarvaṁ khalvidaṁ Brahman* (Verily all this is Brahman) became vibrant living truth to them. They saw Brahman in every living being, in every man and woman, and in every particle of the world. Vivekananda expresses his direct experiences in this respect beautifully in the following poetic lines :

> 'He who is in you and outside you,
> Who works through all hands,
> Who walks on all feet,
> Whose body are all ye,
> Him worship, and break all other idols!'[1]

It is stated in the life of Ramakrishna that after his continuous stay at the stage of superconsciousness (*nirvikalpa*

---

1. *C. W.*, VIII, p. 169.

samādhi) for about six months, so complete was his own identification with the universe, with every being, animate and inanimate, that he was actually in great physical pain when one day one man slapped another man in the process of a quarrel in his presence. On another day when somebody walked over a bed of grass in the temple garden of Dakshineshwar he had the same feeling of acute physical pain in his chest. This identification led him to feel deeply the suffering of the oppressed and the deprived humanity all his life. It is stated in his life, again, that when he was on the way to Varanasi for a pilgrimage with Mathur Babu, a *zamindar*, he sat in the midst of hunger-stricken people, the victims of a famine, near Deoghar and refused to proceed further until Mathur agreed to feed those people and give them hair-oil and clothings. The suffering of the poor people was always his only worldly concern. He therefore persuaded Vivekananda (then known as Naren) to return to the world of suffering humanity from the realm of complete absorption in fathomless Brahman and dedicate himself to the service of the said humanity. And like his master Vivekananda had always felt complete identification with every man in suffering, in misery, and had sympathy even in man's 'errors and excesses'.

Birth of a New Revolutionary Philosophy :

Thus the whole of the religious philosophy of Ramakrishna and Vivekananda in the end converges on one point, viz., 'man', 'the only God that exists'. In a fiery language Vivekananda said—'There had been enough of sterile God of solitary prayers. Let them worship the living God, the coming God, the *Virāṭ* living in all living souls.'[2] Speaking about Ramakrishna Will Durant pointed out, 'He tolerated sympathetically the polytheism of the people, and accepted humbly the monism of the philosophers, but in his own living faith God was a spirit incarnated in all men and the only true worship of God was the loving service of mankind.'[3]

---

2. Romain Rolland—*Life of Vivekananda*, p. 96.
3. *Sri Ramakrishna in the Eyes of the Brahmo and the Christian Admirers*, Firma K. L. Mukherjee, p. 2 (1976).

It is clear that in the Philosophy of Ramakrishna and Vivekananda man as well as his universe was deified. If there is One Reality only, then obviously the universe is permeated by that Reality. Just as *Īśopaniṣad* says, 'Whatever exists in the world is covered by God.' (I-1) Hence Vivekananda gave his call—'Deify it [universe]; it is God alone.' [4] Thus here is a bold acceptance of life as it is, since life itself is holy. All creative activities, all struggles are, according to this wonderful philosophy, only efforts to manifest the innate divinity of man. It is a wonderful positive world-view since in it there is no denouncing of the world, no turning back from the struggles, miseries and afflictions of man. Also man's daily life, in this philosophy, becomes sacred and every work becomes a form of worship.

It is to be particularly noted that everything is positive and nothing negative in this philosophy which proclaims, above all, man's right to every kind of freedom—freedom from every kind of bondage, freedom from servitude to other men, society, nature, etc. All these form the core of Ramakrishna-Vivekananda's philosophy.

It must be realized that Ramakrishna and Vivekananda demonstrated directly realized truth and did not merely elucidate this or that speculative philosophy. In a letter to Mary Hale Vivekananda wrote—'I have a message, and I will give it after my own fashion. I will neither Hinduise my message, nor Christianise it, nor make it any "ise" in the world. I will only my-ise it and that is all.'[5]

For this purpose he moulded Vedanta on the basis of Sri Ramakrishna's and his own realizations, adding new meaning to it. Marie Louise Burke has shown how this moulding was done. She says, 'Never before had it (Vedanta) been broadened into a philosophy and religion which included every faith of the world and every noble effort of man—reconciling spirituality and material advancement, faith and reason, science and mysticism, work and contemplation, service to man and absorption in God.'[6]

4. *C. W.*, II, p.146.
5. ibid., V, p. 72.
6. Marie Louise Burke—*Swami Vivekananda In America* : *New Discoveries* (second edition), p. 608 (1958).

What emerged was not the same old monism or Advaita Vedanta known heretofore, a new depth and a new dimension had been added to it. Now, this new depth and new dimension, and this all-inclusive comprehensiveness made Vivekananda's doctrine distinctly his own. It is not new in its genesis but it is all new in its comprehensiveness and in the unity of the opposites which it successfully blends.

As pointed out by M. L. Burke, 'As Swamiji later conceived it, Vedanta was the one unifying force of all the diverse religions, the inevitable and ultimate inclusion of science, the justification of all social, moral, psychic and philosophical efforts of man to realize his own glory, and the method by which that glory might be fully attained.'[7]

As inevitable consequences of this new formulation of Vedanta we got :

(1) a revolutionary concept of man;
(2) a revolutionary concept of religion;
(3) a revolutionary concept of revolution itself.

The first two we will discuss in the next two chapters, and the last one at a later state. These revolutionary concepts have important bearing for man's social life and its transformation.

7. ibid., Part I, p. 469 (1983 edition).

CHAPTER 3

The Revolutionary Concept of Man

I

CONCEPT OF DIVINITY OF MAN

'Divinity of man' is the core of the new revolutionary philosophy of Vivekananda. By this doctrine Vivekananda makes man almost almighty. Man's inherent strength is infinite and his latent capacities are also infinite. In the *Atharva Veda* we find man declaring—'Mighty am I, superior by name upon the earth, all-conquering am I, completely conquering every region.' (XII. i. 54) This might of man, his sovereignty over nature, is the crux of this new philosophy as propounded by Vivekananda. He places man, as we shall see in the course of our analysis, above environment and makes him the moulder of his own destiny. He says—'Never forget the glory of human nature. We are the greatest God that ever was or ever will be. Christs and Buddhas are but waves on the boundless ocean which *I am*.'[1]

According to Vivekananda, this power, this energy, this strength latent in every man must be manifested and he did not like a mild approach in this respect. It must be manifested here and now. Ramakrishna also disliked the attitude of 'slowly and gradually it will come about'. One should be bold and up and doing, one should have what he stated, 'a dacoit-like attitude'. Vivekananda, just as his master did, emphasized this dogged determination. The smashing truth that he taught was that man is divine and every one should assert this here and now.

He demanded also that man should take full responsibility of himself on his own shoulders. Here he lays down two practical maxims which form the quintessence of his philosophy of man-making :

---

1. *C. W.*, VII, p. 78.

1. Get hold of yourself.
2. Get hold of the Self.

From these two we come upon a few more valuable maxims of great practical importance in man's life :

1. Self-effort.
2. Self-reliance.
3. Self-mastery.

The two words that were constantly on the lips of Swamiji were 'strength' and 'fearlessness'—the words which he considered were the quintessence of the Upanishads. 'If there is one word,' he says, 'that you find coming out like a bomb from the Upanishads, bursting like a bomb-shell upon masses of ignorance, it is the word "fearlessness".'[2] The doctrine that added a new dimension to the concept of man was the doctrine of *Śakti* or strength. 'This is the great fact', he said, 'strength is life, weakness is death. Strength is felicity, life eternal, immortal; weakness is constant strain and misery : weakness is death.'[3] Man, in his opinion, is the repository of infinite strength since he is one with Brahman.

In the post renaissance period in the West scientific discoveries propounded a mechanistic, materialistic and deterministic view of Reality. Hence came attempts to interpret 'man' more and more materialistically, mechanistically, and economically. And such theories were accredited as 'scientific'.

II

MATERIALISTIC INTERPRETATION OF MAN

Materialistic interpretation of 'man' reached perhaps its culmination in the writings of Ludwig Feuerbach, the German philosopher, whose later-day writing led to the coining of the pun : 'Man is what he eats.'[4] The great danger of such a materialistic interpretation of 'man' for man himself and for human civilization as a whole has been brought out very aptly by

---

2. ibid., III, p. 160.
3. ibid., II, p. 3.
4. Richard Falkenberg—*History of Modern Philosophy*, Progressive Publishers, Calcutta, 1953, p. 595.

Professor Sorokin in a poignant statement : 'Mankind should be grateful to the sensate [materialistic] culture for its wonderful achievements [in the fields of science and technology]. But now . . . when its product is poison gas rather than fresh air, when through its achievements it has given into man's hands terrific power over nature and the social and the cultural world without providing with self-control, with power over his emotions and passions, sensate appetites and lusts—now in the hands of such a man, with all its achievements of science and technology, it is becoming increasingly dangerous to mankind itself and to all its values.'[5] In a strikingly revealing observation he then goes on to point out—'The sensate culture did its best in the way of degrading man to the level of a mere reflex mechanism, a mere organ motivated by sex, a mere semi-mechanical, semi-physiological organism, devoid of any divine spark, of any absolute value, of anything noble and sacred.'[6]

Thus it has been made very clear by Professor Sorokin that the crisis of our age, the looming danger of total annihilation in an atomic war, is the result of the degradation of man under materialistic or sensate culture. The solution obviously lies in the elevation of man and for this a switch over from materialism to spirituality is badly needed. Professor Sorokin is most emphatic when he speaks on this matter—'If the conquest of the forces of nature is the main function of the sensate [materialistic] culture, the taming of man, his "humanization", his ennoblement as the participant in the Divine Absolute, has always been the function mainly of the ideational or idealistic [spiritualistic] culture . . . . Hence the urgency of the shift . . . from the subjugation and control of nature by man to the control of man by himself.'[7] He adds convincingly—'This control is impossible without a system of universal perennial values. Such values are irreconcilable with the sensate mentality and culture which by their nature are relative, utilitarian, hedonistic and expedient only.'[8] Hence the need of the hour is absolute, eternal and spiritual values which form the basis of ethics.

Long before Sorokin, Swami Vivekananda declared in a

---

5. P. A. Sorokin—*The Social and Cultural Dynamics*, p. 625.

6. ibid. 7. ibid. 8. ibid.

prophetic tone, 'The whole of western civilization will crumble to pieces in the next fifty years if there is no spiritual foundation.'[9] And within fifty years after this prophecy two devastating world wars occurred fulfilling his prophecy. And the massacre of Hiroshima and Nagasaki in the Second World War was just an indication of what might happen to mankind if the prophetic warnings are allowed to go unheeded.

Marxian Concept of 'Man' : As we all know, the basis of Marxian philosophy is the materialistic, mechanistic, and the deterministic science of the nineteenth century, many of the basic propositions of which, as we shall see later on, stand exploded today as a result of the progress made by science in the present century. He was primarily influenced by the progress of science as at that time and by the other great event of history at that time, viz., technological and industrial revolution. His interpretation of man is accordingly materialistic. But Marx was very much different from the older materialists, like Feuerbach, who, while holding that there was nothing excepting that which we perceive through our senses, preached a personal ethics of resignation and contemplation and for this passive attitude Marx criticized Feuerbach very severely. Marx, on the contrary, was an extreme activist who could not put up with any philosophy which was not mainly concerned with the amelioration of man's material circumstances of life. Hence came this famous oft-quoted utterance from him : 'The Philosophers have only interpreted the world in various ways; the point, however, is to change it.'[10]

Defining man, Marx said, '...human essence is no abstraction inherent in each single individual. In its reality it is the ensemble of the social relations.'[11] According to him, the forces of external nature which controls man's life lead him to feel helpless and that is how the terrestrial forces assume the form of supernatural forces. The seed of man's alienation from universe germinates in

9. *C. W.*, III, p. 159.
10. K. Marx and F. Engels, *On Religion*, Foreign Languages Publishing House, Moscow, second impression, p. 72.
11. Quoted in *Chintānāyak Vivekananda*, Ramakrishna Mission Institure of Culture, 1984, p. 687.

this feeling of helplessness. 'But it is not long before', he adds, 'that side by side with the forces of nature, social forces begin to be active, forces which confront man as equally alien, and at first equally inexplicable, dominating him with the same apparent natural necessity as the forces of nature.'[12]

The Problem of Alienation : According to the Marxist definition, alienation is a condition where man's own act becomes to him an 'alien' power, standing over and against him, instead of being ruled by him. In a mature society today, according to Marx, the following types of alienation are found to exist in the life of a working man :

1. alienation from the process of work;
2. alienation from the production of work;
3. alienation from himself;
4. alienation from others.

As it is evident from the above, according to Marx, alienation is rooted (1) firstly, in man's ignorance about nature and (2) secondly, in economic exploitation. Hence the solution lies in (1) spreading scientific knowledge and (2) collective action against economic exploitation. And, in his opinion further, only in a classless society where private property is destroyed there is a complete return of man to himself.

In Marx's philosophical system, 'man is a social animal' and his 'self-regarding impulses work themselves out through channels determined by the social environment to which he is subject'.[13] Evidently, Marx is an environmentalist and in his system man's role is not that of a free agent, man is free only within the parameter of the material conditions prevailing in society. But the question is : 'Is it ever possible for a subordinate agent to be free from alienation since his free will shall always be superseded by society even in its classless stage?' In the opinion of the Austrain Marxist thinker Ernest Fisher, for example, a new alienation is created when power passes, by institutionalization, from revolutionary organs into the hands of central authority.[14]

---

12. Marx and Engels, *On Religion*, Foreign Languages Publishing House, Moscow (second impression), p. 147.
13. ibid.
14. Ernest Fisher, *Art Against Ideology*, London, 1969, p. 90.

Existentialistic Concept of Man : After the Second World War existentialism, a humanistic philosophy by declaration of its exponents, attracted the attention of the world. There are both atheists and theists among the existentialists. Both the schools, however, directed their attention towards solving the mystery of human existence. They were influenced by Nietzsche, Kafka, and in my humble opinion by Neo-Vedanta, which, as pointed out by Romain Rolland, has been imperceptibly 'one of the most life-giving and fertilizing streams' in the 'burning soil of Europe and America in those days'.[15] The influence has been imperceptible, its mark of impress is, however, written in bold letters on the texture of world thought today, which cannot escape the sharp eyes of a serious researcher.

According to Jean Paul Sartre, the leading exponent of the atheistic school, 'There being no God, there is at least one being whose existence comes before its essence, a being which exists before it can be defined by any conception of it.'[16] That being to him is 'man'. To Heideggar, another existentialist, it is 'Human Reality'. 'Man is nothing else but what he proposes, he exists only in so far as he realizes himself, he is therefore nothing else but what life is', declares Sartre. His doctrine declares that there is no reality except in action.[17] Thus, man is what he makes of himself and man is responsible for what he is. 'This is subjectivism', and 'subjectivism' means freedom of individual, according to Sartre. For man 'there is no other legislator for him than himself', asserts the existentialist philosopher. This freedom is the value of all values to him.

All these seem an echo of Vivekananda. For example, as we have seen already, to Vivekananda man was the highest God. 'We are the greatest God that ever was or ever will be'—he said. On freedom he said—'The question was practically this : "What is this universe? From what does it arise? Into what does it go?" And the answer was : "In freedom it arises, in freedom it rests,

15. Romain Rolland—*Life of Vivekananda*, p. 220.
16. *Existentialism* by Jean Paul Sartre. *The Age of Analysis*, Selected by Morton White, The New American Library of World Literature, New York, 1955, p. 134.
17. ibid.

and into freedom it melts away." '[18] Again he said—'All human life, all nature . . . is struggling to attain to freedom.'[19] Thus more than anybody else he has emphasized 'freedom' as the essence of human life.

Man's responsibility to determine his own destiny has been the keynote of Vivekananda's philosophy. 'We are our own help', he said. 'If we cannot help ourselves, there is none to help us.' Referring to the *Gītā* he said, 'Thou thyself art thy only friend, thou thyself thy only enemy. There is no other enemy but this self of mine, no other friend but myself.'[20] Thus man is the maker of his own destiny, he is what he makes himself. This is the essence of the doctrine of Sartre also.

Kierkegaard, the leader of the other school of existentialism, who exerted a great deal of influence on Christian theology in this century lays stress on the individual man here and now, man in his passion, anxiety, boredom, and loneliness. In his opinion, 'awareness of one's own existence becomes most acute in periods of extreme inner tension, when anxiety and dread, having passed beyond the stage of local concern for particular ends, now have become total or so to say, metaphysical.'[21] And in his opinion only by passing through 'such dark nights of the soul' one can fully know the self. Hence according to him, one knows the self by direct experience. He was not interested like Marx in the process of historical development since he did not believe that the root cause of human ailment lay in external forces. Like Vivekananda he was interested in the inner transformation of man, i.e., in the 'morphology of spiritual progress'.[22]

Kierkegaard's difficulty was that he failed to relate man to God convincingly. Criticizing Kierkegaard on this point, Morton White remarks—'The great problem of Kierkegaard is to relate God's is-ness, if I may use the term for the moment, to human existence, and this he tries to solve by appealing to the Incarnation. Christ's person is the existent outgrowth of God who is. By what is admittedly a mysterious process the abstract God enters a concrete existence. We must accept this on faith

18. *C. W.*, II , p. 125. 19. ibid., p. 127. 20. ibid., I, p. 478.
21. *The Age of Ideology*, p. 228. 22. ibid.

and faith alone ... .'[23] Thus there is a logical gap in Kierkegaard's metaphysical system. The missing link, as it appears to us, is the Vedantic doctrine of identity of Man and God, or *Jīva* and Brahman.

Yet Kierkegaard shocked the world by calling man to face the fact of his own existence as a conscious being and by stressing the need for looking inward.

Difficulties of the Western Concepts: Thus it is evident that the West has been groping in darkness in search of a rational philosophy which would provide a satisfactory explanation of man and his relation to the universe and assure him of a joyous and meaningful life and which would at the same time guarantee emancipation of the common man from tyranny and oppression. They switched over from the Hegelian idealism to the materialism of Feuerbach and Marx and again to the subjectivism of the existentialists but in vain—the answer that they were yearning for did not come. Nietzsche has been vocal about the necessity of a philosophy of a joyous life for man but he could not deliver the goods since his role was destructive and not constructive. His message that 'God is dead' or that man needed a more joyous life than that promised in the New Testament could not bring joy or solace to man as his philosophy gave no indication with regard to the means of attaining it.

Speaking about Marx and Nietzsche, Henry D. Aicken significantly observes—'None of these men was content merely to amend tradition; each, in his own way tried to destroy it. What they sought to accomplish as philosophers was not just a new way of ideas or a new critique of reason, but virtually the creation of a new kind of man.'[24] But this they failed to accomplish, the creation of new kind of men was not given to them, since by destruction nothing can be created. They preached sensate values which lead man to degradation. All that they could accomplish was to destroy man's faith in God, in Universal Reality, and in his own innate goodness. Surely it is not possible to create a new kind of men by incessantly telling them that they are nothing but semi-physiological organisms,

23. *The Age of Analysis*, p. 120.

24. *The Age of Ideology*, p. 184.

insignificant worms overpowered by nature, society, history, environment, and above all by his own sub-conscious, raging with lunatic passions.

Kierkegaard's subjectivism satisfied theological demands but with its logical gap could not satisfy the demands of a rational mind. Thus the common man who was divested of all his glory was thrust back into the belief that he had no escape from nature, society, and his wild passions. The last mentioned idea was the contribution of Sigmund Freud to add to the cup of man's misery. This was the culmination of the sensate concept of man which destroyed man's faith in his inner goodness. Freud's theory indirectly corroborated the Christian theological doctrine of original sin of man and man's helplessness to redeem himself. As a result many returned to the fold of old religious faiths against the dictates of reason.

Surely all these doctrines do not promise man joy, hope, strength and freedom, for which he has an innate yearning. The verdict that he is nothing but a plaything of the forces over which he has no control, virtually condemns him to an inglorious existence which gradually might lead to his personality disintegrated. All those whom Freud studied were actually the victims of sensate culture. Freud's main tenets have come to be largely modified today, but the mischief was already accomplished, it gave a booster to the spread of sensate values most. And since there is always a big knowledge-lag among the common people, it still has a hold over them.

III

NEO-VEDANTIC CONCEPT

Materialistic philosophy having totally failed to satisfy man's needs and aspirations, a switch over to spiritualistic philosophy providing nourshing and elevating values, was urgently called for. As has been aptly pointed out by Marie Louise Burke, 'The time-spirit draws its own prophet to earth; and the prophet, in turn personifies the time-spirit.'[25] When Vivekananda arrived on the world scene towards the end of the

25. *Bulletin of the Ramakrishna Mission Institute of Culture*, Calcutta, June 1974, p. 141.

nineteenth century with his philosophy of neo-Vedanta, the answer to the heart-grinding searches of the modern man was found since neo-Vedanta harmonized science and religion, reason and faith, the secular and the spiritual needs of man into wonderfully integrated comprehensive system of thought.

In a trumpet voice Swami Vivekananda declared : 'Ye divinities on earth—sinners!'[26] As beautifully put by Professor Benoy Kumar Sarkar, an eminent Indian sociologist, 'The first four words summoned into being the gospel of joy, hope, virility, energy and freedom for the races of men. And with the last word he demolished this whole structure of soul-degenerating cowardice-promoting, negative, pessimistic thought.' 'On the astonished world', Professor Sarkar points out, 'the little five-word formula fell like a bomb-shell.'[27] It was a true bomb-shell on the orthodox world believing in the theory of original sin as well as on the new world of agnostics—who did not believe in the presence of any divine spark in man. And he threw it on an august assembly of world's intellectuals and elites. Standing firmly on the ancient Vedantic philosophy, Vivekananda coined these five words as a solution to the problem of modern men and to the crisis of modern civilization.

Neo-Vedanta and the Problem of Alienation : Neo-Vedanta pronounces spiritual oneness of the universe. Herein lies the solution to the problem of alienation. Vivekananda says, 'If you go below the surface, you find that Unity between man and man, between races and races, high and low, rich and poor, gods and men, and men and animals. If you go deep enough, all will be seen as only variations of the One... .'[28]

The awareness of this oneness led Vivekananda to accept the whole world as his own. As Sister Nivedita points out, 'No institution, no environment, stood between him and any human heart.'[29]

---

26. *C. W.*, I, p. 11.
27. *The Might of Man in the Social Philosophy of Ramakrishna-Vivekananda*, Madras, 1936, p.15.
28. *C. W.*, II, p. 153.
29. Sister Nivedita, *The Master As I Saw Him,* 1939, p. 217.

The awareness of the essential unity of mankind made him accept all religions as true and admire every distinctive cultural pattern. He declared : 'The Bible, the Vedas, the Koran, and all other sacred books are but so many pages, and an infinite number of pages remain yet to be fulfilled.' Thus he accepted all the diverse races of men, all the diverse cultures, all the diverse religions as one, he accepted all men however different from him as his brethren. Thus it is evident the problem of alienation just melts away where there is such universal acceptance, where unity becomes a living truth.

IV

DYNAMIC CONCEPT OF MAN

Vivekananda's concept of man is a concept of volcanic dynamism. A person is to realize his divine self and thereby attain *mukti* or liberation. This is the whole object of his life. Heaven and hell and all other such matters are nothing but theological myths. As stated by Sister Nivedita—'He preached *mukti* instead of heaven; enlightenment instead of salvation; the realization of Immanent Unity, Brahman, instead of God.'[30]

Man must struggle for liberation, must fight his way out, he cannot rest, cannot give up the fight, because this struggle is the nectar of his life. He has to move on and on without a moment's break. This is the crux of Vivekananda's philosophy. And his philosophy is a song of this struggle, a virtual marching song of the soul : 'Sharp as the blade of a razor, long and difficult and hard to cross, is the way to freedom. . . . Yet do not let these weaknesses and failures bind you. . . . We will then certainly cross the path, sharp as it is like the razor, and long and distant and difficult though it be. Man becomes the master of gods and demons.'[31] Thus his message in this respect is the same as that of *Aitareya Brāhmaṇa* in which it is stated that 'Wandering one findeth honey, wandering the sweet Udumbara fruit, consider the pre-eminence, of the sun who wearieth never of wandering.' Therefore, 'Oh man! march on and on.'

It must be noted that this volcanic dynamism impels a man

30. ibid., p. 225. 31. *C. W.*, I, p. 342.

to move from idea to idea, to break down the shackles of dead customs, traditions, superstitions, dogmas and meaningless rituals. A true revolutionary that he was, Vivekananda asserted man's right to rebel against nature as well as the tyranny of traditions, customs, usages, etc. And what he said in this connection was again a bomb-shell—'Everything is conscious which rebels against nature : there, consciousness is manifested.'[32] He thundered , '...this obedience to law carried far enough would simply make us matter—either in society, or in politics, or in religion.' Denouncing the theory of inviolability of laws made by the sages, a very popular Indian idea at the time, he said : 'Eternal law cannot be freedom. . . . If there is to be an eternal law binding him all the time, where is the difference between him and a blade of grass?' 'Rishi, Muni [sages] or God', he thundered again, 'none has power to force an institution on society. When the needs of the time press hard on it, society adopts certain customs for self-preservation. Rishis have only recorded those customs.'

Not Supremacy of Society over Man but Supremacy of Man over Society : In expounding his philosophy of mobility and vital dynamics Vivekananda exploded also the theory of supremacy of society over man. According to Marx and Durkheim as well, the life of the individual is tyrannically determined by society. Vivekananda was dead against such social determinism. Instead of man's life being determined by society, society is made, moulded and remoulded to serve his purpose—the purpose of his self-realization, according to Vivekananda. Ridiculing the idea of a perfect society so popular in the West at that time, he said, ' "A good world ", "a happy world ", and "social progress ", are all terms equally intelligible with "hot ice" or "dark light ". If it were good, it would not be the world.'[33] 'Society is good at a certain stage', he throws a bomb-shell at the social reformist, 'but it cannot be our ideal; it is a constant flux. . . . What the world wants is thought-power through individuals. . . . The history of the world is that of six men of faith, six men of deep pure character.'[34] Thus he boldly explodes the doctrine of

32. ibid., VI, p. 453.
33. ibid., VIII, p. 383.
34. ibid., VI, p. 144.

externalistic doctrine of reform so popular in those days among the materialists and seeks equally boldly to establish his theory of internalistic human development and progress through the manifestation of the soul-power of man.

Thus we find that Vivekananda places man above nature, above society, above tradition, and above environment and makes him the moulder of all these and moulder of his own destiny always.

V

TWENTIETH CENTURY SCIENTIFIC CONCEPT OF MAN

Regarding the twentieth century scientific concept of man we may refer to the well-known scientist Erwin Schrödinger, Senior Professor of the Dublin Institute for Advanced Studies. At the end of his book *What is Life*, which is a study on the physical aspect of the living cell, he makes several significant observations regarding the philosophical implications of his study. The sum and substance of what he says is : Every individual, however different, are aware of two facts, (1) first, 'my body functions as a pure mechanism, according to the laws of nature' ; (2) second, 'I know, by incontrovertible direct experience, that I am directing its motions.' The inevitable conclusion is, according to him, 'Hence I am God, Almighty', although this is blasphemy according to the Christian terminology. But this is what modern biology implies and this is the essence of Vedanta— *Aham Brahmāsmi* (I am Brahman).[35] In his own words— 'In itself, the insight is not new. The earliest records to my knowledge date back some 2500 years or more. From the early great Upanishads the recognition of Ātman=Brahman (the personal self equals the omnipresent, all-comprehending eternal Self) was in Indian thought considered, far from being blasphemous, to represent the quintessence of deepest insight into the happenings of the world. The striving of all the scholars of Vedanta was, after having learnt to pronounce with their lips, really to assimilate in their minds this grandest of

35. *Bṛhadāraṇyakopaniṣad.*

all thoughts.'[36] The same view has been expressed by Professor F. Capra in his sensational book *Tao of Physics* where he goes on to say after reviewing some of the theories of modern physics—'Thus the mystic and the physicist arrive at the same conclusion, one starting from the inner realm, the other from the outer world. The harmony between their views confirms the ancient Indian wisdom that Brahman, the ultimate reality without, is identical to Ātman, the reality within.'[37] Thus Man is Ātman and Brahman, his real self is not the body but the soul which is identical with the Universal Soul, as shown by Vivekananda.

VI

CONCLUSIONS

Thus it is evident that the modern scientific concept of 'man' is virtually the same as the Vedantic concept and more so as propounded by Vivekananda. The upshot of this identity of Brahman and Ātman is that there is infinite strength and infinite possibilities in a man for becoming great and good. Hence Vivekananda gave his call—'Ay, let every man and woman and child, without respect of caste or birth, weakness or strength, hear and learn that behind the strong and the weak, behind the high and the low, behind everyone, there is that Infinite Soul, assuring the infinite possibility and the infinite capacity of all to become great and good.'[38] The implication of this for the 'rights' of men are very important as we shall see later on.

ORDINARY MAN IN VIVEKANANDA'S PHILOSOPHY

One wonderful aspect of Vivekananda's revolutionary concept of 'man' is that it recognizes the ordinary man's right to worldly happiness. And this recognition fosters in man a unique sense of his own dignity and worth. 'Each man is great in his own place', he declares giving the ordinary man an honour not given so far.

Not only the ordinary man but his daily activities, his humble daily pursuits, are sought to be deified by Vivekananda. Truly, to

36. Erwin Schrödinger—*What is Life*, Cambridge University, 1945.
37. Fritzof Capra, *Tao of Physics*, second edition, p. 296.
38. *C. W.*, III, p. 193.

Vivekananda, as pointed out by Sister Nivedita, '...the workshop, the study, the farmyard, and the field are as true and fit scenes for the meeting of God with man as the cell of the monk or the door of the temple.'[39] As a result, the old dichotomy between secular and spiritual breaks down. Everything is spiritual in this world and nothing is secular. Thus every man's daily pursuit becomes the ladder to the highest goal, i.e., attainment of liberation. This nullifies the exclusive claim that is advanced by a handful of spiritual men for monopolizing wealth and knowledge. Everybody has equal right in this matter as in all other matters.

Thus strength, fearlessness and freedom are the three cardinal qualities of man, according to Vivekananda. As he says, '...physical freedom, mental freedom, and spiritual freedom are the watchwords of the Upanishads.'

EVERY MAN—THE CREATOR OF HIS OWN DESTINY

Finally, Vivekananda utters one of the most vital truths about human life when he says—'And all the responsibility of good and evil is on you.' He considers this doctrine of individual responsibility as one of great hope. 'What I have done I can undo.' 'Take the whole responsibility on your own shoulders, and know that you are the creator of your own destiny'—he adds emphatically. 'All the strength', he continues, 'and succour you want is within yourselves. ... The infinite future is before you....'[40] 'Each man's master is his own soul', he declares finally. Commenting on this declaration Romain Rolland aptly observes—'This respect for human individuality and its freedom is admirable. No other religion has possessed it to this degree, and with Vivekananda it was a part of the very essence of religion. His God was no less than all living beings and every living being ought therefore to be free to develop.'[41]

Vivekananda's philosophy is thus a gospel of hope, of optimism, which urges man to recreate his being and venture upon to create a better future for himself and for mankind as a whole. His concept of 'man' is scientific and of great significance for the future of man.

---

39. ibid., I, *Introduction*, xv. 40. ibid., II, p. 225.

41. Romain Rolland, *Life of Vivekananda*.

CHAPTER 4

The Revolutionary Concept of Religion

Vivekananda's concept of religion is, in truth, a revolutionary one and is just the opposite of the Marxian concept.

I

ORIGIN OF RELIGION : VIVEKANANDA AND KARL MARX

According to Karl Marx, religion originated in 'fear' and 'it is the opium of the people'.[1] According to Vivekananda, on the other hand, religion originated in fearlessness, in man's bold attempt to go beyond the limitations of nature. While giving his own view he took into consideration the two theories that were given by two different schools of thought, known at the time, and were accepted by the scholars at the time regarding the origin of religion, viz., (1) the theory of ancestor worship; (2) the theory of nature worship.[2]

Ancestor Worship and Nature Worship : According to the first school of thought, ancestor worship was the beginning of religion. It was in vogue among the Babylonians, Egyptians, Chinese, Hindus and the primitive races in America. In ancient days the people of these regions believed that the spirit lived even when the body was dissolved. According to the second school who mostly depended on ancient literature, stressed that the genesis of religion was in nature worship. The different forces of nature were deified and worshipped as they appeared to the people in the ancient days to be mysterious.

VIVEKANANDA'S VIEW

According to Vivekananda, these two views can be

1. K. Marx and F. Engels, *On Religion*, Foreign Language Publishing House, Moscow, second impression, p. 9.
2. *C. W.* II p. 58.

reconciled in a third view and this view is his own. He claims that in this third view is to be found the true story of germination of religion. In his own words, religion is originated in the struggle to transcend the limitations of nature.[3] Explaining he says, 'Either, man goes to seek for the spirits of his ancestors, the spirits of the dead, that is, he wants to get a glimpse of what there is after the body is dissolved, or, he desires to understand the power working behind the stupendous phenomena of nature. Whichever of these is the case, one thing is certain, that he tries to transcend the limitations of the senses.'[4]

Dream Theory : According to him, it is 'very natural that the first glimpse of religion should come through dreams'.[5] It appeared as natural only to the enquiring mind in ancient days that if even during the dream state when the body was apparently dead, the mind went on with all its intricate workings, the same working would go on when the body was actually dissolved. This was the starting of man's searching into the inner world and after some time man discovered higher states than either the waking or the dreaming states. In all the organized religions of the world, the prophets and the seers are declared to have gone through these higher states that are different from the waking or sleeping, and in these higher states, it is claimed, they came face to face with a series of facts that belonged to the spiritual world. In the holy books we find recordings of these experiences and there is striking similarities in these recordings all over the world. 'Thus', says Vivekananda—'a tremendous statement is made by all religions; that the human mind, at certain moments, transcends not only the limitations of the senses, but also the power of reasoning. It then comes face to face with facts which it could never have sensed, could never have reasoned out.'[6] Now these facts are, he claims, the basis of all the religions of the world. And, according to Vivekananda, they can be put to the test of reason.

As pointed out by Vivekananda what is important is this fact that the existing religions of the world claim for the human mind this peculiar power of transcending the limits of the senses and the limits of the faculty of reasoning and this power they put

3. ibid., p. 59. 4. ibid. 5. ibid. 6. ibid., II, p. 61.

forward as a statement of fact. And the facts that were revealed to them through the superconscious experience were related to something which was infinite—Infinite Moral Law or Abstracted Presence, or Omnipresent Being or Abstract Essence.

The prime question is : did religion originate in fear? Or in man's bold attempt to go beyond the limitations of the senses? In a masterly analysis, referring profusely to the writings of the western anthropologists, philosophers and the social-scientists, Vivekananda shows that the idea of the soul is common among the Hindus, Buddhists, Egyptians, Persians, Greeks, Hebrews and the Sufis.

Fear Theory : *A Semitic Concept* : But there is a difference between Aryan and Semitic concepts of the soul. According to the Semitic races, the soul could not exist without a body. Hence the attempt of the Egyptians to preserve the mummies. But among the Vedic Aryans we find the concept of immortality of the soul which is separate from the body. Fear, therefore, dominates the Semitic thought lest the body gets destroyed. Their literature is full of agonies and cries expressed by men in constant fear of destruction of the body which means total annihilation. The Vedic Aryans who believed in the concept of the soul apart from the body were not dominated by this fear psychosis. The Semitic concept was, as pointed out by Vivekananda, grossly materialistic. Marxian theory is based on this Semitic concept.

The Aryan Concept : Speaking of the Vedic Aryans Vivekananda observes—'We must turn now for the source of the higher ideas of the soul to another race, whose God was an all-merciful, all-pervading Being manifesting Himself through various bright, benign, and helpful *Deva*s, the first of all the human race who addressed their God as Father—"Oh, take me by the hands even as a father takes his dear son"; with whom life was a hope and not a despair; whose religion was not the intermittent groans escaping from the lips of an agonised man during the intervals of a life of mad excitement; but whose ideas come to us redolent with the aroma of the field and the forest; whose songs of praise—spontaneous, free, joyful, like the songs which burst forth from the throats of the birds when they hail this beautiful world illuminated by the first rays of the lord of the day—come down to us even now through the vista of eighty centuries, as fresh calls from heaven; we turn to the ancient Āryas.'[7] This rather long statement based on ancient Indian literature makes it crystal clear that religion with the Vedic Aryans originated not in fear but in the joy of life, in the spirit of enquiry. This directly contradicts the Marxian theory that religion originated in fear.

Religion originated in Fearlessness : According to Vivekananda, religion originated in fearlessness and the essence of religion is, as stated in the Upanishads, the message—*Abhīḥ* or 'Be fearless'.

As stated by Vivekananda religion is not only fearlessness, it is also awakening of the soul, it is manifestation of strength and energy, it is attaining freedom, it is struggling, fighting out the way marching ahead towards this goal. Thus it is thoroughly dynamic. And that which is dynamic—is awakening of the soul—can never be the opiate of the people. As stated by Vivekananda, 'Religion is not in doctrines, in dogmas, nor in intellectual argumentation; it is being and becoming, it is realization.'[8] Elucidating he says—'Temples or Churches, books or forms are simply the kindergarten of religion, to make the spiritual child strong enough to take higher steps.... .'[9] The process of being and becoming is a dynamic process and dynamism is not the property of anything akin to opium.

Religion is Dynamism : A Process of Being and Becoming : Thus religion is the extremely dynamic process of transformation of man—of manifestation of his divinity. In a strikingly revealing statement Vivekananda says—'Religion is the greatest motive power for realizing the infinite energy which is the birthright and nature of every man.'[10] Religion in this sense is positive and not negative. 'It is not the teachings of men, but a growth, a development of something higher within our nature that seeks outlet.'[11] It is apparent that religion in this sense is extremely practical, it is, in fact, a practical science.

---

7. ibid., IV, p. 262.
8. ibid., II, p. 43.
9. ibid.
10. ibid., p. 67.
11. Swami Vivekananda, *The Necessity of Religion.*

II

WHAT RELIGION IS NOT

Not Dogmas and Doctrines : Vivekananda has laid down also what religion is not. It is not dogmas, doctrines, rites, rituals and other externals. These externals are helpful at the kindergarten stage of religion, which stage man must soon cross and come to the higher stage when he realizes—'spirit as spirit'. Thus Vivekananda's view of religion is not theological, it is spiritual. Religion in this dynamic sense forms the foundation of Vivekananda's social philosophy.

Religion is not Priestcraft : Religion is not also priestcraft. 'Priestcraft', Vivekananda points out, 'is in its nature cruel and heartless. That is why religion goes down where priestcraft arises.'[12] Priestcraft, in fact, according to Vivekananda, is the absence of religion. It is an irreligious phenomenon. Priestcraft is based on a claim of privileges on the ground of superiority attained in the spiritual field. Vivekananda makes it a point to show that this claim of superiority is not tenable in terms of Vedanta. '...as to spirituality', says Vivekananda, 'no privilege should be claimed there. ... All beings, great or small, are equally manifestations of God; the difference is only in the manifestation. ... The most ignorant man, the most ignorant child, is as great a messenger of God as any that ever existed, and as great as any that are yet to come. ... Wherever there is a being, that being contains the infinite message of the Most High.'[13] Vivekananda declares, 'The work of Advaita [Vedanta], therefore, is to break down all these privileges.'[14]

It is clear from this statement that priestcraft is a privilege-making, and religion a privilege-breaking force. None before Vivekananda did lay down this dichotomy, and show this difference, between religion and priestcraft. Marx and some other critics have made a mess of the two and held religion responsible for all the vices of priestcraft. Raising his voice in protest against such critics Vivekananda says—'. . . for all the devilry that religion is blamed with, religion is not at all in fault : no religion

---

12. *C. W.*, I, p. 428. 13. ibid., p. 424. 14. ibid.

ever persecuted men, no religion ever burnt witches... . What then incited people to do these things? Politics, but never religion... .' Politics certainly has to be blamed for all the atrocities that have been perpetrated in history in the name of religion and they have always been instigated by the priests.

RELIGION AND THEOLOGICAL DOCTRINES

Theological doctrines also are not the essence of religion. Vivekananda challenged all the theological doctrines such as the Christian doctrine of original sin, salvation, of rewards in heaven and punishment in hell and such other irrational and weakening doctrines. 'Ye! divinities on earth! sinners! It is a sin to call a man so; it is a standing libel on human nature', he declared in one of his immortal speeches at the Chicago Parliament of Religions in 1893. Quoting the first five words of the speech 'Ye! divinities on earth!—sinners?', Professor Benoy Kumar Sarkar, as we have seen already, observes that these five-words formula was like a bomb-shell that shocked the Parliament of Religions. 'The first four words', he says, 'summoned into being the gospel of joy, hope, virility, energy and freedom for the races of men. And yet with the last word, embodying as it did a sarcastic question, he demolished the whole structure of soul- degenerating, cowardice-promoting, negative, pessimistic thoughts. On the astonished world the little five-word formula fell like a bomb-shell. The first four words he brought from the East and the last word he brought from the West. All these are oft repeated expressions, copybook phrases both in the East and in the West. Yet never in the annals of human thought was the juxtaposition accomplished before Vivekananda did it in this dynamic manner and obtained instantaneous recognition as world's champion.'[15]

RELIGION AND CREED

Again, religion to Vivekananda was not mere this or that creed. 'I make the distinction', he said, 'between religion and creed. Creed is something antagonistic and combative. Religion

---

15. Benoy Kumar Sarkar—*The Might of Man in the Social Philosophy of Ramakrishna-Vivekananda*, published by the Ramakrishna Math, Mylapore.

is of the Self—which is in every religion.' And, therefore, he criticizes those who take only an intellectual interest in religion. 'Religion is with these people', he observed, 'a sort of intellectual opium-eating, and there it ends.'[16] It is really interesting to note that like Karl Marx, Vivekananda also thought that at times religion may turn out to be the opium of the people. But that happens, according to Vivekananda, when it is only lifeless intellectualism. When it is practical, living, then it is different.

III

GOSPEL OF ŚAKTI

'Vivekananda's gospel', points out Dr Sarkar, 'is that of energism, of mastery over the world, over the conditions surrounding life, of human freedom, of individual liberty, of courage trampling down cowardice, of world-conquest. And those who are acquainted with the trends of the world thought since the middle of the nineteenth century, are aware of the fact that it was just along these lines that the West was groping in the dark to find a solution. The most formidable exponent of these wants and shortcomings was the German man of letters and critic, Nietzsche, his famous writing *Als Sprach Zorathustra* (1885) and other works have awakened mankind to the need of a more positive human and joyous life's philosophy than that of the New Testament. This joy of life for which the religious, philosophical and social thought was anxiously waiting came suddenly from an unexpected quarter, from the unknown young man of India. And Vivekananda was acclaimed as the pioneer of a revolution—the positive and constructive counterpart to the destructive criticism of Nietzsche.'[17] The revolutionizing gospel of this young monk—was the doctrine of *Śakti*, a religion which sought to establish the supreme might of man.

Marie Louise Burke points out that the first impact of Vivekananda's thought on the West was a new urge for religion.

---

16. *C. W.*, III, p. 63.
17. Benoy Kumar Sarkar—*The Might of Man in the Social Philosophy of Ramakrishna-Vivekananda*, published by the Ramakrishna Math, Mylapore.

Suddenly after the Parliament of Religions when Vivekananda was lecturing all over America there was a rise in the number of persons attending the Churches. Prior to this there was a similar religious upsurge but that was due to the spread of a fear psychosis as a result of Christian preaching that the doom of man was hell-fire. The upsurge that occurred during the period of Vivekananda's preaching in America was entirely inspired by a philosophy of love and joy and that philosophy was Vivekananda's philosophy which preached that there was eternal hope for man since he had before him an eternal life of joy.

Vivekananda has shown that religion is love, joy, and power or *Śakti*. Sister Christine, one of the direct disciples of Vivekananda, writes in her reminiscences—'Our conception of spirituality was not only clarified [through knowing Swamiji] but transcended. Spirituality brings life, power, joy, fire, glow, enthusiasm—all the beautiful and positive things, never inertia, dullness, weakness. Then why should one have been so surprised to find a man of God with a power in an unusual degree? Why have we in the West always associated emaciation and anaemic weakness with spirituality? Looking back upon it now one wonders how one could ever have been so illogical. Spirit is life, *Śakti*, the divine energy.'[18] As noticed by Christine, Swamiji himself manifested that power. Marie Louise Burke observes—'But the divine energy he manifested also made his every word a thunderbolt, and then perhaps no one knew this better than he.'[19] Swamiji once said to Mrs Hansbrough, a Vedanta student of Northern California, 'You have heard that Christ said—"My words are spirit and they are life", so are my words spirit and life, they will burn their way into your brain and you will never get away from that.'[20] Writing on this topic Professor Benoy Kumar Sarkar observes—'The key to Vivekananda's entire life, his decade-long preparations down to 1893 and his decade-long work down to his death in 1902 is to be found in this Śakti-Yoga, energism, the vigour and strength of freedom. All his thoughts and activities are expression of this energism. Like our Puranic

18. Marie Louise Burke, *Swami Vivekananda* : *His Second Visit To The West*, p. 450.
19. ibid.
20. ibid.

Viśvāmitra or the Aeschylean Prometheus he wanted to create new worlds and distribute the fire of freedom, happiness, divinity and immortality among men and women.'[21]

IV

THE WATCHWORD OF RELIGION

So the watchword of religion is all these : power, joy, life, strength, and freedom. Hence Vivekananda criticized the Christian theological concepts—of original sin, salvation, of rewards in heaven and punishment in hell and such other weakening doctrines. He did not spare the materialist. Hitting them with his bomb-shells he declared—'... ye are not the bodies, matter is your servant, not you the servant of the matter.'

He criticized vehemently also the attempt that was common in the West in his time—the attempt to secularise religion. All emphasis was laid on doing humanitarian activities in the West and the name of religion was uttered by courtesy only. Summarizing the then tendencies of religion both in the East and in the West very briefly he said—'Religions of the world have become lifeless mockeries.' He was therefore not at all aggrieved over the fact that some of the precepts of theology and some religious superstitions were exploded by science. It helped him to clear the Augean Stable of superstitions, myths and meaningless rituals that came to be associated with religion through the priests. No wonder that Marx declared war against such a religion and Vivekananda did the same, only his criticisms are perhaps much more scathing.

V

THE NECESSITY OF RELIGION

In this connection Vivekananda sought also to point out that—'Without the knowledge of the Spirit, all material knowledge is only adding fuel to fire, only giving into the hands of selfish man one more instrument to take what belongs to

21. *The Might of Man in the Social Philosophy of Ramakrishna-Vivekananda*, pp. 16-17.

others, to live upon the life of others, instead of giving up life for them.'[22] Here he unfolds the dangers of materialism and the great utility of religion to the modern man. In another significant statement he shows how religion could enrich human life—'This infinite power of the spirit, brought to bear upon matter, evolves material development, made to act upon thought, evolves intellectuality, and made to act upon itself, makes of man a God.'[23]

Pitirim A. Sorokin, the renowned sociologist, has expressed the same view, as pointed out earlier also. In his monumental sociological work, *Social and Cultural Dynamics*, he has made it a point to elaborate that materialism degrades whereas religion ennobles man and therefore religion is absolutely necessary to make a man a man. According to him, modern civilization which is facing a crisis due to degradation of man caused by sensate or materialistic culture needs religion for its security. 'Mankind should be grateful', he observes, 'to the sensate culture for its wonderful achievements. But now when it is agony, when its product is poison gas rather than fresh air, when through its achievement it has given into man's hands terrific power over nature and the social and cultural world, without power over his emotions and passions, sensate appetites and lusts—now, in the hands of such a man, with all its achievement of science and technology, it is becoming increasingly dangerous to mankind itself.'[24] The dangers of materialism for mankind has been very clearly brought out in this statement.

Dwelling on the merits of an ideational (or spiritualistic) culture he says, 'The most urgent need of our time is the man who can control himself and his lusts, who is compassionate to all his fellow men, who can see and seek for the eternal values of culture and society, and who deeply feels his unique responsibility in this universe. If the conquest of the forces of nature is the main function of the sensate culture, the taming of man, his "humanization", his ennoblement as the participant in the Divine Absolute has been the function mainly of the ideational or the idealistic culture.'[25] 'The sensate culture',

22. *C. W.*, IV, p. 84.
23. ibid., p. 351.
24. P. A. Sorokin, *Social And Cultural Dynamics* (abridged edition), p. 628.
25. ibid.

continues Sorokin, 'did its best in the way of degrading man to the level of a mere reflex machanism, a mere organ motivated by sex, devoid of a spark, of any absolute values, of anything noble and sacred. Such a debasement now becomes increasingly dangerous for the sensate man himself. Hence the urgency of the shift from sensatism to ideationalism or idealism from the subjugation and control of nature by man to the control of man by himself.'[26]

Modern man is, therefore, in dire need of returning to the fold of religion. And Vivekananda has shown that—'Religion is fundamental in the very soul of humanity; and as all life is the evolution of that which is within it, of necessity, expresses itself through various peoples and nations.'[27]

According to Vivekananda, religion in this fundamental spiritual sense—in the sense in which it is one single expression of the spirit of man—is to play a very significant role in the life of the modern man. 'It is sometimes said', explains Vivekananda in a revealing statement, 'that religions are dying out ... of the world. To me it seems that they have just begun to grow. ... So long as religion was in the hands of a chosen few or of a body of priests, it was in temples, churches, books, dogmas, ceremonials, forms and rituals. But when we come to the real, spiritual, universal concept, then, and then alone, religion will become real and living; it will come into our very nature, live in our every movement, penetrate every pore of our society, and be infinitely more a power for good than it has ever been before.'[28]

VI

THE CONCEPT OF UNIVERSAL RELIGION

Thus, as shown by Vivekananda, so long as religion is in the hands of the priests and confined within the temples, churches and the holy books, religious differences may appear to be insurmountable and may be posing serious problems. But, as Vivekananda perceived, 'spiritual unity is the ultimate ground of all diversity.' This unity is the goal of all human knowledge. It

---

26. ibid. 27. *C. W.*, VI, p. 46. 28. ibid., II, p. 68.

underlies all religious doctrines and experiences, all metaphysical conceptions, all ethical ideals, and scientific truths. As experienced and explained by Vivekananda, One self unites all forms of existence, penetrates all phases of life. 'If you go below the surface', he says, 'you find that Unity between man and man, between races and races, high and low, rich and poor, gods and men, and men and animals. If you go deep enough, all will be seen as only variations of the One, and he who has attained to this conception of Oneness has no more delusion.'[29]

Unity of Mankind : Hence Swami Vivekananda did not find any fundamental difference between one section of humanity and another, between one religion and another. Without the recognition of the spiritual oneness of mankind there cannot be any unification of the world. As shown by Vivekananda, it is the only common ground where racial, social, economic, political and cultural differences can melt. And this unification of the world was one of the greatest dreams that was dreamt by Vivekananda.

VII

UNITY IN VARIETY

In truth, he dreamt of a unity in variety and not of uniformity, not the disappearance of all individual distinctiveness, which is impossible. Variety of cultures will remain and there is no harm in it. Different religions will also remain without any detrimental effect on society. In his concluding address at the Parliament of Religions he declared— 'The Christian is not to become a Hindu or a Buddhist, nor a Hindu or a Buddhist to become a Christian. But each must assimilate the spirit of the others and yet preserve his individuality and grow according to his own law of growth.'[30] 'If the Parliament of religions', he further added, 'has shown anything to the world it is this : It has proved to the world that holiness, purity and charity are not the exclusive possessions of any church in the world, and that every system has produced men and women of the most exalted character. In the face of this

29. ibid., p. 153.

30. ibid., I, p. 24.

evidence, if anybody dreams of the exclusive survival of his own religion and the destruction of the others, I pity him from the bottom of my heart, and point out to him that upon the banner of every religion will soon be written ... "Help and not Fight", "Assimilation and not Destruction", "Harmony and Peace and not Dissension".'[31]

Thus, diversity of religions will remain but the different religions will co-exist as diverse courses of worship of the One Infinite, as experienced by Ramakrishna. The result is not a uniform pattern of religion for diverse people but the acceptance of all religions as true by all. The Universal Religion is thus a confederation of religions, if we may say so.

Expressing his own wonderful concept of universal religion he says—'I accept all religions that were in the past, and worship with them all; I worship God with everyone of them, in whatever form they worship Him. ... The Bible, the Vedas, the Koran, and all other sacred books are but so many pages, and an infinite number of pages remain yet to be unfolded. I would leave it open for all of them. We stand in the present, but open ourselves to the infinite future. We take in all that has been in the past, enjoy the light of the present, and open every window of the heart for all that are to come in the future.'[32] Ramakrishna also was a Hindu to a Hindu, a Moslem to a Moslem, a Christian to a Christian, to a devotee a great devotee, to a *Jñānī* (man of knowledge) a *Jñānī*.

The Core of Religion : The central theme of this universal religion is the divinity of man, for this is the core of every religion. The knowledge of this divinity is the secret of man's development, secular as well as spiritual. It gives him infinite faith in himself and the awareness that he has infinite potentialities. He is thus invested with great strength which finds expression in creativeness of various types and dimensions enriching the society also.

Universal Form of Worship : *Service to Man—Practice of 'Jīva is Shiva'* : Swami Vivekananda has also introduced a universal form of worship. Since every human being has the same divinity in him, we can worship God by serving man. 'You may invent an image', he says, 'through which to worship God, but a

31. ibid.

32. ibid., II, p. 374.

better image already exists, the living man. You may build a temple in which to worship God, and that may be good, but a better one, a much higher one, already exists, the human body.'[33]

This religion is new in this sense that it does not depend on priests, churches, books, dogmas, ceremonials and rituals. It dispenses with all these auxiliaries prone to be misued. It is also new in this sense that it includes every positive thought. 'The religious ideals of the future', says Vivekananda, 'must embrace all that exists in the world and is good and great, and at the same time, have infinite scope for future development. All that was good in the past must be preserved; and the doors must be kept open for future additions to the already existing store.'[34]

The new world needed a new religion and Vivekananda has given that—a comprehensive dynamic religion of man, intensely practical for human growth and development.

VIII

RELIGION IS A SCIENCE

In relating what religion is, Vivekananda made a startling statement for the modern man—'All human knowledge is but a part of religion. ... Science and religion are both attempts to help us out of the bondage; only religion is the more ancient, and we have the superstition that it is the more holy. In a way it is, because it makes morality a vital point, and science does not.'[35] Thus, according to Vivekananda, science is a part of religion, religion being more comprehensive. Perhaps more startling for the modern man is the statement that 'religion itself is a science'. Depicting the nature of the science of religion Vivekananda says—'Religion is the science which learns the transcendental in nature through the transcendental in man.'[36] Explaining his ideas further he adds—'This science of religion is based on the analysis of the human soul. It has no creed.' Giving the concept of religion, an infinitely broad dimension, he adds, 'No man is born to any religion; he has a religion in his own soul.'[37]

33. ibid., p. 313.
34. ibid., p. 67.
35. ibid., VII, p. 103.
36. ibid., VIII, pp. 20-21.
37. ibid., VI, p. 82.

RELIGION IS REALIZATION AND BEING AND BECOMING

Proceeding further with his startling revelations Vivekananda shows that like any other science experimentation and realization are the first and the last words of religion. 'Stand up and reason out, having no blind faith'[38]—he urges everybody having the spirit of enquiry. What Vivekananda seeks to drive at is this, that the spirit of scientific enquiry is of utmost importance in religion, more than in any other science. 'In true religion', he asserts, 'there is no faith or belief in the sense of blind faith. ... To believe blindly is to degenerate the human soul. Be an atheist if you want, but do not believe in anything unquestioningly. … You not only hurt yourselves thereby, but you injure society, and make danger for those that come after you. Stand up and reason out, having no blind faith. Religion is a question of being and becoming, not of believing.'[39]

IX

UNIVERSAL-SCIENCE-RELIGION

Religion as propounded by Vivekananda is universal, as we have seen already, and at the same time it is a science, hence it has been very aptly given the name 'Universal-Science-Religion' by Romain Rolland.[40] Vivekananda has given the basic tenets of this religion beautifully in a nutshell in the following manner— 'Each soul is potentially divine. The goal is to manifest this Divinity within, by controlling nature, external and internal. Do this either by work, or worship, or psychic control, or philosophy—by one or more or all of these—and be free. This is the whole of religion. Doctrines, or dogmas, or rituals, or books, or temples, or forms, are but secondary details.'[41] This Universal-Science-Religion is of supreme significance to modern man who has a scientific bend of mind and relies on reason and not on blind faith. It is a practical science, it is to be real in the life of the modern man every moment.

---

38. ibid., IV, p. 216.
39. ibid.
40. Romain Rolland, *Life of Vivekananda*, p. 258.
41. *C. W.*, I, p. 257.

X

RELIGION AND REASON

This was obviously the rationalistic religion which was being sought after by the West, but in vain. Rationally, one can deny a creator God sitting in heaven, virtually a tyrant bestowing his mercy and punishment like a wily child. One can even deny a God immanent in nature, but can never deny his own self, of which he has a conscious awareness in the inmost corner of himself, he is certainly aware of his own existence all the time, this awareness can never leave him even for a single moment. And therefore a religion which proclaims that this Self is Existence, Knowledge and Bliss, is acceptable to him. This is what Vedanta teaches directly and every other religion also in one or other form.

In his philosophical expositions of religion Vivekananda pays first homage to Reason. In a bold statement, characteristic of him, he asserts—'Is religion to justify itself by the discoveries of reason, through which every other science justifies itself? Are the same methods of investigation, which we apply to sciences and knowledge outside, to be applied to the science of Religion? In my opinion this must be so, and I am also of opinion that the sooner it is done the better. If a religion is destroyed by such investigation, it was then all the time useless, unworthy superstition; and the sooner it goes the better. I am thoroughly convinced that its destruction would be the best thing that could happen.'[42] Dwelling on the results of such investigations he adds confidently, 'All that is dross will be taken off, no doubt, but the essential parts of religion will emerge triumphant out of this investigation. Not only will it be made scientific—as scientific, at least, as any of the conclusions of physics or chemistry—but will have greater strength, because physics or chemistry has no internal mandate to vouch for its truth, which religion has.'[43]

Regarding the question how exactly speaking religion satisfies reason, he points out —'The first principle of reasoning is that the particular is explained by the general—until we come to the universal. A second explanation of knowledge is that the explanation of the thing must come from inside and not

---

42. ibid., p. 367.

43. ibid.

outside....' Elucidating the second principle further he says, '...what is meant by science is that the explanations of things are in their own nature, and that no external beings or existences are required to explain his phenomenon. The chemist never requires demons, or ghosts, or anything of that sort to explain his phenomenon. The physicist never requires anyone of these to explain the things he knows, nor does any other scientist. ... Every science wants its explanation from inside.'[44]

In his opinion religion can satisfy both these cardinal principles of rationality—(1) the principle of generalization, and (2) the principle of immanent change. As to how the first principle is satisfied he says, 'The generalization principle ought to be satisfied along with the principle of evolution. We have to come to an ultimate generalization, which not only will be the most universal of the generalizations, but out of which everything else must come.... The Brahman of the Vedanta fulfils that condition, because Brahman is the last generalization to which we can come to. It has no attributes but Existence, Knowledge and Bliss Absolute.' 'Existence,' he explains, '... is the very ultimate generalization which the human mind can come to.'[45] What is meant by knowledge is what we see in the universe as the essential unity of things. This oneness is the one fact that is being proved everyday by modern science. Thus the first principle of generalization is satisfied by Vedanta.

As to the second principle, he says—'That the explanation of a thing comes from within itself is still more completely satisfied by Vedanta. The Brahman, the God of the Vedanta, has nothing outside of Himself; nothing at all. All this indeed is He : He is the universe : He is the universe Himself.'[46] Therefore all the change that we perceive in the universe is only immanent, that is manifestations of the Brahman.

Thus Vivekananda's Vedantic concept of religion, as claimed by him, satisfies completely the principles of reasoning so that it may be acceptable to all in the modern age.

This concept is revolutionary in the sense that it meets all the challenges of modern science and principles of reasoning. It is certainly a revolutionary concept that religion itself is a science.

---

44. Swami Vivekananda, *Reason and Religion.*
45. *C. W.*, I, p. 372.
46. ibid., p. 374.

CHAPTER 5

The Convergence of Science and Vedanta

I

THE CHALLENGE OF SCIENCE

In the twentieth century both science and religion seem to have converged. Scientists like Erwin Schrödinger, Charles Townes and Fritjof Capra have made explicit statements to this effect. But the situation was different in the nineteenth century at the time of Vivekananda's arrival in the West. There was total compartmentalization of religion and science. To the educated people they were incompatible. In a brilliant exposition of the situation Marie Louise Burke points out : 'The fundamental problem for the western world was whether the universe was ultimately governed by mechanical laws or by a supreme benevolent Intelligence. It could not be both. One reason that these two world-views—scientific and religious—were incompatible was that the former, for all its supposed lack of dogmatism, rejects that which cannot be known empirically or explained rationally and it so happens that it can find no shred of evidence for the existence of the spiritual forces. Thus in order to embrace an effective personal God—transcendent or immanent —modern man had to compromise his hard-won scientific outlook and betrary his reason.'[1] Naturally educated people declared that they professed no religion.

For this crisis in the western thought-world at the time three factors, viz., (1) nineteenth century science, (2) Christian theological doctrines which were found contradictory to science,

---

1. *Foundation-Day Souvenir*, 1980, Ramakrishna Mission Institute of Culture, Gol Park, Calcutta.

(3) and the dualistic philosophical doctrines which had a great influence over the mind of the scientists, may be held responsible, as it would clearly appear from our subsequent analysis.

II

NINETEENTH CENTURY SCIENCE

In the nineteenth century, science proclaimed that the universe was an automatic machine made of tangible matter and operating under immutable laws. The four main propositions of the nineteenth century science were :

(1) the Nebular Theory of the Universe;
(2) the Atomic Theory of Physics;
(3) the Darwinian Theory of Evolution in Biology;
(4) the Behaviourist Theory of Psychology.

The essence of all these theories taken together is: this universe and the planet we inhabit have a long process of evolution. Life occupies an infinitesimal small fraction of this cosmic universe, and has sprung out of an accidental, chemical and thermal combination. The protoplasmic cell manifested first symptoms of life. This germ of life multiplied and evolved into species under the pressure of natural environment till it developed a nervous system. Our thinking and feeling are caused by the movement of the nerve cells of our brains and by the secretion of the glands. Thus sensible universe, life and mind, all resolve into matter and mechanical motion.

Christian Theological Doctrines : Christian theological doctrines of original sin and the necessity of taking refuge in a monarchical God to save one's soul from hell-fire could not show their rational basis and hence were rejected. These doctrines therefore contributed towards increasing the rift between science and religion.

Western Philosophical Dichotomy and Its Impact on Science and Society :

The development of the philosophical thought in the West led at this time to an extreme formulation of Spirit/Matter dualism as reflected best in the philosophy of Rene Descartes (17th century). This view influenced the scientists in general and they were led to treat matter as something dead and separate from themselves and to see the material world as consisting of multitude of objects 'assembled into a huge machine'. Such a mechanistic view was propounded by Newton who laid the foundation of classical physics. Now if there is a machine there must be an inventor and operator of the machine. Hence with this concept of the universe the concept of a monarchical God is inevitably linked up.

This mechanistic view led to the fragmentation of the world with far-reaching consequences. First of all, Descartes's principle 'I think, therefore I am' has led to the separation of the mind from the body and this means inner fragmentation. There has been a fragmentation in the world outside also since the world is viewed by the philosophers and the scientists as a conglomeration of multitude of objects and events.

This fragmentation had important social repercussions. As Professor F. Capra says beautifully in an illuminating statement that the natural environment is treated as if it consisted of separate parts to be exploited by different interest groups. The fragmented view is further extended to society, which is split into different nations, races, religions and political groups. The belief that all these fragments—in ourselves, in our environment, and in our society—are really separate can be seen as the essential reason for the present series of social, ecological and cultural crisis. It has alienated us from nature and from our fellow human beings. It has alienated us from nature and from our fellow human beings. It has brought a grossly unjust distribution of natural resources, creating economic and political disorder; an ever-rising wave of violence, both spontaneous and institutionalized, and an ugly, polluted environment in which life has often become physically and mentally unhealthy.[2]

This is a very clear exposition of the repercussions of the fragmentation process consequent of the development of philosophy and science in the nineteenth century West mentioned above, on socio-cultural, ecological and politico-economic fields.

---

2. Fritzof Capra, *The Tao Of Physics* (2nd edition), p. 9.

Spread of Materialism : Since rational people could not sacrifice reason in order to accept religion, soon materialism prevailed in society dislodging religion.

In a brilliant analysis Alwyn Jones has described the consequences of this materialism. It has led with the aid of science and technology first of all to industrial mode of production and consumption. In his opinion, in spite of its blessings specialisation of skill in highly industrialized society has led to a 'reduction of reason, a reduction of the whole to one of its parts has taken place'.[3]

This is, therefore, the result of a mechanistic-materialistic concept of the world—the extreme fragmentization of man and decline of rationality.

SOCIAL CONSEQUENCES OF MATERIALISM

Regarding its social consequences Jones observes, 'It cannot contain within itself a reason or rationality which would, in Max Weber's terms, "incorporate the overall or substantive interests of mankind". It cannot do this because the institutions of advanced industrial civilization are oriented to the promotion, above all else, of material growth and progress, and it is this single-minded attachment to materiality at the expense of other human ends or purposes such as spiritual or aesthetic, which has become a destablizing influence in the culture as a whole.'[4]

Neither the idealistic philosophers, like Kant or Hegel, nor the materialists could close up the rift between science and religion. Galileo retained God as the first cause, his function being to push the mechanical world into action. Kant also divided the universe into two worlds. One was the world of time, space and causation in which God had no place. There was another world, the real world, which the senses could not perceive, which was the world of God. Through our moral sense and religious intuition only we could get sometimes an inkling of this world. Hegel conceived of an Absolute Idea which unfolds itself into the finite and through a dialectical process evolves into the perfect Absolute.

3. 'The Violence of Materialism in an Advanced Industrialised Society : An Eco-Sociological Approach'—*The Sociological Review*, February 1987.
4. ibid.

This also could not satisfy the rational mind since it is absurd that the infinite will become finite. Showing the logical gap Vivekananda argued, 'Attempts have been made in Germany to build a system of philosophy on the basis that the Infnite has become the finite . ... but philosophers naturally ask for a logical fundamental basis for the statement that the finite can fully express the Infinite. The Absolute and the Infinite can become this universe only by limitation . ... and for the limited to be the unlimited is simply absurd, and can never be.'[5]

None of these philosophical doctrines were, therefore, able to solve the problem. None could satisfy the rational mind of the modern man and at the same time satisfy his deeper urges. The modern man was, therefore, inevitably committed to the mechanistic, materialistic and deterministic world-view.

III

HISTORICAL SIGNIFICANCE OF VIVEKANANDA'S ADVENT IN THE WEST

Vivekananda gave the modern West the solution to its complex problem of thought and life arising out of the incompatibility between science and religion. As we have seen already, the situation in the West was that a modern man had to compromise his hard-won scientific outlook and betray his reason if he was to accept God. 'Orthodox Christianity prescribed that'—says Marie Louise Burke.[6] Vivekananda vehemently protested against this idea. He said in his characteristic manner, '...it is better that mankind should become atheists by following reason than blindly believe in two hundred millions of gods on the authority of anybody.'[7]

Vivekananda offered solution to the problem by pointing out that the universe governed by the mechanical forces and the universe governed by the non-mechanical forces were the same, they were actually the different readings of an unchanging and

5. *C. W.*, II, p. 99.
6. *Foundation-Day Souvenir*, 1986, Ramakrishna Mission Institute of Culture, p. 9.
7. *C. W.*, II, p. 336.

indivisible Reality. The ultimate Reality, he showed, is One—beyond all forms, beyond all names. It is absolute, infinite, eternal and unchanging. In the words of Swamiji himself, '... this universe itself is the Absolute, unchangeable, the noumenon; and the phenomenon constitutes the reading thereof.'[8] Explaining he said, 'In dualism, the universe is conceived as a large machine set going by God, while in qualified monism, it is conceived as an organism, interpreted by the Divine Self.' 'And ... the non-dualists say, all this is nonsense. ... "This universe does not exist at all; it is all illusion. The whole of this universe . . . and all the other beings born and dying, all this infinite number of souls coming up and going down, are all dreams." There is no *jīva* at all. How can there be many? It is the one Infinity. As the one sun, reflected on various pieces of water, appears to be many, and millions of globules of water reflect so many millions of suns, and in each globule will be a perfect image of the sun, yet there is only one sun, so are all these *jīva*s but reflections in different minds.'[9] Elaborating he further said, 'But a dream cannot be without a reality, and that reality is that one Infinite Existence. You, as body, mind, or soul, are a dream, but what you really are, is Existence, Knowledge, Bliss. ...That those who receive this knowledge are one with the universe.'[10] Interpreting Swamiji, Marie Louise Burke points out : 'Seen in one way, from one state of consciousness, the universe appears as a mass of matter, moving and changing according to its own laws, seen from a different standpoint it appears to be composed of ideas, of thought forms, seen from a yet higher standpoint, it is pure consciousness as is a wax garden (to use a simile of Sri Ramakrishna) composed through and through of wax.'

Thus it is clear that according to Vedanta, as interpreted by Vivekananda, reality is One. Science also laid down even in the nineteenth century the same idea—that there was only one reality but that reality was matter. Hence Vivekananda said—'Science is nothing but the finding of unity'. Explaining he said, 'Do you not see whither science is tending? The Hindu nation proceeded through the study of the mind, through metaphysics and logic. The European nations start from external nature, and now they

---

8. ibid., p. 338. 9. ibid., I, pp. 401-03. 10. ibid., p. 403.

too are coming to the same results. We find that searching through the mind we at last come to that Oneness, that Universal One, the Internal Soul of everything.... Through material science we come to the same Oneness. Science today is telling us that all things are but the manifestation of one energy which is the sum total of everything which exists... .'[11]

Hence he arrived at the conclusion that science and religion are not incompatible. He said, 'It seems to us, and to all who care to know, that the conclusions of modern science are the very conclusions the Vedanta reached ages ago; only, in modern science they are written in the language of matter.'[12]

Vivekananda was confident that one day science will also speak in the language of religion and that religion and science will shake hands. While speaking of the need of fellow-feeling between religions he said that this was also needed between religion and materialistic sciences. In this connection he makes a very significant statement in which he says, 'To bring about this harmony, both will have to make concessions, sometimes very large, nay more, sometimes painful, but each will find itself the better for the sacrifice and more advanced in truth. And in the end, the knowledge which is confined within the domain of time and space will meet and become one with that which is beyond them both, where the mind and senses cannot reach—the Absolute, the Infinite, the One without a second.'[13] Dwelling on the same topic he adds in another statement : 'This union will give us the highest philosophy. Science and religion will meet and shake hands. . . . This will be the religion of the future, and if we can work it out, we may be sure that it will be for all times and peoples. This is the one way that will prove acceptable to modern science, for it has almost come to it. When the scientific teacher asserts that all things are the manifestation of one force, does it not remind you of the God of whom you hear in the Upanishads : "As the one fire entering into the universe expresses itself in various forms, even so that One Soul is expressing Itself in every soul and yet is infinitely more besides?" '[14]

How clear was Vivekananda's conception of the unity of

---

11. ibid., II, pp. 140-41.
12. ibid., III, p. 185.
13. ibid., II, p. 69.
14. ibid., p. 140.

science and religion, is evident from a letter written by him to Mr Sturdy in February 1896 in which he writes, 'I am working a good deal now upon the cosmology and eschatology of the Vedanta. I clearly see their perfect unison with modern science.... I intend to write a book later on in the form of questions and answers. ... The first chapter will be on cosmology, showing the harmony between Vedantic theories and modern science.' He laid down his ideas in the form of a chart in the said letter which is produced below :

Brahman	=	The Absolute
Mahat or Īśvara	=	Primal Creative Energy
Prāṇa and Ākāśa	=	Force and Matter

Explaining he says, '... all these spheres or layers of the universe are only so many varying products of Ākāśa and Prāṇa. ... the lowest or most condensed is the Solar sphere, consisting of the visible universe, in which Prāṇa appears as physical force, and Ākāśa as sensible matter. The next is called the Lunar sphere, which surrounds the Solar sphere. This is not the moon at all ... Prāṇa appears in it as psychic forces, and Ākāśa as *tanmātra*s, or fine particles. Beyond this is the Electric sphere ... a condition in which the Prāṇa is almost inseparable from Ākāśa... . Next is Brahmaloka, where there is neither Prāṇa nor Ākāśa, but both are merged in the mind-stuff, the primal energy. And here— there being neither Prāṇa nor Ākāśa—the *jīva* contemplates the whole universe and *samaṣṭi*, or the sum total of *mahat* or mind. This appears as a Puruṣa, an abstract universal soul, yet not the Absolute, for still there is multiplicity. From this the *jīva* finds at last that Unity which is the end.'[15]

Thus, Vivekananda showed in the nineteenth century that there was no incompatibility between science and religion, both being enquiries into the realm of the same reality. He showed also, as we have seen in the previous chapter, that there can be a

15. ibid., V, pp. 102-03.

rationalistic religion so that in accepting it a modern man will not have to go against the dictates of reason and hard-won scientific attitude. Vedanta is that rationalistic religion since it preaches the same thing as the science preaches, viz., that reality is One. Some scientists of the contemporary period agreed with this view of Vivekananda. In one of his lectures Vivekananda has revealed this. He said, 'I have myself been told by some of the best western scientific minds of the day, how wonderfully rational the conclusions of the Vedanta are. I know one of them personally who scarcely has time to eat his meal or go out of his laboratory, but who yet would stand by the hour to attend my lectures on the Vedanta; for, as he expresses it, they are so scientific, they so exactly harmonize with the aspirations of the age and with the conclusions to which modern science is coming at the present time.'[16] And we will presently see also that religion, as claimed by Vivekananda, is empirical and observation and experiment are its important instruments as in the case of natural sciences.

Thus we find that the pestering problem of the modern West, the crisis in its thought and life, was successfully solved by Vivekananda. Herein lies the historic significance of his advent in the West.

IV

TWENTIETH CENTURY SCIENCE AND RELIGION

Science and Vedanta came much closer in the twentieth century through the advancements made in the field of science. Contrary to the nineteenth century assertion that science has reached the pinnacle of its development, it has come to be admitted today that behind the phenomenal world another world lies hidden which has set the stage for the former and about this hidden world very little has come to be known as yet. It is the world which the scientists call the 'Real World'. And it may therefore rightly be said that the science in the twentieth century has come face to face with the veil of *māyā* and it is now attempting to have a glimpse of what is behind by raising the veil. Speaking on *What is Life*, Schrödinger, a well-known scientist, observes, 'Consciousness is

16. ibid., III, p. 185.

singular of which plural is unknown, that there is only one thing and that, what seems to be a plurality, is merely a series of different aspects of this one thing, produced by a deception (the Indian *māyā*), the same illusion is produced in a gallery of mirrors. . . .'[17] Here we find a noted scientist actually using the concept of Indian *māyā* in Vedanta while making a scientific exposition.

As a result of what has happened in science in the twentieth century, the whole perspective of thought in the scientific world has got transformed. Einstein set the stage for this new perspective with his relativity theory. According to the relativity theory, in the words of Professor Capra, '... space is not three-dimensional and time is not a separate entity. Both are intimately connected and form a four-dimensional continuum "space-time". In relativity theory, therefore, we can never talk about space without talking about time and vice versa.' 'Furthermore, there is no universal flow of time', he adds, 'as in the Newtonian model. Different observers will order events differently in time if they move with different velocities relative to the observed events. In such a case, two events which are seen as occurring simultaneously by an observer may occur in different temporal sequences for other observers. All measurements involving space and time thus lose their absolute significance.'

Next should be mentioned Plank's quantum theory which also revolutionized science. 'Max Plank discovered', says Professor Capra, 'that the energy of heat radiation is not emitted continuously but appears in the form of "energy packets". Einstein called these energy packets "quanta" and recognized them as a fundamental aspect of nature.'[18] In this connection Plank has made an important declaration, 'In the world of atoms, the law of causality has definitely failed.'[19]

Still another theory to revolutionize the scientific world was Heisenberg's 'uncertainty principle'. As stated by Professor Capra, the precise mathematical form of the relation between the

---

17. Erwin Schrödinger, *What is Life*, Cambridge University (1946), p. 90.
18. *The Tao Of Physics*, p. 56.
19. *Parliament of Religions*—Swami Vivekananda Centenary Committee, 1965, p. 307.

uncertainties of position and momentum of a particle is known as Heisenberg's uncertainty principle. 'It means that, in the sub-atomic world we can never know both the position and momentum of a particle with great accuracy.'

Net Results of these Theories : After Eienstein's theory of relativity, Plank's quantum theory, Heisenberg's uncertainty principle, De Broglie's work on the nature of light and Niels Bohr's principle of complementarity shattered the materialistic, mechanistic and the deterministic shackles of the nineteenth century science. Summarizing the net trend Professor Pitirim A. Sorokin observes : 'For this modern science matter has become but a condensed form of energy which dematerializes into radiation. The material atom is already dissolved into more than thirty non-material, "cryptic, arcane, perplexing, enigmatic, and inscrutable" elementary particles : the electron and the anti-electron, the proton and the anti-proton, the photon, the meson, etc., or into "the image of waves which our thought projects afar".'[20] Continuing with his summarization Professor Sorokin further observes—'Around a bend of quantum mechanics and at the foot of the electronic ladder the basic notions of "materialistic and mechanistic science", such as "matter", "objective reality", "time", "space" and "causality" are no longer applicable and the testimony of our senses loses its significance.'[21] 'As to the deterministic causality', Sorokin adds, 'it is already replaced in the modern science by Heisenberg's principle of uncertainty by fanciful quantum jumps, by a mere chance-relationship or in the psycho-social phenomena by voluntaristic "free-willing law of direction" exempt from causality and chance.'[22]

This revolutionary trend is not only characteristic of modern physics, but also of biology, psychology and the social sciences. Noting the trends in these other sciences Sorokin comments, 'In contrast to the superannuated, though still intoned, clitches of mechanistic, materialistic, and deterministic biology, psychology, and sociology, the rising, significant theories in these disciplines clearly show that the phenomena of life, organism, personality, mind and socio-cultural processes are irreducible to, and cannot

20. *Vedanta and the West*, No. 139, p. 9.
21. ibid., pp. 9-10.
22. ibid., pp. 9-10.

be understood as, purely materialistic, mechanistic and sensory realities. According to these theories they have, besides their empirical aspects, the far more important—mindfully, rational and even super-sensory and super-rational—aspects.'[23]

New Concept of Total Reality : Previously materialistic science denied the existence of any non-sensory reality. At the present moment this concept is abandoned by all the scientists as too narrow and too inadequate. In the words of Sorokin again, 'Today this total reality is thought of as the infinite X of numberless qualities and quantities : spiritual and material, temporal and timeless, everchanging and unchangeable, personal and super-personal, spatial and spaceless. Of its innumerable modes of being three basic forms appear to be important : (a) empirical-sensory, (b) rational-minded, and (c) super rational-supersensory.'[24] This concept is considered by the scientists much nearer to the concepts of reality in all the great religions of the world.

Theory of Cognition : Inevitably with the change in the concept of total reality there has been a change in the scientific theory of cognition. In his masterly analysis Sorokin throws light also on this aspect of changed trend in modern science. Today, according to him, it is admitted that there are at least three different channels of cognition : sensory, rational, and supersensory-superrational. 'The empirical aspect of total reality', observes Sorokin, 'is perceived by us through our sense organs and their extensions : microscopes, telescopes, etc. The rational aspect of the reality is comprehended by us mainly through our reason : mathematical and logical thought in all its rational forms. Finally, the glimpses of the superrational-supersensory forms of the reality are given to us by the true supersensory-superrational "Intuition" or "divine inspiration", or "flash of enlightenment of all creative geniuses : founders of great religions ... giants of philosophy and ethics, great scientists, artists, moral leaders and other eminent creators in all fields of culture".'[25] This 'supersensory-superrational' intuition is spoken of as the instrument of supreme knowledge in various religions and it is called by various names in different religions : 'no-knowledge' in Taoism, 'samādhi' in Hinduism, 'enlightenment' in

---

23. ibid., p. 10. 24. ibid. 25. ibid., p. 11.

Christianity. Today we find a scientific confirmation of such supersensory-superrational concepts in vogue in old religions. This is evident in the following statement of Professor Capra—'Probing inside the atom and investigating its structure, science transcends the limits of our sensory imagination. From this point on, it could no longer rely with absolute certainty on logic and common sense. Atomic physics provided the scientists with the first glimpses of the essential nature of things. Like the mystics, physicists are now dealing with a nonsensory experience of reality and, like the mystics, they had to face the paradoxical aspects of this experience.'[26]

Theory of Human Personality : A change has come also in the concept of human personality. From the Freudian concept of human personality dominated by pan-sexual unconscious libido today we have come upon a new concept in which man is not merely an animal organism but also a rational thinker and doer, and moreover is a supersensory-superrational being who is 'an active participant in the supreme, creative forces of the cosmos', capable of transcending unconscious and conscious levels and pass on to superconscious states in moments of direct perception of reality.

V

CONSCIOUSNESS AS THE SOURCE OF MATTER

A few years back Dr George Wald, a Nobel-laureate in Biology and Medicine and a Professor of the Harvard University, made a revealing statement in Calcutta while lecturing at the Indian Statistical Institute. According to a newspaper report, Dr Wald said, '... it was good physics, and not vague mysticism to consider "consciousness" as the source of matter.' Speaking on the 'Life in the universe', he said that to believe in consciousness as the source of universe was better than the notions of astrophysics which believed in continuous creation of hydrogen in the universe from nothing or of the theoritical physicists who believed the elementary particles came from the space.[27] This is clearly in accordance with Vedanta since Vedanta upholds that

26. *The Tao Of Physics*, pp. 38-39.
27. *The Statesman*—a date between 1 and 12 November, 1979.

reality of the universe is at substratum 'consciousness'. Eddington, the famous physicist, also said, 'All through the physical world runs that unknown content, which must surely be the stuff of our consciousness.'[28]

Modern Science and Eastern World-View : Thus we notice today a definite trend towards convergence of modern science and eastern world-view. Dr Capra has made the most outspoken statement in this respect in his sensational book *Tao of Physics*, mentioned already. Dr Capra said that the basic elements of eastern world-view, emerging more generally from mystical thought, provide a consistent and relevant philosophical background to the theories of contemporary science.[29] While introducing the book he says moreover—'We shall see how the two foundations of twentieth-century physics—quantum theory and relativity theory—both force us to see the world very much in the way a Hindu, Buddhist or Taoist sees it, and how this similarity strengthens when we look at the recent attempts to combine these two theories in order to describe the phenomena of the submicroscopic world : the properties and interactions of the subatomic particles of which all matter is made. Here the parallels between modern physics and eastern mysticism are most striking, and we shall often encounter statements where it is almost impossible to say whether they have been made by physicists or by eastern mystics.'[30]

THE EASTERN WORLD-VIEW : ORGANIC CONCEPT

In contrast to the mechanistic and materialistic world-view of the nineteenth century science, the eastern world-view is organic. According to Vedanta, as we have seen already, Reality is one, it appears as many through the veil of *māyā*. This happens due to ignorance. Attainment of Knowledge leads to the realization of this unity. As stated by Professor Capra, 'In the eastern view, then, the division of nature into separate objects is not fundamental and any such objects have a fluid and ever-changing character. The eastern world-view is therefore intrinsically dynamic and contains time

---

28. *Space-Time and Gravitation* (quoted by Swami Ranganathananda in his book *Science and Religion*), p. 125.
29. *The Tao Of Physics*, p. 11.
30. ibid., pp. 4-5.

and change as essential features. The cosmos is seen as one inseparable reality—forever in motion, alive, organic; spiritual and material at the same time. '[31] 'Correspondingly', Professor Capra specifically points out, 'the eastern image of the Divine is not that of a ruler who directs the world from above, but of a principle that controls everything from within'.[32]

Recent changes in science has led to a replacement of the mechanistic concept by an organic concept as we have already noted. In view of this, Professor Capra asserts that '... eastern thought—and, more generally, mystical thought—provides a consistent and relevant philosophical background to the theories of contemporary science; a conception of the world in which scientific discoveries can be in perfect harmony with spiritual aims and religious beliefs.'[33] Elucidating the point he observes, 'The two basic themes of this conception are the unity and interrelation of all phenomena and the intrinsically dynamic nature of the universe. The further we penetrate into the submicroscopic world, the more we shall realize how the modern physicist, like the eastern mystic, has come to see the world as a system of inseparable, interacting, and ever moving components, with the observer being an integral part of the system.'[34]

We have seen already that Swami Vivekananda emphasized these points at the end of the nineteenth century. He claimed that Vedanta was the most scientific religion since it preached unity of the universe in Brahman—the Existence Absolute, the Knowledge Absolute, and the Bliss Absolute. It was also the most scientific religion since it preached also that 'This universe has not been created by any extra-cosmic God, nor is it the work of any outside genius. It is self-creating, self-dissolving, self-manifesting, One Infinite Existence, the Brahman. *Tattvamasi Śvetaketo*—That thou art, O Śvetaketu!'[35]

In Vivekananda's time science had just discovered that in the midst of the variety of forces there is unity. In his own words, 'It has just discovered that what it calls heat, magnetism, electricity, and so forth, are all convertible into one unit force... .'[36] He pointed out

31. ibid., pp. 10-11.
32. ibid., p. 11.
33. ibid.
34. ibid.
35. *C. W.*, III, pp. 423-24.
36. ibid., p. 399.

that this idea was to be found in the *Saṁhitā* in the concepts of Prāṇa and Ākāśa. But as regards unity of force and matter, he points out, 'our modern science is mute'. But he predicted that this unity will soon be found and in the twentieth century it has been found.

To Swami Vivekananda fragmentation of mind and body was not possible since mind also was matter in a tenuous form and mind was the instrument of still another unity.

He held that 'Time, space and causation cannot be said to be independent existences. ... The present has no existence apart from the past and the future. It is all one complete whole, the idea of time has been imposed upon us by the form of our understanding.' After Einstein's theory of time-space unity, modern conception of time had to accept the unity of a compounded past, present and future.

VI

IMPACT ON RELIGION

What does all these developments leading to Scientific-Vedanta *rapprochement* imply for religion? Today we find that instead of dislodging religion, science has come to stand as a proof of it. According to Amaury de Riencourt, the latest development in science 'would be an objective validity to the general mystical experience when stripped of mythological trapping of the various cultures and religions in which it is expressed'.[37] According to him further, 'This would amount to a mutual confirmation of the latest scientific revolution and the overall mystical experience.' Going one step further he adds, 'It might also be areas of potential collaboration between scientists and mystics if a connection between their respective frames of reference can be established.'[38]

Schrödinger also finds, as we have seen already, plenty of support for the basic Vedantic vision. He points out specifically 'that the plurality perceived by us is an illusion'. Quoting Vedanta philosophy and its famous analogy of the universe as similar to a many-faced crystal which shows multitudes of

37. Amaury de Riencourt, *The Eye of Shiva*, p. 41. 38. ibid.

pictures of what is a single reality without multiplying, he attempts to establish it.[39]

VII

SCIENCE AND RELIGION—BOTH EXPERIMENTAL

According to Riencourt, both science and religion are thoroughly empirical enquiries. 'Both are experimental', he points out, 'both observe with detatchment—easily in the East since ego and personality have to be dismissed as fundamentally unreal.'[40] The view that is popularly held, viz., that science is subject to experimentation while mysticism is not, is being seriously challenged today by the scientists themselves.

To the argument that controlled experiment is not possible in the case of religion and mysticism, Romain Rolland answers that control is possible but that depends on the person who undertakes it. 'It is for you', he says, 'to control its observation. It does not avoid control, rather it seeks it, for it (Vedanta) does not belong to those religious camps that entrench themselves behind the mystery of their revelations. Its doors and windows are wide open to all. Come and see.'[41] Thus the religion of Vedanta accepts the challenge of experimentation.

THE NATURE OF EXPERIMENT IN RELIGION AND MYSTICISM

According to Professor Capra, 'The firm basis of knowledge on experience in eastern mysticism suggests a parallel to the firm basis of scientific knowledge on experiment. This parallel is further enforced by the nature of the mystical experience. It is described in the eastern traditions as a direct insight which lies outside the realm of the intellect and is obtained by watching rather than thinking; by looking inside oneself; by observation.'[42] Professor Capra shows clearly that 'When the eastern mystics talk about "seeing", they refer to a mode of perception which may include visual perception, but which always and essentially

39. *What is Life*, p. 90.
40. *The Eye of Shiva*, p. 126.
41. Romain Rolland, *Life of Vivekananda*, p. 262.
42. *The Tao Of Physics*, p. 22.

transcends it to become a nonsensory experience of reality.'[43] 'What they do emphasize, however,' Professor Capra adds throwing more light on the nature of experience or experiment of the eastern mystics, 'when they talk about seeing, looking or observing, is the empirical character of their knowledge. This empirical approach of eastern philosophy is strongly reminiscent of the emphasis on observation in science and thus suggests a framework for our comparison.'[44]

The appropriateness of this comparison may be questioned since the physicists work in a team and with the aid of a highly sophisticated technology, their experiments are repeatable, but the mystic obtains his knowledge through introspection without any external aid and his experiment, it is generally believed, is not repeatable. To this pertinent question Professor Capra's answer in brief is : 'Repetition of experiments in subatomic physics is not also easy, it requires many years of training just as the mystic requires many years of training under an experienced and able guide' and 'as in the case of the scientific training the dedicated time does not guarantee success'. But, 'If the student is successful', rightly points out Professor Capra, 'he or she will be able to repeat the experiment.' And as Professor Capra reveals further, 'The repeatability of the experience is, in fact, essential to every mystical training and is the very aim of the mystics' spiritual instruction.'[45]

Furthermore, Professor Capra takes pain to show that 'A mystical experience, therefore, is not any more unique than a modern experiment in physics. . . . The complexity and efficiency of the physicist's technical apparatus is matched, if not surpassed, by that of the mystic's consciousness—both physical and spiritual—in deep meditation. The scientists and the mystics, then, have developed highly sophisticated methods of observing nature which are inaccessible to the lay person.'[46]

VIII

ROLES OF FAITH IN SCIENCE AND RELIGION

Charles Townes, a Nobel-laureate in physics and Professor of

---

43. ibid. 44. ibid., pp. 22-23. 45. ibid., p. 23. 46. ibid.

physics at the Massachusetts Institute of Technology, U.S.A., dwelling on the popularly known theories of divergence between science and religion points out in an illuminating article[47] that they centre round the role of faith and revelation in religion. According to him, both faith and revelation have an essential role to play not only in religion but in science also. 'The essential role of faith in religion', he observes, 'is so well known that taking things on faith rather than proving them is usually taken as characteristic of religion as distinguishing religion from science. But faith is essential to science too, although we do not generally recognize the basic need and nature of faith in science.'[48] Citing the example of Einstein, the greatest scientist of the present century, Professor Townes further observes, 'Einstein affords a rather explicit example of faith in order, and many of his contributions come from intuitive devotion to a particularly appealing type of order.'[49] 'Einstein spent the last half of his life', adds Dr Townes, 'looking for a unity between gravitational and electro-magnetic fields. Many physicists feel he was on the wrong track, and no one yet knows whether he made any subsequent progress. But he had faith in a great vision of unity and order, and he worked intensely at it for thirty years or more. Einstein had to have the kind of dogged conviction that could have allowed him to say with joy, "though he slay me, yet will I trust in him".'[50]

Role of Revelation in Science and Religion : Regarding the role of revelation in science and religion Professor Townes shows in an illuminating account that scientific discoveries are, just like the religious truths, very much the results of revelations. 'Religious discoveries', he says, 'often come by great revelations; scientific knowledge, in the popular mind, comes by logical deductions, or by accumulation of data or of data which is analysed by established method in order to draw generalizations called laws. But such a description of the scientific discovery is a travesty of the real thing. Most of the important scientific discoveries can come about very differently and are much more closely akin to revelation.'[51] Gautama Buddha had revelation

47. *Prabuddha Bhārata*, March 1967, p. 145. 48. ibid., p. 148.
49. ibid., p. 149. 50. ibid. 51. ibid.

after years of toil and enquiry. Similarly, according to Townes, a scientist after years of investigations regarding a troubling problem suddenly comes upon the answer. 'Such ideas', emphasizes Professor Townes, 'more often come during off-moments than while confronting data.' Citing an example he says, 'A striking and well-known discovery of the "benzene ring" by Kekule, who while musing at his fireside was led to the idea of a vision of snakes taking their tails in their mouths.'[52] 'We cannot', he adds, commenting on the nature of such revelations leading to scientific discoveries, 'yet describe the human process which leads to the creation of an important and substantially new scientific insight. But, it is clear that the great scientific discoveries, the real leaps do not usually come from the so-called "scientific method" but rather more as did Kekule's—with perhaps less picturesque imagery, but by revelations which are just as real.'[53]

Are Scientific Postulates proved and Religious Postulates unproved?

It is popularly held that scientific discoveries can be definitely proved whereas religious ideas have only the faith of their prophets to support them. It is also a popular belief that definite 'proof' gives the scientific ideas a certain kind of absolutism and universalism which is lacking in the case of religious ideas. According to Townes, the entire process of 'proving' based on mathematical postulates and laws of logic are on shaking grounds. 'Mathematical or logical proof', he goes on to state, 'involves choice of some set of postulates, which hopefully are consistent with one another and which apply to a situation of interest. In the case of natural science, they are presumed to apply to the world around us. Next, on the basis of agreed laws of logic, one can derive or "prove" the consequences of these postulates.'[54] Some mathematicians have shown that, in the most generally used mathematics, it is fundamentally impossible to know whether or not the set of postulates chosen are even self-consistent. Referring to this Townes observes, '... only by constructing and using a new set of master postulates can

52. ibid. 53. ibid. 54. ibid.

we test the consistency of first set. But these in turn may be logically inconsistent without the possibility of our knowing it. Thus we never have a real base from which we can reason with surety.'[55] 'Godel doubles our surprises', adds Dr Townes, 'by showing that ... there are mathematical truths which fundamentally cannot be proved by the approach of normal logic.'[56] Thus Godel has convincingly proved the limitations of human logic on which we depend for arriving at our so-called 'proof' of scientific truth.

Validity of scientific postulates, it is believed, can also be proved through experiments. Regarding the nature of scientific experiments Professor Townes observes, 'We derive experiences to test our experiments and believe those laws or hypotheses are correct which seem to agree with our experience. Such tests can disprove an hypothesis or can give us useful confidence in its applicability and correctness, but never proof in any absolute sense.'[57] In his opinion religious beliefs may also be viewed as working hypotheses, tested and validated by experience. 'The validity of religious ideas', says Charles Townes, 'must be and has been tested and judged through the ages by saints and by individual experience.'

He admits that perhaps controlled experiment on religious ideas is not possible at all and we have to rely on human history and personal experience. Here it must be noted that personal experiences recorded in various countries and in the different countries agree to a surprising extent. Dwelling on this point Vivekananda said, 'As mathematics in every part of the world does not differ, so the mystics do not differ. ... Their experience is the same; and this becomes law.'[58] But, as Professor Townes points out, this lack of controlled experiment is to be found in the case of certain natural sciences as well as in the social sciences, and in these cases also we have to depend on experience and observation in testing hypothesis instead of easily reproducible experiments.

As we have seen already, Dr Capra also expressed the same opinion. He has pointed out that everybody has moments of intuitive insight even in moments when we understand a joke and all scientific discoveries are the results of this intuitive insight.

---

55. ibid., p. 150. 56. ibid. 57. ibid. 58. *C. W.*, VI, p. 81.

The eastern mystics cultivate this faculty through meditations by silencing the rational mind. A stage comes at last where there is an identification of the observer with the environment and direct perception of the reality is obtained.

There is also difficulty of giving the mystic's experience a proper expression. They cannot be expressed in words as Sri Ramakrishna said. Professor Capra has thrown light on it in his brilliant analysis in his book *Tao of Physics*. He points out that in this matter scientist faces the same difficulty. 'Since words are', he observes, 'always an abstract, approximate map of reality, the verbal interpretations of a scientific experiment or of a mystical insight are necessarily inaccurate and incomplete. Modern physicists and eastern mystics alike are well aware of this fact.'[59] His concluding remarks in this respect are very significant : 'Whenever the eastern mystics express their knowledge in words—be it with the help of myths, symbols, poetic images or paradoxical statements—they are well aware of this limitations imposed by language and "linear" thinking. Modern physics has come to take exactly the same attitude with regard to its verbal models and theories. They, too, are only approximate and necessarily inaccurate. They are the counterparts of the eastern myths, symbols and poetic images .... The same idea about matter is conveyed, for example, to the Hindu by the cosmic dance of the god Shiva as to the physicist by certain aspects of quantum-field theory. Both the dancing god and the physical theory are creations of the mind : models to describe their authors' intuition of reality.'[60] This is a direct blow to the popular view that science proves with absolute certainty while religion deals with myths and unrealities which cannot be proved. Here a physicist asserts that theories of physics are as much a creation of the mind as the concept of a dancing God by a mystic. Physical theories are models to describe their author's intuition of Reality as much as the concept of dancing Shiva is the Hindu mystic's intuition of Reality.

IX

SCIENTIFIC CONCEPT OF CONSCIOUSNESS

Regarding the nature of consciousness new light has been

---

59. *The Tao Of Physics*, p. 27. 60. ibid., pp. 30-31.

thrown by scientific discoveries. Riencourt observes, '... the root of consciousness is wholly beyond what we term physical nature, that is the space-time universe that our senses apprehend, and that consciousness is related to life as meaning is to expression. Consciousness intrudes into our space-time universe by means of organic development, but springs from another dimension altogether, coming, as it were, from inside out. Consciousness, as such, is deathless since it belongs to a plane of reality that is beyond life and death as well as beyond time and space—death being merely the withdrawal of consciousness from the space-time universe of phenomena that we can observe from outside, what dies and is reborn however, is the expression of consciousness, that is organic life.'[61]

Thus it is obvious that a mysterious spiritual force appears to sustain life and consciousness, and this the mystic comprehends in his ecstatic experiences. As Riencourt points out specifically, 'Physics now accepts the fact that we have to restore consciousness to the fundamental position in the universe, rather than see it simply as a secondary material epiphenomenon derived from a particular arrangement of atoms and particles in the brain.'[62]

X

THE CONCEPT OF 'MĀYĀ' AND MODERN SCIENCE

The theory of *māyā*, one of the basic tenets of Vedanta philosophy, has also got now the scientists' approval. Reflecting on modern physics Professor Capra points out—'Such a theory of subatomic particles reflects the impossibility of separating the scientific observer from the observed phenomena.... It implies, ultimately, that the structures and phenomena we observe in nature are nothing but creations of our measuring and categorizing mind.'[63] Drawing a comparison with the theory of *māyā,* Professor Capra further observes, 'The eastern mystics tell us again and again that all things and events we perceive are

---

61. *The Eye of Shiva*, p. 184.
62. ibid., p. 30.
63. *The Tao Of Physics*, p. 266.

creations of the mind, arising from a particular state of consciousness and dissolving again if this state is transcended. Hinduism holds that all shapes and structures around us are created by a mind under the spell of *māyā*, and it regards our tendency to attach deep significance to them as the basic human illusion.'[64] We have already noted the view of Schrödinger in this respect. In his book *What is life* he uses the term 'Indian *māyā*' to explain his views on the nature of life and consciousness.

XI

MODERN SCIENCE ON THE TRANSCENDENT NATURE OF REALITY

Throwing light on the transcendent nature of Reality, Professor Capra says, 'The space-time of relativistic physics is a similar timeless space of a higher dimension. All events in it are inter-connected, but the connections are not causal. ... When they are taken as four-dimensional patterns without any definite direction of time attached to them, there is no "before" and no "after", and thus no causation.'[65] Thus Reality transcends space, time and causation. In support of his views in this connection he quotes Swami Vivekananda. 'Similarly', he says, 'the eastern mystic asserts that in transcending time they also transcend the world of cause and effect. Like our ordinary notions of space and time, causation is an idea which is limited to a certain experience of the world and has to be abandoned when this experience is extended.' 'In the words of Swami Vivekananda', he quotes, '"Time, space, and causation are like the glass through which the Absolute is seen. ... In the Absolute there is neither time, space, nor causation".'[66]

XII

THE CONVERGENCE

Thus today we find Vivekananda's prediction has come true. Science and Vedanta has come to shake hands. The world-views of modern science and of eastern mystics, the best expression of

---

64. ibid. 65. ibid., p. 173. 66. ibid.

which is to be found in Vedanta, are the same. 'Both emerge', as Professor Capra points out, 'when one inquires into the essential nature of things—into the deeper realms of matter in physics; into the deeper realms of consciousness in mysticism—when one discovers a different reality behind the superficial mechanistic appearance of everyday life.'[67] They have other similarities. In the words of Professor Capra, 'To begin with, their method is thoroughly empirical. Physicists derive their knowledge from experiments; mystics from meditative insights. Both are observations, and in both fields these observations, are acknowledged as the only source of knowledge.'[68] 'The mystic looks within', as Professor Capra describes it, 'and explores his or her consciousness at its various levels, which include the body as the physical manifestation of the mind. ... In contrast to the mystic, the physicist begins his inquiry into the essential nature of things by studying the material world.' They arrive at the same goal though they come to it through different routes. 'Penetrating into ever-deeper realms of matter, he [the physicist] has become aware of the essential unity of all things and events. More than that, he has also learnt that he himself and his consciousness are an integral part of this unity. Thus the mystic and the physicist arrive at the same conclusion; one starting from the inner realm, the other from the outer world.'[69] Then he makes the sensational statement that the harmony between their views confirms the ancient Indian wisdom that Brahman, the ultimate reality without, is identical to *ātman*, the reality within.[70]

Same ideas were expressed by Vivekananda in 1896 when he said, 'Science is nothing but the finding of unity. As soon as science would reach perfect unity, it would stop from further progress, because it would reach the goal. Thus chemistry could not progress further when it could discover one element out of which all others could be made. Physics would stop when it would be able to fulfil its services in discovering one energy of which all the others are but manifestations, and the science of religion become perfect when it would discover Him who is the one life in a universe of death, Him who is the constant basis of

67. ibid., p. 295. 68. ibid. 69. ibid., p. 296. 70. ibid.

an ever-changing world. One who is the only Soul of which all souls are but delusive manifestations. Thus through multiplicity and duality, that the ultimate is reached. This is the goal of all science.'[71]

'All science', Vivekananda asserts, 'is bound to this conclusion in the long run. Manifestation, and not creation, is the word of science today, and the Hindu is only glad that what he has been cherishing in his bosom for ages is going to be taught in more forcible language, and with further light from the latest conclusions of science.'[72]

The long and short of this illuminating statement is that the goal of science and goal of religion are the same and therefore it is inevitable that the two will converge. What in addition is emphasized here is that science will stand proof of religion.

Going one step further Professor Capra points out, '...there is an essential harmony between the spirit of eastern wisdom and western science. ... modern physics goes far beyond technology, that the way—or *Tao*—of physics can be a path with a heart, a way to spiritual knowledge and self-realization.'[73]

Swami Vivekananda, after forcefully establishing that Advaita Vedanta is the only scientific religion, said in a similar tone, 'Thus you see that this and this alone, and none else, can be the only scientific religion. And with all the prattle about science that is going on daily at the present moment in modern half-educated India, with all the talk of rationalism and reason that I hear everyday, I expect that whole sects of you will come over and dare to be Advaitists and dare to preach it to the world in the words of Buddha ... "For the good of many, for the happiness of many". ... That is the Advaita position. Have mercy on others.'[74]

Science and mysticism are two complementary manifestations of human mind, of its rational and intuitive faculties. The modern scientists have made extreme specialization of the rationalized mind, mystics have made extreme specialization of the intuitive mind. The two must combine in future to make man a perfect being and to have a more perfect knowledge of the Universal Reality.

---

71. *C. W.*, I, pp. 14-15.
72. ibid., p. 15.
73. *The Tao Of Physics*, p. 12.
74. *C. W.*, III, p. 424.

Finally, Vivekananda emphasized again and again that the Reality, the Absolute was not a matter of speculation but of supersensuous experience. 'The mind is not to be ruffled by vain arguments, because argument will not help us to know God. It is a question of fact and not of argument. All arguments and reasoning must be based upon certain perceptions without which there cannot be argument. Reasoning is the method of comparison between certain facts, which we have already perceived. If these perceived facts are not there already, there cannot be any reasoning. If this is true of the external phenomena, why can it not be so with the internal? The chemists take certain chemicals and certain results are produced. This is a fact : you see it, you sense it and make that the basis of which to build all your chemical arguments. So with the physicists, so with all other sciences. All knowledge must stand on perception of certain facts, and upon that we have to build our reasoning. But, curiously enough, the vast majority of mankind think, especially at the present time, that no such perception is possible in religion, that religion can only be apprehended by vain arguments. ... Religion is a question of facts and not of talk. We have to analyse our soul and find what is there. ... There are certain religious facts which have to be perceived, and upon them religion will be built.'

'This is one great idea to learn to hold on to, the idea of realization.'

'This is the watchword of Vedanta—realize religion, no talking will do.'

The important conclusion that follows is that if science is valid, so is religion. As we have seen the confluence of the two is also inevitable. Vedanta propounded by Vivekananda is the scientific religion with the covergence of science and religion. And the keynote of this religion is realization. Finally it is a practical science—'a path with a heart', its motto being 'for the good of the many, for the happiness of the many', uttered by Buddha.

Swami Vivekananda thus developed Vedanta as a background philosophy of modern science. He did it in advance anticipating many of the developments of twentieth century science. Talking about Vedanta he boldly declared that this and this alone can be the only scientific religion.

Considering the developments of modern science Amaury de Riencourt raises a very important question : 'Can a connection between the scientific and mystical frames of reference be established over and beyond a certain metaphysical parallelism?' In answer he then goes on to show that 'Indian mysticism, at least as far as its leading representatives are concerned, has evolved as much in the past hundred years as the science of physics itself, in a direction that points towards an inevitable convergence of the two.' And he further points out specifically that 'From its (Indian mysticism) modern awakening with Sri Ramakrishna and Swami Vivekananda, eastern mysticism has begun to adopt its revelations to the entirely different cultural framework provided by science and technology, without in any way sacrificing what is valid in its traditional understanding of the phenomenon itself.'[75]

In this way we find that what Swami Vivekananda said in respect of Vedanta being the most suitable background philosophy of modern science is being confirmed by modern western scholars, by the scientists today.

75. *The Eye of Shiva*, p. 190.

CHAPTER 6

The Problem of Contradictions

I

CONTRADICTIONS IN LIFE

Till the twentieth century, science in all its phases of development, was unable to solve one basic problem of life, viz., the problem of contradictions. The universe, as it appears to us, is not only a multiplicity of existence but also a bundle of contradictions like good and bad, life and death, pleasure and pain, darkness and light, and so on and so forth. If we admit anything 'is', we must simultaneously admit 'it is not'. Science being silent on this point, it was left to the philosophers, both in the East and in the West to deal with the problem. No social thinker also could bypass it. It has been, in fact, one of the main preoccupations of a stern materialist like Karl Marx also. The most outstanding philosopher in the West who attempted a solution of the riddle was Hegel, the well-known German philosopher. Hegelian dialectics were attempted to be improved upon by Marx in order to make it suitable for explaining his theories about social contradictions. Swami Vivekananda also has attempted a solution on the basis of Vedanta with important bearing on his social philosophy. Twentieth century science seems to be in full agreement with this solution, as we shall see below.

II

HEGEL'S SOLUTION : THE DIALECTICS

According to Hegel, 'The true reality is reason, all being is the embodiment of a pregnant thought, all becoming a movement of the concept, the world a development of thought.'[1] All

1. Richard Falkenberg, *History of Modern Philosophy*, p. 489.

important to Hegel was the concept of 'the Absolute'. To Hegel, 'this absolute is movement and life' and the absolute is immanent in Reality. According to Hegel further, 'Absolute or the logical idea exists first as a system of antemundane concepts, then it descends into the unconscious sphere of nature, awakens to self-consciousness in man, realizes its content in social institutions, in order, finally in art, religion, and science to return to itself enriched and completed : i.e., to attain a higher absoluteness than that at the beginning!'[2] Thus the absolute is a process and all that is real is the manifestation of this process.

The process manifests itself through the threefold rhythm—thesis, antithesis and synthesis. This is Hegel's dialectical method. 'All reality is development, and the motive force in this development (of the world as well as of science) is opposition, contradiction. Without this there would be no movement, no life. Thus all reality is full of contradiction... .'[3] According to Hegel, to any concept, there is a contradictory concept. It is at once negated, but it is not totally annulled, it is conserved. 'This is effected by thinking the contradictory concepts together in a third higher, more comprehensive and richer, concept... .'[4] In this synthesis the ... opposition or contradiction melts. 'But the synthesis is still not a final one', states Faulkenberg in presenting Hegel's views, 'the play begins anew; again an opposition makes its appearance, which in turn seeks to overcome, etc. Each separate concept is one-sided, defective, represents only a part of the truth, needs to be supplemented by its contrary, and, by its union with this, its complement, yields a higher concept which comes nearer to the whole truth but still does not quite reach it. Even the last and the richest concept—the absolute Idea—is by itself alone not the full truth; the result implies the whole development through which it has been attained.'[5]

According to the Hegelian logic further, the most general concept is 'pure being', unqualified by any characteristic. But we cannot think of a 'pure being' unqualified by any characteristic. Hence 'being' without quality is equivalent to nothing or 'not-being', but it turns into 'being' again for in being thought out it exists as 'something thought'. Pure being and pure nothingness

2. ibid. 3. ibid., p. 493. 4. ibid. 5. ibid., p. 494.

are the same thing according to Hegel since both are unqualified and propertiless. 'The transition from being to nothing and from nothing to being is "becoming".'[6] 'Becoming' means unity of both and hence it contains the essence of both. 'In a similar way it is further shown that quality and quantity, are reciprocally dependent and united in measure (which may be popularly illustrated thus : progressively diminishing heat becomes cold).'[7]

Thus it is clear that Hegelian dialectics consist of three laws:

1. the law of the unity of the opposites;
2. the law of the negation of negation;
3. the law of transformation of quantity into quality.

III

MARX AND ENGELS ON DIALECTICS

According to Marx and Engels, Hegel's laws of dialectics 'are not drawn from nature and history, but imposed on the latter as thought. ... The category to him was antecedent, while the dialectics of the real universe was its mere reflection. Actually the opposite is true; the dialectics of the mind is only the reflection of the real world both of nature and of history'. Since the universe was true to Marx he decided to invert the dialectics in order to apply it to explain social transformations.

Engels, who studied the contemporary science very carefully, proclaimed that the laws of the dialectics are universal, equally applicable to society and nature. 'Natural science', says Engels, 'has now advanced so far that it can no longer escape the dialectical analysis.'[8] Engels wrote this on the basis of the three main scientific discoveries of the time, viz., (1) 'the transformation of energy' and 'the unity of all motion in nature', (2) the organic cell as the unit, out of the multiplication and differentiation of which all organisms, except the very lowest, arise and develop, (3) 'the theory of evolution, which was first presented in connected form and substantiated by Darwin'.[9]

---

6. ibid., p. 496.
7. ibid.
8. *Marxist Philosophy*, edited by George Hanna (1968), Russian Edition, pp. 40-41.
9. ibid.

Engels and Lenin took the three laws of Hegelian dialectics and showed their working in nature and society. First, the law of the unity of the opposite was considered.

Opposites are the internal aspects, tendencies, forces of an object, which are mutually exclusive, but at the same time presuppose each other, e.g., 'north and south poles which are mutually exclusive and at the same time interconnected'.[10] The inseverable interconnection of these aspects makes up the unity of the opposites.[11] 'Opposites not merely exist side by side, but are in a state of constant contradiction, struggle is going between them. The struggle of opposites is the inner content, the source of the development of reality.'[12] Lenin pointed out that all motions whether social or natural pass through contradiction and unity.[13]

The second law, the negation of negation, means that a change negates a given state. For instance, when out of a grain of barley a plant germinates, there is negation. The plant is the negation of the grain. This plant produces large number of grains and when these have ripened it dies. This is negation of negation. As a result of this negation of negation, we have in place of a single grain a large number of them.

The third law—the law of transformation of quantity into quality, means that when quantitative changes go beyond a certain point there occurs a qualitative change as if by a sudden leap. The rise of the organic form out of the inorganic matter, origin of the living cell from the inanimate objects, the differentiation of organism into various species, growth of the nervous system, the growth of the intellect, mind and consciousness—all these illustrate the operation of this law according to Marx and Engels.

IV

THE VEDANTIC SOLUTION AS PRESENTED BY SWAMI VIVEKANANDA

As we have seen above, according to Hegel, thesis and anti-thesis are the imperfect expressions of the more perfect synthesis.

---

10. ibid. 11. ibid. 12. ibid.
13. Dr Atindra Nath Bose, *Crossroads of Science and Philosophy*, p. 61.

The question arises : can the imperfect ever express the perfect? Hegel's answer is in the affirmative. According to him, as we have seen already, the Reality, the Absolute, the Idea, the Infinite Perfection, proceeds to realize its perfect nature through history. Vedanta shows that this is logically untenable because perfection is infinity and manifestation means limits. If the perfect Absolute manifests itself, then 'it becomes unlimited limits which is impossible, absurd'. According to Vedanta, what is perfect is always perfect, it can never be imperfect and what is imperfect is always imperfect, it can never be perfect. Therefore, the Vedantic explanation of the co-existence of the opposites is that this contradiction is only seeming and not real. The opposites are one and the same thing, they are identical and are always in perfect harmony. Hence the question of manifestation of the imperfect through contradictions gradually to attain perfection, does not arise at all. It is *māyā* that the Reality which is unity and perfection appears like contradictions. The logical inconsistency involved in the Hegelian dialectics is removed by the theory of *māyā*, the best exponent of which in the modern era is Swami Vivekananda.

This is what the Swami says explaining *māyā*, 'In the objective society there will always be a mixture of good and evil—objective life will always be followed by its shadow, death. ... In objective life every bullet has its billet—evil goes with every good as its shadow. ... This mixture of good and evil, of life and death, knowledge and ignorance is what is called *māyā* or the universal phenomenon.' Explaining the matter further, Swamiji observes, 'Good and evil are not two things, but one, the difference being only in manifestation—one of degree and not of kind. Thus the same truth manifests—both in our relative error and knowledge, the same bliss manifests itself in good and evil; and the same real existence appears as both life and death.'[14] Actually, contradictions are not true, harmony and oneness are true. If contradictions were true then there could not have been ever any harmony or real unity between the two opposites.

Hence the Vedantic conclusion emerges : that the contradictions are mere appearances and not true at bottom and

---

14. *Letters of Swami Vivekananda* (third edition), pp. 317-18.

that the universe as we think of it does not exist. 'The Absolute does not change or re-evolve', says Swamiji . 'In the little amoeba is that infinite perfection latent.' According to Vedanta, therefore, the Absolute, the Perfect, has not become the universe (as Hegel thinks), we see the unchangeable Perfect as the universe due to *māyā* or ignorance.

It is to be noted that this theory of *māyā* does not imply idealism. It does not say that the universe does not exist, it exists but at the same time it is not what we take it for. For instance, as Vivekananda states, in the darkness of night, a stump of tree is looked upon as a ghost by some superstitious persons, as a policeman by a robber, as a friend by some one waiting for his companion; in all these cases, the stump of the tree did not change, but there were apparent changes, and these changes were in the minds of the people who saw it. In the same manner absolute truth never changes, yet it appears as changing, as manifesting itself through contradictions. All these changes—all these contradictions, are, therefore, projections of our mind—*māyā*, and not true. Hence there is no birth, no death, no beginning, coming into being, and then ending, ceasing and passing away and then becoming, as is supposed by Hegel.

This logical inconsistency in Hegel led him to formulate several very absurd postulates regarding historical processes and human institutions. For example, he asserted, 'It may be said of universal history, that it is exhibition of spirit in the process of working out the knowledge of that which it is potentially' and 'the shape which the perfect embodiment of spirit assumes is the state' (the political organ).[15]

Vedanta professes, on the other hand, that the world as it appears is forever imperfect and therefore the sum-total of good and evil in the universe is always the same. Not an iota of the total amount of evil can decrease, nor can the good that exists in the world increase by an iota, in spite of all the historical evolution that takes place. Again, according to Vedanta, every finite object is imperfect, the state (the political organ) which is a finite phenomenon has always its deficiencies. It is absurd to say,

15. *Philosophy of History* by Hegel (reproduced in *The Age of Ideology* by Henry D. Aicken, Chapter on Hegel), p. 89.

Vedantists would assert, that the state (the political organ) is the perfect embodiment of the spirit or the absolute.

It is clear from the above that the first law of the Hegelian dialectics, viz., 'the law of the unity of the opposites', has not been formulated in a very convincing manner by its exponent. It is not consistent with logic. As regards the other two propositions of Hegelian dialectics, viz., 'the law of negation of negation', and 'the law of transformation of quantity into quality', we find, in the same manner, that they cannot satisfy our reason. They are practically mere assertions and no satisfactory rational explanation is provided by Hegel to support them. Vedanta, as interpreted by Swami Vivekananda, shows that it is not possible for a cell to develop into a higher organism, for unconscious beings to manifest consciousness, unless the highest form of existence, the highest form of consciousness, lies already in it as a potential force, for something can never come out of nothing.

V

VEDANTIC THEORY OF EVOLUTION AND INVOLUTION

According to Vedanta, therefore, evolution does not mean emergence of completely new objects out of nothing, that being impossible. It only means that the potential becomes manifest, that the finer form of existence becomes grosser. Explaining this Vivekananda says, 'Everything in nature begins, as it were, from certain seeds, certain rudiments, certain fine forms, and becomes grosser and grosser ... and then again goes back to that fine form, and subsides.'[16] According to this Vedantic logic, when out of a grain of barley a plant emerges, there is no negation of the grain. The grain is the finer form of the plant, which is again the grosser form of the grain. Hence, what happens at the time of the germination of the grain is that the finer form of existence becomes grosser. Similarly, when the plant dies leaving several grains there is no 'negation of negation', because the plant is not destroyed, only it re-enters into its finer form of existence. If the plant had been destroyed it would not have been possible for the

16. *C. W.*, II, p. 204.

grains to grow into plant again, for out of a state of negation or complete annihilation nothing can come back.

The basis of this whole theory is the undeniable truth upheld by the Sāṁkhya philosophy that something can never come out of nothing.

It is evident from the above that to every process of evolution there is a corresponding process of involution. Explaining this an throwing light on human evolution Swami Vivekananda says : 'Applying the law we dwelt upon under macrocosm, that each involution presupposes an evolution, and each evolution an involution, we see that instinct is involved reason. What we call instinct in men or animals must therefore be involved, degenerated, voluntary actions, and voluntary actions are impossible without experience.'[17] Similarly, '... protoplasm was the involution of the highest intelligence.'[18] The little cell, which becomes afterwards the man, was simply the involved man and becomes evolved as a man later on. We see then, that nothing can be created out of nothing.'

The inevitable conclusion that follows is that everything exists through eternity and will exist through eternity : nothing is ever destroyed. That is also the view of science. According to the law of conservation of energy, the total amount of energy in the universe can never alter, nothing can be added, no part of it can ever be destroyed. Even in Economics, production does not mean creation of new objects out of nothing, it means transformation of raw materials and other ingredients into new forms, it means creation of new utilities only. Thus we can have only change of forms and not creation of new materials, we cannot have quantitative changes, but only qualitative changes. And even when we have qualitative changes, something does not come out of nothing, only potential qualities become manifest.

Thus change there must be since that is the law of the universe. 'Only', in the words of Vivekananda, 'the movement is in succeeding waves and hollows, going back to finer forms, and coming out into gross manifestations.' Thus the process of involution and evolution is going on throughout the whole nature.

---

17. ibid., p. 221.

18. ibid., p. 209.

This leads Swami Vivekananda to a startling conclusion. This can be best expressed in his own words conveying his wonderful logic : 'The whole series of evolution beginning with the lowest manifestation of life and reaching up to the highest, the most perfect man, must have been the involution of something else. The question is : The involution of what? What was involved? God.'[19] The sum-total of the intelligence displayed in the universe must be the involved Universal Intelligence unfolding itself. This Universal Intelligence is what we call God. Explaining this theory Vivekananda says further, '...call it by any other name, it is absolutely certain that in the beginning there is that Cosmic Intelligence. This Cosmic Intelligence gets involved and it manifests, evolves itself, until it becomes the perfect man, the "Christ-man", the "Buddha-man".'

Two conclusions were derived by Vivekananda from this theory : (1) first, that cause and effect are one and the same thing, that the manifested or the grosser state is the effect and the finer state the cause, (2) second, if we can find the end we can find the beginning and vice versa. If in the end there is the perfect man like Buddha the perfect man must have been in the protoplasm also; 'that perfect man', he says, 'who is at one end of the chain of evolution was involved in the cell of the protoplasm, which is at the other end of the same chain'.[20] Thus we cannot escape the inevitable conclusion that the universe in its true nature is the Cosmic Intelligence or God in the words of the theologians, and undifferentiated Brahman, i.e., Existence Absolute, Knowledge Absolute and Bliss Absolute in the words of Advaita Vedanta.

VI

VEDANTIC DIALECTICS : THE BASIS OF VIVEKANANDA'S SOCIAL PHILOSOPHY

The Vedantic dialectics, as it appears from the above, are composed of three doctrines : (1) The doctrine of *māyā*, (2) the doctrine of involution and evolution, (3) The doctrine of immanent change. The Vedantic explanation of the problem of contradictions and of the nature of Reality is contained in these

---

19. ibid., p. 208.

20. ibid., p. 209.

three doctrines, which have been made logically unassailable by Vivekananda. Just as the Hegelian dialectics (being uprooted from the Hegelian Idealism and rooted in Scientific Materialism) form the basis of Marxian social philosophy, in the same manner these Vedantic dialectics form the basis of Vivekananda's social philosophy.

From the analysis that we have made above about Hegelian and Vedantic dialectics it is clear that the Hegelian laws—(1) the law of the unity of the opposites, (2) the law of negation of negation, (3) the law of transformation of quantity into quality—do not provide a logically satisfactory explanation of the problem of the opposites in the universe. Vedantic doctrines—(1) the theory of *māyā*, (2) the doctrine of evolution and involution and (3) the doctrine of immanent change provides a better logical apparatus for the purpose of explaining the universe appearing as a bundle of opposites.

VII

TWENTIETH CENTURY SCIENCE AND THE PROBLEM OF THE OPPOSITES

In modern physics, Niels Bohr's theory of complementarity has thrown light on the problem of the opposites. Explaining the notion of complementarity with regard to atomic reality as propounded by Niels Bohr, Professor Capra says—'He considered the particle picture and wave picture as two complementary descriptions of the same reality, each of them being only partly correct and having a limited range of application. Each picture is needed to give a full description of the atomic reality, and both are to be applied within the limitations given by the uncertainty principle.'[21] According to Bohr, this notion of complementarity may be an useful concept outside physics also. In this connection Professor Capra points out that similar concepts are found in ancient Chinese thought. 'It played an essential role', says Professor Capra, 'in ancient Chinese thought which was based on the insight that opposite concepts stand in a polar—or complementary relationship to each other.' We have seen that on this insight is based Vedantic conceptions of *māyā* and 'unity in variety'. Swami

Vivekananda's statement in this respect has been quoted above.

Referring to the latest atomic theory Professor Capra adds—'The exploration of the sub-atomic world has revealed a reality which repeatedly transcends language and reasoning, and the unification of concepts which had hitherto seemed opposite and irreconcilable turns out to be one of the most startling features of this new reality. ... Examples of the unification of opposite concepts', he says continuing, 'in modern physics can be found in the sub-atomic level, where particles are both destructible and indestructible, where matter is both continuous and discontinuous and force and matter are but different aspects of the same phenomenon. ... Space and time themselves are two concepts which had seemed entirely different, but have been unified in relativistic physics. This fundamental unity is the basis of the unification of the opposite concepts mentioned above.' Comparing the experience of the mystics with the concept of dynamic unity of the opposites in modern physics, Capra again goes on to observe, 'Like the unity of opposites experienced by the mystics, it takes place on a "higher plane", i.e., in a higher dimension, and like that experienced by the mystics it is a dynamic unity, because the relativistic space-time reality is an intrinsically dynamic reality where objects are also processes and all forms are dynamic patterns.'[22]

It is not possible to visualize the four dimensional world of relativistic physics where the opposites are united. Dwelling on this point Professor Capra says : 'Physicists can "experience" the four-dimensional space-time world through the abstract mathematical formalism of their theories, but their visual imaginations—like everybody else's—is limited to the three-dimensional world of the senses. Our language and thought patterns have evolved in this three-dimensional world, and therefore we find it extremely hard to deal with the four-dimensional reality of relativistic physics.'[23] This is so because the multi-dimensional experience transcends the sensory world and therefore they cannot be expressed in ordinary language or the language of the sensory world.

---

21. Fritzof Capra, *The Tao Of Physics*, p. 145.
22. ibid., pp. 134-35.
23. ibid., pp. 135-36.

Physics has been so far able to give an idea of a higher dimensional reality but 'experiencing' or 'visualizing' that reality has been the business of the eastern mystics who practised in deep meditation how to transcend the sensory world and directly had experiences of the super-sensory, super-rational reality.

But the mystics also failed to convey their experience in words, since the super-sensory, super-rational experience cannot be expressed in the language of the sensory world as we have seen in the previous chapter. Hence Sri Ramakrishna, the greatest of all the modern mystics, said allegorically : 'Once a salt doll went to measure the depth of the ocean. ... It wanted to tell others how deep the water was. But this it could never do, for no sooner did it get into the water it melted. Now who was there to report the ocean's depth?'[24] Again he said very significantly throwing immense light on the issue, 'What Brahman is cannot be described. All things in the world—the Vedas, the Purāṇas, the Tantras, the six systems of philosophy—have been defiled, like that has been touched by the tongue, for they have been read or uttered by the tongue. Only one thing has not been defiled in this way, and that is Brahman. No one has ever been able to say what Brahman is.'[25]

Regarding the unity of the opposites, Ramakrishna said, 'The world consists of the illusory duality of knowledge and ignorance. It contains knowledge and devotion, and also, attachment to "woman and gold"; righteousness and unrighteousness; good and evil. But Brahman is unattached to these. Good and evil apply to the *jīva*, the individual soul, as do righteousness and unrighteousness. But Brahman is not at all affected by them. ... The sun sheds its light on the wicked as well as on the virtuous.'[26]

Sri Ramakrishna describes the condition of the mystic who has a direct experience of the ultimate unity where opposites melt. He says, 'When a man has true (transcendental) knowledge, he feels everything is filled with consciousness.'[27] Obviously, this consciousness is single, hence there cannot be any feeling of opposites.

---

24. Swami Nikhilananda, *The Gospel of Sri Ramakrishna*, p. 29.
25. ibid., p. 28. 26. ibid. 27. ibid., p. 568.

This, as we have seen already, is also the scientist's viewpoint. We have already quoted Schrödinger who said, '...consciousness is singular of which the plural is unknown; that there is only one thing and that what seems to be a plurality, is merely a series of different aspects of this one thing, produced by a deception (the Indian *māyā*), the same illusion is produced in a gallery of mirrors... .'[28]

Individual selves are, therefore, identical with the Universal Self, the one single entity that exists, whose nature is pure consciousness. In Christian terminology it is a blasphemy to say, 'Hence I am the God Almighty'. But it is not so with the Indian Vedantic thought as well as according to modern scientific view of single consciousness. Speaking about it Schrödinger observes, 'In itself the insight is not new. The earliest records to my knowledge date back some 2500 years or more. From the early great Upanishads, the recognition of Ātman=Brahman (the personal self equals the omnipresent, all corresponding eternal Self) was in Indian thought considered, far from being blasphemous, to represent the quintessence of deepest insight into the happenings of the world. The striving of all the scholars of Vedanta was, after having learnt to pronounce with their lips, really to assimilate in their minds this grandest of all thoughts.'[29]

Hence, to the non-dualist eastern experience and the non-dualistic scientific thinking today the opposites are at bottom identical, they appear as opposites in the sense-world. Beyond the sense-world there is no existence of two or many, hence existence of opposites is impossible, there exists in that plane of higher dimension only the undifferentiated Reality, Brahman of the Vedantists without any attribute—the Brahman which is Existence, Knowledge and Bliss Absolute.

VIII

VALIDITY OF THE NINETEENTH CENTURY SCIENCE AND MARXISM

Has the nineteenth century science lost its validity? The question assumes great importance in view of the fact that

28. Erwin Schrödinger, *What Is Life*, p. 90.   29. ibid.

Marxism, a philosophy which is today widely followed in a large number of countries, is based on it.

Throwing light on the question of validity of the nineteenth century science Professor Capra observes : 'The mechanistic world-view of classical physics is useful for the description of the kind of physical phenomena we encounter in our everyday life and thus appropriate for dealing with our daily environment, and it has also proved extremely successful as a basis for technology. It is inadequate, however, for the description of physical phenomena in the submicroscopic realm.... In everyday life, then, both the mechanistic and the organic views of the universe are valid and useful; the one for science and technology, the other for a balanced and fulfilled spiritual life. Beyond the dimensions of our everyday environment, however, the mechanistic concepts lose their validity and have to be replaced by organic concepts which are very similar to those used by the mystics. This is the essential experience of modern physics....'[30] Dealing with the same matter, Riencourt observes, '... it (modern physics) does not actually abolish the Newtonian structure but overcomes and preserves it as being only a special case within the much larger framework provided by Relativity and Quantum Theory.'[31]

However, as we have pointed out already, the philosophical basis of Marxism is on the mechanistic, materialistic and deterministic science of the nineteenth century which has been invalidated so far as the submicroscopic world is concerned. There has not been any attempt so far on the part of the Marxists to assess the impact of twentieth century developments in science on the Marxist philosophy. The fact that the Marxist concept of reality stands invalidated today seems not to have dawned upon the followers of Marx.

The Marxist Concept of Reality : According to the Marxist concept, the external world and the forms of being can never be created and derived by thought out of itself, as has been assumed by the idealists like Hegel, rather '... matter and nature in general are objective and independent of man and his consciousness though mind and consciousness are the products of human brain.'

30. *The Tao Of Physics*, pp. 294-95.
31. A. de Riencourt, *The Eye of Shiva*, p. 45.

Hence, says Engels, 'If we deduce the world schematism not from our minds but from the real world, deducing the basic principles of being from what it is, we need no philosophy, but positive science.'[32] And according to this positive science, at the time the world was composed of matter, and motion was the mode of existence of matter.

IX

MARXIST CONCEPT OF THE OPPOSITES AS APPLIED TO SOCIETY

Struggle of the opposites as the source of development

We have already noted the shortcomings of Hegelian logic. Instead, the Hegelian dialectics were adopted by Marx to explain this motion related to matter since in the words of Engels, 'Natural Science has now advanced so far that it can no longer escape the dialectical synthesis.'

The three laws of Hegelian dialectics, viz., (1) the law of the unity of the opposites, (2) the law of negation of negation, and (3) the law of transformation of quantity into quality were adopted by Marx to explain the universe. According to the Marxist philosophy, through the operation of these three laws, complete new objects come into being out of nothing.

It is contradiction or struggle of the opposites, according to this philosophy, that comprises the main source of development of matter and consciousness. 'Development is the "struggle" of "opposites" ', says Lenin.[33] 'The history of science and of society', he adds, 'proves that the struggle of opposites is the source of development. For example, the struggle or the interaction of mechanical, electrical and nuclear force of attraction and repulsion plays a very great part in the formation and continued existence of atomic nuclei, atoms and molecules. The struggle of these forces, modern cosmogonic theories show, was an important source of the formation of the solar system.'[34]

---

32. F. Engels, *Collected Works.*
33. V. I. Lenin, *Collected Works*, Vol. 38, p. 360.
34. V. I. Lenin, *Marxist Philosophy*, pp. 96-97.

Similarly, '... opposite process of assimilation and dissimilation are inherent in living organisms. It is their struggle, their interaction that constitutes the specific source of development in everything living.'[35]

According to Marx, 'The process of evolution of the human society is the same as that of nature, i.e., the dialectical process. Every existing tendency in society (i.e., thesis) produces its opposites (i.e., antithesis) in its process of continuous change. The conflict between the two leads to its disruption and to its suppression by another which is a synthesis of both. Contradictions in material production, especially the forces of production and the relations of production, are among the most important of the contradictions of social development. In antagonistic-class societies the contradiction between the forces and the relations of productions is expressed in the struggle of hostile classes, which leads to social revolution, and the replacement of the old social system by the new.'[36]

ECONOMIC DETERMINISM

According to Marx, the method of production in economic life determines the general character of the social, political and spiritual aspects of life. The political, legal, moral and cultural systems grow upon the economic substructure.

In the process of development of the system of production, changes in the forces of production, i.e., instruments, technical knowledge, etc., take place which call for changes in relations of productions (i.e., class relations). Each social system gathers defenders whose interests are bound up with its continuance. These classes cling to their powers and privileges and give resistance to those who demand a share in the fruits of their common effort. They also use the coercive machinery of the state to suppress their rival classes. Hence, the political and social institutions have a tendency to lag behind the evolution of productive forces, and are brought to correspond to it only by a sharp jerk of a revolution.

35. ibid., p. 97. 36. ibid.

The doctrine of class struggle

According to Lenin, 'Classes are groups of people one of which can appropriate the labour of another owing to the different places they occupy in a definite system of social economy.'[37] The relation of a class to the means of production is the chief feature determining its place and role.

The history of class societies is the history of class struggle. The class struggle is the driving force, the source of development of class society.

The class struggle is irreconcilable. As Marx and Engels say, 'Freeman and slave, patrician and plebian, lord and serf, guild-master and journeyman, in a word, oppressor and the oppressed, stood in constant opposition to one another, carried on an uninterrupted, now hidden, now open fight, a fight that each time ended, either in a revolutionary reconstitution of society at large or in the common ruin of the contending classes.'[38]

Thus the doctrine of the class-struggle is basically an extension of the Marxist concept of the role of the opposites in nature. We shall have a glimpse of Vivekananda's views on social contradictions in a subsequent chapter.

---

37. V. I. Lenin, *Selected Works*, Vol. 3, p. 248.
38. K. Marx and F. Engels, *Collected Works*.

CHAPTER 7

Significance of the Convergence of Science and Vedanta for Society

THE SIGNIFICANCE OF MODERN SCIENCE FOR SOCIETY

The world-view of modern science which converges on the world-view of Vedanta and on mysticism in general, is not yet reflected in existing society. Society is still based on the mechanistic, materialistic and fragmented world-view of the nineteenth century. That is why society is so much fragmented and there is so much discord, dispute, breach of peace and dominance of violence in the various spheres of present-day social life. Emphasizing these points at the end of his remarkable contribution, viz., *The Tao Of Physics*, towards understanding the significance of convergence of twentieth century science and mysticism, Professor Capra says : 'I believe that the world-view implied by modern physics is inconsistent with our present society, which does not reflect the harmonious interrelatedness we observe in nature. To achieve such a state of dynamic balance, a radically different social and economic structure will be needed : a cultural revolution in the true sense of the word. The survival of our whole civilization may depend on whether we can bring about such a change. It will depend, ultimately, on our ability to adopt some of the *yin* attitudes of eastern mysticism; to experience the wholeness of nature and the art of living with it in harmony.'[1]

The Need for a Cultural Revolution : To bring the society in tune with the organic concept of the twentieth century science it is necessary to strike a dynamic balance between the different parts of the society. A cultural revolution is urgently called for to make a new kind of men with the sense of this organic world-

1. Fritzof Capra, *The Tao Of Physics*, p. 298.

view. Mysticism is a way of life. Like mysticism this organic view of modern science must be made a way of life, if there is to be a radical change in social relationships and social institutions.

The question that is of supreme importance today is how to bring about this cultural revolution, to create a new breed of men with whom modern science will be a way of life. Even the scientists today do not understand the social, philosophical, cultural, and spiritual implications of their own theories. Even they—many of them at least—still go on supporting a society which is based on the mechanistic, materialistic and fragmented world-view of the preceding century. They do not realize that science today points beyond this view towards oneness of the universe, oneness of humanity. The majority of the people in the West, a vast majority of the elites all over the world including India, the land of spirituality, still cling to the outdated mechanistic, materialistic and fragmented world-view. It seems that they are not aware of the implications of the latest developments in science at all.

First thing necessary is that it must be hammered to these people constantly that there is no real conflict between science and religion. 'In fact', as Riencourt says, 'they appear to complement one another in an unexpected application of Niels Bohr's theory of complementarity.'[2] In this connection he quotes Einstein, the greatest scientist of this age, who says: 'The most beautiful and most profound emotion we can experience is the sensation of the mystical. It is the sower of all true art and science. He, to whom this emotion is a stranger, who can no longer wonder and stand rapt in awe, is as good as dead. To know what is impenetrable to us really exists, manifesting itself as the highest wisdom and the most radiant beauty which our dull faculties can comprehend only in their most primitive forms—this knowledge, this feeling is at the centre of true religiousness.'[3]

It should be borne in mind that the greatest scientist of this age wants us to realize that the mystical sensation is at the root of all creativity in the fields of art and science. A man without this, is more dead than alive.

---

2. A. de Riencourt, *The Eye of Shiva*, p. 39.

3. ibid., pp. 39-40.

Thus it is clear that a cultural revolution which would drive deep into our mind all these wonderful ideas must be based on a philosophy which integrates science and religion—science and mysticism in general.

We have seen already that such a philosophy is Vedanta as remoulded by Swami Vivekananda, a better coined term for which is 'Universal-Science-Religion', coined by Romain Rolland, as it integrates science and religion and as its keynote is universality. Vivekananda has established Vedanta as the most scientific religion of the world, suitable for the modern man with true rational and scientific attitude. It is wonderfully in conformity with the twentieth century science.

II

THE VEDANTIC SOCIAL ORDER

What kind of social order does this Universal-Science-Religion imply? We are reminded here of what Vivekananda fervently urged in one of his lectures : 'Science means that the cause of a thing is sought out by the nature of the thing itself. As step by step science is progressing, it has taken the explanation of natural phenomena out of the hands of spirits and angels. Because Advaitism has done likewise in spiritual matters, it is the most scientific religion. This universe has not been created by any extra-cosmic God, nor is it the work of any outside genius. It is self-creating, self-dissolving, self-manifesting, One Infinite Existence, the Brahman, *Tattvamasi Śvetaketo*— "That thou art, O Śvetaketu!" '[4] What is uttered by him next is very significant for our present purpose. 'And with all the prattle about science that is going on daily at the present time in modern half-educated India, with all the talk about rationalism and reason that I hear every day, I expect that whole sects of you will come over and dare to be Advaitists, and dare to preach it to the world in the words of Buddha . . . "For the good of many, for the happiness of many." '[5]

Now it is clear that the practical implication of Vedanta, the most scientific religion, is this wonderful idea that society must

4. *C. W.*, III, pp. 423-24.

5. ibid., p. 424.

be based on this motto given 2500 years ago by Buddha—viz., 'for the good of many and for the happiness of many'.

From his conclusion that Vedanta is the most scientific religion, how does he jump on this idea?

This is actually the logical derivation from the Vedantic conception of Ātman/Brahman identity which is upheld by scientists like Schrödinger and Capra. Swami Vivekananda had no doubt in his mind that science would uphold it one of these days since he had the insight to see that it was the truth—truth only—this Ātman/Brahman identity.

This concept of Ātman/Brahman identity led him to reduce the whole of the abstruse Vedanta Philosophy to two very simple and basic principles, viz.,

1. the divinity of man;
2. the essential spirituality of life.

From these two principles the social significance of Vedanta is evident. If Vedanta is made practical, it follows obviously—

1. that every state, every society, every religion must be based on the recognition of this all powerful presence latent in man, i.e., divinity;
2. that in order to be fruitful, all human interests should be guided and controlled according to the ultimate idea of spirituality of life.[6]

Obviously, a society based on the Vedantic principles, would be a society based on equal human rights for everybody. For, as argued by Vivekananda, if behind the strong and the weak, behind the high and the low, behind everyone there is that Infinite Soul, assuring the infinite possibility and capacity of all to become great and good, as is proclaimed by Vedanta, then no privilege, on mental, physical, spiritual, social, economic, or any other ground whatsoever can be claimed. Bringing out the wonderful logic behind his argument Vivekananda further observes, 'The same power is in every man, the one manifesting more, the other less; the same potentiality is in everyone. Where is the claim to privilege?'[7] Thus Vedanta strikes at the very root of privileges. And it is clearly evident that the Vedantic society is a privilege-free society.

---

6. Romain Rolland, *Life of Vivekananda*, p. 290. 7. *C. W.*, I, p. 423.

Analysis of Privileges : According to Vivekananda, the idea of privilege is the bane of human life. And there are many kinds of privileges claimed in society. Analysing this point further he says : 'Of course there is first the brutal idea of privilege, that of the strong over the weak. There is the privilege of wealth. If a man has more money than another, he wants a little privilege over those who have less. There is the still subtler and more powerful privilege of intellect; because one man knows more than others, he claims more privilege. And the last of all, and the worst, because the most tyrannical, is the privilege of spirituality. If some persons think they know more of spirituality, of God, they claim a superior privilege over everyone else.'[8]

Thus Vivekananda identifies four kinds of privileges prevailing in society :

1. privileges claimed on the basis of differences of physical strength (most brutal, claimed by the physically strong over the weak);
2. privileges based on the differences, of possession of wealth (claimed by the moneyed man over the poor);
3. privileges based on the basis of differences of the power of the intellect (claimed by the elites over the illiterates);
4. privileges based on the differences of the power of spirituality (most cruel, claimed by the spiritual men, i.e., the priests) over lay men.

As Vedanta preaches divinity of man, which means every body has the same potential capacity to be great and good, it can never sanction any of these privileges. Hence, Vivekananda declares, 'None can be a Vedantist and at the same time admit of privileges to anyone, mental, physical or spiritual, absolutely no privilege for anyone.' Thus a society based on Vedantic ideal is a society free of privileges. 'The work of Advaita', declares Vivekananda further, 'is to breakdown privileges', i.e., to bring about a new social order based on equality of opportunities for everybody.

THE CHARACTERISTICS OF A VEDANTIC SOCIAL ORDER

It is not possible to bring absolute sameness in society.

---

8. ibid.

Differences or variations there must be. Only the privileges claimed on the differences will have to go. Explaining this idea of a Vedantic society, Vivekananda goes on to say : '... the absolute sameness of conditions, if that be the aim of ethics, appears to be impossible. That all men should be the same, could never be, however we might try. Men will be born differentiated; some will have more powers than others; some will have natural capacities, others not; some will have perfect bodies, others not.'[9] Thus 'the sameness as regards external forms and position can never be attained'.

'But what can be attained', points out Vivekananda, 'is elimination of privilege.'[10] In every society in all ages there is a struggle, all the time going on, for the elimination of privileges. 'The difficulty is not', Vivekananda points out further, 'that one body of men are naturally more intelligent than another, but whether this body of men, because they have the advantage of intelligence, should take away even physical enjoyment from those who do not posses that advantage. The fight is to destroy that privilege. That some will be stronger physically than others, and will thus naturally be able to subdue or defeat the weak, is a self-evident fact, but that because of this strength they should gather unto themselves all the attainable happiness of this life, is not according to law, and the fight has been against it. That some people, through natural aptitude, should be able to accumulate more wealth than others, is natural; but that on account of this power to acquire wealth, they should tyrannize and ride roughshod over those who cannot acquire so much wealth, is not a part of the law, and the fight has been against that. The enjoyment of advantage over another is privilege, and throughout ages, the aim of morality has been its destruction. This is the work which tends towards sameness, towards unity, without destroying variety.'[11]

Now this is the idea of the Vedantic society. In it there will be unity in variety, but absolutely no privilege for anybody on any ground.

---

9. ibid., p. 434. 10. ibid., p. 435. 11. ibid.

IV

VEDANTIC SOCIETY AND CLASSLESS SOCIETY

The Vedantic society is not, however, the classless society in the Marxist sense of the term. In the classless society no privilege on grounds of wealth is admitted. But in the Vedantic society no kind of privilege is to be admitted—neither privilege on grounds of physical strength, nor of wealth, nor of intellectuality, nor of spirituality. It seeks to abolish privilege in a more comprehensive sense. Next in the privilege-free Vedantic society, as conceived by Vivekananda, all human interests will be guided and controlled by the ultimate idea of spirituality of life. But in the Marxist type there is no place for religion and spirituality. We have seen in the previous section the great need for combining religion and science for the benefit of society and this Vedanta does in an admirable manner.

A society based on religion and science and for that matter on Vedanta does not mean that in such a society economic and secular interests will be neglected. For Vedanta proclaims everything to be spiritual and seeks to breakdown the fictitious demarcation between the secular and the spiritual. Hence interpreting Vivekananda, Nivedita says : 'If the many and the One be indeed the same Reality, then it is not all modes of worship alone, but equally all modes of work, all modes of struggle, all modes of creation, which are paths of realization. No distinction, henceforth, between sacred and secular. To labour is to pray. To conquer is to renounce. Life is itself religion.'[12]

In terms of this doctrine, therefore, even economic progress is essential for this order of spiritual socialism. We all know how eager Vivekananda was to bring a transformation in the economic life of the people in India. Elaborating the thesis of Vivekananda further, Nivedita makes the revealing comment : 'To him, the workshop, the study, the farmyard, and the field are as true and fit scenes for the meeting of God with man as the cell of the monk or the door of the temple.'[13] Economic progress is as much the aim of a Vedantic society as spiritual progress. For realizing his divinity man must have economic facilities as well as social and other facilities.

---

12. ibid., *Introduction*, p. xv.

13. ibid.

CHAPTER 8

Impact of Vedanta on Sociology and Political Science

In the chapters preceding we have tried to show how Swami Vivekananda expanded Vedanta to include science and religion reconciling faith and reason, eastern and western knowledge, to make it an integrated philosophy for mankind as a whole. As a result he was able to expand the concept of 'Man' and 'Man's Life' to infinity. He declared, 'Never forget the glory of human nature. We are the greatest God that ever was or ever will be. Christs or Buddhas are but waves on the boundless ocean which I am.' And this idea is of supreme importance today for shaping a new social order and new political system.

In the light of neo-Vedanta or Universal-Science-Religion, he has succeeded in expanding also our concepts of 'History', 'Society', 'Evolution', as well as some of the most important political concepts like 'Right', 'Liberty', 'Equality', 'Law', 'Democracy', 'Socialism' and 'Revolution', as we will see subsequently.

He was able to throw new light on the basic nature and purposes of 'Society', 'State' and 'Government' and the individual's relation to these collective bodies. And a thoroughly new and for that matter 'revolutionary' concept of 'revolution' itself has been advanced by him, throwing light on hitherto unknown aspects of the laws and instruments of social revolutions.

Thus without being, primarily speaking, a social scientist Vivekananda, the master-mind, was able to state the most vital truths about man's social life enriching thereby both 'Sociology' and 'Political Science'. It may be stated here, even at the cost of repetition, that Vivekananda has not uttered a single word without the support of reason or history or which runs counter to science. He was all his life a true seeker of Truth and a follower of Truth and Truth only. All his life he served no other master save Truth. 'A search for the stern truth is the best fruit of the best scientific training'—said Sister Nivedita, the great disciple of Swami Vivekananda, who found that great spirit of 'search for the stern truth' embodied in him. Swami Vivekananda's social philosophy, his political and economic ideas bear ample testimony to the truth of this statement. This will be evident to us as we proceed to discuss his historical, sociological, political and economic ideas in the subsequent chapters.

Part II
The Historical Ideas

CHAPTER 9

The Historical Ideas : Basic Concepts

I

SWAMI VIVEKANANDA AND HISTORY

Speaking of Swami Vivekananda, Sister Nivedita very aptly said, 'History was his own fort'. History was one of the subjects that he offered for his graduation and he had a vast study in this discipline. How vast it was can be assessed from the fact that before his graduation, when he was still a boy in his teens, he had studied all the enormous volumes of *History of Rome* by Gibbons.

Yet Vivekananda was not primarily an historian, his chief concern being to save mankind from the destructive path of materialism.Yet his prophetic insight combined with his vast study and power of original thinking has led him to come upon strikingly original findings. Indeed the most striking feature of his contributions to this field of study is remarkable originality.

His historical consciousness was born in his spiritual consciousness. He sought to observe how divinity of man had manifested itself from time immemorial. 'The history of civilization', he said, 'is the progressive reading of spirit into matter.' Toynbee, the greatest historian of the present century, expressed a similar view long afterwards.[1]

II

NATURE AND DEFINITION OF HISTORY

Regarding the nature of history, Toynbee says : 'I do not think that history in the objective sense of the term is a succession of facts, nor history writing the narration of these

1. Arnold Toynbee, *A Study of History*, Vol. 10, page 1.

facts. Historians, like all human observers, have to make reality comprehensible, and this involves them into a continuous judgement about what is true and what is insignificant.'[2] And regarding the nature of reality, he observes, 'For all we know, reality is the undifferentiated unity of the mystical experience.'[3] Toynbee takes pain to point out further that in every phenomenon, there is something unique and this means 'mentally incomprehensible'. According to him, '... it is the historians who have made it their business to be not only the exponents of the elements of uniqueness, but also its champions.'[4]

Regarding defining history properly, Toynbee says, 'The most obvious definition of history is that it is the study of human phenomena as we see them on move through time and space.' 'History must', he says, 'aim at preserving the complexity of individual events while also constructing them into a design which possesses a certain coherence of meaning.'[5]

SWAMI VIVEKANANDA'S APPROACH

Swami Vivekananda's approach is the composite approach consisting of describing history of different nationalities to identify their distinctive national traits and then finding an unity between them as various expressions of Man as a divine essence. As Sister Nivedita points out : 'Thus, a nationality, in the Swami's eyes, had all the sacredness of a church—a church whose inmost striving was to express its own conception of ideal manhood.'[6]

Hence Vivekananda did not believe in studying history of nationalities in isolation. His historical studies are therefore studies of the history of mankind as a whole.

Utility of Historical Research : Regarding the utility of historical research, Vivekananda says, 'Then what is the use of so much historical research, you may ask. Because we have to get at the truth; it will not do for us to remain bound by wrong ideas due to ignorance. ... You have to keep your eyes always fixed on truth only, and shun all superstitions completely.'

---

2. ibid. (abridged edition), p. 477. 3. ibid., p. 485. 4. ibid.
5. ibid. 6. Sister Nivedita, *The Master As I Saw Him*, p. 229.

Thus the pursuit of truth is the aim of the historian in carrying on his investigations according to Vivekananda.

III

IS HISTORY AN OBJECTIVE SCIENCE ?

According to eminent historians[7], there cannot be any absolute objectivity in history since the historian cannot help seeing his collected data regarding events and happenings with the coloured glass of his own mind, which is limited by his knowledge and experience and above all by his world-view. But a somewhat relative objectivity is possible and this is essential. Close adherence to facts and happenings should certainly be maintained and this can be maintained in analysing situations. Here no bias, passion or prejudice—religious, racial or communal, regional or national, doctrinal or dogmatic—should intervene to cause deviation from close adherence to facts. This is exactly what Vivekananda means to say in the passage just quoted in the previous section.

No Absolute Truth in History : Just as there cannot be any absolute 'objectivity' in history there cannot be any absolute truth in history. Absolute Truth—God or Brahman or Ātman is the subject-matter of metaphysics. In the relative world truth is only relative and history deals with the relative world and therefore historical truths are relative truths. And the historian cannot know even the whole of this relative truth since of no time or space total facts or informations about the situations are available. And it may be noted here that Vivekananda has stated repeatedly that this world is a relative one and its truths are also relative.

HISTORY AS A SCIENCE

In recent period there has been a marked tendency to speak of history as a science. This is mainly due to the influence of Marxism which speaks of 'Historical Materialism' based on

7. Dr Nihar Ranjan Roy—'Truth, Objectivity and Science in History', an article in *Religion and Society in Ancient India* (Sudhakar Chattopadhyaya Commemoration Volume). I owe my indebtedness to this article in writing this section.

'Scientific Materialism'. 'Science' is the magic word of this century which enamours everyone who has the knowledge of the three R's.

Causes of events or situations are sought to be found by history and when the historians are trying to establish causality they have to show facts that lie behind their findings. Attempts have been made recently to employ tools and technology that really belong to the realm of physical or biological science to archaeology which is related to history. And statistical methods have been sought to be applied to history.

But does that make history a science? In recent years there has been a marked tendency in India to recast Indian history according to the Marxist doctrine of 'Historical Materialism'. These historical studies are being called 'scientific' since they are based on a 'scientific' model according to these writers themselves.

As we have already seen in chapter 4, scientific methods are composed of : (1) close observation, (2) experimentation, and (3) repeatability of the phenomenon under scrutiny.

In the case of history it must be borne in mind that close observation of the entire situation at a particular time and space is not possible since, as we have noted already, the entire facts are not available. Moreover, the situation under study can be studied in a static condition only and as a disjointed fact. The historian cannot see the totality of the situation, hence observation in the historical field is basically different from the observation in the field of biological or physical sciences where the entire phenomenon can be wholly observed.

Secondly, experimentation with historical facts or events is by nature of things impossible since historical events cannot be reproduced.

Thirdly, because of the same logic, repeatability of historical facts or events is out of the question. Although there is a popular saying that 'history repeats itself', but exact repetitions of historical events is unknown up to now.

Herein lies a marked difference between history and the social sciences also. Although controlled experimentation as in the case of physical sciences may not be possible in sociology and political science, 'yet within limitations of their respective disciplines they can achieve a high degree of probability, can make intelligent hypotheses and formulate legitimate inductive generalizations'.[8] But even these facilities are not available to history since in history every event or situation is unique, in the sense that it occurs once only.

SCIENTIFIC MATERIALISM OF MARX : AN EXPLODED DOCTRINE

Moreover, we should remember that the mechanistic-materialistic-deterministic science, which form the basis of 'Scientific Materialism' of Marx stands exploded today by the twentieth-century developments in science as seen in the previous part of the book. Hence the infallibility of Marxist historiography based on this science can no longer hold ground. Historians using this method are to note that their findings which they claim to have absolute certainty or being 'scientific' are far from being so. A group of writers in the West headed by Lucas and Gramschi have already engaged themselves in remoulding the Marxist thinking in view of the changed situation. Engels himself laid the ground for such efforts. In one of his letters (August 5, 1890, to Mr Schmidt) he says emphatically, 'In general, the word "materialistic" serves many of the younger writers in Germany as a mere phrase with which anything and everything is labelled without further study, i.e., they stick on this label and then consider the question disposed of.... All history must be studied afresh, the conditions of the existence of the different formations of society must be examined individually before the attempt is made to deduce from the political, civil-law, aesthetic, philosophic, religious, etc., views corresponding to them. Upto now but little has been done here because only a few people have got down to it seriously.... However, all this will right itself.'[9]

But it seems that this appeal has fallen to deaf ears mostly, especially in countries like India, where writers following Marx

8. *Religion and Society in Ancient India*—Edited by Pranabananda Jash and others, p. 29.
9. *Selected Works of Marx and Engels*, Vol. II, p. 442.

try strictly to adhere to the exploded dogma of 'Scientific Materialism' as originally laid down by Marx.

At the end of his book on *Ludwig Feuerbach and the end of Classical German Philosophy*, Engels makes his own concept of the material universe clear which, unlike Feuerbach's, is that of a process, 'as a matter undergoing uninterrupted historical development'. He further asserts that with each epoch-making discovery even in the sphere of natural science it (materialism) has to change its form. Engels's ideas are not shared today by many Marxists.

IV

IMPACT OF MODERN SCIENCE ON HISTORY

After the revolutionary discoveries in science in the twentieth century which has demolished the mechanistic-materialistic view of the world, there is a definite trend towards a spiritualistic view of the world in modern science and today scientists like F. Capra and many others are hailing eastern mysticism as the background philosophy of modern science (vide part I).

Obviously, therefore, there must be a corresponding change in historiography. This point even though emphasized by historians like Toynbee and sociologists like Sorokin, has not made much impression upon the Marxist historians, particularly in countries like India. It is high time to realize that the word 'scientific' does not necessarily mean 'Scientific Materialism' and that 'history' is not equivalent to 'Historical Materialism'.

The Meaning of Scientific History : Then what is to be meant by scientific history? It means that from the first step of making data-research to the end of presentation of the findings, reason and objectivity and adherence to facts must be strictly observed. And 'reason' here means 'historical reason', i.e., it cannot be proved by experimentation. It means, therefore, that there must be adherence, as far as practicable, to what actually happened in history. It must not be tainted by any preconceived idea, which often makes people to conceal facts. The most important quality that must always be present in an historian is open-mindedness. He must always be, at any cost, true to facts, his vision must be unfailingly a clear vision and not a tainted vision—tainted by any dogma or doctrine.

V

VIVEKANANDA'S HISTORICAL STUDIES

Swami Vivekananda was not, as we have mentioned earlier, a mere historian first and foremost, just as he was not a mere political scientist or a sociologist. But he had a philosophy of history just as he had a political philosophy and a social philosophy of his own. He had a master mind and the 'combined insight of a sociologist, of a philosopher and of a mystic', as pointed out earlier. Due to this unique insight he was able to make certain predictions absolutely accurately about some of the future events, e.g., about the proletariat revolution taking place either in China or in Russia or devastating world wars breaking within the next fifty years since his time. It may be noted here that the Marxian thesis was that the proletariat revolution would take place in mature capitalist countries like England, Germany, and U. S. A. But actually the revolution took place in Russia, an underdeveloped country, and later on in China, a similar country. Thus history proved Vivekananda's prediction true and not the Marxian.

To the prophetic vision of Vivekananda, the past, the present and the future of mankind was like the open pages of a book and they were in a meaningful relation.

But whatever he spoke was spoken very briefly almost in the form of aphorisms.

VI

THE SOCIOLOGICAL METHOD OF STUDYING HISTORY : VIVEKANANDA'S METHOD

In spite of his marked brevity, strict adherence to objectivity is crystal clear in his studies. All his statements were based on data, whose authenticity was verified. And his method was what has now come to be known as the 'sociological method', i.e., the method of studying history from 'the bottom up' or studying history in the contemporary life of the masses. In his lecture entitled *The Problem Of Modern India And Its Solution*, he says, 'If the word history is understood to mean merely narratives of kings and emperors, and pictures of society—tyrannized over from time to time by the evil passions, haughtiness, avarice, etc., of the rulers of the time, portraying the acts resulting from their good or evil propensities, and how these reacted upon the society of that time—such a history India perhaps does not possess. But every line of that mass of the religious literature of India, her ocean of poetry, her philosophies and various scientific works reveal to us—a thousand times more clearly than the narratives of the life-incidents and genealogies of particular kings and emperors can ever do—the exact position and every step made in advance by that vast body of men who, even before the dawn of civilization, impelled by hunger and thirst, lust and greed, etc., attracted by the charm of beauty, endowed with a great and indomitable mental power, and moved by various sentiments, arrived through various ways and means at that stage of eminence.'[10]

Thus it is clear that Vivekananda did not follow the western method of studying political history—history of victories and defeats of kings and emperors and of the wars they fought to conquer the territories of other nations. In search of history he first of all turned the pages of ancient literature in which was hidden the records of achievements and glories of an entire race, entire mass of people, living within the territory of a country.

Next, he turned to the study of nature, of surrounding and natural environments, the natural resources—the rivers, the changes in the course of rivers—for studying history. For example, while talking of the history of the ancient Greeks he says, 'In a small country lying in the eastern corner of the Mediterranean Sea, beautiful and adorned by nature, and garlanded by well-formed and beautiful-looking islands, lived a race of men who were few in number, but of a very charming aspect, perfectly formed, and strong in muscles and sinews, light of body, yet possessing steadiness and perseverance, and who were unrivalled for the creation of all earthly beauties, as well as

10. *C. W.*, IV, p. 399.

endowed with extraordinary practicality and intellect. The other ancient nations used to call them Yavanas, but they called themselves Greeks.'[11] Here he reads history of Greece in the natural surroundings and racial traits.

Next, he took to studying history in the life of the common men in the contemporary period, and in their character, their institutions and social organizations. Nivedita, his disciple, who learnt from him and recorded many of his utterances regarding history of various peoples, remarks in her notable historical study *Footfalls of Indian History* : 'The character of a people is their history as written in their own subconscious minds and to understand that character we have to turn on it the limelight of their history.'[12]

Vivekananda's Method—Objective and Scientific : It is clear that Vivekananda's method was objective and scientific. Since he always stuck to facts collected from studying literature or natural environment or from direct study of the life of the masses. And as a roaming monk, he had an unique opportunity to study the lives of the masses by directly coming into contact with them.

He always went to the sources, to the Vedas and Purāṇas, the *Jātaka*s and such other available literatures. For identifying some of the tribes that came from outside, he read *Rājataraṅgiṇī*, a recorded history of Kashmir. From *Chaṇḍīmaṅgal* of Mukundaram he gave an account of the change in the course of the river Ganga and its impact on the lives of the people living on the bank of that river. He depicted the nature of ancient Indian polity by referring to the Vedas, Purāṇas, the epics—*Rāmāyaṇa* and *Mahābhārata* and the Buddhist literature as well as the folklores. He studied the history of other ancient countries with equal care. For studying the history of Babylonia, Assyria, Egypt and Palestine he read the *History of the Far East* by Maspero. At first he read the English translation but when he learnt that the translator was a Christian with a bias and had therefore eliminated those portions of Maspero's book which went against the Christians, he read the original book in French. This shows

11. ibid., p. 401.
12. *Sister Nivedita's Works* (1st edition), Vol. IV, p.1—Edited by Pravrajika Atmaprana.

how meticulous he was about the authenticity of the materials he used. As is evident from his historical studies, viz., *The Historical Evolution Of India*, *Modern India*, *The Problem Of Modern India And Its Solution*, *The East And The West*, *The Memoirs Of European Travel*, etc., he utilized vast materials with equal meticulous care.

From all these studies it is clear that Vivekananda always used the vast canvas of world history as the background even when he studied the history of a particular nation, ancient or modern. And one would be simply awed by the vast study that lies behind the observations made by him often very briefly.

Vivekananda never knew 'fear' when he made his historical statements. In one of his letters to Mary Hale, for example, he wrote criticizing severely the British rulers in India— 'There has been a reign of terror in India for some years. English soldiers are killing our men and outraging our women— only to be sent home with passage and pension at our expense.'[13] And then he wrote, 'Suppose you simply publish this letter—the law just passed in India will allow the English Government to drag me from here to India and kill me without trial.'[14] Knowing it fully well that he may be punished severely for criticizing the British rulers under the then laws he nevertheless did criticize them fearlessly without caring for the consequence.

Fearlessness in stating facts, undenyingly, is one of the essential characteristics of an historian who professes to be 'scientific'. Just as he should not have any bias or prejudice, he should not have fear of anybody or anything, otherwise the historical truth can never come out in full. Vivekananda had this essential but rare quality to the maximum degree, as is apparent from his historical studies mentioned above.

No Determinism : *Man, a Free Agent to Vivekananda* : To Vivekananda, man is a free agent, as we have seen while discussing his concept of man, and history is an expression of the free will of man. Toynbee also expresses the same view when he says that the birth of civilization is due to exercise of free will since living beings cannot be subject to inexorable law.[15]

---

13. *C. W.*, VIII, p. 476.
14. ibid., pp. 476-77.
15. *A Study of History*, p. 47.

How does this free will of man express itself? As stated by Toynbee again, 'The dynamic process starts with challenge and response or because the undifferentiated unity of the pure Being is broken up into separate categories opposing each other. This play of opposites is called in Greece "love and hate", in China as "Yin and Yang", in the modern West as "thesis and antithesis".'[16] According to Vedanta, as interpreted by Vivekananda, it is due to *māyā* that the undifferentiated unity of the pure Being appears as many and as opposites. The philosophical aspects of this theory we have discussed already. Human history is a play of opposites, of rise and fall, of growth and decay, it is an expression of virtue and vices, of heroic achievements and deplorable failures, according to Vivekananda.

16. ibid.

CHAPTER 10

The History of Civilizations

As pointed out earlier, Vivekananda's approach in his historical studies is total and not fragmented—an approach not much known in his time but made popular by Toynbee in the twentieth century. 'I reject', says Toynbee, 'the present-day habit of studying history in terms of national states; these seems fragments of something larger, civilization. In so far as man needs to classify information before interpreting it, this large-scale unit seems to me to be less disturbing than a smaller scale.'[1] Fragmentation of history leads to distortion since it gives a partial view of man's journey through time.

I

EASTERN AND WESTERN TYPES OF CIVILIZATIONS

Long before Toynbee, Vivekananda accepted civilization as the unit of his study. In his *The East And The West*, he classified broadly two distinct types of civilizations :

1. the Asiatic or the Indian civilization—the eastern type, and
2. the western type originating from the Greek civilization.

The distinction has been drawn on the basis of the central ideal that has been working at the foundation of these two distinct types of civilization.

The ideal of the western type is the pursuit of happiness or *dharma* in Indian terms, and the ideal of the eastern is *mukti* or the pursuit of liberation. Defining *mukti* he says : 'That which teaches that even the happiness of this life is slavery... .' Explaining he says, '... happiness, wherever it may be, being within the laws of nature, is subject to death and will not last

---

1. *Arnold Toynbee, A Study of History.*

ad infinitum. Therefore man must aspire to become *mukta*, he must go beyond the body; slavery will not do.'[2]

Both the ideals are necessary for mankind : At the very beginning he makes it clear that both the ideals are necessary for the progress of humanity. He clearly asserts that '... the fall of our country ... is due to the utter want of this *dharma*.'[3] Since it is not possible for the entire population to follow the path of *mokṣa*, or liberation, *dharma* is necessary. *Dharma* means pursuit of happiness as well as of incessant work. Performance of *swadharma*, that is, 'activities according to one's own inclination', as stated in the *Gītā*, is a great virtue for the ordinary man. The Vedas recommended fourfold goals of life—*dharma*, *artha*, *kāma*, *mokṣa*, and emphasized the necessity of harmonizing and balancing them in one's life. Performance of *swadharma* is the path of welfare of men in all societies. In every land it is the ladder to the ultimate freedom. India deviated from this path and gave all importance to the ultimate ideal of *mokṣa* since the Buddhist period, which was wrong. Since everybody tried to pursue the path of *mokṣa* and not *dharma*, the country lagged behind others in the race of attaining material prosperity.

According to Vivekananda, different nations within a particular civilization may have some differences in their central ideal. For example, he mentions that 'political independence is the ideal of the French nation'. 'To the English just and equitable distribution of wealth', and 'the business principle', but both these ideals are fundamentally different from the eastern or the Indian. To the Indians, he observes, '... political and social independence are well and good, but the real thing is spiritual independence—*mukti*.'[4]

Fundamental Unity between the two types of Civilizations : At the very outset Vivekananda makes it also clear that in spite of differences of civilizations, mankind is basically one. 'As the same fire', he puts it beautifully, 'is manifesting itself in different forms, so the same one great Force is manifesting itself as political independence with the French, as mercantile genius and expansion of the sphere of equity with the English,

2. *C. W.*, V, p. 446. 3. ibid., p. 447. 4. ibid., p. 458.

and as the desire for *mukti* or spiritual independence with the Hindu.'[5] This implies the need for mutual appreciation of each other by the different nations belonging to different civilizations and mutual working for progress and prosperity of all.

Each race has a mission : He believed that 'each race has a peculiar mission to fulfil in the life of the world'.[6] Hence each nation has an important role to play in the life of others. And therefore, 'He had hopes of democratic America, he was enthusiastic over Italy of art, culture, and liberty—the great mother of Mazzini. He spoke of China as the treasury of the world. He fraternized with martyred Babists of Persia. He embraced in equal love the India of the Hindus, the Mohammedans, and the Buddhists. He was fired by the Moghul Empire... . He could comprehend and defend the grandeur of Chenghis Khan and his dream of Asiatic unity. He made Buddha the subject of magnificent eulogy : "I am the servant of the servants of Buddha".'[7] Thus according to Vivekananda, the achievements of the different nations in the different fields of life enriched mankind as a whole and not merely the particular nations only. He emphasized that the nations must be aware of it and learn to live in harmony and cooperation with each other.

The same idea has been harped on in the recent years by Toynbee. Referring to the present-day world where distance has been annihilated by the progress of science and technology, Toynbee says, 'In a world thus united in both space and time, the study of human affairs must be comprehensive. ... In order to save mankind we have to learn to live together in concord in spite of traditional differences of religion, civilization, nationality, class and race. In order to live together in concord successfully, we have to know each other, and knowing each other includes knowing each other's past, since human life like the rest of the phenomenal universe can be observed by human minds only as it presents itself to them on the move through time.' Thus, 'All of human history is relevant to present and

---

5. ibid., pp. 459-60. 6. ibid., III, p. 108.
7. Romain Rolland—*Life of Vivekananda*, p. 149.

future human needs', and 'The knowledge of the history of mankind should be one of mankind's common possessions.' 'We shall have to', Toynbee points out further, 'value them and love them as being parts of mankind's common treasure and therefore being ours too.'[8] This was exactly the view of Vivekananda as is evident from the account given by Romain Rolland which we have quoted just now.

According to Swami Vivekananda, the particular manifestation of this force which has moulded a national character in a particular way cannot be altered and should not be altered for the benefit of mankind as a whole. India should not be westernized. India should remain India and contribute its quota to human civilization and culture. But that does not mean that India should learn nothing from other nations. 'The man who says', points out Swami Vivekananda, 'he has nothing more to learn is already at his last gasp. The nation that says it knows everything is on the very brink of destruction!'[9] But he emphasizes at the same time that whatever we accept from others must be moulded in the national way. One should not give up his own national ideal but must assimilate others' without being off one's own feet. In this respect his motto was—'To modernize the old and to nationalize the modern'.

Acceptance and Assimilation : Actually give and take, acceptance and assimilation—is the process which is going on all the time in history. He has cited an example which speaks of his vast knowledge of history. Speaking about how Shiva and Kālī worships have been accepted by other nations from India, he says in a humorous tone, 'Once this Old Shiva, riding on His bull and taboring on his *damaru* travelled from India, on the one side, to Sumatra, Borneo, Celebes, Australia, as far as the shores of America, and on the other side, this Old Shiva battened His bull in Tibet, China, Japan, and as far up as Siberia, and is still doing the same. The Mother Kālī is still exacting Her worship even in China and Japan : it is She whom the Christians metamorphosed into the Virgin Mary, and worship as the mother of Jesus the Christ.'[10]

---

8. ibid., p. 47. 9. *C. W.*, V, p. 463. 10. ibid., p. 445.

II

EVOLUTION OF CIVILIZATIONS

The Concept of Evolution in History : The theory of evolution, which formed the basis of almost all the philosophical doctrines of India made indent into the physical and social sciences in the West in the nineteenth century. As a result it came to be believed in the West, as is pointed out by Vivekananda, that 'man is not born into a civilized state all of a sudden'[11], from savage stage, man has gradually evolved into a civilized state.

Tracing this evolution of civilization Swami Vivekananda throws new light on the different distinct stages of this development. The basis of his analysis is mostly ancient literature. His findings which are strikingly original are given below :

Primitive or the Pre-Civilized stage : *Position of Women*: Primitive man in the earliest days knew simple weapons of wood and stone only, lived in mountain caves, wore skins and depended on hunting. Gradually they learnt the use of metals. The use of iron came to be known much later. Ancient Babylonians, Egyptians and the Greeks did not know the use of iron. Next they learnt agriculture and tending cattle. In the earliest stage marriage was not known, children were known after their mother. Gradually wealth and women became the possessions of the males. As stated by Swami Vivekananda that women became as much the property of man as his slaves and chattels. Thus even in the primitive stage the status and position of women were inferior to that of men.

Emergence of Society and the dawn of Civilization : In the next stage society began to be formed and there were varieties of development in the different parts of the world. Those living on the sea shores depended on fishing, the mountaineers kept large flocks of sheep, those living in the forests took to hunting and those living in the plains depended on agriculture.

Civilization dawned among the last group of people since their struggle for existence was less hard, they had time for

11. ibid., p. 520.

thought and culture. But they were physically weak, as they lived on grains and not on animal diet.

The hunter, the shepherd and the fisherman in times of scarcity of food took to piracy and robbery and plundered the more civilized plains' people who in self-defence formed large unions and thus small kingdoms came to be established. This was the genesis of the political organ which came to be known as the 'state'. It was the 'coercive agency of the society'.

Two types of races : *Devas and Asuras* : Those who became civilized, lived on grains, dwelt in villages and towns, wore woven clothes and had the disposition of contemplation have been classed by Vivekananda as *deva*s, i.e., person with *daivī* or divine traits. The other group, who dwelt in the hills, deserts or sea-shores, lived on animal diet and wore hides and skins of wild animals and were habituated to plunder, piracy and robbery, were classed as *asura*s having non-divine inclinations. The basis of his classification is ancient literature.

Fusion of the two and the emergence of the Modern Society : But there were fusions between the two all the time; '... men of different types', Vivekananda says, 'and dispositions, civilized and savage, born with the nature of the *deva*s and the *asura*s have become fused together and form modern society.'[12] He makes it clear, therefore at the very outset that no nation is of purely *daivī* nature and no nation is purely *āsurī* nature and for that matter no nation can claim superiority over others. Referring in this connection to a saying of Ramakrishna, he observes, 'And that is why we see, in every society God playing in these various forms—the sādhu Nārāyaṇa, the robber Nārāyaṇa, and so on.'

The Dawn of Civilization in Asia on the River Banks : According to Swami Vivekananda, civilization dawned in Asia, on the plains near large rivers and fertile soils—on the banks of the Gaṅgā, the Yangtse-kiang and the Euphrates. The foundation of civilization was agriculture and the people depending on it manifested mostly *daivī* nature. For this view Vivekananda has been accused of preaching Asia-centrism just as European

12. ibid., p. 526.

historians are often accused of preaching Europe-centrism. But as a follower of truth only Vivekananda stated what he found out to be the truth through his investigations into the vast ancient literature of the world.

Location of European Civilization : It has also been shown by Vivekananda that most of the European civilization originated either in the hilly areas or sea-coasts, among the people depending on piracy and plunder, i.e., manifesting *āsurī* traits. The original home of the *āsurī* people was, according to him, Central Asia and the deserts of Arabia. This shows that according to Vivekananda, Asia was not only the mother of civilizations, it was the mother of uncivilized children also.

The descendents of *asura*s, the shepherds and hunters, in horde after horde chased the *deva*s and scattered them all over the world and the latter carried the banner of civilization to the different parts of the world. This shows exactly how Asia became the mother of human civilization.

Swami Vivekananda has studied not only the history of the growth of human civilization but also the different manifestations of it in different lands and regions. We give below a brief account of it.

III

EARLIEST CIVILIZATIONS

Dravidians, Babylonians and the Sumerians : The civilization of Egypt and that of ancient Babylonia are the oldest according to the scholars since the ruins of houses, etc., date back to 6000 B.C.[13] But Vivekananda advances completely a different theory. He points out that 'Madras Presidency is the habitat of that Tamil race whose civilization was the most ancient and a branch of whom, called the Sumerians, spread a vast civilization on the banks of the Euphrates in very ancient times.' He presents the following facts in support of his views : the 'Sumerian astrology, religious lores, morals, rites, etc., formed the foundation for the Assyrian, and the Babylonian

13. ibid., VII, p. 368.

civilizations' and that 'their mythology was the source of the Christian Bible'. Thus, according to Vivekananda, civilization of the Tamils in India was the oldest in history.

Dravidians and Egyptians : Vivekananda has also given the view that 'another branch of these Tamils spread from the Malabar coast and gave rise to the wonderful Egyptian civilization'. In support of his view he points out that a god called 'Shibu' was worshipped in the early days of Egyptian civilization. Obviously this 'Shibu' is 'Shiva', worshipped by the Indians. This is no doubt a positive proof of Indian influence over the Egyptians of ancient days.

Egypt was the granary of the world and the birth-place of sculpture. It was known for its Pyramids, the art of preserving the dead bodies, the university and the library in Alexandria. Emperor Aśoka sent preachers to Egypt in its later days. In many respects Greek civilization was indebted to Egypt. Egypt was destroyed along with the university and the library of Alexandria by the Christian barbarians and a woman savant called Hypatia was most brutally murdered. In this account given by Vivekananda is shown how fusion of races enriched the Egyptian civilization.

The Jewish Civilization : According to Swami Vivekananda, the Jewish civilization was much more recent compared to that of the Babylonians, since the date of composition of Bible was 500 B. C. to several years after the Christian era and since Bible includes entire Babylonian cosmology. The concept of 'Satan', according to him, is totally a Persian concept.

Persian Civilization : Persian civilization was indebted, in the opinion of Vivekananda, to both ancient Greece and India. Persia was later on invaded by the Arabs and it adopted the Mohammedan religion, 'with the result that the Mussulman religion took quite a new shape; the religion of the Arabs and the civilization of Persia became intermingled'.[14] Thus it is evident that fusion and intermingling was an eternal process in history. Vivekananda's objective in relating history of different civilizations was to draw our attention to this fact.

---

14. ibid., V, p. 508.

Greek Civilization : the Mother of European Civilization : As shown by Swami Vivekananda, 'a civilized race from Asia Minor founded in the land north of Mediterranean a higher order of civilization, viz., the Greek civilization'. Giving in brief the essential feature of the ancient Greek civilization, Vivekananda says : 'The Greek lives entirely in this world. He does not care to dream. Even his poetry is practical. His gods and goddesses are not only human beings, but intensely human, with all human passions and feelings almost the same as with any of us. He loves what is beautiful, but, mind you, it is always external nature : the beauty of the hills, of the snows, of the flowers, the beauty of forms and figures, the beauty in the human face... . And the Greeks being the teachers of all subsequent Europeanism, the voice of Europe is Greek.'[15] Thus, Vivekananda makes it clear in his exposition that the foundation of the modern European Civilization is on the ancient Greek Civilization.

Roman Civilization : '... in Italy', writes Vivekananda, describing the growth of the Roman Civilization, 'a barbarous tribe known as the Romans conquered the civilized Etruscans, assimilated their culture and learning, and established a civilization of their own... .'[16] Though they brought Greece under their subjugation, the Greeks were their teachers and therefore Roman civilization was enriched by assimilating Greek culture and learning. Its achievements have been 'politics, military science, art of colonization and foreign conquest'.[17] Europe as a whole was brought under the suzerainty of Rome.[18] This unification under Rome helped the spread of Greek culture and learning all over Europe.

Spread of Christianity : Central Asia and Arabia was the home of the *asuras*. They invaded Europe and being pushed by them the barbarians of northern Europe fell upon Roman Empire and destroyed it. Jews being conquered by Rome was driven away from Jerusalem, as a result they and their new religion—Christianity, spread all over Europe.[19] This was thus another civilizing force for Europe according to Vivekananda—this

15. ibid., IV, pp. 142-43.
16. ibid., V, p. 527.
17. ibid., VII, p. 371.
18. ibid., V, p. 527.
19. ibid.

sublime influence of the religion preached by Jesus Christ based on the doctrine of love and brotherhood.

Rise of the Modern European Race : From the fusion of the different hordes of *asuras* the modern European race arose. They were still barbarians. Two heads of the Christian churches, the Pope of Italy and the Patriarch of Constantinople, began gradually to exercise authority over their kings, queens and the people.[20] This also might have helped the process of civilizing in Europe.

Rise of Mohammedanism : Mohammedanism arose in the deserts of Arabia and with great force and vigour they fell upon Europe, and along with the tide the learning and culture of India and ancient Greece were carried into Europe. Fusion of Greek and Indian culture exercised a civilizing influence over the European races in the opinion of Vivekananda. A few centuries after, when the Turks and Tartars were converted from Buddhism to Mohammedanism, they conquered the Hindus, the Persians and the Arabs.

Rise of the Modern European Civilization : Subsequently the Tartars seized the throne of Arabian Caliph and took possession of Jerusalem. 'Hordes of European barbarians,' describes Vivekananda, 'rushed towards Asia Minor to deliver Jerusalem from the hands of the infidels.' They failed but Europe began to be civilized coming into contact with the Asian civilization. The English, French, German and other savage nations who dressed themselves in hides and skin and ate raw flesh came into contact with the Asian civilization, and became gradually civilized. In this connection Vivekananda made two startling statements : (1) 'An order of Christian soldiers of Italy and other countries, corresponding to our Nāgās, began to learn philosophy; and one of their sects, the Knights Templars, became confirmed Advaita Vedantists, and ended by holding Christianity up to ridicule.' (2) 'Moreover, as they had amassed enormous riches, the kings of Europe, at the orders of the Pope, and under the pretext of saving religion, robbed and exterminated them.'[22] Comment from the historians on these interesting statements are so far lacking.

---

20. ibid., p. 528. 21. ibid., pp. 529-30. 22. ibid., p. 530.

The Italian Renaissance : As viewed by Vivekananda, with the Mussalman invaders the learning and arts of ancient Greece entered into Italy, overpowered the barbarians, 'and with their quickening impulse, life began to pulsate in the dead body of the world-capital of Rome'. 'But this new birth was for Italy only a rebirth; while for the rest of Europe, it was the first birth.'[23] Thus the European civilization was born in the sixteenth century A.D., i.e., during the reign of the Mogul Emperors in India.[24]

Spanish Civilization : The Moors, a Mohammedan tribe, established a civilized kingdom in Spain, cultivated various branches of knowledge and founded the first university in Europe. In the art of war, in architectural buildings, they left a strong mark of their impress.[25] According to Vivekananda, the emergence of the Spanish civilization was for that matter a land-mark in human history.

Varieties of Slave Society : Swami Vivekananda has shown in his *The East And The West* that while the Mohammedans had contracts between the feudatory chiefs and their armies, in the matter of wars ordinary people were let alone, in Europe the king and his groups of feudatory chiefs were on one side and turned all the subject-people into their slaves. Everyone had to live under the shelter of a military feudatory chief as his man and then was he allowed to live; he had to be always ready to fight at any time for him.[26] Thus, slavery was much more widespread and ruthless in Europe than in Asia.

IV

ETHNOLOGY AND HISTORY

In his *Memoirs of European Travel*, Swami Vivekananda has relied on ethnology as a developed science as well as on ancient literature in depicting history of various countries.

This science of ethnology classifies different races on the basis of physical traits. These races are, as described by Swami Vivekananda, (1) Negroes, found in Africa, and Negrites (little Negroes) found in ancient days in certain portions of Arabia,

23. ibid., p. 509. 24. ibid. 25. ibid., p. 530. 26. ibid., p. 531.

portions of the banks of Euphrates, Southern Persia, whole of India, Andamans, parts of Australia; (2) Mongolians and Mongoloid (little Mongoles) both occupied greater part of Asia, e.g., Nepalese, Burmese, Siamese, Malayas, Japanese, Huns, Tartars, Turks, Manchus, etc., belong to this stock. Many among them were nomads; (3) Dravidians, inhabitants of ancient Egypt, Babylonia, and Southern part of India; (4) the Semitic races who lived in north Arabia and the modern Jews and ancient Babylonians, Assyrians, Phoenicians belong to this stock; their languages also have a common stock; (5) finally, the Aryans who spoke a language allied to Sanskrit.

The point that was sought to be emphasized by Vivekananda was that all the modern races sprang from an admixture of these various ethnic groups. Thus to him racial purity was a myth. According to him, a race which has a preponderance of one or the other races, has the language and the physionomy of the same stock, is called after that race.[27] Besides physical features, similarities of religious ideas may also be noted among the various people belonging to the same stock. For example, 'The religion of all the Semitic races' Vivekananda points out, 'with slight minor variations, was almost the same. The Babylonians, Jews, Phoenicians, and Arabs of a later date used the same form of worship. Almost every god was called Moloch... .'[28]

V

CIVILIZATION OF MODERN EUROPEAN COUNTRIES

Swami Vivekananda in his historical studies made observations not only on ancient civilizations but also on almost every modern European country, bringing out the essential characteristics of each.

Civilization of France : Regarding France in his assessment he says, 'To understand this Europe, one has to understand her through France, the fountain-head of everything that is highest in the West. The supreme power that rules the world is Europe, and of this Europe the great centre is Paris. Paris is the centre of

27. ibid., VII, p. 368.

28. ibid.

western civilization. Here, in Paris, matures and ripens every idea of western ethics, manners and customs, light or darkness, good or evil.'[29] They are the worshippers of beauty, everywhere in everything there is an attempt at beauty, an attempt at art . Again, Swami Vivekananda points out, 'France is the home of liberty. From here, the city of Paris, travelled with tremendous energy the power of the People, and shook the very foundations of Europe. . . . the spirit of the French Revolution is still working among the other nations of Europe.'[30] Revolutionary spirit that emerged out of the French Revolution predominates over art, literature, philosophical ideas and political notions of modern Europe.

German Civilization : In contrast, according to Swami Vivekananda, 'German civilization is full of muscle'.[31] Germany's supremacy and influence was all over Europe and America all the time. Vivekananda mentions that : 'Today Germany is the dictator to all Europe, her place is above all!' Referring to Germany's great achievements he notes that 'Germany has given man and woman compulsory education, making illiteracy punishable by law'. In the opinion of Vivekananda, predominance of Germany in the manufacturing industries and expanding monopoly of German merchandise even over the English colonial territories made Germany to attain its power.[32]

Austria, Hungary, Bulgaria, Serbia, Turkey and other countries : Giving glimpses of all these countries Vivekananda remarks : 'There are three civilized nations in Europe—the French, the Germans and the English. The rest are almost as badly off as we are and the majority of them are so uncivilized that you can find no race in Asia so degraded.'[33] They were at the time both economically and culturally backward. Under development was the order of the day extensively all over the world including Europe excepting a small portion of it.

Vivekananda, however, very much appreciated the Hungarians' revolutionary attempts to get themselves free from Austria's domination and in this connection he made a memorable statement regarding the value of freedom. 'Freedom

---

29. ibid, p. 382.
30. ibid., V, p. 511.
31. ibid., VII, p. 382.
32. ibid.
33. ibid., p. 391.

with but one meal a day and tattered rags on is a million times better than slavery in gold chains.'[34] This is being proved by the events in eastern Europe today when one by one the different countries are removing the shackles of communistic totalitarianism and dictatorship in their bid to be free.

Europe : a Military Camp : Tracing the history of various countries of Europe, Vivekananda concludes that 'the whole of Europe was gradually transformed into a vast military camp — and this is even now the case'.[35] 'Throughout Europe there is a craze for soldiers', he said, 'soldiers everywhere'.[36] France, after having suffered a defeat from Germany, in anger made every citizen a soldier. Naturally Germany had to be prepared also and conscription was in vogue everywhere at the time. England being an island, is continually strengthening her navy. He pointed out also that Russia with largest population could amass biggest army and the titular states like Serbia and Bulgaria, which the European powers created by dismembering Turkey were also to have well-equipped and trained army in order to retain their identity as a separate nation state.

The Turks : In connection with relating the history of Hungary, Swami Vivekananda referred to the racial stock to which the Hungarians belonged to, viz., the Turks. He then went on at length to describe the history of the Turks whose original home was Turkistan or Changwoi in the Turkish language. The story of their fusion with the Aryan and the Semitic races, their extreme love of war, their conquest of western India and founding kingdoms there, the story of the famous emperor Kaṇiṣka who founded the Mahāyāna school of Buddhism, the story of their conversion to Mohammedanism and the decline of learning and culture among them, their conquest of Persia and the similar decline in culture overtaking the people of Persia, their conquest of Constantinople and of India (the Mogul emperors of India belonged to this stock)—all these have been related with supporting facts by Swami Vivekananda.[37] This is an account which speaks very highly of Swami Vivekananda's vast scholarship in history and the depth of his historical vision.

---

34. ibid., p. 392.
35. ibid., V, p. 530.
36. ibid., VII, p. 392.
37. ibid., p. 394.

VI

THE VAST CANVAS OF WORLD HISTORY

Thus in his review of various civilizations Vivekananda has laid open the vast canvas of world history beginning from time immemorial. Civilization after civilization has emerged, all have been the achievements of the human race as a whole. Mankind has marched on the path of progress through various routes, winning new ground with each step. This is the vision that we get after going through Vivekananda's account of history of the different nationalities and civilizations from the beginning.

CHAPTER 11

Historical Evolution of the Indian Civilization

I

The Indian people : The Indian people, according to Vivekananda, like every other people in the world, come from a mixed stock. Throughout the long and the chequered history of India there has been fusion between the Dravidians, Tartars, aboriginals and the Aryans. The Aryans were however the dominant type and while assimilating the language, manners, customs, and religions of others, they left a strong mark of their own impress on everything.

The Aryans : The theory that the Aryans were invaders coming from outside India has been challenged by Swami Vivekananda. And his arguments seem unassailable. He makes it clear that there is no reference about it in any of our ancient literary work—neither the Vedas nor the later works of the ancient times. He also refutes the theory that Rāmachandra's war against Rāvaṇa described in the epic *Rāmāyaṇa* was the war of conquest of the uncivilized non-Aryans by the civilized Aryans. He points out that 'The civilization of Laṅkā was rather higher, and surely not lower, than that of Ayodhyā.'[1] He also points out that the Vānaras (monkeys) and other southern Indians were Rāmachandra's allies and their territories as well as the territory of Rāvaṇa were not annexed by him. Although the aborigines who attacked the sages performing the sacrifices, were killed by the kings, but there is no evidence that their territories were annexed. Actually, according to Vivekananda, the civilization of India was created and enriched by both the Aryans and the non-Aryans and the contributions of the latter to the Indian civilization were as important as that of the former.

The National Character : The keynote of the national character

1. *C. W.*, V., p. 536.

of these people, as shown by Swami Vivekananda from the very beginning has been three qualities, viz., (1) inquisitiveness, (2) analytical power, and (3) bold poetic insight, which led them to develop various arts and sciences. It is well known how their contributions to astronomy, other branches of mathematics and chemistry enriched the world in those very early days of human civilization. These dominant qualities made the people contemplative and to make bold attempts to go beyond the limitations of the senses and have a glimpse of what is beyond. The Indian climate also gave a higher direction to the genius of the race. In the words of Vivekananda : 'In a land where nature was propitious and yielded easy victories the national mind started to grapple with and conquer the higher problems of life in the field of thought.'

Vedic period : The earliest record about Indian civilization are the Vedas but at that time when the Vedas were composed India was well ahead on the march of civilization. This is evident from the available facts. As pointed out by Swami Vivekananda, 'An organized pantheon, elaborate ceremonials, divisions of society into hereditary classes necessitated by a variety of occupations, a great many necessaries and a good many luxuries of life are already there.'[2] It implies that 'Many forms of religion and society must have been left behind in the onward march, before we find the race as depicted in the scriptures, the Vedas.'[3]

Spiritual trend : We have just now seen that the Indian climate and the abundance of natural endowments made struggle for existence rather easy here and hence the people turned towards a life of contemplation and engaged themselves with the deeper problems of life. It is natural only that in such a society priests or the Brahmins who professed to lead a spiritual life would be given the highest position. This predominant preistly class developed elaborate systems of rituals and ceremonials and wanted the people to observe them. But the kingly class also engaged themselves in philosophical speculations which struck at the root of ceremonialism and ritualism. Hence these two major classes came into conflict with each other. The priests in defence of ceremonialism in the economic interest of themselves opposed the kingly efforts to root it out.

---

2. ibid., VI., p. 159.
3. ibid.

The materialists and the triangular fight : A third class of people recruited from both the kings and the Brahmins depicted spiritualism as a fraud and upheld the attainment of material comforts as the highest goal of life. The people being tired of observing ceremonialism at the behest of the priests and 'wondering at the philosophies of the king' sought to join enmasse the camp of the materialists. And there started, as Vivekananda describes it, '... that triangular fight in India between ceremonials, philosophy, and materialism which has come down unsolved to our own days.'[4] Here it is evident that materialism was also a creation of the upper classes and the theory that it was a philosophy of the common people is a myth.

Krishna and Buddha : Krishna and Buddha were the prophets of India who attempted a solution of the tangle. First of all, the people were taught to see in differences the same truth in various garbs. But there were the claims of the kingly class for superiority and the people were intolerant of both the kingly and the priestly privileges. Krishna opened the gates of spiritual knowledge to all irrespective of sex or caste but he left the same question on the social side undisturbed. Buddha preached against ritualism and privileges of the priests and hereditary castes but he did not intend to destroy Vedic religion. His aim was to reform it, and he did not want to overturn the social order, though he attempted hard to bring social equality. This is briefly the core of Vivekananda's assessment of the two great prophets.

The Mahābhārata War : In ancient India the centre of national life was always intellectual and spiritual, and not political. 'The outburst of national life', he points out, 'was round [the] colleges of sages and spiritual teachers. We thus find the *samiti*s of the Pañchālas, of the Kāśyas (of Varanasi), the Maithilas standing out as great centres of spiritual culture and philosophy, even in [the period of] the Upanishads. Again these centres in turn became the focus of political ambition of the various divisions of the Aryans.' In the great epic *Mahābhārata* is described a war of supremacy between the Kurus and the Pañchālas in the process of which they destroyed each other. This is to be noted that according to Vivekananda, this was a war between the Kurus and the Pañchālas

4. ibid., p. 160.

and not between the two rival groups of the same Kuru dynasty as depicted in the great epic.

Supremacy of Magadha : Afterwards supremacy was attained by the Magadha kings and the field of Buddhist activity was the same region. The new priest power, i.e., the order of the Buddhist monks and nuns joined hands with the political power of the Maurya kings who made Buddhism a world-wide religion. In the words of Vivekananda, 'The popularity of Buddhism and its fresh vigour made the Maurya kings the greatest emperors that India ever had.' It is obvious that in this brief assessment Vivekananda is extremely objective and realistic. He was a great admirer of Buddha but here he shows no trace of hero-worship.

Revival of Vedic Religion and the decline of Buddhism : He describes the downfall of Buddhism with the same spirit of objectivity. According to him, Buddhism lost its individuality due to its extreme adaptability and overzealousness to 'be of the people'. The Vedic religion in the meantime had got rid of many of its objectionable features. With the Scythian invasion, Pāṭaliputra was destroyed and Buddhism declined. The Scythians who were the sun-worshippers, found affinity with the sun-worshipping sects of the Brahmins, and when the latter agreed to adapt and spiritualize many of their customs, they stood by the Brahmins.

Revival of priesthood : Thus with the Schythian conquest there was a revival of the priestly power. The nation was once again under the clutches of the priests and the exclusive monks of the new order. Their demand for privileges was sky-high and to that the masses were deprived of their rights and were oppressed.

Rise of a renascent India with Śaṅkara and Rāmānuja : Then there came a period of darkness about which we know very little. In the poetic language of Vivekananda this period is described in the following manner : 'Then there is a period of darkness and shifting shadows ; there are tumults of war, rumours of massacres; and the next scene rises upon a new phase of things.' The supremacy of the Magadha was gone, most of northern India was under petty chiefs. Buddhism was almost extinct. The nation was under the clutches of double priesthood of Brahmins and monks. However, in the next period, 'a renascent nation rose to glory—with the valour and blood of the heroic Rajputs, the new philosophical impulse organized by

Śaṅkara, and with the arts and literature of the courts of Mālava.'

Attempt to revive ritualism : Priesthood in Hindu society having grown to be hereditary by this time, an attempt was made to revive the rituals of the Vedic period, failing which neo-Hinduism made philosophic portions of the Vedas its basis. According to Vivekananda, the process of assimilation and reformation went on for over thousand years.

The problem of unification of the nation : So long the question was simple, of Aryanizing the other types of races. But now it was different. There was no longer a compact race of the same stock, speaking the same language and with the same social and religious aspirations. In its place there was a vast mass of people divided by race, colour, speech, spiritual instinct, and social ambitions into 'hopelessly jarring factions'. And this heterogeneous elements had to be unified and welded into one gigantic nation. This task was accomplished by Buddhism. But with its decline the problem was manifest again.

Rights of the masses and Śaṅkara and Rāmānuja : The movement of Śaṅkara, however, could not serve the masses, because of its adherence to strict caste-laws and because it attempted communication through the Sanskrit language, which was no longer the language of the masses. Moreover, the philosophy of Śaṅkara had no emotional appeal. This was a bold criticism made by Vivekananda although he was a great admirer of Śaṅkara, whom he considered the boldest and the greatest philosopher of the world.

The philosophy of Rāmānuja, according to Vivekananda, was more practical, had an emotional appeal, it denied categorically the privileges of birth in the spiritual sphere. And since its vehicle was the people's language it succeeded in drawing the masses to the fold of the religion of the Vedas once again. And with it unification was also accomplished. Thus the spiritual upheaval of Śaṅkara and Rāmānuja was followed by the usual Indian sequence of united races and powerful empires.

Mohammedan invasion : Round about this period Mālava empire relying on ritualism flourished in northern India for a short time. Then after some time there came a series of invasions and northern India was in the grip of the central Asiatic conquerors of Islamic religion. South India then became the centre of Indian spiritual civilization. The Mohammedans then tried hard to subjugate the South but never got a strong foothold there.

Religious movements of the Mohammedan period : The religious movements that arose in northern India at the time aimed at preventing the people from embracing Mohammedanism *en masse* which brought in its trail social equality for all. Kabīr, Dādu, Chaitanya, Nānak, all preached equality of all men although their philosophies differed in many respects. But they did not lay down any new thought and aspiration, according to Vivekananda. They were in his estimate, 'mere apologists only struggling to obtain permission to live'. This is no doubt a very bold and objective assessment again.

Sikhs and Marathas : *the nature of the religious ideals* : Towards the end of this period of the rule of the Mohammedans there occurred the rise of Sikhism through the genius of Guru Govinda Singh, and the result of his spiritual work was followed by the well-known political organization of the Sikhs. There was also a rise of the Marathas under Śivājī, who sought to re-establish Hindu domination over India.

Throughout the history of India, as it is unveiled by Vivekananda, a spiritual upheavel was almost always succeeded by a political unity and extensive empires coming into existence which in turn helped to strengthen the spiritual aspirations that brought it into being. But in his estimate the spiritual revival that preceded the rise of the Maratha and the Sikh empires were extremely reactionary, mass-fanaticism and hatred for the alien being its basis. Hence they lost their motive power as soon as they succeeded in destroying the rule of the Mohammedans. And soon their influence had gone and they lost their grip over the life of the nation.

Modern period—arrival of the European races : Towards the end of the Mogul Empire there came the various European races as traders in India and they clashed with each other for attaining supremacy over the land. Ultimately the British came out as victorious.

The spiritual movements of the modern period : At this time the religious movements that came into being in India took the same line of self-defence that was taken up by the northern Indian sects during the period of Mohammedan rule. They were in Swami

Vivekananda's estimate, 'the feeble tones of a dying people pleading for permission to live'. 'They are ever eager', he adds, 'to adjust their spiritual or social surrounding, according to the tastes of the conquerors.' And he predicted that 'No wonder that these sects have mushroom lives to live.'[5] True to Vivekananda's predictions the influence of the reformists of the nineteenth century who sought to reform Hinduism declined gradually and today towards the end of twentieth century they are no significant force in the social or religious life of the country.

II

THE UNIQUE HISTORICAL INSIGHT OF SWAMI VIVEKANANDA

We find therefore that to the deep and unique historical insight of Swami Vivekananda were revealed : (1) the selfish economic interests of the priests in defending ceremonialism even in the early days of Indian history; (2) the desire of the kingly philosophers to attain social supremacy; (3) the protest of the oppressed masses in joining the materialist camp; (4) the social question remaining unsolved even after Krishna's attempt to grant equality of rights in spiritual matters and Buddha's and Vaiṣṇavites' attempt to bring about social equality; (5) the failure of Śaṅkara to touch the problems of the masses; (6) the apologetic character of the religious reformers of the Mohammedan period; (7) the reactionary and narrow fanatic character of the Sikh and Maratha uprisings; (8) the apologetic character of the reform movements of modern India and their attempts at appeasing their foreign masters. All these may not seem palatable to all. But Vivekananda was fearless in stating the truths which his study of history revealed to him.

III

THE SOCIAL PROBLEM AND THE RELIGIOUS MOVEMENTS IN INDIA

The historical investigations of Swami Vivekananda reveals how the religious movements have made attempts to solve the social

5. ibid., p. 167.

problem, viz., the problem of granting the masses equal spiritual and social rights throughout the ages. From the earliest days the struggle between the masses and the ruling classes has gone on over the question of privileges claimed by the upper classes. The peculiar feature of India in this respect was that this question was not attempted to be solved politically. Religious reformers and not the politicians, made attempts to solve it. This was so, since; as pointed out by Swami Vivekananda, 'the centres of national life were always the intellectual and spiritual and not political', and since the 'political and social power has been always subordinated to spiritual and intellectual'.[6] Hence social revolution always came in this country after a spiritual revival. 'Such changes revolutionizing society', says Swami Vivekananda in *Modern India*, 'have been happening in India again and again, only in this country they have been effected in the name of religion, for religion is the life of India, religion is the language of this country, the symbol of all its movements.'[7] Citing examples from history he says—'What could have saved Indian society from the ponderous burden of omnifarious ritualistic ceremonialism, with its animal and other sacrifices, which all but crushed the very life out of it, except the Jain revolution, which took its strong stand exclusively on chaste morals and philosophical truth? Or without the Buddhist revolution what would have delivered the suffering millions of the lower classes from the violent tyrannies of the influential higher castes?'[7a]

IV

POLITICS IS NOT THE ONLY INSTRUMENT OF SOCIAL REVOLUTION

Thus it is evident from Indian history, as brought out by Swami Vivekananda, that politics is not the only instrument of social revolutions, religion has been in India all through an efficient instrument in this respect. He has described how the spiritual upheavals associated with the names of Chārvāka, Buddha, Jaina, Śaṅkara, Rāmānuja, Chaitanya, Nānak, Kabīr, Dādu, Brāhmo

6. ibid., p. 161. 7. ibid, IV., p. 462. 7a. ibid.

Samāj, Ārya Samāj have ushered in social revolutions in different periods of history since the earliest days.

Play of the two opposing forces : The lesson of history is, as viewed by Swami Vivekananda, that society is always subject to the working of two opposing forces—viz., 'privilege-making' and 'privilege-breaking' forces. At times the privilege-making forces gain upperhand and at other times the opposite force. The dynamic play of these two opposing forces makes society going.

The role of materialism in India as a privilege-breaking force : Swami Vivekananda, an eminent exponent of spiritualism in modern India, has no hesitation in making this historical truth known that when priesthood in its period of decadence makes the life of the masses unbearable with their demand of sky-high privileges, materialism comes to the rescue of these oppressed masses in setting them free from meaningless ceremonialism and the clutches of the priestly class. 'As a rule spirituality brings a class of men who lay exclusive claim to the special powers of the world ... then, society has to help itself, and materialism comes to the rescue.' But materialism creates new problems. Materialism helps a nation to attain material prosperity. But, as stated by Vivekananda, 'Along with the prosperity, will rise to white heat all the inborn jealousies and hatred of the human race. And the world will be destroyed had not spirituality come to the rescue.' Thus we find that materialism also gives rise to claims of privileges and results in cruelty and oppression. Spirituality saves mankind at such times. Therefore what history reveals, according to Vivekananda, is that materialism and spirituality both play a double role—as a both privilege-making and a privilege-breaking force. This speaks volumes of the attitude of detachment of Vivekananda as an historian. He makes no attempt to hold brief for spiritualism when it degenerates into a privilege-making force.

V

BRITISH RULE IN INDIA : A MANIFESTATION OF IMPERIALISM

Regarding the British rule in India Swami Vivekananda had no illusion, he did not consider it a blessing like the nineteenth century reformers. He was aware of the imperialistic character of the British rule. In his opinion, 'British rule in modern India has only one redeeming feature, though unconscious; it has brought India out once more on the stage of the world; it has forced upon it the contact of the outside world.'[8] But this was the only redeeming feature in his opinion, the other consequences were disastrous.

Merciless exploitation : First of all, Vivekananda makes it clear that 'No good can be done when the main idea is blood-sucking.' This brings out the essence of British rule in India. Merciless exploitation was the true character of British rule in India.

According to him, 'A few hundred, modernized, half-educated, and denationalized men are all the show of modern English India—nothing else.'[9] Unfolding the exploitation, devastation and atrocities that were committed by the British in India, Vivekananda observes, 'In spite of the centuries of anarchy that reigned during the struggles of the English to conquer, the terrible massacre the English perpetrated in 1857 and 1858, and the still more terrible famines that have become the inevitable consequence of British rule (there never is a famine in a native state) and that take off millions, there has been a good increase of population, but not yet what it was when the country was entirely independent—that is, before the Mohammedan rule. Indian labour and produce can support five times as many people as there are now in India with comfort, if the whole thing is not taken off from them.'[10]

Stating how basic liberty and freedom of the people were denied by the British he says, 'This is the state of things—even education will not more be permitted to spread; freedom of the press stopped already (of course we have been disarmed long ago), the bit of self-government granted to them for some years is being quickly taken off. We are watching what next! For writing a few words of innocent criticism, men are being hurried to transportation for life, others imprisoned without any trial; and nobody knows when his head will be off.'[11]

Depicting the reign of terror that was let loose on India at the time by the British he goes on to say, 'There has been a reign of

8. ibid, VIII., p. 475. 9. ibid., p. 476. 10. ibid. 11. ibid.

terror in India for some years. English soldiers are killing our men and outraging our women—only to be sent home with passage and pension at our expense.'[12] Refuting the theory that the English has spread education in India he says, 'All property and lands granted by the previous governments for supporting education have been swallowed up, and the present Government spends even less than Russia in education.'[13] And what type of education? An education in which, in the words of Vivekananda, 'the least show of originality is throttled'.

The cruelty of the oppressions has again been described by him thus, '. . . they have their heels on our necks, they have sucked the last drop of our blood for their own pleasures, they have carried away with them millions of our money, while our people have starved in villages and provinces.'[14]

Finally, giving a summary view of the British rule in India he comments, 'You look about India what has the Hindoo left? Wonderful temples, everywhere. What has the Mohammedan left? Beautiful palaces. What has the Englishman left? Nothing but mounds of broken brandy bottles.'[15]

It appears from the above review of the British rule in India made by Swami Vivekananda that the British rule in India did not leave the impression of a high level civilization of the ruling British nation. He had a glimpse of what imperialism means from his experience of British rule in India. And he had an horror of imperialism and its consequences. He condemned British rule and imperialism wholeheartedly.

---

12. ibid.
13. ibid., p. 477.
14. Marie Louise Burke—*New Discoveries*, 2nd edition, p. 25.
15. ibid.

CHAPTER 12

The Philosophy of History

I

In this chapter we will note some of the important findings of Swami Vivekananda which emerged out of his historical studies. And then we shall also make an attempt to have a glimpse of his philosophy of history.

SOME IMPORTANT FINDINGS

1. *Religion is not responsible for social oppressions* : Regarding the alleged role of religion in engineering social oppressions, Swami Vivekananda observes, '... for all the devilry that religion is blamed with, religion is not at all in fault: no religion ever persecuted men, no religion ever burnt witches, no religion ever did any of these things. What then incited people to do these things? Politics, but never religion; and if such politics takes the name of religion, whose fault is that?'[1] And as shown by him, politicians in collusion with the priests are responsible for all these atrocities. They did perpetrate atrocities to subserve their selfish interests.

2. *Distinction between the Graeco-Roman and the Asian Civilizations* : Regarding the distinction between the Graeco-Roman civilization and the Asian civilization he points out, 'The voice of Asia has been the voice of religion. The voice of Europe is the voice of politics. Each is great in its own sphere. The voice of Europe is the voice of ancient Greece.'[2] The voices are different, but the note that each has sounded has been important towards the development of the entire humanity—this is his contention.

3. *Each Nation has a mission* : His vast knowledge of the history of civilizations led him finally to the conclusion that

1. *C. W.*, IV, p. 125.

2. ibid., p. 142.

'each nation has a mission for the world' and 'so long as that mission is not hurt, the nation lives', despite vicissitudes. 'But as soon as its mission is destroyed, the nation collapses.'[3] In support of his theory he points out that 'Rome's mission was imperial power, expansion. And so soon as that was touched, Rome fell to pieces, passed out. The mission of Greece was intellect, as soon as that was touched, Greece passed out. So in modern times, Spain and all these modern countries.'[4] And he points out that the mission of India is religion, or spiritual life. Since time immemorial religion has been the centre of life of the Indian people. So long as this mission is not destroyed India will live, it will go strong in spite of all its problems, difficulties and vicissitudes. As soon as it is destroyed, it will die a natural death. Hence the central mission of a nation should be carefully safeguarded by its members.

4. *India—a cultural unity without a political unity* : Indian society started as a cultural unity without having any political unity. This sort of situation is good for social and cultural progress; but its price is the chronic warfare between the local states. The political unity was restored at a later period during the regime of Aśoka. This restoration takes place repeatedly once the original unity is achieved. During the period of intermediate lapses there may be anarchic situation causing a break in the tradition. But this never happened in the case of India. There never occurred in its long history a complete break with the past. The same tradition has continued from time immemorial right up to the present.

5. *The continuity of the Indian and the Chinese Civilizations* : Thus an important conclusion of Vivekananda that emerged from his study of history is regarding a peculiar feature of the Indian and the Chinese civilizations, viz., their continuity, their capacity for survival. According to Vivekananda, this happens in the case of peaceful nations. 'When you study the civilization of India', he says, 'you find that it has died and revived several times; this is its peculiarity. Most races rise once and then decline for ever. There are two kinds of people; those who grow continually and those whose growth comes to an end.

3. ibid., VIII, p. 75.

4. ibid., pp. 74-75.

The peaceful nations, India and China, fall down, yet rise again; but the others, once they go down, do not come up—they die.'[5] Here Vivekananda makes it clear that only peaceful nations possess this quality. Pursuit of peace makes a nation to survive. No doubt it is a very illuminating finding which explains rightly the causes of continuity of certain nations as against the others.

6. *India's deficiency* : The historical studies of Vivekananda made him convinced that the Indian ideal was not a perfect one since it led to the negligence of the masses. According to him, the high ideal of spiritual life was not for the masses, they have a right to worldly happiness which was not recognized in India of old. 'But you see', he says, 'how those vast millions are forced to accept the opposite point of view by tyranny. ... This is the tyranny of the great, tyranny of the spiritual, tyranny of the intellectual, tyranny of the wise. ... Now, I say', he declares emphatically, 'that this thing has got to stop. There is no use in sacrificing millions and millions of people to produce one spiritual giant.'[6] As argued by Vivekananda, material prosperity and equitable distribution of national income was needed to do justice to the masses which India had neglected in the past.

7. *The Shudras or the Proletariats are oppressed throughout the Indian history* : Again he is very critical of India regarding the oppression of the Shudras, or the working classes by the upper classes. In *Modern India* he says : 'And where are they through whose physical labour only are possible the influence of the Brahmin, the prowess of the Kshatriya, and the fortune of the Vaishya? What is their history, who, being the real body of society, are designated, at all times, in all countries, as "baseborn"? For whom kind India prescribed the mild punishments, "Cut out his tongue, chop off his flesh", and others of like nature, for such a grave offence as any attempt on their part to gain a share of the knowledge and wisdom monopolized by her higher classes—those "moving corpses" of India and the "beasts of burden" of other countries—the Shudras, what is their lot in life?'[7] With this merciless criticism he makes it clear that India's degradation was due to this reason, viz., the denial of the rights of the proletariat and this was the actual reason for India's

5. ibid., pp. 92-93. 6. ibid., p. 76. 7. ibid., IV, pp. 466-67.

misfortune of being under foreign domination for centuries. When foreigners invaded the country, the masses did not give their support to their oppressors, viz., the kings who were in alliance with the priests in the matter of oppressing them.

8. *Merit of modern Western Civilization* : Appraising the modern western civilization Vivekananda observes : 'From the day when education and culture, etc., began to spread gradually from patricians to plebians, grew the distinction between the modern civilization as of western countries, and the ancient civilization as of India, Egypt, Rome, etc. ... The chief cause of India's ruin has been the monopolizing of the whole education and intelligence of the land, by dint of pride and royal authority, among a handful of men.'[8] The great merit of modern Europe according to him, has been that it made education universal, accessible to all high or low. Here we find that Vivekananda is very critical of India and is full of praise for the West. Those who accuse him of Asia-centrism or India-centrism may please note.

9. *No Civilization in history has been perfect or the ideal one* : After all his historical studies Swami Vivekananda finally concludes that no civilization, neither the eastern nor the western, has been perfect. In his opinion the eastern and the western civilizations both must have mutual exchange of ideas to reach a higher stage of development. 'India has to learn from Europe the conquest of external nature, and Europe has to learn from India the conquest of internal nature. Then there will be neither Hindus [Indians] nor Europeans—there will be the ideal humanity which has conquered both the natures, the external and the internal.'[9] That was his watch-word, his dream that man should conquer both external and internal nature. A combination of eastern and western civilizations so that mankind may attain a higher state of development was his sole desire.

II

SWAMI VIVEKANANDA'S PHILOSOPHY OF HISTORY

The Wave Theory : According to Swami Vivekananda, history like the universe is moving in cycles of wave forms.

8. ibid., p. 482.

9. ibid., V, p. 216.

'The universe', he says, 'according to the theory of the Hindus, is moving in cycles of wave forms. ... The march of human affairs is like that. The history of nations is like that: they rise and they fall; after the rise comes a fall, again out of the fall comes a rise, with greater power. This motion is always going on.'[10]

What do these movements in history reveal? They reveal this important truth, according to Vivekananda, that : 'In every nation's spiritual life, there is a fall as well as a rise. The nation goes down, and everything seems to go to pieces. Then, again, it gains strength, rises; a huge wave comes, sometimes a tidal wave—and always on the topmost crest of the wave is a shining soul, the Messenger.'[11] Thus there is a rise of the wave when the prophet appears and there is simultaneously all-round progress. Even material progress follows a spiritual upheaval. Indian history as mentioned already, bears ample testimony to it.

Role of the Prophets in moulding history : Historians so far have not paid much attention to the fact of the advent of a Messenger and his role in moulding history. It is not just an accident that such 'Messenger of life' do appear. They are created by the social forces and then they recreate the society. According to Vivekananda, 'Creator and created by turns, he is the impetus that makes the wave rise, the nation rise : at the same time, he is created by the same forces which make the wave, acting and interacting by turns. He puts forth his tremendous power upon society; and society makes him what he is. These are the great world-thinkers. These are the Prophets of the world, the Messengers of life, the Incarnations of God.'[12] Here he makes it clear that society makes them just as they re-make society.

Prophets are many : Vivekananda has made this also clear that contrary to the popular belief in some parts of the world to the effect that there can be only one Prophet, history reveals that Prophets are many and they are destined to be many. Showing the reason he points out that 'By studying the lives of all these great Messengers, we find that each, as it were, was destined to play a part, and a part only; that the harmony consists in the sum total, and not in one note. As in the life of races—no race is born alone to enjoy the world. ... Each race has a part to play in this divine

10. ibid., IV, p. 120. 11. ibid. 12. ibid.

harmony of nations. Each race has its mission to perform, its duty to fulfil. The sum total is the great harmony.'[13] Thus according to Vivekananda, all the prophets contributed in elevating humanity—human society as a whole. The contribution of each has been unique and much needed for progress.

Role of the Prophets in fighting against Priesthood : The priests keep the people ignorant and are responsible for the controlling position of the grinding superstitions in their mind. Prophets try to set the people free from these chains. History holds out evidence of this. For example, Vivekananda points out, '... among the Jews there was a continuous struggle between the priests and the prophets; and the priests sought to monopolize power and knowledge... . The culmination of the struggle was the victory of Jesus of Nazareth.... This great prophet killed the dragon of priestly selfishness, rescued from its clutches the jewel of truth, and gave it to all the world, so that whosoever desired to possess it would have absolute freedom to do so, and would not have to wait on the pleasure of any priest or priests.'[14]

In India also the Brahmins, who began the spiritual investigations in India, began later on to arrogate powers and privileges to themselves. In the words of Vivekananda, 'If a Brahmin killed a man, he would not be punished. The Brahmin, by his very birth, is the lord of the universe! Even the most wicked Brahmin must be worshipped!',[15] and as stated by him, 'Buddha was the triumph in the struggle that had been going on between the priests and the prophets in India.' Sri Krishna succeeded in the struggle during his life-time, and the priestly power was almost effaced from India during the Jain and Buddhist revolutions. Buddha preached the gist of philosophy of the Vedas to one and all, without any distinction. Both Krishna and Buddha denied exclusive privileges of the Brahmins.

The important role of the prophets as an opponent of priestly power, as an opponent of crystallized privileges in the name of religion has thus been brought out by Swami Vivekananda. No other historian or anybody else has done it before him or after.

Spirituality moulds history : Men like Christ and Buddha have proved also that 'History of the world is a history of the few

13. ibid., pp. 120-21. 14. ibid., VIII, p. 94. 15. ibid., p. 95.

men who have faith in themselves.' They have moulded history and mankind to a tremendous extent. And they were all men with tremendous spiritual power. It is spirituality that moulds history. This truth was discovered by Vivekananda. 'Confucius', he says, 'Moses, and Pythagoras; Buddha, Christ, Mohammed, Luther, Calvin, and the Sikhs; Theosophy, Spiritualism, and the like; all these mean only the preaching of the Divine-in-Man.'[16]

Role of the common man in making history : Swami Vivekananda was not a mere historian, he was himself a prophet of the stature of a Buddha, a Christ and had a vision of the Infinity. The entire human history was like the open pages of a book to him. Hence the most vital truths regarding human history were revealed to him. To this prophetic vision was revealed also the great truth that 'The history of the world is not of its great men, of its demi-gods, but it is like the little islands of the sea, which build themselves to great continents from fragment of the sea drift. Then the history of the world is in the little acts of sacrifice performed in every household.'[17] Therefore, according to him, every one must be brought to manifest this 'divine power'. 'Give back', he urged, 'the divine consciousness to all the poor, the downtrodden, the oppressed, and the sick.'[18] For when they are elevated human civilization obviously would reach its pinnacle of glory.

Progress and War in Vivekananda's philosophy of history : Vivekananda did not consider competition as an essential motive force for progerss. He was totally convinced that every war retards progress. 'The more I study history', he observed, 'the more I find that idea [of competition] to be wrong. Some say that if man did not fight with man, he would not progress. ... but I find now that every war has thrown back human progress by fifty years instead of hurrying it forwards. The day will come when men will study history from a different light and find that competition is neither the cause nor the effect, simply a thing on the way, not necessary to evolution at all.'[19] In his philosophy of history, therefore, violence, war and competition have no place. History reveals gradual development of a new social order based

16. ibid., p. 229.
17. ibid., p. 240.
18. ibid., p. 229.
19. ibid., V, p. 278.

on cooperation, peace and mutual aid. Vivekananda had a vision of this great event at the end of his historical studies.

III

HISTORICAL POSITIVE SPIRITUALISM

Only Spiritual Civilizations do survive : Vivekananda's historical investigations led him to the important conclusion that a purely materialistic civilization cannot last long, it must be by its own nature, short-lived. 'The history of the world,' points out Vivekananda, 'is our witness. Nation after nation has arisen and based its greatness upon materialism, declaring man was all matter. ... All such civilizations, therefore, as have been based upon such sand foundations as material comfort and all that, have disappeared one after another, after short lives, from the face of the world; but the civilization of India and the other nations that have stood at India's feet to listen and learn, namely, Japan and China, live even to the present day, and there are signs even of revival among them. Their lives are like that of the Phoenix, a thousand times destroyed, but ready to spring up again more glorious. But a materialistic civilization once dashed down, never can come up again; that building once thrown down is broken into pieces once for all.'[20] The history of the great civilizations of Greece and Rome are a pointer in this matter. Both crumbled down to pieces never to get back their glorious days again. Toynbee also ascribes this to spiritual demoralization on the morrow of success. And he points also to the facts that the basis of Greek civilization was the worship of the ephemeral self and that of Roman civilization was the idolization of an ephemeral institution, viz., the Roman Empire. According to Vivekananda, this sort of civilizations have the seed of disintegration within themselves and they succumb never to recoup again after a short peirod.

Socialism needs a Spiritual Foundation : From his lesson of history Vivekananda was led to argue that even a socialistic phase of society cannot last unless it is based on religion. 'Everything goes to show', he said, 'that socialism or some form of rule by the

---

20. ibid., III, p. 380.

people, call it what you will, is coming on the boards. The people will certainly want the satisfaction of their material needs, less work, no oppression,no war, more food. What guarantee have we that this, or any civilization, will last, unless it is based on religion, on the goodness of man?' 'Depend on it', he says emphatically, 'religion goes to the root of the matter. If it is right, all is right.'[21]

As we all know, the present-day situation in the socialist countries are volatile. Seventy-two years after socialist revolution in Russia and forty years after the revolution in China, it is discovered today that there is rampant corruption and inefficiency within the system which is arresting economic growth and threatening their respective national integration. Corruption and all that signifies demoralization of man—the most important factor determining the fate of a civilization—are the order of the day in the countries of eastern Europe under communist domination. Reading danger in the situation Soviet Russia is trying the policy of liberalization through the policies of *Perestroika* and *Glasnost*. Religious freedom has already been granted there. China is going the opposite way at the present moment, it is trying the weapon of repression and oppression which never can quiet down a popular protest, it rather increases the strength of the protesting people, and a peaceful movement is converted into a violent revolution—such is the lesson of history. Romania had already a blood bath for winning its emancipation from the communist totalitarianism, which it succeeded in shaking off as in Poland, Czechoslovakia, Hungary and other countries of eastern Europe.

Spirituality is the man-making force : Ultimately therefore, we come to what Vivekananda said : that every civilization must have a spiritual basis since spirituality is the man-making force. Systems do not provide stability, but good and strong men who are the products of a spiritual civilization. What is required for the success of socialism is good men. And for producing good men what is needed is a spiritual basis which today maybe provided by the Universal-Science-Religion as propounded by Vivekananda. Spiritual freedom as well as other kinds of freedom are essential for the success of socialism.

---

21. ibid., V, p. 202.

Russia had an inkling of what was going to happen and that is why maybe that the intellectuals of the country are turning towards the wholesome teachings of Ramakrishna-Vivekananda. E. P. Chelishev, one of their leading intellectuals, said in a recent interview : 'We do not consider Vivekananda and Ramakrishna Paramahamsa to be mere religious leaders as they are commonly looked upon. They are prophets of human emancipation, of equality and of human progress. ... The message of Ramakrishna and Vivekananda is the message of peace, amity and world-brotherhood ... in the context of the present nuclear menace which is gradually engulfing the earth, it is very much essential to disseminate the message of Ramakrishna-Vivekananda all over the world. ... There is no doubt that their message was necessary and relevant in India and the world of their time, but it is still more necessary and relevant in the present Indian context and in the context of the contemporary world. That is why a large number of Soviet scholars and thinkers have dedicated themselves to the study of Ramakrishna, and particularly Swami Vivekananda.'[22]

What does this mean for the future of the socialistic world? A switch over from a faith in historical materialism to a faith in historical spiritualism? For Ramakrishna-Vivekananda preached one thing only, the positive religion of the Vedanta or Universal-Science-Religion. Did Vivekananda declare for this reason that in the future era India will be the centre from which light will emanate and illuminate the world?

The philosophy of history of Vivekananda which seeks to explain and interpret the future in a satisfactory manner may be given an appropriate name, viz., the historical-scientific-spiritualism. In this positive philosophy of history material forces of civilization are not neglected but the emphasis is on spiritualism on which depends stability of civilizations.

22. *Prabuddha Bhārata*, January 1986, p. 70.

Part III

The Sociological Ideas

CHAPTER—13

The Sociological Ideas—I : Culture and Civilization

I

THE CONCEPT OF CULTURE AND CIVILIZATION

Swami Vivekananda has given a spiritualistic interpretation of the terms 'culture' and 'civilization' on the basis of his objective historical studies. His ideas resemble in some respects the ideas, of Oswald Splengler, the writer of the sensational book *The Decline of the West*, of Toynbee, perhaps the greatest historian of this century, and of Sorokin, one of the most outstanding sociologists of the present day. Vivekananda was a forerunner coming ahead of them in the nineteenth century.

'This universe', says Vivekananda, 'is simply a gymnasium in which the soul is taking exercise... .'[1] Hence, according to him, culture is a process of spiritualization of man.

Splengler also interpretes cultures as spiritual phenomena, rooted in a definite 'landscape'. According to him, 'Culture is a spiritual orientation of a group of people who have achieved some unitary conception of their world which is reflected in and which shapes all their activities, such as art, religion, philosophy, politics and economics.'[2]

To Arnold Toynbee a civilization is essentially a religious and ethical system with influence over a larger area than a nation. Such a system is unified by customs, institutions, and ideologies. There are others who think civilization has only a political connotation. 'These writers', according to Ogburn and

---

1. *C. W.*, V, p. 308.
2. *History*: *Its Philosophy, Theory and Methodology*—Satish K. Bajaj, published by the Indian Institute of Language Studies, p. 66.

Nimkoff, 'confine the term civilization to only a part of culture such as government, art, ethics, or religion.'[3]

Culture is, it seems, a more comprehensive concept than civilization, it is a super organic system, of which material achievements, family organization, economic organization, political organization, custom, religion, philosophy, ethics, science, art—every possible creative expression of man, are parts. Sorokin, therefore, in defining culture observes : 'In the broadest sense it may be the sum-total of everything which is created or modified by the conscious or unconscious activity of two or more individuals interacting with one another or conditioning one another's behaviour.' According to this definition, science, philosophy, arts, religion, techniques—everything constitute culture.[4] According to Ogburn and Nimcoff, 'These selected parts of culture called civilization, are, of course, different from culture as a whole. The concept of civilization as a sort of ethical values is different, too, from an objective concept of culture.' They are also of the opinion that 'The whole culture of a people at any time is a particular configuration of its parts : material culture, family organization, economic organization, political organization, custom, religion, philosophy, science, art.' 'The patterns which these make are highly varied. India, China, Egypt, Greece, Rome—all had different configurations.'[5]

The Concept of Highest Culture : Swami Vivekananda does not consider material aspects of culture unnecessary, rather he considers them very much necessary. But the most important are the spiritual values. According to him, even material prosperity is not secured unless there is spiritualization of man. Spiritualization of man makes him conscious of his own innate infinite strength and potentiality and when a man becomes fully conscious of this, he cannot sit idle, it drives him to manifest his power in creative activities which bring forth material prosperity and cultural achievements of various types. According to Vivekananda, the conception of highest culture is to be found in

---

3. *Handbook of Sociology* (Indian Edition), p. 553.
4. *The Social and Cultural Dynamics* (abridged), p. 2.
5. *Handbook of Sociology*, p. 553.

the conception of Brahminhood.[6] 'The great ideal of India—Brahminhood.' He writes explaining, 'Propertyless, selfless, subject to no laws, no king except the moral'[7]—such is the ideal man, the Brāhmaṇa. According to him, 'Brahminhood is the solution of the varying degress of progress and culture as well as that of social and political problems.'[8] And he makes it clear that Brahminhood cannot be the exclusive privilege of a few, of a particular group or class. Everyone has a right to it and everyone must have the opportunities to manifest it—opportunities to raise himself up to this highest ideal. And if we want our civilization to advance, everyone must be granted the opportunities to rise to the level of Brahminhood. 'If the Brahmin', he says, 'is he who has killed all selfishness and who likes and works to acquire and propagate wisdom and power of love—if a country is altogether inhabited by such Brahmins, by men and women who are spiritual and moral and good, is it strange to think that that country is above and beyond all laws, what police, what military are necessary to govern them? Why should anyone govern them at all?'[9] Herein we find a hint towards the idea of a stateless society, a society in which 'state simply withers away', to borrow a Marxist term. But this is possible when every man is raised to the highest cultural level. Herein the concept is different fundamentally from the Marxist idea of a stateless society which is attained when class differences are totally effaced.

Vivekananda is totally convinced that without this ethical and spiritual culture it is not possible to make any progress. 'No amount of force', he points out, 'or government or legislative cruelty will change the conditions of race, but it is spiritual culture and ethical culture alone that can change wrong racial tendencies for the better.'[10] According to him further, 'It is culture that withstands shocks, not a simple mass of knowledge. . . . Knowledge is only skin-deep, as civilization is, and a little scratch brings out the old savage.'[11] Hence he argues strongly in favour of giving the masses 'culture'—the highest culture that has been so far conceived.

---

6. *C. W.*, IV, p. 309. 7. ibid. 8. ibid.
9. ibid., V, p. 308. 10. ibid., p. 303. 11. ibid., III, p. 291.

Sorokin after identifying three universal types of culture-patterns known in history, viz., sensate (materialistic), ideational (spiritualistic) and idealistic (a mixture of the former two), makes it clear that the ideational or the spiritualistic culture makes a man a man with control not only over external nature but also over himself, and that in order to make the achievements of the sensate culture, viz., science and technology safe for humanity, this spiritualistic culture is absolutely necessary. In the hands of sensate man science and technology have proved to be instruments of annihilation.[12] Hence spiritual culture is necessary for the humanization of the animal in man.

This is, in fact, a confirmation of Vivekananda's views on the value of spiritual and ethical culture.

VIVEKANANDA'S IDEA OF CIVILIZATION : A SPIRITUAL CONCEPT : According to Vivekananda, the value of everything is to be decided by 'how far it is a manifestation of God'. Hence he defined civilization 'as the manifestation of that divinity in man'.[13] In an interview in the West the interviewer told him, 'You aim at producing very perfect individuals by *sannyāsa*, concentration and so forth. Now the ideal of the West seems to be the perfection of the social state; and so we work at political and social question, since we think that the phenomena of our civilization depends upon the well-being of our people.' To this Swami Vivekananda replied : 'But the basis of all systems, social and political, rests upon the goodness of men. No nation is great or good because parliament enacts this or that, but because its men are great and good. . . . Religion goes to the root of the matter. If it is right, everything is right.'[14] In reply to the question 'What is civilization?', he said on another occasion : 'The more advanced a society or a nation is in spirituality, the more is that society or nation civilized. No nation can be said to have become civilized only because it has succeeded in increasing the comforts of material life by bringing into use lots of machinery and things of that sort.'[15] Making the idea clear he said on still another occasion, 'Civilization, true civilization,

12. ibid., p. 628.
13. ibid., V, p. 308.
14. ibid., p. 192.
15. ibid., VI, p. 462.

should mean the power of taking the animal-man out of his sense-life—by giving him visions and tastes of planes much higher—and not external comforts.'[16] 'The lower the civilization of man', he made it further clear, 'the greater is the power of the senses.' 'A nation may', he went on to say, adding emphasis to his concept, 'conquer the waves, control the elements, develop the utilitarian problems of life seemingly to the utmost limits and yet not realize that in the individual, the highest type of civilization is found in him who has learned to conquer self.'[17] He concluded, therefore, that 'The history of civilization is the progressive reading of spirit into matter.'[18]

A. N. Whitehead declares : 'In each age of the world, distinguished by high activity, there will be found at its culmination, and among the agencies leading to that culmination, some profound cosmological outlook, implicitly accepted, impressing its own type on the current springs of action.'[19] Quoting this statement Arnold Toynbee says : 'Following Whitehead's lead, I should define civilization in spiritual terms.'[20] Thus it is clear that the view that the process of civilization is a process of spiritualization, i.e., the view of Swamiji, is more or less accepted today by a number of most distinguished thinkers of the modern era.

Materially speaking, V. G. Childe thinks civilization means 'Urban Revolution'.[21] According to Swami Vivekananda, as seen in the previous chapter, germination of civilization is to be found with the development of the art of agriculture. That is what at least history of Asian civilization reveals. Egypt also bears testimony to this; it was the granary of the world and this development of agriculture helped its civilization to grow. Toynbee points out that 'there has been citiless societies that has nevertheless been in the process of civilization'.[22] In India urbanization came later when the kingly class attained supremacy in society superseding the Brahmins. Instead, India attained a high level civilization in the Vedic age when cities were unknown. This is also the view of A. L. Basam, the noted Indologist, in his notable book *The Wonder that was India.*[23]

---

16. ibid., IV, p. 284. 17. ibid., p. 242. 18. ibid., p. 200.
19. ibid., VIII, p. 429. 20. Arnold Toynbee, *A Study of History*, p. 44.
21. ibid. 22. ibid. 23. ibid.

II

CIVILIZATION : GERMINATION, GROWTH, AND DECLINE

Reviewing the entire history of human civilization and the different varieties of its manifestations in different geographical areas, Swami Vivekananda has brought out the forces that helped to form civilization, as well as the forces that have accounted for their growth and decline.

FORMATIVE FORCES AND GROWTH FACTORS

Among the formative forces and the forces of growth he identifies, in his studies on history, the following :

(1) Natural Environment; (2) Fusion of the Races; (3) Conquests and Invasions; (4) Religion; (5) Commerce; (6) Contributions of the Proletariat.

Natural Environment : While tracing the earliest history of man, as we have seen already, Vivekananda has shown that civilization first dawned among the people living in the plains since their struggle for existence was not hard and since they had ample time for contemplation and thought. Arts, sciences, engineering skill as well as spirituality and religion originated among these people. Natural environment favoured the Asiatic people living in the plains and on the river banks of Ganges, Yangtsekiang and Euphrates and that is why earliest civilization is found to have germinated among the Asiatic people living in these regions.

Racial Stock : Recial stock was an element since the race with divine inclinations, being favoured by natural environment, turned towards developing learning and culture. With the development of learning new acquisitions were made in almost every field of life, temporal and spiritual. In the process of this acquisitions the divine inclinations of the people were of great help. They stuck to highest ideals and worked hard to reach the highest pinnacle of civilization.

Conquests and Invasions : Conquests and invasions were also an important factor especially in the early periods. For example, the conquest of Greece by the Romans helped the conqueror to be civilized through assimilation of culture and learning of the conquered. Thus, 'though conquered the Greeks were the teachers'. In the same way the Turks who conquered parts of western India, by getting converted to Buddhism, got civilized as is evident from the efforts of emperor Kaṇiṣka to found the Mahāyāna Buddhist school and his other spiritualistic endeavours.

Religion : Religion has always been a civilizing factor. As stated just now, the Turks got civilized when they were converted to Buddhism. Religion has been the most effective civilizing force since it enables man to control himself. The religion of Mohammad civilized the Arab nomads and Christianity the barbaric races of Europe. There are plenty of such instances in history. To Vivekananda this factor has played an important role throughout the history.

Commerce : According to Vivekananda, commerce, particularly Indian commerce, has been an important factor in the growth of civilizations since very ancient times. 'Of all the causes', he says, 'which have worked for the present state of human civilization from the ancient times, the commerce of India is perhaps the most important.' He makes it clear also that 'from time immemorial India has beaten all other countries in point of fertility and commercial industries'.[24] 'Uptill a century ago, the whole of the world's demand for cotton cloth, cotton, jute, indigo, lac, rice, diamonds, and pearls, etc., used to be supplied from India. Moreover, no other country could produce such excellent silk and woollen fabrics, like the kincob, etc., as India.' 'Naturally, therefore', he points out, 'from ancient times, whatever country became civilized at any particular epoch, depended upon India for those commodities.' 'Most people', he adds, 'are ignorant of the extent to which the opulance of ancient countries like Babylon, Persia, Greece, and Rome depended on Indian commerce. After the downfall of Rome, Baghdad in Mohammedan territory, and Venice and Genoa in Italy, became the chief western marts of Indian commerce.'[25] Mentioning the trade routes he further points out : 'This trade used to follow two main routes—one was through land, via Afghanistan and Persia, and the other was by sea—

24. *C. W.*, VII, pp. 356-57. 25. ibid., p. 357.

through the Red Sea. . . . And when the Turks made themselves masters of the Roman Empire and closed the trade-route to India for the Italians, then Christopher Columbus . . . a Spaniard or a Genoese, tried to explore a new route to India across the Atlantic, which resulted in the discovery of the American continent. ...It is, therefore, that the aborigines of America are to this day designated as Indians.'[26]

The statements of Vivekananda quoted above make it clear that commerce was an important factor in the growth of civilizations since very old days.

Contributions of the Proletariats : Finally, while talking about the genesis and growth of civilization, Vivekananda speaks highly of the contributions of the labourers and particularly of the Indian labourers who produced and manufactured those essential commodities on which every civilized nation was dependent. 'Ye labouring classes of India', he says, 'as a result of your silent, constant labours Babylon, Persia, Alexandria, Greece, Rome, Venice, Genoa, Baghdad, Samarquand, Spain, Portugal, France, Denmark, Holland, and England have successively attained supremacy and eminence.'[27]

CAUSES OF DECLINE

Regarding the causes of decline of civilization Swami Vivekananda mentions the following : (1) a race becoming enervated by being slave to wealth and luxury; (2) barbarian attacks and destruction; (3) dissociation of the ruling class from the working class or the proletariat who, according to him, is the foundation of the society, source of all power.

Demoralization due to wealth and luxury : *Internal Cause* : He has explicitly stated in his *The East and the West* that the cause of the decline of the Roman Civilization has been moral decline. 'In the efflux of time', he says, 'the Romans became enervated by being slaves to wealth and luxury.' This cause, it seems logically, have been the driving force behind the decline of other civilizations as well. Vivekananda believed that with the growth of life is sown simultaneously the seed of death.[28] And

26. ibid. 27. ibid., p. 358. 28. ibid., IV, p. 454.

this is a universal truth that with growth starts the process of degeneration. In the case of civilizations, the creative abilities of the men in power decline as has been pointed out by Toynbee. This is the immanent cause of the decline of civilization.

Invasions and Conquests by the Barbarians : *External Cause* : To this immanent cause were superimposed invasions and conquests which led to the crash of many civilizations known in history. For example, the Asian invasion and invasion by the northern European races at a time when demoralization has eaten up the vitality of the nation, led to the total crashing down of the mighty Roman Empire.

Dissociation of the ruling classes from the masses : There is a third cause, viz., the dissociation of the ruling classes from the masses which happens when the former put exclusive claims on wealth and culture depriving the masses from their due share. Swami Vivekananda observes, 'Whether the leadership of society be in the hands of those who monopolize learning or wield the power of riches or arms, the source of its power is always the subject masses. By so much as the class in power severs itself from this source, by so much it is sure to become weak.'[29] 'It is the evidence of history', he says, 'that at a certain time every society attains its manhood, when a strong conflict ensues between the ruling power and the common people. The life of the society, its expansion and civilization, depend on its victory or defeat in this conflict.'[30] The result is revolution and many civilizations succumb to it. 'Where the society is healthy and strong', Vivekananda reveals, 'there soon follows a fierce contest between the king and his subjects, and, by its reaction and convulsion, are flung away the sceptre and the crown... .'[31] And he reveals also that 'If the society is weak and debilitated, it silently suffers all ill-treatment at the hands of the king, and as the natural consequence, both the king and his people go down and down and fall into the most degraded state, and thus become an easy prey to any nation stronger than themselves.'[32] The alternative to revolution in a weak society is: being conquered by foreign invaders. And this is how India became an easy prey to

---

29. ibid., p. 470.
30. ibid., pp. 461-62.
31. ibid., p. 465.
32. ibid., pp. 464-65.

invaders of all sorts. As the masses were denied their due share in the country's wealth and culture and as the ruling class became dissociated from the masses by withholding these from them, when the invaders came down like avalanches on the soil of the country, the deprived masses did not put forward any resistance worth the name.

It is interesting to note that regarding the decline of civilizations Toynbee observes : 'The masses become estranged from their leaders, who then try to cling to their position by using force as a substitute for their lost power of attraction. I trace the fragmentation of society into a dominant minority, an internal proletariat and an external proletariat consisting of the barbarians on the fringes, and I sketch the social reactions of these diverse groups to the ordeal of disintegration.'[33]

This is in a sense a confirmation of Vivekananda's theory as depicted above that dissociation of the ruling class from the masses may lead to the disintegration of a one-time flourishing civilization.

III

CIVILIZATION AND CLASS SOCIETY

Vivekananda has shown in his sociological treatise *The East and the West*, that in the earliest civilized society there evolved a very simple division of labour as the society became divided into different classes according to the occupation of the people. Three major classes emerged consisting of the ruler, the trader and the producer. The first two were the non-producing classes and depended entirely on exploiting the fruits of labour of the third, viz., the producing class. Describing the class-structure in early days Vivekananda states : 'One tilled the ground, a second guarded the produce from being robbed, a third took it to another place, and a fourth bought it. The cultivator got almost nothing; he who guarded the produce took away as much of it as he could by force; the merchant who brought it to the market took the lion's share. . . . The protector came to be known as the king; he

33. Arnold Toynbee, *A Study of History*, p. 211.

who took the commodities from one place to another was the merchant. These two did not produce anything—but still snatched away the best part of things, and made themselves fat by virtually reaping most of the fruits of the cultivator's toil and labour.'[34]

Gradually complex division of labour evolved and class divisions multiplied and society became complex. In the words of Swami Vivekananda, 'Now, with the march of events all these matters grew more and more involved, knots upon knots multiplied, and out of this tangled network has evolved our modern complex society.'[35]

Thus it is evident that as revealed by Vivekananda that all along from the very beginning the civilized society has been a class society and class society means exploitation. Thus with civilization, as it developed through history, goes exploitation and depriving of the masses of their due share in their own produce.

Toynbee also points out that 'We have . . . to equate civilization with a state of society in which there is a minority of the population, however small, that is free from the task not merely of producing food, but of engaging themselves in any other of the economic activities, e.g., industry and trade—that have to be carried to keep the life of the society going on the material plane at the civilizational level. These non-economic specialists—the professional soldiers, administrators, and perhaps, above all, priests—have certainly been city-dwellers in the cases of most of the civilizations known to us.'[36] Thus it is evident that civilization means a society divided into various different classes, economic and non-economic, and in ancient days when urban centres grew up, the non-producing classes lived in the cities while the producing classes mostly lived in the rural areas.

The nature of class predominance in civilized society: Swami Vivekananda has studied the nature of class divisions in civilized society in detail in his remarkable historical and sociological treatise 'Modern India' and has pointed out that in different

34. *C. W.*, V, p. 525. 35. ibid. 36. *A Study of History*, p. 47.

periods there has been predominance of different classes. 'But from a careful study of the history of the world', he goes on to state, 'it appears that, in conformity with the law of nature, the four castes, the Brahmin, Kshatriya, Vaishya, and Shudra, do, in every society, one after another in succession, govern the world.'[37] Here he speaks of four classes and not three as stated earlier. Here he adds the priestly class, who played a predominant role in every country at one time or other.

But the length of the period of supremacy of a particular class has varied in different countries as shown by him. He shows that 'Among the Chinese, the Sumerians, the Babylonians, the Egyptians ... the Jews, the Arabs—among all these ancient nations, the supreme power of guiding society is, in the first period of their history, in the hands of the Brahmin or the priest.'[38] In the second period, the ruling power is in the hands of the Kshatriya, i.e., 'either the absolute monarch or oligarchical government by chosen body of men'. Third period is the period of Vaishya rule which is manifested in the modern era in countries like England where the traders predominate. As shown by Vivekananda, Troy and Carthage in ancient times, Venice and a few other states in latter days, were flourishing commercial centres but in these cases, the monopoly of commerce was in the hands of the descendants of royal family or the Kshatriyas and not in the hands of the Vaishyas.[39] Hence there was no supremacy of the Vaishyas over society at the time.

In Egypt, as pointed out by Vivekananda, priestly power had supremacy for a short period, in China the royal power 'centralized by the genius of Confucious, has been controlling and guiding the priestly power ... for more than twenty-five centuries'. Lamas of Tibet, representative of priestly power, were subject in every way to the Chinese emperor for two centuries. In India priestly power had control for a very long time and for that matter Kshatriyas came in control late and hence Indian Empire emerged long after the Chinese, Egyptian, Babylonian and other Empires had risen.[40] With the Jewish people, the royal

37. *C. W.*, IV, p. 449.
38. ibid., pp. 449-50.
39. ibid., p. 450.
40. ibid., 'Modern India'.

power, though tried hard, could never succeed in wrestling power from the priests.[41]

In the modern period with almost all the countries India also came under Vaishya supremacy. In the case of India it came to be established through the British rule. The world is yet in the third epoch although in the twentieth century a number of countries came under proletariat or Shudra supremacy. Vivekananda predicted that the dawn of the Shudra era was inevitable but he did not live to see it, although he knew it for certain that it would first dawn either in Russia or in China. And that is what actually happened, supremacy of the Shudras came to be established first in Russia and then in China.

As shown by Vivekananda, the foundation of priestly power is on intellectual strength and spiritual power and with the supremacy of the priests there occurs the first advent of civilization, 'the first mastery of spirit over matter', since 'the first offshoot of the universal welfare and good is nursed by his spiritual power, by his devotion to learning and wisdom, by his renunciation, the watchword of his life'.[42] But sooner or later, a time comes, when the priests begin to realize the secret of their power and they put up claim for sky-high privileges over others and in the course of time they get demoralized and their spiritual power also declines due to lack of exercise. This is the period when their interests clash with the interests of the other classes because of their exclusive claims on privileges. And ultimately the kingly class, the Kshatriyas, snatches away their supremacy with the help of the proletariat, the masses.

'...during the Kshatriya supremacy', Swami Vivekananda points out in reference to Indian history, 'a strong desire for pleasure pursuits has made its appearance at the first stage, and later have sprung up inventions and developments of arts and sciences, as the means for its gratification.'[43] So there was development of arts and industries during this period. As described by Vivekananda : 'Thousands of intelligent men left the toilsome task of the ploughman and turned their attention to the new field of fine arts, where they could display the finer play of their intellect in the less laborious and easier ways. Villages

41. ibid. 42. ibid. 43. ibid., p. 459.

lost their importance; cities rose in their stead.'[44] Thus urbanization was achieved during the supremacy of the kingly power in India when luxury industries developed.

In India is to be noticed a peculiar feature of the kingly class. Swami Vivekananda has drawn our special attention to it. Being taken over by world-weariness when their sense-enjoyment reached a saturation point towards the end of their life the kings took to a life of renunciation and absorption in meditation. They realized the profound truths which are embodied in the Upanishads and the *Gītā*, the Jaina and the Buddhistic scriptures and they were all against the ritualism of the priests. And this was a point of conflict between the priests and the kings since disappearance of the elaborate rites and ceremonials meant a death-blow to the priests' profession. In their own economic interest, the priests invented and defended elaborate ceremonials.

Class-Conflicts : Swami Vivekananda has shown that the subjects were equally oppressed by both the priests and the kings. According to him, 'Wisdom, knowledge, wealth, men, strength, prowess and whatever else nature gathers and provides us with, are only for diffusion... .'[45] Hence when the priests are in power and the masses are repressed there starts a conflict between the priests and the people and out of that conflict kings come to attain supremacy. Since they oppose ceremonialism the people support the king. And when again during the period of kingly supremacy 'oppression steps into the place of protection—sucking of their blood in place of preservation, conflict between the ruling power and the common men starts and gradually takes a severe turn'. In such a situation there are two possibilities according to Vivekananda. First, as we have seen earlier, 'If the society is weak and debilitated, it silently suffers all ill-treatment at the hands of the king, and as the natural consequence, both the king and his people go down and down and fall into the most degraded state, and thus become an easy prey to any nation stronger than themselves.' It so happened in the case of India. To any student of history this is evident from the series of invasions by foreign powers who conquered and

44. ibid., p. 460.

45. ibid., p. 464.

ruled India for centuries. The second possibility is overthrowing of the oppressor from power by a revolution. Thus, 'Where the society is healthy and strong, there soon follows a fierce contest between the king and his subjects, and, by its reaction and convulsion are flung away the sceptre and the crown; and the throne and the royal paraphernalia become like past curiosities preserved in the museum galleries.'[46] This is evident in the history of the revolutions in various countries.

Next the Vaishya power comes to ascendency. The power of the Vaishya lies in wealth, the modern system of manufacturing allows the Vaishya to accumulate huge wealth in the form of profit. Vivekananda describing the secret of the Vaishya power, writes in his characteristic way as if a Vaishya is speaking to the priest and the king : 'Do you see those lofty and extensive mills? Those are my hives. See, how swarms of millions of bees, the Shudras, are incessantly gathering honey for those hives.'[47] The statement makes it clear that the Vaishyas have power by dint of their accumulated wealth to buy the labour of millions of working people who contribute to generate further profit and accumulation of wealth for him. Here Vivekananda unveiled the essence of capitalism or of Vaishya rule.

Just as civilization advanced through the advancement of learning during the period of priestly power and through the development of agriculture, art, industries, urbanization and commerce during the period of kingly rule, during the period of Vaishya rule civilization advances through unprecedented economic prosperity in which accumulation of wealth and capital plays the pivotal role. Moreover, as pointed out by Vivekananda, with merchandise is carried learning and culture of one country to another by the Vaishya. Hence there is maximum diffusion of culture under Vaishya rule. This also helps civilizations of various countries to advance. For example with the British, who were representative of the Vaishya power, there came to India knowledge of science and technology which was of great help to the Indian civilization for advancing in the present century.

During all these periods—the period of the priestly rule, the

46. ibid., p. 465.

47. ibid., pp. 465-66.

period of the kingly rule, and the period of the Vaishya rule the proletariat are deprived of their due share in the country's wealth and culture and they are tyrannized and oppressed and cruelly exploited. The result is a class conflict, which sometimes takes very serious turn. This proletariat class has come into conflict with the Vaishya class in the present era. This phase of the class-struggle he saw with his own eyes both in the West and in the East. 'The lower classes are', he points out, 'gradually awakening to this fact and making a united front against this, determined to exact their legitimate dues. The masses of Europe and America have been the first to awaken and have already begun the fight. Signs of this awakening have shown themselves in India, too, as is evident from the number of strikes among the lower classes nowadays.'[48] And he was certain about the consequences. Hence he said : 'But what great changes are taking place slowly, all over the world, in pursuance of nature's laws ! Countries, civilizations, and supremacy are undergoing revolutions.'[49]

The proletariat was to win in the class-struggle of this epoch. Vivekananda arrived at this conclusion from his vast knowledge of contemporary history and direct knowledge about the proletariat. Hence he declared prophetically, 'Yet, a time will come when there will be the rising of the Shudra-class, with their Shudra-hood', and 'Socialism, Anarchism, Nihilism, and other like sects are the vanguard of the social revolution that is to follow.'[50]

Class-War and History : Hence it is evident that history, as viewed by Swami Vivekananda, is a story of class-wars and ascendency of different classes in succession.

Arnold Toynbee has shown in his *A Study of History* that the dominant non-economic minority in society, consisting of the professional soldiers, administrators and above all the priests in different societies, who are creative and therefore have the allegiance of the majority during the period of growth of a civilization, undergoes a decline in respect of their spiritual creative power and faculty of extracting allegiance of the

---

48. ibid., VII, p. 149. 49. ibid., p. 358.
50. ibid., IV,.pp. 468-69.

majority during the period of decadence and they therefore have recourse to using force. Thus the conflict between the ruling class and the ruled starts.[51]

This theory of association between disintegration of a society and class-strife was related by St Simon from his direct experiences of the social strifes prior to the French Revolution, it was further developed by Karl Marx, and given a perfect shape. As stated by Toynbee, '... this schism in itself is the result of two negative movements. First, the dominant minority attempts to hold by force—the privilege which it has ceased to merit, and then the proletariat repays injustice with resentment, fear with hate, and violence with violence when it executes its art of secession.'[52] As we have seen above, the essence of Vivekananda's theory is the same. His study at the time revealed facts that were later on confirmed by the eminent historians.

IV

THE DOCTRINE OF THE PROGRESS OF CIVILIZATION

Swami Vivekananda in his historical investigations has challenged the European doctrine of the progress of civilization which in effect is a theory of the superiority of the European civilization. And therefore, his challenge was to this concept also. Many eminent Indians at the time of Vivekananda fell under the spell of this concept. They believed that Europe was advanced in the march of civilization, while India was lagging behind.

Challenging the concept he says in a bold statement, 'What is the meaning of the "progress of Civilization", which the Europeans boast so much about? The meaning of it is the successful accomplishment of the desired object by the justification of wrong means, i.e., by making the end justify the means.' And the examples he cites are revealing : 'It makes', he says, 'acts of theft, falsehood, and hanging, appear proper under certain circumstances; it vindicates Stanley's whipping of the hungry Mohammedan guards who accompanied him, for stealing a few mouthfuls of bread; it guides and justifies the well-known

---

51. *A Study of History*, p. 224.

52. ibid., p. 228.

European ethics which says, "Get out from this place, I want to come in and possess it", the truth of which is borne out by the evidence of history, that wherever the Europeans have gone, there has followed the extinction of the aboriginal races.'[53] He is merciless here in exposing the European civilization. It is motivated, he reveals, by selfishness pure and simple and is supported by the instrument of violence and oppression.

The European Civilization : Summarizing his findings on European civilization he says, 'The European civilization may be likened to a piece of cloth, of which these are the materials: its loom is a vast temperate hilly country on the sea-shore; its cotton, a strong warlike mongrel race formed by the intermixture of various races; its warp is warfare, in defence of one's self and one's religion. The one who wields the sword is great, and the one who cannot, gives up his independence and lives under the protection of some warrior's sword. Its woof is commerce. The means to this civilization is the sword; its auxiliary—courage and strength; its aim—enjoyment here and hereafter.'[54]

The Eastern or the Aryan Civilization : Here Swami Vivekananda uses the term Aryan civilization to mean the civilization of eastern countries like India.

In contrast to the Europeans, the Aryans are, as pointed out by Vivekananda, peace-loving, dependent on agriculture, contemplative, devoting time for seeking higher truth, believing that 'Enjoyment lies not in physical development, but in the culture of the mind and the intellect.'[55] And with the Aryan 'The hero was', says Vivekananda, throwing light on the basic nature of Aryan civilization, 'the protector of the weak in danger—the Kshatriya. Ruling over the plough and the sword was *dharma*, the protector of all. He is the King of kings; he is ever-awake even when the world sleeps. Everyone was free under the protection of *dharma*.'[56]

Socio-Political Ideals of the Eastern Civilization : In the above statement Vivekananda has beautifully brought out the

---

53. *C. W.*, V, p. 531.
54. ibid., pp. 533-34.
55. ibid, p. 534.
56. ibid.

socio-political ideals of the eastern or the Aryan civilization. Righteousness or *dharma* was the central idea which moulded these socio-political ideas. This is in contrast with the western ideas depending on physical force and the sword.

Summarizing the Aryan civilization Swami Vivekananda observes, 'The loom of the fabric of Aryan civilization is a vast, warm, level country, interspersed with broad, navigable rivers. The cotton of this cloth is composed of highly civilized, semi-civilized, and barbarian tribes, mostly Aryan. Its warp is *Varṇāśramāchāra,* and its woof, the conquest of strife and competition in nature.'[57]

Varṇāśrama : An Institution for the protection of the backward classes : *Varṇāśrama* means the old Aryan institution of the *varṇa* and *āśrama,* i.e., of four castes and stages of life. The former comprises the Brāhmaṇa, Kṣatriya, Vaiśya, and Śūdra, and the latter, Brahmacharya (student life), Gārhasthya (householder's life), Vānaprastha (hermit life), and Sannyāsa (life of renunciation). Swami Vivekananda has brought out the significance of this institution in full. It was evolved to give protection to the weak, the backward, and the non-Aryans from extinction. Thus even the aborigines and the aliens found a place in the Aryan society under this institution. 'This system of division into different *varṇa*s', he explains, 'is the stepping stone to civilization, making one rise higher and higher in proportion to one's learning and culture.' He concludes with the observation : 'In Europe, it is everywhere victory to the strong, and death to the weak. In the land of Bhārata, every social rule is for the protection of the weak.'[58] This is so because Indian civilization has been mainly an ethical and spiritual civilization, of course, with no mean material achievements. Western civilization has been mainly a material civilization. It must be mentioned here that Vivekananda appreciated the cultural wealth of the West as much as that of the East as we have noted already and he considered a combination of both was necessary to make human civilization advance in the future.

---

57. ibid., p. 536.

58. ibid., p. 537.

V

MARXIAN VIEW OF THE ORIENTAL AND THE INDIAN CIVILIZATIONS COMPARED TO VIVEKANANDA'S VIEW

Since Marxian view has exerted a great influence all over the world, Marx's views on India may be taken into consideration here. Marxian view is in contrast with the view of Vivekananda, since Marx has proceeded on a partial view of civilization, taking into consideration only material achievements which is only a part of civilization.

Indian Disunity : First of all, to Marx India appeared as a country extremely disunited. 'A country', he says, 'not only divided between Mohemmedan and Hindoo, but between tribe and tribe, between caste and caste, a society whose framework was based on a sort of equilibrium, resulting from a general repulsion and constitutional exclusiveness between all its members.'[59] Such a country, such a society, according to him, was predestined to be a prey of the invaders. Indian history is a history of invasions throughout the ages according to him.

Indian Religion : According to Marx, further, the reason for the tale of woe of the Hindusthan 'is anticipated in the ancient traditions of the religion of Hindusthan'. 'That religion', he says, 'is at once a religion of sensualist exuberance, and a religion of self-torturing asceticism, a religion of the "Lingam" and of Juggernaut, the religion of the Monk and Bayadere (dancing girls).'[60] Here Marx makes religion of the land responsible for the foreign domination over the country.

Obviously this is a very distorted view and a travesty of facts about Hindu religion. Evidently Marx's knowledge of the Hindu religion was very superficial and very poor. He had no idea about either the high philosophy of Vedanta in its various forms or the different aspects of the great religion of the land, the meaning of the symbols and the rites, etc. He has read this great religion in its aberrations only and for his information about it he had depended on Christian Missionary propaganda.

Basic Unity of India : Regarding the alleged disunity of the

59. Marx and Engles—*Selected Works*, Vol. I, p. 319.
60. ibid., p. 312.

country also Marx has failed to have a glimpse of the basic unity of the people in spite of its endless varieties, which Vivekananda saw after having a direct experience of the mass life in the sub-continent as a wandering monk. And the fact of this unity was revealed also to Romain Rolland, a foreigner like Marx. In his *Life of Vivekananda* while referring to Vivekananda's experiences in this matter he writes : 'From North to South the ancient land of India was full of gods, yet unbroken chain of their countless arms formed only one God. He realized their unity of flesh and spirit. He realized it also in communion with the living of all castes and all outside caste.'[61] To any serious student of Indian history and culture this is no secret.

Social History of India : Referring to the social history of the country Marx opines, 'Indian society has no history at all, at least no known history. What we call its history, is but the history of the successive intruders who founded their empires on the passive basis of that unchanging and unresisting society.'[62] But, as we have seen already, Vivekananda has depicted the dynamic social history of India from time immemorial up to the present in his historical studies. He has shown how social revolutions took place in the country at the wake of spiritual upheavals all through the historical period from the very beginning.

Mythology as a source of Social History : *Vivekananda's Views* : The social history of any country must have to be found in the ancient literature and mythology and not in the chronicles of kings and their victories and defeats. This point of view about history of a country has been emphasized today by Arnold Toynbee in his *A Study of History*. Vivekananda made this point clear that '. . . what is mythology to one race, or period, is or was history to other races or periods. Even in cases of human teachers, much of their history is taken as mythology by successive generations.'[63] But this important source has been totally neglected by Karl Marx. Swami Vivekananda has depicted, depending on this important source, the history of the class-struggles in India from the earliest period of history with

61. Romain Rolland—*Life of Vivekananda.*
62. *Selected Works of Marx and Engels*, Vol. I, p. 319.

all the special features of a particular period of class-rule, pointing out the causes of rise and downfall of a particular class at a particular point of time. A country with such a history is undoubtedly dynamic.

Impact of British Invasion of India : Analysing and comparing the nature of foreign invasions of India by the barbarian races, Marx observes, 'All the civil wars, invasions, revolutions and conquests, famines, strangely complex, rapid and destructive as the successive action in Hindusthan may appear, did not go deeper than its surface.'[64] Why? To this self-imposed question Marx's answer is, 'Arabs, Turks, Tartars, Moguls, who had sccessively overrun India soon became Hindooized in terms of the eternal law of history, the conquerors are conquered by the superior civilization of their subjects. The British were the first conquerors superior, and therefore, inaccessive to Hindu civilization. They destroyed it by uprooting the native industry, and by levelling all that was great and elevated in the native society.'[65] Further elucidating his standpoint about the matter Marx states, 'England has broken the entire framework of the Indian society without any symptom of reconstitution yet appearing. This loss of his old world, with no gain of a new one, imparts a particular kind of melancholy to the present misery of the Hindu, and separates Hindusthan, ruled by Britain, from all its ancient traditions, and from the whole of its past history.'[66]

Marxian assessment proved wrong by subsequent history of Indian Civilization: Subsequent history of India has proved how erroneous this assessment was. In spite of the disintegration of the isolated village communities and decay of the old handicraft industries, in spite of rapid industrialization with the help of modern technology, in spite of all the consequent economic and social changes, Indian civilization is not a ruin, its ancient traditions, culture and religion are still alive, being revitalized by the nineteenth century Indian renaissance. Thus Indian civilization instead of being dead, having been rejuvenated, has become once more dynamic. Hence Indians are not cut off from

---

63. *C. W.*, IV, p. 374.
64. *Selected Works of Marx and Engels*, p. 313.
65. ibid.
66. ibid., pp. 313-14.

their past culture and tradition. Religion is still a dynamic and dominant force in the country. We may note here what A. L. Basham, the famous Indologist, has stated in his illuminating book *The Wonder that was India.* Writing in 1967 he observes, 'Today there are few Indians, whatever their creed, who do not look back with pride on their ancient culture. ... Politically and economically India faces many problems of great difficulty, and no one can forecast her future with any certainty. But it is safe to predict that, whatever that future may be, the Indians of coming generations will not be unconvincing ... but will be men rooted in their own traditions, and aware of the continuity of their culture. . . . We believe', he continues, bringing to light one of the important achievements of India that 'Hindu civilization is in the act of performing its most spectacular feat of synthesis. In the past it has received, adapted and digested elements of many different cultures—Indo-European, Mesopotamian, Iranian, Greek, Roman, Scythian, Turkish, Persian and Arab. With each new influence it has somewhat changed. Now it is well ahead on the way top assimilating the West.'

It assimilated the West but did not lose its own ground. Pointing out this aspect of Indian civilization Basham further observes, 'Hindu civilization will, we believe, retain its continuity. The *Bhagavat Gītā* will not cease to inspire men of action, and the Upanishads the men of thought. . . . The people will still love the tales of the heroes of the *Mahābhārata* and the *Rāmāyaṇa.* . . . Caste is vanishing. . . . The old family system is adapting itself to new conditions. In fact, the whole face of India is altering, but the cultural tradition continues, and it will never be lost.'[67] This long statement shows how wrong was Marxian assessment of the Indian situation made in the middle of the nineteenth century.

Referring to world's debt to India, Basham goes on to say 'The whole of South-East Asia received most of its culture from India. Early in the sixth century B. C., colonists from western India settled in Ceylon. Other cultural influences, from China and the Islamic world, was felt in South-East Asia, but the

---

67. A. L. Basham—*The Wonder that was India*, Sidgwick and Jackson, London, 1967 edition, Reprint 1985, p. 485.

primary impetus to civilization came from India.' Regarding Indian influence over the West he says, 'Similarities between the teaching of Western philosophers and mystics from Pythagoras to Plotinus and those of the Upanishads have been noted. . . . The possibility of Indian influence on Neo-Platonism and early Christianity is not ruled out.'

Continuing with the same point he further observes : 'Many authorities may doubt that Indian thought had any other effect on that of the ancient West, but there can be no doubt of its direct and indirect influence on the thought of Europe and America in the last century and a half, although this has not received adequate recognition.' Here he refers to the influence of Ramakrishna -Vivekananda on the West.

Basham mentions also what India has contributed to the world in material terms. '. . . India has conferred many practical blessings on the world at large, notably rice, cotton, the sugar-cane, many spices and the domestic fowl; the game of chess and most important of all the decimal system of numeral notation, the invention of an unknown Indian mathematician early in the Christian era.'[68]

Is Oriental Civilization too low? : According to Marx, the orient is a region where 'civilization was too low'. This seems surprising since civilization first dawned in the orient reaching a high level in countries like China and India. Swami Vivekananda has shown in his historical reviews, as we have seen already, that Asia has been the mother of civilizations, that Europe was often fed by Asiatic and Indian ideas which put them on the process of civilization.

Organization of Government in Asia : While describing the organization of government in Asia from time immemorial Marx points out that it had only three departments : (1) that of finance or 'the plunder of the interior; (2) that of war or the plunder of the exterior'; (3) and finally, the department of public works. Three reasons have been assigned by Marx for the existence of public works department in the East, which was unknown in the West, where construction of canals, etc., were the concern of private enterprise : (1) 'climate and territorial conditions,

---

68. ibid., pp. 485-86.

especially the vast tract of desert, extending from the Sahara, through Arabia, Persia, India and "Tartary", to the most elavated Asiatic highlands; (2) the civilization being too low, private enterprise did not emerge; (3) the territorial extent being too vast to call for voluntary association and private enterprise'.[69]

Errors in Marxian statement : First of all, at least India is not a country of deserts, its deserts being confined to a very small part of Rajasthan and Gujarat only. Besides these small areas compared to the vast tracts of the country, India has been known to the ancient world as a very fertile country with rich agricultural resources, Indian merchandise for international trade included rice and other agricultural products as well as different types of manufactured goods. Egypt has been known as the granary of the world in ancient times as seen already. It is surprising to note that instead of appreciating the high skill of the Egyptians and the people of the other oriental countries in converting desert areas into fertile lands with prosperous agriculture, Marx considers this as a symptom of low civilization! Besides, Egypt was the birth-place of sculpture, India the birth-place of the sciences like astronomy, other branches of mathematics and chemistry—'all of great service in the building of modern European civilization',[70] as pointed by Vivekananda, besides its glorious achievements in art, literature and philosophy. Do all these speak of low oriental civilization?

As shown by Karl Marx, the British when coming to power in India accepted the two departments of finance and war from their predecessors, neglected the third one, viz., public works. This truly proved disastrous for India. It is also true that the competition from Lancashire and Manchester caused a decline in her flourishing urban handicrafts and the population living on this industry had to return to the villages and fall on agriculture.

Indian Village Organization : Karl Marx quotes verbatim from an official report of the East India Company to the House of Commons to describe the village organizations in India from time immemorial : 'A village comprised of several hundred or thousand acres of arable and waste lands, politically viewed

---

69. Marx and Engels—*Selected Works*, 1950 edition in two volumes, p. 314.
70. *C. W.*, VI, p. 158.

resembles a cooperation or . . . a township. Its establishment of officers and servants consists of . . . the *patail*, or head inhabitant, who has generally the superintendence of the affairs of the village, settles the disputes of inhabitants, attends to the police and perform the duty of collecting revenues. . . . The *kurnam* keeps accounts of cultivation . . . the *tallier* and the *totie* (?) the duty of the former consists in gaining information of crimes and offences, and in escorting and protecting persons travelling from one village to another; the province of the latter, consisting in guarding the crops and in measuring them. The boundary man, who preserves the limit of the village. . . . The superintendent of tanks and waterhouses distributes the water for the purposes of agriculture. The Brahmin who performs the village worship. The schoolmaster, who is seen teaching the children in a village to read and write in the sand. The calender Brahmin, an astrologer, etc., ... under this simple form of municipal government the inhabitants of the country have lived from time immemorial.'[71] From this description it appears to us that the village communities were highly organized and had a simple but efficient system of administration. But Karl Marx thinks otherwise of the system.[72]

A. L. Basham has given an account of the ancient Indian polity, administrative system and the village administration which gives an opposite picture compared to that given by Marx. Describing the village councils and their functions and the manner in which they discharged their duties he says, 'These . . . councils not only arbitrated disputes and managed social affairs outside the jurisdiction of the government, but were responsible for revenue collection, assessing individual contributions and negotiating the village's collective assessment with the king's representatives. They had virtual ownership of the wasteland, with right of sale, and they were active in irrigation, road-building and other public works. Their transactions, recorded on the walls of village temples, show a vigorous community life, and are a permanent memorial to the best side of early Indian politics.'[73] This speaks volumes about the Indian village

71. Marx and Engels, *Selected Works,* Vol. I, p. 316.
72. ibid., p. 317.
73. ibid.

administrative system. Equally efficient was the state government, city administration as we have a glimpse of all these in Basham's account (Chapter IV).

Describing the onslaught of the British on the village organization, Marx observes, 'English interference having placed the spinner in Lancashire and the weaver in Bengal, or sweeping away both Hindoo spinner and weaver, dissolved these small *semi-barbarian, semi-civilized* communities by blowing up their economical basis and thus produced the greatest and to speak the truth, the only social revolution ever heard in Asia.'[74]

Evidently it is a travesty of facts to describe the weavers and spinners of Bengal as '*semi-barbarian, semi-civilized* communities'. The high standard of their artistic products, their high-level skill, speaks otherwise of them. Moreover, the weavers in East Bengal mostly came from the Muslim community and not the Hindu as was supposed by Marx.

Social Revolutions in India : Secondly, it is a travesty of fact to say that India and Asia as well, have known their only social revolution when the British broke down the old economic structure of India. India had known many class conflicts and social revolutions resulting in the overthrowing of the class in power and in the installation of a new class in power. Besides, Indian economy sustained a high-level international commerce which speaks of its efficiency. Since Indian economy reached stabilization at a high-level commerce, industry and agriculture, and remained in that stage for a long time, it does not mean that there was no evolution before that stage was reached. We have already noted that India experienced urbanization during the period of the supremacy of the kingly class. And urbanization never goes without a social revolutionary impact, as is known to everyone. This social revolutionary impact has been brought to light by Swami Vivekananda. We have quoted this in another context. We quote here again the full statement about it even at the cost of repetition : 'Thousands of intelligent men', he goes on to state, 'left the toilsome task of the ploughman and turned their attention to the new field of fine arts, where they could display the finer play of their intellect in the less laborious and

74. A. L. Basham—*The Wonder that was India*, p. 107.

easier ways, villages lost their importance, cities rose in their stead.' 'Hence the rising of magnificent palaces', Vivekananda states further, 'to take the place of thatched cottages. . . . Delightful gardens, pleasant groves, beautiful galleries, charming paintings, exquisite sculptures, fine and costly apparel began to displace, by gradual steps, the natural beauties of rugged woods and the rough and coarse dress of the simple rustic.'[75] All these speaks of a high-level material civilization attained through urbanization and of the far-reaching social revolution that came along with it, when there was an important change in the composition of the producing classes and rural/urban distribution of population, the ploughmen becoming urban artisans and becoming city dwellers.

Why did India submit to the conquerors? : It is a historical fact that no civilized nation could ever resist the onslaught of a barbaric race. Egypt succumbed to the attacks of Christian barbarians, Greece to the Romans, civilized Romans to the attacks of the Asian and north-European barbarians as has been shown by Swami Vivekananda (vide chapter 10). India, a highly civilized and an ancient nation could not for the same reason resist the onslaught of foreign invasions coming from the barbaric races and was conquered several times. But as Marx himself has stated the conqueror was absorbed by the superior civilization of the country.

The British, who conquered India at a time when the country became very weak under the misrule of the later Mogul emperors, did not come with a superior civilization. Vivekananda, as seen already, has bombarded such a theory. And as we have pointed out earlier Indian civilization has survived the British onslaught, the vitality of it being proved by the renaissance when it became dynamic again, making new acquisitions. Of course, it is true, in this case, the vanquished could not absorb the conqueror within itself as it has done in earlier days. The English civilization had that power of resistance and vitality. But the meeting of the two—Indian and British, a highly developed ethical and spiritual civilization and a developed material civilization with the knowledge of superior

75. *C. W.*, IV, p. 460.

technology, proved to be of benefit to both. As India benefited by acquiring the superior technology from the British, Indian philosophy and culture nourished western culture and civilization as is evident from the writings of Max Mòller, Tolstoy, Romain Rolland, Isherwood and Aldous Huxley and even the poet T. S. Eliot.

The old structure of Indian economic system, which proved its efficiency through its capacity of sustaining a flourishing commerce throughout the ages, succumbed to the technological revolution that was ushered into India through the instrumentation of British rule. But technological revolution was inevitable for every country sooner or later and it was due to come to India also, British rule or no British rule. In a world united by the improvement of communication it was not possible to keep it confined to the territories of those countries which first experienced it. Today technological revolution has engulfed the territories of every nation on earth, whether under British domination at one time or not.

Marxian assessment based on insufficient and wrong informations : Karl Marx evidently has gone on several false premises and wrong infomations in his analysis of Asia and India.

1. He proceeded with the pre-conceived idea that all Asiatic countries had low civilizations whereas the contrary was true.

2. He went on with the pre-conceived idea that European civilization was a superior one which also was not true.

3. By civilization he meant only material civilization, he did not accept the view that civilization was basically a spiritual and ethical concept.

4. He had no idea about the fact that even in material achievements India did not lag behind.

5. He proceeded to assess Indian religion with a very poor knowledge of it. From his comments on Hindu religion it seems he had cent per cent faith in the false propaganda of the Christian missionaries of the period against which Vivekananda fought tooth and nail while in the West. This is evident blatantly from Marx's following comment on Hindu religion, 'We must not

forget that these little communities were contaminated by caste and slavery, that they subjugated man to external circumstances, that they transformed a self-developing social state into a mere changing destiny, and thus brought about a brutalizing worshipping of nature, exhibiting degradation in the fact that man, the sovereign of nature, fell down on his knees in adoration of Kanuman (Hanuman), the monkey, Sabala, the cow.'[76] The lack of knowledge about Hindu religion exhibited here is lamentable. The mistakes committed in mentioning the proper names is a pointer to the fact.

6. His source of information was mostly British officials' report—the officials who were themselves equally ignorant about India.

7. He failed to note that Islam did not lose its identity but India assimilated what is best in Islamic culture.

Karl Marx who was generally speaking a great scholar and a man with the vision of a sage was not very much conversant with Indian history and culture and therefore his main contention regarding India, that the Indian civilization was totally destroyed beyond repair by the British, has been proved erroneous by subsequent history when India experienced a renaissance and a revitalization of her civilization and became dynamic once again with new vigour and strength since nineteenth century onwards.

VI

CONCLUSIONS REGARDING HIGH CIVILIZATION

In conclusion, we may say that the criterion of a high civilization, as pointed out by Vivekananda, is not only material attainments but ethical standard and spiritual height reached by the people in a particular region. What the world needs today to enable the human civilization to rise to the highest pinnalce of glory is a combination of the ethical and spiritual civilization of the East and the material civilization of the West which was in truth the dream of Vivekananda.

---

76. *Selections from Marx and Engels*, Vol. I. p. 317.

CHAPTER 14

The Sociological Ideas—II : Society : Nature and Functions : Laws of Social Evolution

I

SOCIETY : ITS NATURE AND FUNCTIONS

McIver's Concept : Society is the basic organization which nurtures and sustains individuals. It is an organization of the individuals with a control over the lives of the individuals. 'Social beings, men', says McIver, the renowned sociologist, 'express their nature, by creating or re-creating an organization which guides and controls their behaviour in a myriad way.'[1] Further, according to him, 'This organization *society* liberates and limits the activities of men, sets up standards for them to follow and maintain ; whatever the imperfections and tyrannies it has exhibited in human history, it is a necessary condition of every fulfilment of life.'[2] 'Society is', he further adds, 'a system of usages and procedures, of authority and mutual aid, of many groupings and divisions, of controls, of human behaviour and liberties. This ever changing complex system we call society. It is the web of social relationship. And it is always changing.'[3]

Vivekananda's Concept : Vivekananda's concept, stemming out of his Vedanta philosophy, may be compared with that of McIver. 'The manhood of man', Vivekananda says, 'the womanhood of woman, the reality of everything is the Lord—and that this Lord we are trying to realize from time without beginning in the objective world... .'[4] 'The fact being', he continues to say, 'that the Lord is in us, we are He, the eternal

1. McIver—*Society* (1950), p. 5. 2. ibid. 3. ibid.
4. *Letters of Swami Vivekananda* (3rd edition), p. 316.

subject, the real ego, never to be objectified, and that all the objectifying process is a mere waste of time and talent. When the soul becomes aware of this, it gives up objectifying and falls back more upon the subjective. This is the evolution, less and less in the body and more and more in the mind—*man* the highest form, meaning in Sanskrit *manas*, thought—the animal that thinks and not the animal that "senses" only. This is what in theology is called "renunciation". The formation of society, the institution of marriage, the love for children, our good works, morality and ethics are all different forms of renunciation. All our lives in every society are the subjection of the will, the thirst, the desire. This surrender of the will or the fictious self—of the desire to jump out of ourselves as it were—the struggles still to objectify the subject—is the one phenomenon in this world of which all societies and social forms are various modes and stages. Love is the easiest and smoothest way towards the self-surrender or subjection of the will, and hatred, the opposite.'[5]

In this rather long statement, the following basic features of society have been brought out by Vivekananda:

1. Firstly, society is an objective projection of the 'Reality' which is subjective.
2. Secondly, attempts at objectificaiton never succeeds fully, hence society is always imperfect and it will remain so in future. 'Objective society', he says, 'will always be a mixture of good and evil—objective life will always be followed by its shadow, death... .'[6]
3. Thirdly, attempts at objectification are given up by individuals after a certain stage to turn to subjective reality. This is called 'renunciation' in theology, but this is the essence of 'evolution' in sociological terms. Man evolves mentally.
4. Fourthly, human evolution after a stage is not physical any more, but mental and spiritual.
5. Finally, social laws are attempts to control the desire of man so that he is able to proceed along the path of this evolution or renunciation, whatever we may choose to call it.

---

5. ibid., p. 317. 6. ibid. 7. ibid.

It is evident that Vivekananda has given here a masterly analysis of the basic purposes and functions of society, as well as of its true and intrinsic nature. According to this analysis, society enables us to control our desires and to proceed along the path of realization of Truth and Reality. This is the basic purpose served by society. In his opinion further, 'Love is the easiest and smoothest way towards the self-surrender or subjection of the will, and hatred, the opposite.'[7] Thus 'love', 'self-sacrifice', 'control of desire' are the virtues which are imparted to the individuals by society so that the individuals may get elevated properly to manifest his divine potentialities. Finally, he is of the opinion that 'That society is the greatest, where the highest truths become practical. . . . and if society is not fit for the highest truths, make it so; and the sooner, the better.'[8]

It is interesting to note that Professor Pitirim A. Sorokin, almost repeats the words of Vivekananda when he says, 'The minimum of unselfish love is absolutely necessary for the durable existence of any society and that at this present catastrophic moment of human history an increased altruism of the individuals and the groups and extension of the unselfish love of everyone for everyone is a necessary condition for the prevention of the nuclear wars and liberation of mankind from its greatest ills, bloody conflicts, . . . insanity, misery... .'[9]

It is evident also that both Vivekananda and McIver hold that society 'liberates and limits'. Only the basic purposes of society are stated by Vivekananda with more clarity as it is evident from his following utterances :

1. Religion is the greatest cohesive force in society.[10]
2. 'Truth does not pay homage to any society, ancient or modern, society has to pay homage to Truth or die.'[11]
3. 'The whole social fabric is based upon that idea of restraint... .'[12]
4. 'Whatever in society is good and great and sublime is the working out of that love... .'[13]

---

8. *C. W.*, II, p. 85.
9. P. A. Sorokin—'Three Basic Trends of Our Time', *Vedanta and the West*, No. 139.
10. *C. W.*, II, p. 57.
11. ibid., p. 84.
12. ibid., p. 109.
13. ibid., III, p. 73.

II

THE FOUNDATION OF SOCIETY : GOODNESS OF MAN

What Swami Vivekananda emphasizes most as the basis of society, is the goodness of man. He says : '. . . the basis of all systems social, political, rests upon the goodness of man.' 'No nation', he adds, 'is good or great because parliament enacts this or that but because its men are great and good.' Here he shows that religion has got a very significant role to play in man's social life since religion shapes a man from an animal. Sorokin, Toynbee and a host of other thinkers assign the same significant role to religion, as seen already.

III

SOCIETY : NOT AN END IN ITSELF

Vivekananda in his reflections on society emphasizes further the following points :

1. It is the development of the individual, of one and all, of course, and not of the few which constitute progress.[14]

2. Social development or perfection is not the goal of humanity since society and social institutions cannot be perfect. However, 'That society is the greatest, where highest truths become practical.'[15]

3. Finally, society is only a stage of human evolution. 'Society', says Vivekananda, 'is only a stage of growth through which we are passing. . . . If the social state were permanent, it would be the same as if the baby remained a baby. . . . Society is good at a certain stage, but it cannot be our ideal; it is a constant flux.'[16] Hence he concludes that it is highly illogical to make society the test of Truth. 'We might just as well judge', he says, 'the good or utility of a scientific discovery by its use to the baby.'[17]

Thus it is apparent that according to Vivekananda, in the ultimate analysis, society is a means to an end, not an end in itself.

---

14. ibid., IV, p. 463.
15. ibid., II, p. 85.
16. ibid., VI, p. 144.
17. ibid.

IV

CLASSIFICATION OF THE CONCEPTS OF SOCIETY

It is possible to identify four different concepts of society—[18]

(1) the mechanistic concept,
(2) the atomistic concept,
(3) the organic concept,
(4) the functional concept.

According to the first, society is a kind of a mechanical system. According to the second, society is a conglomeration of individuals; it does not recognize it as a super-individualistic entity. According to the third, it is a super-individualistic entity, it has a natural origin and all the properties of a living organism. According to the fourth, it is neither an organism nor a mechanical system but a system of interrelated individuals.

Among these four conceptions, the organic one is widely upheld.

The difficulty with the organismic theory is that an organism is subject to the laws of birth, growth and death. It must decay after a period of growth and ultimately be extinct. But this natural process is not true of all societies. Ancient Indian society and Chinese society have resisted total extinction all through history although they have gone through vast changes. Of course, Swami Vivekananda thinks that society, as a whole, is a passing phase in human evolution since it is a constant flux.

V

THEORIES OF SOCIAL CHANGE

Whether the mechanistic or the atomistic or the organismic theory is true, it is certain that like all empirical phenomena, organic or inorganic, society is subject to incessant changes without any stop-gap.

There are various theories[19] regarding the nature and causes of social changes. Some of well-known theories are:

18. P. A. Sorokin—*Contemporary Sociological Theories*, Chapter IV, (Kalyani Publication, Ludhiana, New Delhi).
19. Wilbert E. Moore—*Social Change.*

(1) simple linear growth theory, (2) stage theory, (3) cumulative retro-active evolution theory, (4) cycle theory.

Simple linear growth theory : The simplest representation of evolutionary growth is represented by a straight line marking a gradual and continuous development of man's civilization. This is called the simple linear growth theory.

Stage theory : The stage theory of growth was at one time very popular with the exponents of social evolution and even now very popular with the layman. The early chapters of world history books invariably subscribe to the idea of successive and progressive eras of man's civilization, marked off by relatively sharp breaks between one era and another. In most examples of stage theory the discontinuities are caused by changes in man's relation to his environment, i.e., in technology. Scholars everywhere have felt uneasy about this single cause concept of evolution and have therefore turned to the concept of multiplicity of factors including technology, environment, racial properties, religion, ethical values, etc., as the determinants of social changes.

Cumulative retro-active theory : The cumulative retro-active evolution theory is a complicated one. It can be explained in the context of economic growth and social change in the following manner : in the economic system, an initial agricultural revolution makes possible a diversion of productive factors to manufacturing, which in turn makes agricultural mechanization, chemical fertilization, and rapid delivery of agricultural products possible. It means that there is a second agricultural revolution due to the growth of manufacturing industries which was initiated by an earlier agricultural revolution.

Linear theory : *Unscientific* : The theory of linear evolution is not considered scientific today although almost all the theories of social evolution formulated in the nineteenth and twentieth centuries have actually been of the linear type, with this or that perpetual trend more and more realized in the course of existence of mankind. But empirical studies point out that there is a limit to every linear trend in the socio-cultural process. According to Sorokin, Newton's law explains the reason. Definite movement in one direction is impossible, because frictions and shocks of external forces would disturb the movement and eventually change its direction. Thus, through the gravitational forces, a linear movement becomes circular or eliptical. And the socio-cultural processes individually or in their totality are not absolutely isolated from the outside cosmological and biological worlds, nor from the pressures of the 'social processes themselves (the process is cumulative) in the sense that one change in a particular aspect of social life causes a further change in another aspect'. Thus, as pointed out by Professor Sorokin, 'It is quite improbable that all these innumerable forces could be negligible or constant at any moment, thus maintaining the direction of the processes unchanged.'[20] Thus it is evident that according to science, there cannot be any movement in a straight line and this is true also of the socio-cultural phenomenon, as has been emphasized by Sorokin.

Linear theory of Karl Marx : Following the instance of August Comte and Herbert Spencer the linear theory of socio-cultural evolution flourished at one time. Large number of writers harped on this refrain—'Glory to evolution and progress that leads mankind to never-ceasing betterment and perfection.' Marxian concept of social evolution is also a continuous one, society evolving through the different stages of slave society, feudalistic society, capitalism and socialism which is the pinnacle and this evolution is taking place through variation or improvement in the single factor, viz., technology. Marx is silent about what happens after the summit has been reached. Does the process of evolution stop? Marx does not care to enlighten us on this vital question. Logically society cannot stop evolving at any stage, society being by nature dynamic. It would remain so even when socialism has been attained. Moreover, even if social evolution takes place due to technological improvement only, does it not happen after the stage of socialism is reached? Does the process of technological development stop? This is another pertinent question on which Marx and his followers are silent. Hence Marx leaves us in a blind alley beyond which nothing can be seen. A linear theory of evolution cannot explain the entire course of social evolution. This is its chief shortcoming. Marx

---

20. P. A. Sorokin—*Social And Cultural Dynamics*, p. 652.

was over-influenced by Darwinian theory which led him to this pitfall. His theory of social evolution explains the beginning but fails to explain the end, it cannot answer the question : 'After socialism what next? What will be the next stage of evolution?' He was also over-influenced by the Industrial Revolution which led him to think that technological change was the only cause of social change.

Wave theory of Swami Vivekananda : Vivekananda challenged the concept of linear progress. His arguments based on modern science are as follows : (1) All progress proceeds by successive rise and fall and 'There is no progress in a straight line.'[21] (2) 'A straight line, infinitely projected, must end in a circle.' It returns to the starting point.[22] (3) 'There is *no progress* without corresponding digression.'[23] According to him, we can attain unity but not progress.

Concept of Progress : Hence the word 'progress' carries no meaning in the context of society according to Vivekananda. Criticizing the concept of social progress he says : 'Another theory in modern times has been presented by several schools, that man's destiny is to go on always improving, always struggling towards, but never reaching the goal. This statement, though apparently very nice, is absurd, because there is no such thing as motion in a straight line. Every motion is in a circle. ... Therefore, this idea that the destiny of man is progressing ever forward and forward, and never stopping, is absurd.'[24] And he points out further that : 'On other and practical grounds we see that the theory of eternal progression is untenable, for destruction is the goal of everything earthly. ... See how, from nebulae, the sun, moon, and stars are produced; then they dissolve and go back to nebulae. The same is being done everywhere. The plant takes material from the earth, dissolves, and gives it back. Every form in this world is taken out of surrounding atoms and goes back to these atoms. It cannot be that the same law acts differently in different places. Law is uniform. Nothing is more certain than that.'[25] He concludes, therefore, that there is no

21. *C. W.*, V, p. 271.
22. ibid., I, p. 196.
23. ibid., VIII, p. 383.
24. ibid., I, pp. 195-96.
25. ibid., pp. 196-97.

progression or digression in nature. It is showing again and again the same forms. In fact the word 'law' means that.

Waves of spirituality and materialism : According to Vivekananda, the same form of change as in nature is found in the field of society also. The change that takes place in society is also like a continuous series of waves, waves of spirituality and materialism one succeeding the other. He describes the process thus : 'Two attempts have been made in the world to found the social life. The one was upon religion and the other upon social necessity. The one was founded upon spirituality, the other upon materialism, the one upon transcendentalism and the other upon realism.' Explaining he adds, 'The one looks beyond the horizon of the little material world and is bold enough to begin life there, even apart from the other. The other, the second is content to take its stand on the things of the world and expects to find a firm footing there. Curiously enough, it seems that at times the spiritual side prevails and then the materialistic side—in wave-like motions following each other.' 'In the same country', he adds, 'there will be different tides. At one time, the full tide of materialistic ideal prevails and everything in this life—prosperity, the education that procures more pleasure, more food— will become glorious at first and then that will degrade and degenerate. Along with the prosperity will rise to white heat all the inborn jealousies and hatreds of the human race. Competition and the merciless cruelty will be the watchword of the day. Then people will think that the whole scheme of life is a failure. And the world will be destroyed had not spirituality come to the rescue and lent a helping hand to the sinking world... .' Continuing with his analysis he further adds : 'As a rule, spirituality brings a class of men who lay exclusive claim to the special powers of the world. The immediate effect of this is a reaction towards materialism, which opens the door to scores of exclusive claims, until the time comes when not only all the spiritual powers of the race, but all its material powers and privileges are centred in the hands of a very few; and these few, standing on the necks of the masses of the people, want to rule them. The society has to help itself, and materialism comes to the rescue.'[26]

---

26. ibid., III, p. 157.

It is a very clear account of the process of social change taking place in a wave form and it clearly explains how the one trend is succeeded by the other—materialism succeeding spirituality and the vice versa.

Role of materialism in society : Most wonderful is Vivekananda's dispassionate evaluation of spirituality and materialism as social forces. He has shown very clearly that spirituality also degenerates and makes room for worst kind of privileges and tyranny and then it is materialism which rescues the oppressed masses. No other protagonist of religion has ever conceded that credit to materialism. At the same time he has very ably shown that spirituality rescues the people from the savage strifes, class-wars and conflicts resulting from materialism. Karl Marx noticed only one side of the wave—the degenerated stage of spiritualism in modern society when materialism came to the rescue of the people from the oppression of the priestly class. Vivekananda has given us the total picture. He had a wonderful breadth of vision and historical insight and it was revealed to him that both spirituality and materialism have utility and both have saved the society from destruction in the past. He points out that the world would be destroyed had not spirituality come to rescue when materialism fully grasps society.

The rhythmic theory of Sorokin : *ideational, idealistic and sensate forms of socio-cultural patterns* : In recent years Sorokin has given us a theory of social change very much similar to that of Vivekananda. According to him, there are three different socio-cultural patterns which succeed one another in a rhythmic manner. These are as mentioned earlier : (1) ideational, (2) idealistic, and (3) sensate. The ideational pattern is characterized by the predominance of spirituality and transcendentalism, the sensate pattern is characterized by the predominance of materialism and the idealistic pattern is a mixture of the two.[27]

It is apparent that essentially this theory of Sorokin is the same as Vivekananda's theory of spirituality and materialism prevailing in turn in society. Again, Sorokin's view conforms to that of Vivekananda in respect of the nature of the class-struggle. Both uphold that struggle for privileges among the different

27. P. A. Sorokin—*Social And Cultural Dynamics*, Chapter 2.

classes is most intense in a period of sensate or materialistic culture. Explaining the point Sorokin adds, 'In our developed sensate mentality every day begins a fight for a maximum share of happiness and prosperity. This often leads to conflicts between sects, classes, states, provinces, unions, etc., and often results in revolts, wars and class-struggles, over-taxation which ruins security and in the long run makes economic prosperity impossible.'[28]

Again, Sorokin assigns to religion the same important role in society as was assigned by Vivekananda. Vivekananda said—'Religion makes an animal a man and a man a God.' Sorokin says in the same strain—'The conquest of the forces of nature is the main function of the sensate culture, the taming of man, his humanization, his ennoblement as a participant in the Divine Absolute has always been the function of the ideational and idealistic culture.'[29] On account of this degenerating effect of the sensate culture on man, there arises the necessity for the society to turn to the other forms. As pointed out by Sorokin, 'The sensate culture did its best in the way of degrading man to the level of a mere reflex organism . . . devoid of anything noble and sacred. Hence the urgency of the shift from sensatism to ideationalism or idealism, from the subjugation and control of nature by man to the control of man by himself.'[30]

From the above it is clear that according to both Vivekananda and Sorokin, spirituality is the centre of social gravitation. As soon as the society moves away from it, there develops a tendency to return to it.

VIVEKANANDA'S CONTRIBUTIONS

The principles of immanent change and involution : The reasons behind the wave form, as we gather them from Vivekananda, are : (1) the principle of immanent change, this is a common point between Vivekananda and Sorokin; (2) the principle of involution, without which the principle of immanent change cannot be fully explained. This is Vivekananda's own theory adapted from the ancient Sāṁkhya philosophy of India.

Immanent change : Explaining the principle of immanent

28. ibid., p. 628. 29. ibid. 30. ibid.

change Vivekananda says—'It is in the very nature of things to manifest themselves. The momentum is not from outside, but comes from inside.'[31]

Involution : Explaining the second principle, viz., the principle of involution, Vivekananda says, '. . . each evolution presupposes an involution. We know that the sum total of energy that is displayed in the universe is the same at all times, and that matter is indestructible.'[32] 'Everything begins', he adds, 'as it were, from certain seeds, certain rudiments, certain fine forms, and becomes grosser and grosser as it develops; and then again it goes back to that fine form and subsides.'[33] Pointing out that the whole process would form a cycle or a wave, Vivekananda continues—'Everything in creation goes on in this form, one wave rising, another falling, rising again, falling again. ... The same law must apply to the universe taken as a whole, because of its uniformity.'[34] Explaining the principle further he adds—'this cycle is the evolution out of the involution of the previous cycle, and this cycle will again be involved, getting finer and finer, and out of that will come the next cycle'.[35]

Pointing out that the principle of immanent change is the only logical explanation of the rhythm of socio-cultural process, Professor Sorokin argues : 'Any consistent theory of externalistic change does not solve the problem, but merely postpones the solution, and then either comes to a mystery or to the logical absurdity of putting the proverbial rabbit out of nothing.'[36] According to him, 'It cannot help changing even if all its external conditions are constant.'[37] Arguing further he points out that 'The principle of immanent change of a socio-cultural system is supported by empirical observation. We do not know any empirical socio-cultural system or phenomenon which does not change in the course of its existence or in the course of time.'[38] Finally, he argues—'Life can never be in equilibrium. Complete equilibrium is never attained (by an organism) and would be fatal if it were attained, as it would mean stagnation, atrophy and death.'[39]

---

31. *C. W.*, V, pp. 277-78. 32. ibid., II, p. 427. 33. ibid., p. 426.
34. ibid., p. 206. 35. ibid., p. 427.
36. P. A. Sorokin—*Social And Cultural Dynamics*, p. 672.
37. ibid., p. 633. 38. ibid., p. 634. 39. ibid., p. 635.

But Sorokin failed to reach the final stage of the logical conclusion of this line of argument which is the principle of involution. Immanent change is not possible without involution. This is shown in a masterly analysis by Vivekananda : 'The seed is the fine form out of which the big tree comes, and another big tree was the form which is involved in that seed. The whole of this universe was present in the cosmic fine universe. The little cell, which becomes afterwards the man, was simply the involved man and becomes evolved as a man.'[40] He concludes : 'We see then, that nothing can be created out of nothing. Everything exists through eternity, and will exist through eternity.'[41] It is clear that immanent change is possible if and only when there is involution. Because of involution it is possible for the same socio-cultural forms to appear repeatedly in history.

No infinite possibilities of variations : Sorokin argues that the socio-cultural process cannot have infinite possibilities of forms and mutations. With infinite possibilities there cannot be any repetition or rhythm. 'Unrepeated rhythm', says Sorokin, 'is no rhythm at all.' He shows also that a finite system cannot be endowed with an infinite or unlimited capacity of transformation, for in that case 'the finite would contain in itself an infinite, which is a logical nonsense'.[42] Therefore, the same pattern must emerge repeatedly. But if a particular pattern is destroyed when the other pattern overtakes it, it cannot reappear because of the same logic of immanent change, viz., 'nothing can come out of nothing'. Hence when one pattern manifests, the others remain dormant, they do not become extinct, or it may be said that they remain in an involved state. Thus there cannot be any evolution without an involution, the two are complementary processes. Sorokin himself mentions that even in the sensate period, spirituality is not totally extinct, it remains confined to a few specially gifted persons so that it may gradually gain ground again and become dominant once again, the vice versa is also true.

It is evident, therefore, that in the socio-cultural field as in the other fields of nature a state of involution precedes every stage of evolution. The same principle, the same law, operates in

40. *C. W.*, II, p. 208. 41. ibid., p. 208.
42. P. A. Sorokin—*Social And Cultural Dynamics*, p. 672.

every department of nature. The process cannot be otherwise in the case of socio-cultural developments. Vivekananda's argument in this respect appears unassailable: '... every evolution presupposes an involution. Nothing can be evolved which is not already there. Here, again, modern science comes to our help. You know by mathematical reasoning that the sum total of the energy that is displayed in the universe is the same throughout. You cannot take away one atom of matter or one foot-pound of force. You cannot add to the universe one atom of matter or one foot-pound of force. As such, evolution does not come out of zero; then, where does it come from ? From previous involution.'[43] Thus it is apparent that Sorokin's logical theory has a gap which is filled in by Vivekananda's theory of involution.

PROPERTIES OF ORGANIC CHANGE

An organic system is a growing concern, and as such it cannot help changing. Hence there emerge two important principles of this organic change as discussed above :

1. *Principle of immanent generation of consequences* : It means that 'As long as it exists and functions, a socio-cultural system incessantly generates consequences which are not the results of the external factors to the system, but the consequences of the existence of the system and of its activities.'[44]

2. *Principle of immanent self-determination of the system's destiny*: It means, 'As soon as a socio-cultural system emerges, its essential and "normal" course of existence, the forms, the phases, the activities of its life, career or destiny are determined mainly by the system itself, by its potential nature and the totality of its properties.' According to Sorokin further, the externalistic forces cannot in many cases 'reverse or fundamentally change the sequence of the phases of the immanent destiny of the system'.[45]

VI

DISTINCTIVE NATIONAL SOCIO-CULTURAL PATTERNS

Distinctive national socio-cultural patterns obviously emerge

43. *C. W.*, II, pp. 227-28. 44. P. A. Sorokin—*Social And Cultural Dynamics.*

as a consequence of operation of these two principles. Vivekananda emphasized this long ago when he said, 'Europe has always been the source of social power and Asia of spiritual power', and again, 'The Greek sought political liberty' and 'The Hindu has always sought spiritual liberty'.[46] In his opinion, a particular socio-cultural system can develop only along its own path of development. In order to show that it can never be externalistic, Vivekananda uses the following diagram :

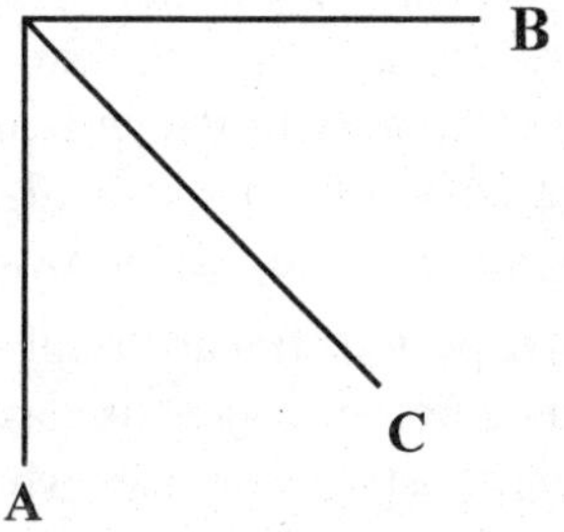

Explaining the diagram Vivekananda says, 'The line of their [of a particular socio-cultural pattern] own development runs in one way, A. Must the new accession of force be a compensating one, B? This would produce a development midway between the two, C—a geometrical alteration merely. But it was not so.'[47] National life was a question of organic forces and not of mechanical forces. It is a pointer to the immanent destiny of a particular socio-cultural system. Hence he firmly said, 'National life was a question of organic forces. We must reinforce the current of that life itself, and leave it to do the rest.'[48]

Empirical basis : Vivekananda built up his theory in this respect on the basis of empirical studies. 'I have been', he stated, 'in the countries of the West—have travelled through many lands of many races; and each race and each nation appears to me to have a particular ideal—a prominent ideal running through its whole life; and this ideal is the backbone of the national life. Not politics nor military power, not commercial supremacy nor mechanical genius furnishes India with that backbone, but

45. ibid.
46. *Complete Works of Sister Nivedita* (1st Edition), Nivedita School, Vol. I, p. 341.
47. *C. W.*, IX, p. 381.
48. ibid.

religion... .'[49] Elaborating his thesis further, he stated—'Suppose you can imitate the Westerns, that moment you will die, you will have no more life in you. ... A stream is taking its rise, away beyond where time began, flowing through millions of ages of human history; do you mean to get hold of that stream and push it back to its source, to a Himalayan glacier? Even if that were practicable, it would not be possible for you to be Europeanized.'[50] Now this is what has been called by Sorokin 'the principle of immanent self-determination'. As Sorokin rightly observes, 'External forces cannot change fundamentally the immanent potentiality of the system and its normal destiny.'

But this theory of Vivekananda, evidently logical and scientific, does not exclude the following possibilities :

1. Short-period linear trend, which is found in his exposition of stages of class rule in history.
2. Externalistic influences which may be assimilated in the main stream.
3. It does not also suggest absolutely identical recurrent socio-cultural patterns.

Externalistic influence : Regarding the assimilation of externalistic influence, Vivekananda points out from his study of history that whenever there was a foreign invasion or commercial contact between nations there occurred exchange of ideas and externalistic influence was sought to be assimilated. 'We find', he states in a lucid exposition, 'that whenever either by mighty conquest or by commercial supremacy different parts of the world have been kneaded into one whole race and requests have been made from one corner to the other, each nation, as it were, poured forth its own quota, either political, social, or spiritual. India's contribution to the sum total of human knowledge has been spirituality, philosophy.'[51] Giving examples from past history he says : 'These she contributed even long before the rising of the Persian Empire ; the second time was during the Persian Empire; for the third time during the ascendency of the Greeks; and now for the fourth time during the ascendency of the English, she is going to fulfil the same destiny once more.' Referring to the modern epoch he says : 'As western ideas of

49. ibid., III., p. 137. 50. ibid., p. 172. 51. ibid., p. 171.

organization and external civilization are penetrating and pouring into our country, whether we will have them or not, so Indian spirituality and philosophy are deluging the land of the West. None can resist it, and no more can we resist some sort of material civilization from the West. A little of it, perhaps, is good for us, and a little spiritualization is good for the West; thus the balance will be preserved.'[52] But this externalistic influence cannot totally eclipse the main trend. Pointing out this he adds : 'If you find it is impossible for the European to throw off the few centuries of culture which there is in the West, do you think it is possible to you to throw off the culture of shining scores of centuries? It cannot be.'[53]

Exact repetitions not possible : As regards the third point that exactly identical cultural patterns cannot recur although the main trend remains the same, Vivekananda has shown through historical analysis that religion is the backbone of India, but we have seen many varieties of religious upheavals in history, never the repetition of the identical pattern. For example, earliest in the historical period there was the Vedic religion of sacrifices with a trace of philosophical monism, it was succeeded by the pure monism of the Upanishads, then there came Buddhist and Jaina upheavals denying the authority of the Vedas, then came the period of monistic religion of a different variety with more emphasis on philosophy preached by Śaṅkara; sometime later there came the various schools of Bhakti-cult represented by Nānak, Kabīr, Chaitanya, and others.[54] Thus it is clear that there are many possibilities within the limit of the main trend.

VII

Concept of Progress : *Modern View* : Today notions of progress are not considered scientific but are considered as value-judgements, changes in approved directions.[55] That Vivekananda did not approve the concept of 'progress' in relation to socio-cultural change has been mentioned already. He never subscribed to a single notion which is not scientific. To him, as we have seen earlier, even a trend towards spirituality has a set-back, it is

52. ibid.
53. ibid., p. 172.
54. ibid., IV, p. 462.
55. McIver—*Society*, p. 615.

periodically succeeded by materialism, which is also a limited trend and it is succeeded by spirituality.

It must also be noted that Vivekananda has given us the most satisfactory explanation of the repetitive forms in terms of evolution and involution. It must not be forgotten that Vivekananda has given this view when there was a leaning in general towards the linear and the externalistic theory. Thus Vivekananda as early as in the nineteenth century gave us a competent and a thoroughly rationalistic theory which has been supported by the twentieth century development of science and sociology. His wave theory and theory of involution are undoubtedly notable contributions to the field of sociology.

Not imposed reform but organic growth : The immense significance of the principle of immanent change and the principle of involution may be emphasized here. Social change is organic and not mechanical in character as we have already seen. Hence it is not possible for society to advance by imposing certain institutional changes or reform measures. Any change, to be of enduring value, must grow from within. An externalistic imposed change cannot last long. It was therefore that Vivekananda was never tired of emphasizing that growth was desirable and not imposed reforms; 'I do not believe in reform, I believe in growth'[56], he said emphatically. Growth process is gradual, it is the manifestation of inherent trend or potentiality. Society is dynamic and therefore it grows and manifests. This is the natural law according to which society operates.

VIII

CYCLE THEORIES OF SPENGLER AND TOYNBEE

Here we may examine the views of Spengler and Toynbee who also subscribe more or less to the cycle, rhythm or wave theory.

According to Spengler, cultures are exactly like living organisms and every socio-cultural system passes through the age-phases of an individual living being, that is to say it evolves, which is the stage of birth or becoming, then it flowers into a full grown system, this is its youth, and then it enters into a stage of

56. *C. W.*, III, p. 213.

decadence which is the winter-time of its old age and then it fast moves towards its inevitable doom. Spengler is rejected today for his over-stress on Social Darwinism. A socio-cultural system is organic in nature but it is not actually a living organism. His theory would not explain the case of India or China where the cultural systems have not met the final doom although there have been phases of decadences in their long history but they revived again, showed the vitality of youth again. This has happened repeatedly in the cases of these two countries.

Toynbee, likewise, points out that civilizations follow the natural laws of birth, growth and decay. As we have seen already, according to Toybee, the genesis or birth of civilizations is to be found in the challenge and response which determines human action in an adverse circumstance. After the birth of a civilization, according to Toynbee, its growth takes place through creative persons who are in minority in the society. According to him, breakdown of civilizations takes place due to three major causes : one, decline of the creative power of the minority; two, withdrawal of social support to the ruling group by the majority of the common people, and three, consequent loss of social unity. In any case the laws of birth, growth and decay are operating in the system of Toynbee also. Toynbee has been criticized on the ground that his generalizations do not depend on scientific theorization and also that Toynbee's conceptual foundation lacks adequacy. However, he believes that the history of mankind will be guided by the progressive increase in the provision of spiritualization of mankind.[57]

Vivekananda's contributions, as seen above, are distinctively his own, although there are some similarities between his views and the views of Spengler, Toynbee and Sorokin.

IX

STAGES OF SOCIAL EVOLUTION : VIVEKANANDA'S CLASSIFICATION

While providing a scientific and therefore a satisfactory exposition on society, its basic nature and purposes and the laws

---

57. Satis K. Bajaj—*History : Its Methodology and Philosophy*, pp. 79-82.

of its evolution, Vivekananda points out also the different stages of social development as manifested in history. We have described these stages in the previous chapter. They have the appearance of a short-period linear trend although ultimately these phases also reveal a circular trend.

We have seen in the previous chapter how in a developed society class division evolved. The priests, the kingly classes, traders and labourers are the four common classes which emerged in very ancient days.

From the account of development of class divisions in society, as narrated by Vivekananda, three conclusions, important from the point of view of sociology, can be derived.

1. The first conclusion is that 'society' and its coercive organ 'the state' represented by the king is not the result of a contract made at a particular time by an assembly of the population, as propounded by Hobbes, Locke and Rousseau, it was the result of a gradual process of evolution. The well-known theory of 'social contract' stands rejected today by the social scientists who uphold the historical evolution theory as it provides the most satisfactory explanation of the origin of society.
2. The second conclusion is that at the root of social formation 'conflict' and violence have also played some role as is evident from the reference to the wars between the different groups of people—*deva*s and *asura*s.
3. The third conclusion is, as pointed out in the preceding chapter, that from the beginning of a class-divided society there was exploitation of the labourers, the actual producers, by the priests, the ruling classes and the merchants who are non-producers. Thus the producing classes were deprived of their due share in the total social product since the very beginning of society.

X

FOUR STAGES OF CLASS RULE

In the historic period, as we have seen already, Vivekananda discovered four stages of class rule. His leading conclusion in this respect we may note here :

1. Human society is in turn governed by the four castes—the priests or the Brahmins, the soldiers or the Khsatriyas, the traders or the Vaishyas, and finally by the labourers or the Shudras.
2. After the proletariat stage the cycle will start again, the entire society will be elevated to Brahminhood. Referring to the scriptures he points out that originally there was only one class, the Brahmins, and society will again be elevated to that stage. It must be borne in mind that a one-class society is virtually a classless society.
3. Each stage has some merits and some demerits, no stage is an unmixed blessing.
4. But there are reasons to justify the stage of the proletariat rule in spite of its deficiencies, since the proletariat has been the deprived class all through the human history. Hence justice requires that they should have ascendancy at the present moment.

Merits and demerits of the different stages of class rule : According to Vivekananda, during the period of priestly rule (i.e., Brahminical rule), the foundation of the sciences were laid. Pointing out the deficiencies of this class rule he says : 'But there is tremendous claim of exclusive rights on hereditary grounds—tremendous claim to privileges.'[58]

'The next one the military or the Kshatriya rule has this merit that during this period arts and culture reach their heights. But the demerit is that the rule is tyrannical and cruel.'

'The merit of the Vaishya rule is that with the trader, the Vaishya, as he goes everywhere, there is good dissemination of culture. Its demerit is that it is awful in its silent crushing power.'

The world has seen already, according to Vivekananda, all these three periods of class rule, the fourth one is yet to come. This is to be the period of the rule of the Shudras. Its merit will be equitable distribution of wealth, its demerit 'perhaps the lowering of culture'.

---

58. *Letters of Swami Vivekananda*, p. 319.

XI

THE CONCEPT OF AN IDEAL SOCIETY AND AN IDEAL 'STATE'

According to Karl Marx, the ideal society is one which is classless and which is attained after the proletariat class rule. According to Vivekananda, 'If it is possible to form a state in which the knowledge of the priest period, the culture of the military, the distributive spirit of the commercial and the ideal of equality of the last, can all be kept in tact minus their evils, it will be an ideal state.'[59] Such is the ideal of an ideal society in which the coercive organ, the state, is not under the control of any particular class and in which are combined all the merits of different class states eliminating their deficiencies. 'But is it possible?' The realist in Vivekananda immediately raises the question. In the actual world no political organization or institution or even a society as a whole can be perfect or ideal. As we have seen already, Vivekananda has made it clear that society is always imperfect, and therefore, any of its organs have to be naturally imperfect. He has made his standpoint clear in the following statement : 'Objective society will always be a mixture of good and evil—objective life will be always followed by its shadow, death, and the longer the life, the longer will also be the shadow. In objective life, however, every bullet has its billet—evil goes with every good as its shadow. Every improvement is coupled with equal degradation... .'

Ideal Society : *A Myth* : 'If good is increasing so is evil. The progress of the world means more enjoyment and more misery too.'[60]

Hence the concept of an ideal society or a state is a myth, an utopia. Marxian concept of an ideal society which is classless and where the state withers away is logically therefore an utopia and this has also been proved by history so far. Even after seventy-two years of Russian revolution and after forty years of the Chinese revolution and the working of the proletariat class rule in various other countries for a prolonged period there is no

---

59. ibid., p. 320.

60. ibid., p. 319.

indication of a purely classless society or of the 'State' entering into the stage of withering away anywhere.

XII

THE ROLE OF THE ECONOMIC FORCES IN SOCIAL LIFE : SWAMI VIVEKANANDA'S VIEW

Swami Vivekananda did not consider the economic forces the only determinant of social life. Nor did he consider religion to be the sole factor. In his opinion economic forces also play a very important role in determining social changes. 'There (runs)', he points out, 'an economic struggle through every religious struggle. This animal called man has some religious influence, but he is guided by economy.' 'Individuals', he explains, 'are guided by something else, but the mass of mankind never made a move unless economy was (involved). You may (preach a religion that may not be perfect in every detail), but if there is an economic background (to it), and you have the most (ardent champions) to preach it, you can convince the whole country.'

Hence we find that he believed in religion and economic forces playing equally important roles in determining social changes. He considered also other factors important, e.g., inter-cultural contacts. He therefore considered a multiplicity of factors playing part but the most predominant factor being the inherent tendencies of a particular socio-cultural system.

Part IV

The Political Ideas

CHAPTER—15

The Concept of State and Government

I

It has already been pointed out that Vivekananda has thrown new light on most of the basic political concepts. The contribution that he has made by bringing out the undiscovered implications of these concepts is invaluable. However, it has so long escaped the notice of the most political philosophers and thinkers. In this part we will concentrate to analyse and assess his thoughts on political concepts.

Concept of the State : We have already traced Vivekananda's ideas on the emergence of the State,[1] the coercive organ of the society. We have seen that according to him, the State evolved among the civilized people, living in the plains, when they were attacked and plundered by the barbaric mountaineers and sea-side dwellers who lived on piracy and robbery. It evolved among the plains people when they formed larger groups in self-defence against the attacks of the plunderers and formed small kingdoms.

The Ideal State—Concept of Vivekananda : We have also scrutinized Vivekananda's concept of an ideal State. No class-state is ideal according to him. A state which combines all the merits of all the different class-states without their shortcomings would be an ideal state. But this concept, he himself does not think is practical. It is therefore, we may conclude, an utopia by his own admission. All States, ancient and modern, are imperfect. States of the future world also would be so.

---

1. Vide Chapters II and III.

II

IDEALISTIC THEORIES OF THE STATE : HEGEL, MARX AND VIVEKANANDA

The idealistic philosophers headed by Hegel hold that the State is an end in itself. According to the earlier philosophers, viz., Plato and Aristotle, in the State alone the individual is capable of living a good life and realizing the highest ends of his existence. State is regarded by them as an organ representing and containing within itself the individuals' all the social aspirations, and at the same time fulfilling all their needs. Hence the State's claim on individual allegiance is based on an absolute authority. Furthermore, the 'State' is according to them, a self-sufficient entity, identical with the entire society.

Hegel treats State as an 'omnipotent and omniscient' entity, 'divine in essence'. And therefore he holds that all its authority emanated from God on account of which he considers obedience to it a sacred duty of the citizens. Hence the individual, according to him, cannot have any right against the State. 'Nothing short of the State is the actualization of freedom', says Hegel. According to him further, the State is itself a real personality and has a real will.

General Will : This absolutist theory, as it is alternatively known, was popularized by the English philosophers, T. H. Green and Dr Bosanquet. Rousseau's theory of 'General Will', elaborated by Hegel, was further developed by Green. 'The General Will is a new entity over and above the sum of the individual wills and it is a new personality over and above the sum of the individual personalities and this is the personality of the State.'[2] Hence the 'General Will' of the State always supersedes the will of the people.

Marx and Engels on the nature of the 'State' : Opposing Hegel, Frederic Engels says, 'The cohesive forces of civilized society is the State, which in all typical periods is exclusively the State of the ruling class, and in all cases remains essentially a machine for keeping down the oppressed, the exploited

2. C.E.M. Joad—*Modern Political Theory.* Chapter on the 'Idealist Theory'.

class.'[3] Thus State does not, it is clear according to this statement, represent the will of all the individuals, but only the interest of the ruling class. In spite of this remark Karl Marx is also a defender of the absolute power of the State, since he wanted complete surrender of all individual rights to the supremacy of the State when proletariat rule is established after a revolution. 'In order to break-down', says Marx, 'the resistance of the bourgeoise, the workers invest the state with a revolutionary cry and a temporary form.' It follows that the State during the period of proletariat dictatorship is justified in using its instrument of coercive power, i.e., oppression and repression under the banner of the State in order to crush down the bourgeoise. 'Since the State is a temporary institution', says Engels, 'which is to be made use of in the revolution in order to suppress forcibly the opponents, it is perfectly absurd to talk about a free popular State.' Engels makes it further clear that society thus far being based upon class antagonisms, has need of the State. But when the proletariat seizes powers, 'It abolishes itself as proletariat, abolishes class distinction and class antagonism, abolishes also the State as State. . . . The State is not "abolished",' he modifies his own statement and says, 'it dies out.'[4] Lenin in his *State and Revolution* makes it clear that when a true classless society comes to be established at the end of the period of proletariat dictatorship, the State which is an instrument of class-rule 'will simply wither away', giving place to a free society of voluntary associations formed for the transactions of public business.[5]

Idealism and Vivekananda's Concept : Vivekananda has been classed as an idealist thinker of the school of Bosanquet and Green by Dr Biman Behari Mazumdar, an eminent Indian professor of Political Science.[6] Dr Mazumdar quotes the following passage from Vivekananda's *Modern India* in support of his view : 'The individual's life is in the life of the whole, ... apart from the whole, the individual's existence is

3. *Selected Works of Karl Marx and F. Engels*, Vol. II (1955), p. 294.
4. *Select Readings from Marx and Engels*, Vol. II, p. 138.
5. C.E.M. Joad—*Modern Political Theory*, p. 93.
6. *Vishwa-Vivek* (Vāk-Sāhitya), a Bengali book, p. 267.

inconceivable— this is an eternal truth and is the bedrock on which the universe is built.'[7] But by the term individual Vivekananda meant the few privileged belonging to the ruling class and by the term 'whole' he meant the underprivileged toiling masses, the multitude. This is apparent from the following statement of Vivekananda made in the same booklet : 'Whether the leadership of society be in the hands of those who monopolize learning or wield the power of riches or arms, the source of its power is always the subject masses. By so much as the class in power severs itself from this source, by so much it is sure to become weak.'[8]

Throughout the entire booklet Vivekananda argues in a forceful manner for the rights of the masses against the few in power. By inference it may be said therefore that he denies that a class-state has any right to absolute obedience of the people. We have seen already that in his view when the interests of the multitude is overthrown and 'when oppression steps into the place of protection' to provide which is the sacred and the bounden duty of the rulers, when 'the ruling class is interested only in sucking their blood in place of preservation', there is always 'fierce contest between the rulers and the subjects, and by its reaction and convulsion, are flung away the sceptre and the crown'.[9] Thus Vivekananda here upholds the rights of the masses to rise in revolution against the oppressive rule of a State dominated by a privileged class.

Hence it is clear that Vivekananda is not by any means an idealist who seeks to support absolute authority of the State over the lives of the people. Dr Mazumdar's view in this respect therefore seems untenable.

III

ORGANIC CONCEPT OF THE STATE : THE RIGHTS OF THE PEOPLE

We have already referred to the organic view of society as upheld by Vivekananda in connection with his views on social

---

7. *C. W.*, IV, p. 463.
8. ibid., p. 470.
9. Swami Vivekananda, *Modern India.*

change. So long organic theory was interpreted to mean by its proponents—among whom are Plato, Hobbes and Rousseau—that individuals are like the cells of an organism and hence have no meaningful existence apart from the whole which implies by inference that they cannot have any rights against the State. Only Herbert Spencer sought to give a different interpretation. He said, 'Society exists for the benefit of its members, not its members for the benefit of Society.'[10] But this individualistic philosophy of Herbert Spencer seemed to Richie and others wholly inconsistent with his organic theory of the State.[11]

Vivekananda, however, uses the organic theory very skilfully to prove that it is the rights of the people which supersede the rights of everybody else in society, even the rights of the State. 'Accumulation of power', he says, 'is as necessary as its diffusion, or rather more so. The accumulation of blood in the heart is an indispensable condition for life; its non-circulation throughout the body means death. For the welfare of society, it is absolutely necessary, at certain times, to have all knowledge and power concentrated in certain families or castes, to the exclusion of others, but that concentrated power is focussed for the time being, only to be scattered, broadcast over the whole of society in future. If this diffusion is withheld, the destruction of that society is, without doubt, near at hand.'[12]

Thus by using the organic concept with great ingenuity he establishes the rights of the masses to wealth, riches, education, culture and power—everything that the privileged classes exclusively enjoy in Society. The privileged class is the ruling class. Hence he says : 'Wisdom, knowledge, wealth, men, strength, prowess, and whatever else nature gathers and provides us with, are all only for diffusion, when the moment of need is at hand. We often forget this fact, put the stamp of "mine only" upon the entrusted deposits, and *pari passu*, we sow the seed of our own ruin!'[13] Here it is clear that the State is, according to him, only the custodian of the wealth of the subjects and the justification for its existence lies in its function of diffusing the same among the subjects, to whom all wealth actually belong.

---

10. Garner—*Political Science and Government*, p. 217.
11. ibid. 12. *C.W.*, IV, p. 458. 13. ibid., p. 464.

Instead the rulers make attempts to grab what is in their custody. Hence he further states, 'The king [meaning the 'State'], the centre of the forces of the aggregate of his subjects, soon forgets that those forces are only stored with him so that he may increase and give them back a thousand fold in their potency, so that they may spread over the whole community for its good.'[14] Thus the rights of the masses are absolute, according to Vivekananda, and not the authority of the State. Thus in his use of the organic theory there is no attempt to support absolutism of the State. He uses the theory with the opposite objective of justifying absolute rights of the people which the State is not justified in circumscribing by any means.

IV

VIVEKANANDA'S VIEW ON THE NATURE OF THE STATE

Since all worldly institutions are imperfect, society and its coercive organ the State are naturally imperfect. Vivekananda has also shown that the State has served as an instrument of exploitation from the earliest times. Describing the emergence of various classes and the origin of the State-power, as we have noted already, he says—'One tilled the ground, a second guarded the produce from being robbed, a third took it to another place, and a fourth bought it. . . . The protector came to be known as the king; he who took the commodities from one place to another was the merchant. These two did not produce anything—but still snatched away the best part of things, and made themselves fat by virtually reaping most of the fruits of the cultivator's toil and labour.'[15] Here Vivekananda has shown very clearly how the State functions in the interest of the ruling class serving in its hand as an instrument of exploitation.

Marx and Vivekananda on the nature of the 'State' : Here we find some similarity between the concepts of Karl Marx and Vivekananda. To both, the State is an instrument of exploitation in the hands of the ruling class. Both consider it as a class-organization.

But there are important differences between the concepts of

---

14. ibid.

15. ibid., V, p. 525.

the two thinkers. To Marx there is no harm if the proletariat State becomes absolute in character in its attempt to crush down the bourgeoise opposition. The State at this stage will be a totalitarian State, according to Marx, and the individuals will have no right to freedom against such a State. Thus this is the same theory of absolutism that was propounded by the idealist philosophers and the defenders of the organismic theory.

Vivekananda was not prepared to subscribe to any such idea which seeks to deny the freedom of the individuals. As we shall see later on, freedom of the individual was the kernel of all his social and political doctrines. 'Freedom is the first condition of growth'—he boldly asserted.

He never thought that privileges could disappear from society for good at any stage and therefore obviously he never thought also that the State could ever wither away. As soon as the old privileges are demolished, new ones are claimed. This is how the society is going on according to the evidence of history. The conflict between the privilege-making and the privilege-breaking forces are going on eternally. So long as these two go on playing, the coercive organ of the society cannot wither away. He never thought that in this imperfect world society can ever be completely perfect. Hence by inference we find that there is no possibility of the State withering away at any stage of social development.

Vivekananda on the Concept of a Stateless Society : In one place only Vivekananda speaks of the possibility of a Stateless society. While speaking about the Indian ideal of Brahminhood, we have seen he said, 'If the Brahmin is he who has killed all selfishness and who lives and works to acquire and propagate wisdom and the power of love—if a country is altogether inhabited by such Brahmins, by men and women who are spiritual and moral and good, is it strange to think of that country as being above and beyond all law? What police, what military are necessary to govern them? Why should anyone govern them at all?'[16] Hence, according to Vivekananda, a society can do without its coercive organ when all men are good and not under any other circumstance. And this is cent per cent

16. ibid., III, p. 197.

true. This is proved in recent history of Russia and China. There is corruption, there is selfishness today in these socialist states by admission of the rulers of these countries. Perfection of the social institutions cannot be attained and therefore ultimately social reforms only cannot solve human problems. For this it is necessary to have better kind of men. Until and unless that is achieved the coercive organ will stay to subserve the interests of the ruling class.

Thus so long as there is imperfection in the world, by inference, we find that according to Vivekananda the State cannot 'wither away'.

Professor Harold Laski on the crisis in the theory of the State : Accepting the Marxist view more or less, Professor Harold Laski opines that 'The State expresses a will to maintain a given system of class-relations.'[17] Any State, according to him, in which the instruments of production are privately owned, cannot by its inherent nature, provide a technique of peaceful change and cannot satisfy demand on the widest possible scale since it must subserve the interests of the private owners. Hence State power has to be captured by a revolution by those who are deprived. According to Professor Laski, it is necessary to limit the power of the State, since if uncontrolled it may turn into a Fascist State of which the capitalist State is only a miniature form and in a Fascist State 'the State power seeks total absorption of the individual within the framework of its coercive apparatus'. 'To limit its power', Professor Laski argues, 'we must destroy the class-structure of society, for the State is simply the executive instrument of the class in society which owns the means of production.'[18] Only then the State will certainly disappear.

This situation, according to Professor Laski, is a situation of crisis in the theory of the State. Marx and Engels, more particularly Lenin in his thesis on 'State and Revolution', have proclaimed the doom of the State. This is not possible to avert, according to Professor Laski. But as we have already pointed out, during the last seventy-two years since the Russian

17. Harold Laski, *Grammar of Politics*, p. iii, Introductory Chapter.
18. ibid., p. xiii.

Revolution and forty years since the Chinese Revolution the State in these countries has become more and more powerful, more and more authoritative. This has happened in the non-socialist countries as well, everywhere authority of the State have been extended and there is no sign of 'withering away' of the State in any country. Hence, there is no crisis threatening the existence of the State. Thus Professor Laski has read a false alarm in the existing secured situation.

Vivekananda thought quite sensibly and reasonably that in an imperfect world new forms of privileges will emerge which means the continuation of the State.

The Marxist theory of the State never takes into consideration human nature and the course of its working in history. This has been taken into account by Vivekananda and given due importance.

V

FORMS OF GOVERNMENT

The Government is the functional instrument of the State. The State functions through the agency of the Government which may have various forms.

Monarchy, Aristocracy and Polity were the three normal forms of Government according to Plato and Aristotle. Tyranny, Oligarchy and Democracy were the corresponding degenerated forms.

Vivekananda discusses in his 'Modern India' the following three forms of Government : (1) Aristocracy (i.e., Rule of the Wise), (2) Monarchy, and (3) Democracy.

Aristocracy : Vivekananda opposed Aristocracy, even if it was the Government of the wise 'seers'. First of all, because it is a rule by the few. In this respect he subscribed to the view of John Stuart Mill that 'A good Government is no substitute for self-government.' He opposed Aristocracy with all the forces that he had under his command. 'All knowledge is possessed', he observed, 'exclusively by some extraordinary great men, and those special personages take birth by the command of God, or in conformity to a higher law of nature. . . . If such a view be correct and certain, there seems to be no necessity for any individual to strive hard to find any new and original truth—all originality is lost to society... .'[19]

Vivekananda's views differ from the views of Plato and Aristotle in this respect. His views in this respect are strikingly original. According to him, even if it is a rule by the best of men with best of intentions and with highest knowledge, it does not prove good for society. Since if they are dictated by the wise, those ruled becomes bereft of all initiative and originality. A society in which the individuals are bereft of initiative and originality cannot advance, there is no doubt that a society ruled by the wise becomes confined within the narrow limits set by the few wise men. Explaining he observes : 'If it is finally settled that the path of human welfare is for ever chalked out by these omniscient men, society naturally fears its own destruction if the least deviation be made from the boundary line of the path, and so it tries to compel all men through rigid laws and threats of punishment to follow that path with unconditional obedience. If the society succeeds in imposing such obedience to itself by confining all men within the narrow groove of these paths, then the destiny of mankind becomes no better than that of a machine. ... The death of such a nation is not far to seek.'[20] Thus it is evident that Vivekananda does not accept a mechanical view of society and does not consider an unconditional subservience to the rule of the wise a virtue.

In *Modern India* he shows further that these men, who after attaining spiritual heights laid the foundation of philosophy and science, after a certain stage, start putting exclusive claims to good things of life, power, wealth, etc., which ultimately lead them to the path of degeneration. And this brings their downfall and thus society declines under their rule. Thus, on account of their exclusive claims, the rule of the wise in time degenerates into a regime of tyranny. The ruling class losing their grip over the source of their power, viz., spiritual knowledge, becomes instrumental in the decline of culture and this decline ultimately stiffles all progress. They monopolize education and culture because of which the subjects also degenerate and become weak.

19. *C. W.*, IV, p. 434.

20. ibid.

Monarchy : The usual practice in textbooks on political science is to discuss Monarchy first, since, perhaps, it is the oldest form of Government. Vivekananda discussed Aristocracy first since his discussions are based on Indian History mostly. In India there were the kings in the earliest days but they were under the control of the Brahmins or the sages. Hence it was virtually an Aristocracy of the Wise which prevailed in the earliest days in India. Later on, of course, a time came when the kings denied the authority of the Brahmins and there came absolute monarchs to rule.

The Doctrine of Divine Right : In his 'Modern India' Vivekananda penetratingly analyses the 'doctrine of the divine rights' on which Monarchy was based. In his opinion this was a clever device of the monarchs for grabbing absolute power. That centralization of power in the hands of a single person leads to oppression and tyrannizing of the masses in the extreme possible manner, has been brought out by him fully. The inevitable consequence, according to him, is either degeneration or revolution. 'Attributing all godship to him', says Vivekananda, 'in his pride, like king Vena (in *Bhāgavatam*), he looks upon other people as wretched specimens of humanity . . . any opposition to his will, whether good or bad, is a great sin on the part of the subjects.' Hence oppression steps in in place of preservation. If the society is weak it declines and is conquered by other powerful races. If the society is strong, revolution overthrows the regime.

Absolute Monarchy, according to Vivekananda, is therefore a regime of tyranny. Further, in his opinion, even if the kings are benevolent and are the dispensors of justice like Rāmachandra and Yudhiṣṭhira in the epics, or Aśoka and Akbar in the historical period, it cannot be ultimately good for the people since people remain dependent on the kings for their welfare and this, in his opinion, is not conducive to growth and welfare. Not only that development gets retarded but such benevolent monarchy is also self-destructive. 'Being always governed by kings of godlike nature', Vivekananda argues, 'to whom is left the whole duty of protecting and providing for the people, they can never get any occasion for understanding the principles of self-government.

Such a nation, being entirely dependent on the king for everything and never coming to exert itself for the common good or for self-defence, becomes gradually destitute of inherent energy and strength. If this state of dependence and protection continues long, it becomes the cause of destruction of the nation, and its ruin is not far to seek.'[21]

Democracy : According to Vivekananda, only democracy is conducive to the development and progress of society. Moreover, in his opinion, democracy is the only natural form of Government for a mature society. 'The voice of the ruled', he opines, 'in the government of their land ... of which the last expression has been echoed with a thundering voice in the Declaration [of Independence] of the American Government, in the words, "That the Government of the people of this country must be by the people and for the good of the people"—cannot however be said to have been totally unrecognized in ancient India.'[22] Actually, this was also the basis of the ancient system of village administration in India known as the Panchayat System. This, according to Vivekananda, is undoubtedly the best form of government since the ruled are in this case self-governed, independent of the patronizing influence of the others, so that their initiative, creativity and capacity grow which propels them on the path of progress.

Democracy not a mere form of Government : Democracy is not merely a form of Government to Vivekananda, it means a social system in which the supremacy of the toiling classes has been established. 'It is the evidence of history', he points out, 'that at a certain time, every society attains its manhood, when a strong conflict ensues betwen the ruling power and the common people. The life of the society, its expansion and civilization, depend on its victory or defeat in this conflict.' In his opinion the masses are the reservoir of all powers. He has shown how the Brahmin and the Kshatriya lost their supremacy being estranged from the subject masses. And the Vaishya who wield power in the present era are similarly getting estranged from the toiling people. It was therefore inevitable that the Shudras will come to seize power one of these days. It is in this connection that

21. ibid., p. 441.

22. ibid., p. 442.

Vivekananda made the prophesy that 'Yet, a time will come when there will be the rising of the Shudra class, with their Shudrahood', and pointed out also that 'Socialism, Anarchism, Nihilism and other like sects are the vanguard of the social revolution that is to follow.' Hence rule by the people means the social supremacy of the toiling people who forms the vast majority of the society. Hence with Vivekananda democracy means also a socialist society. It is not only a form of government but also a form of society.

CHAPTER 16

Democracy, Capitalism and Socialism

I

WESTERN DEMOCRACY

That Vivekananda considers true democracy possible only under Socialism has been mentioned in the previous chapter. This is also clear from his observations on western democracies based on capitalism. 'I have seen your parliament', he observes pointedly, 'your Senate, your vote, majority, ballot; it is the same thing everywhere, my friend. The powerful men in every country are moving society whatever way they like, and the rest are only like a flock of sheep.'[1] With penetrating historical insight he reveals that in the western democracies, 'They that have money have kept the government of the land under their thumb, are robbing the people and sending them as soldiers to fight and be slain on foreign shores, so that, in case of victory, their coffers may be full of gold bought by the blood of the subject-people on the field of battle.'[2] This brief comment has thrown a mass of light on the conditions of the subject-people, who were exploited and murdered. He has made it clear that the nature of democracy under capitalism, as we find it in the western countries, deviates from the ideology and philosophy of democracy preached by its proponets. 'A true democracy exists only when the dominating characteristics is human'—says Dr D. Burns. This is so when 'reason governs the conscience of men'. 'Democracy as an ideal is a society . . . not of similar persons but of equal', adds Burns, who says also that 'in a true democracy no one can avoid his share of the moral responsibility for the action performed in the name and for the interests of all.' 'In a democracy,' as stated by

---

1. *C. W.*, V, p. 461. 2. ibid., p. 462.

Burns again, 'the government is responsible in the political sense, i.e., the government must answer to the people but this makes the moral responsibility of the people more obvious.'[3]

In the capitalist countries, neither does reason govern, nor are the people equal in participating in their so-called 'democratic' governments. Vivekananda was not an admirer of the British or the American type of democracy, although he quoted from the American Constitution in his *Modern India* while trying to define democracy as 'the government of the people, by the people, for the people'. His emphatic view in this respect is revealed in the following caustic remark : 'All these things you hear about constitutional government, freedom, liberty and parliaments are mere jokes.'[4] The remark amply makes clear his actual view on western democracies.

CAPITALISM, IMPERIALISM AND DEMOCRACY

Vivekananda was quite aware of the fact that 'the western world is governed by a handful of Shylocks', i.e., by the capitalists. He was also aware of the nature of the capitalist society 'which', in his own words, 'turns the worker into a mere appendage of machines'. As stated aptly by E. P. Chelishev, '. . . he [Vivekananda] relentlessly exposed the disastrous effects of capitalist competition, the quest for profit, the fabulous luxury of the handful of exploiters and the abject impoverishment and rightlessness of the millions of toilers.'[5] In Vivekananda's own words : 'Tremendous power is being acquired by the manufacture of machines and other appliances, and privilege is claimed today as it never has been claimed in the history of the world.'[6]

Capitalism : Vivekananda did not fail to observe also how capitalism led to the growth of giant combinations with crushing power of exploitation and ferocious struggle for supremacy among the various capitalist nations. As pointed out by Romain

3. Dr D. Burns, *Political Ideals*, Oxford University Press, 1949, pp. 277-78.
4. *Vivekananda Centenary Memorial Volume* (published by the Vivekananda Centenary Committee, 1963), p. 554.
5. Article by E. P. Chelishev in *Swami Vivekananda : Studies in Soviet Union*, edited by Swami Lokeswarnanda.
6. *C. W.*, I, p. 425.

Rolland : '. . . he [Vivekananda] had discovered the spirit of lucre, of greed, of Mammon, with its enormous combinations and ferocious struggles for supremacy. He was capable of rendering homage to the grandeur of a mighty association. . . . But what beauty was there among a pack of wolves?'[7] Thus to Vivekananda these big capitalistic combinations were nothing but a pack of wolves. With these big combinations dominating over the political field, political democracy becomes a mockery, since the masses are too weak to assert their rights against them.

Imperialism : Capitalism at this mature stage (i.e., when giant combinations emerge), manifests symptoms of what has come to be known as 'Imperialism'. As we have seen earlier, he slashed and flayed British imperialism of which he had a direct experience as an Indian. His criticism of the British rule brought out threadbare the consequences of Imperialism as such. This is how he describes the horrors of Imperialism : '... they have their heels on our necks, they have sucked the last drop of our blood for their own pleasures, they have carried away with them millions of our money, while our people have starved in villages and provinces.'[8] Here he shows to what extent 'economic drain' or squeezing of the Indian economy by the imperialistic rulers impoverished India. He has shown also to what extent this exploitation enriched the imperialistic nations.

This squeezing was often made through foreign trade. Describing how this squeezing was executed through the Indian foreign trade he says : 'Up till a century ago, the whole of the world's demand for cotton, jute, indigo, lac, rice, diamonds, and pearls, etc., used to be supplied from India. . . . The fortune of India smiled on Portugal—then came the turn of the French, the Dutch, the Danes, and the English. Indian commerce, Indian revenue and all are now in the possession of the English... .'[9] 'This', he adds, 'the Europeans are unwilling to admit. That India, the India of "natives", is the chief means and resource of their wealth and civilization, is a fact which they refuse to admit, or even understand.'[10]

---

7. Romain Rolland, *Life of Vivekananda*, p. 151.
8. *C. W.*, VII, p. 280.
9. ibid., pp. 357-58.
10. ibid., p. 358.

Thus Vivekananda has shown clearly that the prosperity of the imperialistic countries has been built up with the resources squeezed from the colonial countries like India. It must be remembered that Vivekananda wrote all these long before Lenin wrote his famous treatise 'Imperialism'. This shows the depth of his historical insight, his capacity of visualizing things much ahead of others. Thus long before Lenin, Vivekananda 'unveiled the brutal face of western Imperialism and looked into its eyes, full of rapatious hatred'.[11] Unveiling this brutal face of imperialism he pointed out : 'The wealth and power of a country are in the hands of a few men who do not work but manipulate the work of millions of human beings. By this power they can deluge the whole earth with blood.'[12] No doubt, this is the essence of Imperialism—the capacity for deluging the earth with blood. Its essence is devastating wars between the imperialist powers to get hold over the colonies. All these have been clearly brought out by Vivekananda in his pointed observations quoted above.

Obviously under such a situation democracy means not the government of all the people but of those few only who have power over the labour and life of the millions. Hence he observes that constitutional government, liberty and parliaments are mere jokes, and vote, ballot, majority and all such paraphernalia of representative government are meaningless show-offs.

Lenin's View of Democracy under Capitalism : As regards the nature of democracy under capitalism there is some similarity between the views of Vivekananda and Lenin. 'In capitalist society', Lenin observes, '. . . this democracy is always bound by the narrow framework of capitalist exploitation, and consequently always remains, in reality, a democracy for the minority only—for the possessing classes, only for the rich. Freedom in capitalist society always remains just about the same as it was in the ancient Greek republics : freedom for the slave-owners. The modern wage-slaves owing to the conditions of capitalist exploitation, are so much crushed by want and poverty that democracy is nothing to them . . . that, in the ordinary peaceful

---

11. Romain Rolland, *Life of Vivekananda*, p. 150.
12. *C. W.*, III, p. 158.

course of events, the majority of population is debarred from participating in social and politcal life.'[13] This is also the essence of Vivekananda's statements quoted above.

Lenin's Solution : *the Dictatorship of the Proletariat; Vivekananda's Recommendation* : *More Effective Democracy* : But the difference between them lies in respect of what is to be done in view of the situation. Lenin recommends total banishment of democratic form of government and replacing it by proletariat dictatorship after a revolution. Vivekananda suggests making democratic government more effective with policies for helping an evolutionary process of natural growth of the proletariat regime.

II

SOCIALISM AND THE RULE OF THE PROLETARIAT

We have already seen that Vivekananda predicted that in the coming age it is Shudras or the proletariat who will come to assume power and the vanguards of this great impending event are Socialism, Anarchism and Nihilism and such other doctrines. In fact the precision of Vivekananda's predictions in this matter seem astounding. According to Sister Christine's *Memoirs*, Vivekananda said in 1896 : 'The next great upheaval which is to bring about a new epoch, will come from Russia or China. I cannot quite see which, but it will be either Russia or China.'[14] This proved true, it was first ushered in Russia and next in China. That this precision was due to his deep historical insight and vast knowledge of the life of the masses all over the world is evident from his following remark : 'In both the countries [Russia and China] the huge masses of people are oppressed and downtrodden.'[15] The vast majority in Russia and China were tyrannized and exploited. Hence it was natural that an upsurge of these people was to take place in these countries against the regime of oppression. This is how Vivekananda argued and made

---

13. V. I. Lenin, *State and Revolution*, Chapter 5, Section 2.
14. *Reminiscences of Swami Vivekananda* by His Eastern and Western Admirers, pp. 187-88.
15. ibid.

astoundingly precise prophecies. Dr Bhupendra Nath Dutta, the younger brother of Swami Vivekananda, himself a sociologist and a Marxist, has aptly pointed out that Vivekananda did foretell about the proletariat rule when 'the Bolsheviks had not risen as yet, and the world had not heard anything of the theory of the dictatorship of the proletariat'.[16] As we all know, Marxian prediction was that the proletariat would ascend to power in the mature capitalist countries. History proved Vivekananda's prediction true and not the Marxian one.

Vivekananda not only predicted that 'a time will come when the Shudras in every country . . . will gain absolute supremacy', but also that 'we are to solve the problem of the Shudra, but oh! through what tumults, through what tumults'. Commenting on this utterance Sister Nivedita writes—'He spoke like one gazing direct into the future, and his voice had the ring of prophecy.' And he said this when socialism had not taken a revolutionary turn and Lenin's Gospel of Revolution, viz., *State and Revolution* was still in the womb of the future. Proletariat revolution was yet a dream undreamt of even by its sponsor of 1917. Hence naturally Romain Rolland wondered how could Vivekananda in those early days make prophecies of the days of war and revolutions that were approaching.

Vivekananda's Vision of Mass Uprising : Actually Vivekananda had a clear vision of the future when the toiling masses would march on to power and the upper classes would disappear in the void. He was convinced that the rule of the Shudras was certainly to dawn in India also just as in other countries. In his own inimitable language he described his own vision of this transformation in India—'... upper classes of India', he says addressing the bourgeoise, 'do you think you are alive? You are but mummies ten thousand years old! ... and it is you who are the real "walking corpses". ... You represent the past tense... . Fleshless and bloodless skeletons of the dead body of Past India that you are, why do you not quickly reduce yourselves into dust and disappear in the air? Ay, on your bony fingers are some priceless rings of jewel, treasured up by your ancestors. . . . Now under the British rule, in these days of free education and

16. Dr Bhupendranath Dutta, *Swami Vivekananda—The Patriot-Prophet*, p. 10.

enlightenment, pass them on to your heirs. . . . You merge yourselves in the void and disappear, and let New India arise in your place. Let her arise—out of the peasants' cottage, grasping the plough; out of the huts of the fisherman, the cobbler, and the sweeper. Let her spring from the grocer's shop, from beside the oven of the fritter-seller. Let her emanate from the factory, from marts, and from markets. Let her emanate from groves and forests, from hill and mountains.'[17]

This is the great vision of the future events when the masses would be rising to power on the ashes of the upper classes.

The Process of Transformation as visualized by Vivekananda : In a brilliant exposition Professor Ernest P. Horrwitz has described the process of transformation from the present to the future order of society as envisaged by Vivekananda. 'Vivekananda loathed the bourgeoise', writes Professor Horrwitz, 'and loved the proletariat. The former money-making and pleasure-loving are utterly selfish and a danger to real progress. Peasants, cobblers, sweepers have more self-reliance and capacity for work than the contemptible middlemen who call themselves educated. Through long ages the proletariat has silently worked and produced the world's wealth, without a complaint to their heartless slave drivers. Modern education brings the depressed classes to the fore, and shows the inferiority complex of burgherdom. Money is dead capital, the nation's living wealth is hard personal labour which builds body, mind and soul. Neo-Vedanta preaches the gospel of labour, as the *Gītā* does. Sooner or later the capable and industrious worker will get in position above the middleman, that imbecile and parasite of society. Capital drifts into the hands of the worker whose skill is Yoga. . . . He is a hero, a brave fellow, a lion in human shape, the wealth approaches him. . . .'[18]

It is evident from this exposition that the labourers who have efficiency will be coming inevitably to own capital and control the productive system and there is certainly to take place, as a result, a 'root and branch' reform in society— i.e., a change in

---

17. *C. W.*, VII, pp. 326-27
18. *Sri Ramakrishna in the Eyes of Brahmo and Christian Admirers* by Nanda Mukherjee, Firma KLM Private Ltd. (1975), pp. 114-15.

property relations and in social arrangements. This was very clearly visualized by Vivekananda in his great prophetic vision.

Not Destruction, but Growth : Of course, it is true, that Vivekananda does not think in terms of destroying the present social order through violent means since he believes in growth and not in forcibly imposing something on society. In his opinion, the growth was to take place in pursuance of nature's laws. This is mentioned in his following significant statement : 'Those uncared for lower classes of India—the peasants and weavers and the rest . . . it is they who from time immemorial have been working silently, without even getting the remuneration of their labours! But what great changes are taking place slowly, all over the world, in pursuance of nature's laws! Countries, civilizations and supremacy are undergoing revolutions.'[19] Here he speaks of natural laws operating slowly but surely.

This evolutionary theory of Vivekananda may be criticized, but so may be the 'revolutionary' theory as we shall presently see. Marx also is a supporter of the evolutionary theory when he shows that capitalism will succumb to its inner contradictions giving place to socialism in course of time. This theory was given an extremely revolutionary mould by Lenin. Anyway, there is no doubt that Vivekananda envisaged far reaching changes, social and institutional, to take place so that the entire social order would be transformed in a revolutionary manner.

Lenin and Vivekananda : In view of the far-reaching changes in respect of the social arrangements envisaged by Vivekananda it is not surprising that Professor Ernest P. Horrwitz discovers a great affinity between Vivekananda and Lenin, 'the respective founders of Neo-Vedanta and New Russia'.[20] According to Professor Horrwitz, the aims of Neo-Vedanta was realized in the soils of Soviet Russia in spite of its avowed atheism. 'The Chrysalis of divinity', he says, 'has turned into the butterfly of humanity, that fairest flower in the garden of the soul.'[21] Hence he urges : 'Neo-Vedantists must show themselves worthy of Ramakrishna's legacy. His clients are duty bound to uphold by

19. *C. W.*, VII, p. 358.
20. *Sri Ramakrishna in the Eyes of Brahmo and Christian Admirers*, p. 113.
21. ibid., p. 112.

cultural means, a classless society.'[22] Here, of course, the fundamental difference between Lenin and Vivekananda has come out. The means that were sought to be used by Lenin was violent political revolution, but the means sought to be used by Vivekananda were the 'cultural means'. Obviously 'cultural means' are not by any means violent.

III

WESTERN SOCIALISM

In the West the term 'Socialism' was first used in the Poor Man's Guardian in 1833. According to another opinion, the name 'Socialism' came to be known in the year 1835 when Robert Owen, a successful capitalist, founded 'The Association of all Classes in all Nations'. Actually Socialism was the child of the two great revolutions—(1) Industrial Revolution; (2) the revolution in thought that found best expression in France. St Simon was the fore-runner of the socialist thought. Robert Owen also dreamt of a social order free from the perversions of the competitive society. He wanted to establish producers' co-operatives in order to usher in a new social order. The tradition of this utopian socialism actually began from Plato. In his 'Republic' he elaborated the plan of a social order in which property was to be held in common and injustice was to be unknown. Robert Owen and Fourier and their followers made attempts to work out their plans in actual life but met with failures.

As we know already, Marx is the first scientific writer who made attempts to show that inevitably in the course of social development the socialist ideal would be realized.

Marxist Concept : As we have seen already, the Marxist concept of Socialism is based on (1) the theory of Surplus Value; (2) Materialistic conception of History, and (3) the theory of Dialectics.

Marx's theory has given rise to both (1) evolutionary and (2) revolutionary schools of thought. When Marx describes the evolution of society ushered in through technological changes

22. ibid.

and manifested through various stages, it appears that the socialistic stage is a natural growth. The theory of the evolutionary school following Marx came to be known as collectivism or State Socialism. In contrast to this evolutionary school, the other school, the revolutionary school, points out that the present capitalist society is composed of two opposed classes, the haves and the have-nots. The evolutionary process is slow hence a revolution is necessary to hasten the next transformation of society. The 'haves' are to be made by force to relinquish state-power in favour of the 'have-nots'. This revolutionary theory has come to be known as Communism.

Communism and Revolution : The word 'Communism' was given a special meaning in the *Communist Manifesto* of Marx and Engels. Early Christians used this term to mean a society in which property is held in common. Communism in the Marxist sense is essentially a theory of method—method of transforming one type of society into another, from capitalism to socialism, for example. The two main doctrines of communism are : (1) Class War, and (2) Revolution, i.e., forcible seizure of power by the proletariat. Thus this is a deviation from the other Marxist doctrine that the era of capitalism would end as a result of the contradictions inherent in the very nature of capitalism and socialism would automatically emerge.

Lenin's Concept : Lenin and his followers consider revolution a must for accomplishing the transformation of capitalism to socialism. Again there are two distinct stages of revolutionary process according to this school : (a) a transitional revolutionary stage—the stage of the proletariat domination over the state; (b) a communistic classless stage in which the state as the coercive organ of a class-society disappears.

IV

VIVEKANANDA'S CONCEPT OF SOCIALISM

In spite of the affinity between Vivekananda and Lenin as shown by Professor Horrwitz, there are fundamental differences between western Socialism particularly of the Marxist-Leninist brand and Vivekananda's concept of Vedantic Socialism based on the doctrine of divinity of man. In Vivekananda's privilege-free society based on the Vedantic world view, not only does the toiling classes attain their full rights as in the case of Marxist socialist state, but also in such a social order all human interests are guided and controlled according to the ultimate idea of spirituality of life.

Vedanta as the basis of Communism : Vivekananda was convinced that the western brand of communistic society cannot last unless based on the foundation of spirituality. Vedanta was, in his opinion, eminently suitable for serving as the basis of a communistic society. And he was able to convince some of the revolutionaries on this point. In an interview given in the West he made this revealing statement : 'All the social upheavalists, at least the leaders of them, are trying to find that all their communistic or equalizing theories must have a spiritual basis, and that spiritual basis is in the Vedanta only. I have been told by several leaders who used to attend my lectures, that they required the Vedanta as the basis of the new order of things.'[23] Speaking on the mission of the Vedanta he again said, 'Europe wants it (Vedanta) today just as much our downtrodden masses do, and this great principle is even now unconsciously forming the basis of all the latest political and social aspirations that are coming up in England, in Germany, in France, and in America.' Thus as Vivekananda claims, in their genesis, socialism and communism are Vedantic ideas.

V

INDIVIDUALISM AND VIVEKANANDA'S SOCIALISM

Vivekananda, however, never approved of the sacrifice of the individual to the absolute supremacy of society, which is the essence of the Marxist brand of Socialism. While giving his own views on the matter Vivekananda observes : 'You and I—each is *vyaṣṭi* (the part), society is *samaṣṭi* (the whole). . . . Whether or not *vyaṣṭi* has individual freedom, and if it has, what should be its measure, whether or not *vyaṣṭi* should completely sacrifice its own will, its own happiness for *samaṣṭi*—are the perennial

23. *C. W.*, V, pp. 212-13.

problems before every society. ... These, like big waves, are agitating modern Western society.'[24] Defining Socialism and Individualism from this point of view he says, 'The doctrine which demands the sacrifice of individual freedom to social supremacy is called Socialism, while that which advocates the cause of the individual is called individualism.'[25]

Consequences of Social Supremacy : *Retardation of the Growth of the Individual* : From this point of view he found affinity between Socialism and the old Indian social system. The latter like the socialistic system of Marx was based on the idea of the supremacy of the social system over the individual. Indian social system, in addition, recognized a system of social hierarchy. In this system, as in Socialism, the individuals were required to sacrifice their freedom to the supremacy of the Great Society. The consequence, as pointed out by Vivekananda, has proved disastrous for India from the point of view of individual growth and happiness as well as from the point of view of society's progress. 'The consequence', says Vivekananda, 'one good result, the rest evil. It produced skill in one or two things well, having practised them every day through generations.'[26] Giving examples he says, 'With the simple mechanism of an antediluvian loom, worth one rupee, and the feet put in a pit, it is possible to make kincobs, worth twenty rupees a yard, in this country alone. A torn mat, an earthen lamp, and that fed by castor oil—with the aid of materials such as these, wonderful savants are produced in this country alone.'[27] But this artistic skill and intellectual attainment were not all. Much more important was the life of the multitude. Under the system the multitude had little scope for development of their faculties.

'But all these things', he points out referring to the life of the masses, 'are done by people like lifeless machines; there is no mental activity, no unfoldment of the heart, no vibration of life, no flux of hope; there is no strong stimulation of the will, no experience of keen pleasure, nor the contact of intense sorrow; there is no stir of inventive genius, no desire for novelty, no appreciation of new things. Clouds never pass away from this mind. . . . It never occurs to the mind if there is any better state

24. *Letters of Swami Vivekananda.* 25. ibid. 26. ibid. 27. ibid.

than this, where it does it cannot convince, in the event of conviction, effort is lacking and even where there is effort, lack of enthusiasm kills it out.'[28] Thus he shows that under a system of social supremacy over the individuals, human intellect stagnates, there is no development of the heart, inventive genius is lacking, will, conviction, effort, and enthusiasm die out. What is the result? Society becomes static, it stagnates and declines. These are serious consequences. Hence he asks : 'Can that be called a society which is formed by an aggregate of men who are like lumps of clay?'[29]

Experience of the Soviet Union : That this is exactly the case with the Soviet Union* is apparent from President Gorbachov's reports in 1987 and 1988 to the Party Congress. According to these reports, there have taken place degradation and stagnation of the individual, loss of initiative and effort and decline of rationality in him, resulting in the retardation of economic growth and social progress. And as we shall see presently, the Soviet leaders had to concede liberalisation of the system and curb down the supremacy of society.

This proves the truth of Vivekananda's findings about the evils of absolute social supremacy over the life of the individuals. He firmly declares : 'It is more blessed . . . even to go wrong impelled by one's free will and intelligence than to be good as an automation.'[30] 'Freedom is the first condition of growth,' he reminds us time and again. Truly without freedom no progress is possible.

Individual Liberty—Essential for Socialism : Hence it appears, as shown by Vivekananda convincingly, that without individual liberty socialism is not able to deliver the goods. Hence political democracy is a necessary concomitant of socialism. If socialism is to survive it must sanction revival of democracy.

Vedanta and Individual Liberty : As Vivekananda's socialism is firmly rooted in Vedanta, emancipation of the individual from

28. ibid. 29. ibid.

* Subsequently, the Soviet Union was disintegrated in the year 1991. Presently it is known as Confederation of Independent States.

30. ibid.

every kind of servitude—political, economic, social as well as servitude to nature—is its avowed goal. Vedanta proclaims the supremacy of the spirit over matter and it upholds a spiritual concept, of man as we have already noted. According to this concept, man is a free agent and therefore he must be granted utmost liberty for his free and independent growth. Hence says Vivekananda : 'To advance oneself towards freedom, physical, mental, and spiritual— and help others to do so, is the supreme prize of man.'[31]

Hence Vivekananda does not subscribe to a view of socialism in which individual liberty is sacrificed. His concept of socialism is deeply rooted in individualism, however anachronistic it may sound. This is clear from his following statement also : 'The greatest goodness is the highest freedom. Our aim should be to allow the individual to move towards this freedom.'[32]

VEDANTIC SOCIALISM : SOCIALISM BASED ON INDIVIDUALISM

Vivekananda's concept of Vedantic socialism is therefore a unique one. It is an admixture—a theory blend of socialism and individualism—apparently irreconcilable ideals, but which it is possible to reconcile on the basis of Vedanta as according to it an individual is a manifestation of the total unity, of Brahman.

Dr D. Burns at the end of his analysis of socialism in his treatise on *Political Ideals* observes significantly : 'If we could imagine an ideal at once individualistic and socialistic such would be the effective ideal for most thinking men . . . the individualist is right in aiming at the variety of individuals and so is the socialist in impressing on all their common interest; for the fullest development of each is to be found in the performance of his function in the life of the whole.'[33]

Regimentation : Opposing the trend towards regimentation in the present day socialist states, Burns observes : 'Society is an organic whole; and as in a tree the health of the cells in leaf and root is the health of the whole organism, so also is society, without distinct individuals with fully free and various

31. ibid. 32. *C. W.*, VI, p. 100.
33. Dr D. Burns, *Political Ideals*, p. 275.

development, the whole decays no less than it would without interdependence between its component parts.'[34]

This seems like an echo of Vivekananda's view discussed above. 'Individuality in universality', says Vivekananda, 'is the plan of creation. Each cell has its part in bringing about a consciousness. Man is individual and at the same time universal. It is while realizing our individual nature that we realize even our national and universal nature.'[35] In his opinion further, 'There cannot be life, even in the plant, without the idea of freedom. In the plant or in the worm, life has to rise to the individual concept. . . . you cannot move or live without the idea of freedom.'[36] He urges therefore : 'All must struggle to be individuals—strong, standing on your own feet, thinking your own thoughts, realizing your own Self. No use swallowing doctrines others pass on—standing up together like soldiers in jail, sitting down together, all eating the same food, all nodding their heads at the same time. Variation is the sign of life. Sameness is the sign of death.'

No fetters on Individual Freedom : Hence, according to Vivekananda, no fetters should ever be imposed on individual freedom so that the individual may grow freely to his full stature. Bondage can never bring any good to any one. He makes this clear through the following questions : 'Can dirt be washed by dirt? Can bondage be removed by bondage? Where is the instance?'[37] As he was a realist he could not accept a proposition like this that bondage can bring freedom without an empirical evidence, the evidence of history. For the goal of socialism is after all individualistic—the ultimate liberation of all the individuals in society. And this was the view of Marx himself. 'Marx', says John Elster, 'apparently believed that communism would be characterized by the full and free self-realization of the individual.'[38] But this can never be attained in the end if freedom is sacrificed at the beginning since the grinding supremacy of the society will produce only mental dwarfs, incapable of any creative activity.

---

34. ibid.
35. *C. W.*, VI, p.121.
36. ibid., I, p. 336.
37. ibid., IV, p. 491.
38. John Elster, *Making Sense of Marx* (Cambridge University Press, 1985), p. 522.

Hence Vivekananda opposed the very idea of coercion in any manner however noble might be the cause. He said thundering, 'I say liberate, undo the shackles of the people as much as you can.'[39]

At the end of his essay *On Liberty*, J. S. Mill said, 'The worth of a state in the long run is the worth of the individuals, composing it; and a state which postpones the interests of their mental expansion and elevation to a little more of administrative skill . . . a state which dwarfs its men in order that they may be more docile instruments in its hand even for beneficial purposes—will find that with small men no great thing can really be accomplished, and that the perfection of the machinery to which it has sacrificed everything will in the end avail it nothing, for want of the vital power which, in order that the machine might work more smoothly, it has preferred to banish.'[40] This classical defence of liberty of the individual is also the very essence of Vedantic thought, the best exponent of which in the modern era is Vivekananda. His entire exposition of Vedanta sounds like a saga of human emancipation.

Hence, though an ardent socialist—Vivekananda himself declares himself to be so—he is at the same time an ardent individualist. He has succeeded in blending socialism and individualism into a system where the socialistic ends would be achieved with the full play of individual freedom.

VII

DICTATORSHIP AND TOTALITARIANISM

Obviously the idea of complete freedom of the individuals at all levels and always, does not conform to the idea of dictatorship or totalitarianism at any stage. As aptly pointed out by Burns, 'Socialism will come, it is inevitable but the means prescribed for attaining it, viz., "dictatorship" and "totalitarianism" have been questioned.'[41] 'The end may survive', he adds, 'as a hope even

39. *Letters of Swami Vivekananda*, p. 420.
40. John Stuart Mill, *Utilitarianism, Liberty, and Representative Government*, London, 1931, p. 170.
41. *Political Ideals*, p. 275.

when the means first adopted to attain it have been shown to be ineffective.' Finally he concludes with the significant observation : 'And like all other ideals also its embodiment will probably prove its deficiency; for there is no panacea for human needs, and other dreams will follow and realization even of the most glorious that we could now conceive.'[42]

This seems to conform to Vivekananda's Vedantic view that a society is a constant flux, it can never be perfect and that new dreams were inevitably to replace the old. Vedanta is in essence a 'gospel of perpetual revolution'. Hence he said, 'I am a Socialist not because it is a perfect system, but half-a-loaf is better than no bread.'[43] He was fully aware of the shortcomings of the western socialist ideal of the contemporary period, still he wanted its benefits to be reaped fully by the dispossessed, the Shudras, who were mercilessly exploited for centuries. But he was the last person to lend support to dictatorship or totalitarianism, having always held high the ideal of complete freedom of the individuals, this being the great Vedantic ideal.

VIII

DEMOCRACY AND SOCIALISM

The Marxist Idea : As regards democracy and Socialism, the Marxian view is based upon the conviction that under the conditions of capitalistic exploitation, democracy is not and cannot be a reality. According to Marx, so long as the masses are sunk in poverty and ignorance it is idle to talk about individual freedom, since they cannot under the circumstances use their rights properly to determine their government. They have no freedom to do so since they are compelled to sell their labour to the highest bidder. The structure of government under capitalism may be in form democratic but the repository of authority in society is not the popularly elected government since it is dictated and used by those who have economic power by dint of their capacity to possess and control the means of production.

According to Marx, when the era of capitalism will terminate, the transitional stage would be of necessity that of a

---

42. ibid.

43. *Letters of Swami Vivekananda*, p. 417.

dictatorship since it will be necessary to suppress the bourgeoise. As viewed by him dictatorship of the proletariat would mean a stage of democracy of the exploited, not the democracy of the entire population, for it would not obviously express the real will of the exploiters. 'Thus', as pointed out by C. E. M. Joad, 'before the revolutionary period pure democracy is found to be inoperative, and during the revolutionary period it is declared to be impracticable.'[44] Democracy both before and after revolution are partial, before revolution it expresses the will of the exploiters, after revolution the will of the exploited only.

No future for Democracy in Marxism : As pointed out by Burns, 'Democracy as an ideal is . . . a society not of similar persons but of equals... .'[45] Hence the democratic ideal can be realized only in a society in which all its members are equal, that is to say, in a classless society where every man is equal to the other. But, according to Marx, as we have seen, in a classless society State does not exist, hence there is no need for a government which functions on behalf of the State. Therefore by inference we find that democracy as a form of government has no future according to the strict Marxian doctrine.

IX

RECENT MOVEMENTS FOR DEMOCRACY IN THE SOCIALIST COUNTRIES

In spite of the strict Marxian view in this respect, in almost all the socialist countries today there is a strong demand for democracy as a form of government among the people who all belong to the proletariat class. The trend first made its appearance in the European countries under the domination of the Soviet Union and it came to be known as Euro-communism. But this trend seems to have engulfed Russia itself subsequently. The result being 'Perestroika' and 'Glasnost'—two recently introduced liberal policies of gradual democratization of the political system in the Soviet Union. The movement has, of late, captured the imagination of the young and the elite in China also,

44. C.E.M. Joad, *Modern Political Theory*, p. 97.
45. Dr D. Burns, *Political Ideals*, p. 278.

where, of course, the government has chosen to go the Stalinist way and suppress it forcibly with the aid of the armed forces.

Euro-Communism : The term Euro-communism was coined in June 1975 by a non-communist Italian journalist. But the trend was first visible in the fifties of this century, Euro-communist parties have come to be formed in Italy, France and Spain, and Euro-communist influences are visible on the Communist parties of European countries like Denmark, Sweeden, Norway, Iceland, Greece, Great Britain and Finland, as well as in the non-European countries like Japan, Australia and Venezuela.[46]

THE MAIN TENETS OF EURO-COMMUNISM

No Monolithic World Communist Movement : Euro-communists first of all assert that the concept of a monolithic world Communist movement is wrong. They assert the need for the Communists in each country to determine their own policies based on their particular traditions and on the economic, political and cultural peculiarities and uniqueness of their own country. They also criticize the repressive measures that were used at one time within the Soviet Union and the eastern European countries.

Unification of Socialism and Democracy : But what is of greatest significance is that they proclaim that socialism and democracy may be happily united. They reject the theory of violent revolution and the need for dictatorship of the proletariat. They are convinced that there is a democratic road to Socialism. It may be brought through the will of the majority of the people. When a majority supporting Socialism is represented in the parliament it is Socialism which would obviously come and prevail. Thus consent of the people is an important principle professed by the Euro-communists.

Religion to be Allowed : Moreover, it is important to note that the Euro-communists strongly reject atheism and they support liberal policy with regard to the question of religion.

Pluralistic Democratic Model : Euro-communists in fact advocate a pluralistic democratic model of socialism in which democratic freedom and participation by all citizens in national affairs are guaranteed. In the Euro-communist's view the system

46. Wolfgang Leonard, *Euro-Communism*, New York, p. 1.

in the USSR (before the era of *Perestroika*) and the satellite countries was too monopolistic, too dictatorial, too centralized and too bureaucratic. Hence such a system is not suitable for a modern industrially developed country with a democratic tradition.

On the whole, it is clear that Euro-communists are committed to democracy, pluralism, religious liberalism, indepedence and freedom of the individual. All these are, however, irreconcilable with our past conceptions of communism of the Marxist-Leninist-Stalinist brand.

Rejects the Model of October Revolution : Moreover, the Euro-communists are of the opinion that the model of October Revolution of 1917 in Russia is not the only model for transition to socialism for all countries at all times. For example, the situation in the developed capitalist countries with democratic traditions is basically different from the situation in Russia in 1917, Russia being at the time an underdeveloped country and without any democratic tradition. Hence the model must have to be, of necessity, different in the case of the developed capitalist countries.

Multi-Party System and Voting by Secret Ballot : Finally, Euro-communism recognizes a multi-party system and the system of election by secret ballot. Parliament under Euro-communism is to be the most important instrument for formulating and promulgating the socialist institutions. But that does not mean that radical changes, a thorough transformation of social relations and institutions will not take place. Thus, according to the Euro-communists a transition from capitalism to socialism is possible with the consent of the population and within the parliamentary framework and with a multi-party system. This process may be termed as the process of bloodless revolution with peaceful means. Euro-communists express faith in bloodless revolution with peaceful means.

Though there are differences between various Euro-communist exponents, yet there are agreements on the whole on essential matters like the necessity of preserving the democratic traditions and framework when the transition takes places from Capitalism to Socialism.

LESSONS OF CONTEMPORARY DEMOCRATIC MOVEMENTS IN THE SOCIALIST COUNTRIES

The democratic trends in communism are manifesting themselves in various different ways in the various communist countries. In Karl Marx University in Hungary, for example, *Das Kapital* of Karl Marx is no longer a compulsory text. If any one so desires, may offer it as an optional text. In fact, today in Hungary people are ready to give the Marxist literature its historic value but they are no longer ready to accept it as the only determinant of the path that is to be followed by the State. In the nineteenth century when the Industrial Revolution in Great Britain was on swing the economic conditions prevailing at the time took the shape of a particular type of economic theory and that forms the basis of the Marxist doctrine. But the conditions have now completely changed in the course of a century. For this reason today the Hungarian economists consider Marxist economic doctrines out of date. Besides, in the course of the last four decades when Marxism was actually being applied, it manifested many shortcomings. This is the reason why Marxism is no longer the basis of the State in Hungary.[47] They have also reverted to Market Economy.

Hungary has taken another important decision and in this matter Poland has shown it the way. In Poland a second labour party fought for recognition since 1981 and in this struggle Lech Walesha, the party leader, and thousands of his followers were jailed, ultimately, however, Walesha and his party 'Solidarity', winning. In the recent national election of Polish legislature in the lower house out of the total seats of 261, 'Solidarity' came to secure 260, one seat going to an independent peasant; in the upper house out of a total of 100 not a single seat could be secured by the Communist Party although it was in power during the last forty years. And for the first time in forty years a democratic government has been installed in Poland dislodging the Communist Party.

Hungary has followed the suit of Poland. The country was occupied by Hitler's army in 1944, it was brought under the

47. Article in Bengali by Sri Yoganath Mukhopadhyaya in the daily *Bartamān* dated 2 August 1989.

control of the Soviet Union in 1945. In the general election held in 1945, the Communist Party was defeated, the opposition securing the majority. But Soviet Russia, then under the rule of Stalin, declared the election null and void and took over absolute control of the country. Another futile attempt was made by Hungary in 1949 to come out of the Soviet control but that was baffled with ruthless repression. After that Hungary was under the dictatorship of a Soviet supported leader for 31 years. Soon after Mikhail Gorbachov declared the policy of Perestroika, Hungary again took a bold step and declared that a multi-party system and democratic government would form the basis of the State. Bulgaria's Communist Party now functions under the banner of 'Socialist Party'. It has recently accomplished the most successful transition to democracy. They held free and fair election and actually won. But the Communist victory in Bulgaria is not a victory of Marxism-Leninism. The essential fact remains that the Communist won because they transformed themselves in both policy and rhetoric to the point that they ceased to be Communists in the people's eyes.

One-Party Rule : *Multi-Party Rule* : According to the orthodox Marxist doctrine, in the post-revolutionary period, as we have seen above, one-party rule is natural and this is what is real democracy for the classless society that is sought to be established through the revolution, that is to say the system of proletariat dictatorship is actually a system of proletariat democracy. Since there is justice and there is equality in this system, there is also democracy for the proletariat in it.

But the developments in the post-revolutionary period in the communist countries belie this thesis. Marx spoke of dictatorship of the proletariat, under Lenin's interpretation it was transformed into the dictatorship of the Bolshevik Party, and under Stalin and Mao Ze Dong it turned into the dictatorship of one man, the party chief. And this one man dictatorship in all the different countries continued till the death of the dictator. This is the history not only of the Soviet Union and China, but also of Cuba, Yugoslavia and Hungary. And all the mass uprisings against the dictatorships in Hungary, Poland, Czechoslovakia and recently in China were crushed with the help of the armed forces. This does not prove that the dictatorship is a democracy for the people of the Proletariat Raj. If that had been so, thinkers like Pasternak, Solzhenitsyn, Shakharov and Zao Ziang would not have protested and the democratic movements would not have emerged.

That people are against the regime, that they do not consider that they enjoy their democratic rights under the so called dictatorship of the proletariat, is proved by the fact that in the recently held election of the Super-Parliament in Soviet Russia, where out of a total number of 2250 seats, free election was allowed in the case of 750 seats, many stalwarts of the party were defeated. In Lithuania and Latvia also Communist Party has been drastically defeated by a newly formed party called the 'Popular Front'.[48] Soviet Union has subsequently amended its constitution allowing multi-party system and a Presidential form of Government.

X

DEMOCRATIC TRENDS IN THE SOVIET UNION

Perestroika : As we have mentioned above the democratic trend recently has overtaken Soviet Union itself. Liberalization of Policy called 'Perestroika' is in the process of implementation for sometimes. Mikhail Gorbachov, the Party Chief in the Soviet Union who masterminded the policy, defines 'Perestroika' as a revolution.[49]

In his opinion, 'Decisive acceleration of the socio-economic and cultural development of the Soviet Socirty involves radical changes on the way to a qualitatively a new state.'[50] While calling it a 'revolution' he points out, 'We do not equate "Perestroika" with the October Revolution, an event that was a turning point in the thousand year history of our State and unparalleled in force of impact.' But according to him, this is the second revolution which was necessary to consolidate the achievements of the first one.

48. ibid., article in Bengali by Sri Nirmalendu Bikash Rakshit.
49. 'Perestroika—the Revolution' by B.P.L. Pathak in *Social Scientist*; 'How Far Can Soviet Reform Go' by William D. Oc. in *Problems of Communism*, Nov.—Dec. 1988.
50. Mikhail Gorbachov, *Perestroika*, Collens, 1987, p. 50.

Perestroika as laid down by its proponent has four different parts : I. Re-assessment of the past; II. Re-structuring of the economy, which *Perestroika* literally means ; III. *Glasnost*—which refers to the entire process of democratization of the Soviet Polity; and lastly, a redefining of the relation of 'Socialism and the world'; in other words, redefining the relation of Socialism and Capitalism.

I. *Re-assessment of the Stalin-era* : It has been made in the *1987 Report* of Gorbachov to the Party Congress. According to it, the Stalin-era was characterized by strict centralization, administration by injunction and violation of law which had tragic consequences. Stalin made also, according to it, a wrong assessment of the role of the middle peasant in the economy and the result was collectivization of agriculture which again resulted in tremendous human suffering. It seems from the *Report* that the Stalin phenomenon was the inevitable consequence of the concept of the dictatorship of the proletariat and Lenin's concept of the role of the party. In the words of Gorbachov : 'Contrary to the assertions of our ideological opponents the Stalin-era personality cult was certainly not inevitable. It was alien to the nature of Socialism, represented a departure from its fundamental principles, and therefore, has no justification.' It is admitted also in the *Report* that the 'Party's leading nucleus headed by Joseph Stalin had safeguarded Leninism in the ideological struggle.'[51] The source of atrocities of the Stalin era is, therefore, Leninism. The Russian people as a result of all these policies of repression were suffering from intellectual and economic stagnation. Enterprise, initiative, dynamism and rationalism were lacking. Hence it was necessary to make this reassessment of the past as a part of the programme of the new revolution under the policy of *Perestroika*.

II. *Economic Re-structuring* : It was necessary to restructure the economy in order to shake-off the stagnation that has set in the economic life of the country. To quote Gorbachov—'In the last fifteen years the national income growth rates declined by more than half and by the beginning of the eighties had fallen to a

51. *Report to the Festive Meeting on 70th Anniversary of the Great October Revolution held on November 2, 1987.*

level close to economic stagnation.'[52] 'And all these happened', Gorbachov further points out, 'at a time when scientific and technological revolution opened up new prospects for economic and social progress.'

According to Abel Aganbegyan, a noted Soviet economist, two objective factors responsible for the situation are : (1) the constraint of natural resources; (2) the change in the demography of the Soviet Union which compels reliance hereafter on increasing labour productivity. Another cause seems to be that while after the devastation of the Second World War, Germany and Japan, taking advantage of the situation, rebuilt their industry entirely on a new technological base, Soviet Union only replaced the old structure. Two attempts of reforms were made, first in the fifties and then in the sixties. But these attempts failed since social and political structures were not remoulded to suit the reforms at the economic level.

Hence Gorbachov's 'Perestroika' is an attempt to restructure not only the economic system but also the political and social systems.

Economist Tatyana Zaslavsky's criticism of the Soviet economy was the starting point for defining the policy of *Perestroika*. It contained a blistering criticism of the unreliability of the economic data in the Soviet Union. A recent essay by Nikolay Shmelev removes any doubt about the inadequacies of the centrally planned economic system. He declares that 'All the pricing decisions made since the late 1920's are a "terrible legacy" that must be discarded if the present reform is to have any prospect of success.'

What Aganbegyan, Zaslavekaya and others tried to impress upon was the fact that economic progress could not occur without a free play of the market forces to set prices based on supply and demand.

In his *1988 Report*, Gorbachov describes the economic reforms as consisting of : (1) a deep going reform of the system of economic management, truly radical in scale (2) complete operational autonomy and self-financing of the primary cells of the economy; (3) creation of large cooperative sector under the

52. *Perestroika*, pp. 18-19.

law of cooperatives, for broad use of diverse form of cooperation in all economic fields. The linking of wage to an individual's work is also being emphasized.

Shortcomings of the Central Planning Board : Regarding the shortcomings of the Central Planning Board, Gorbachov in his *Report* observes, 'To expect that the State Planning Committee will be able to trace all inter-sectoral links and choose an optimum variant is to harbour an illusion.' The market system obviously seemed to be more efficient since it provides an incentive for more efficient production.

Among other problems affecting the economic front is a kind of social psychology that has developed with an effect which is hardly desirable—'a psychology of dependence' that have stuck deep roots. This attitude may be described as the 'parasitical attitude'. According to Gorbachov, the prestige of conscientious and high quality work began to decline and a 'wage-levelling mentality' was becoming wide-spread. There is reference in *1988 Report* to those 'who are lazy, wasteful and idle'.

III. *Glasnost* : *Democratization* : Strictly speaking the term *Glasnost* means open discussion in public affairs. But this term can be applied to the entire process of democratization that has been instituted in the political life and institutions in the Soviet Union. These political aspects of *Perestroika* are of immense importance to the Soviet Union. *Glasnost* insists on the importance of mass media, the rule of law, the secret ballot vote, so on and so forth.

IV. *Socialism and the World* : This is considered by many as the most revolutionary aspect of *Perestroika.* The new thinking regarding Socialism and the world falls under two broad heads : (1) a reappraisal of potentialities of Capitalism and of its capacity to adopt and survive; (2) a realization of the threat of annihilation that nuclear destruction poses to the entire human race and to the Planet Earth. It is recognized today under the policy of *Perestroika* that Capitalism and Socialism are the two forms of economic organizations available to the developing third world countries. It is also recognized that the relations between the capitalist nations and the existing socialist nations are of cooperation, co-existence and co-sharing of a common human heritage. And foreign relations of the Soviet Union have undergone a change accordingly as is manifest in its declaration of the policy of disarmament.

The new economic system will be based on, as Aganbegyan describes, 'the most powerful incentive, economic interest'. But it must be remembered that from the point of view of motivation, economic interests include : (1) at the first stage, the satisfaction of basic needs ; (2) at the second stage, satisfaction of the needs which the present level of culture imposes; (3) at the third stage, security which includes provision for a pleasant old age; (4) and at the final stage, satisfaction of the desire of giving a head-start to one's own children. And these claims have been described legitimate by Gorbachov in his *Report*.

Assessment of Perestroika : *Need for an Ideological Basis* : It is apparent from all these about the new thinking and *Perestroika* in the Soviet Union that human needs are not determined by the level of technology but by certain ideological presumptions. It is true, as Erich Fromn points out, 'that as long as everybody wants to have more, there must be class-war, and in global terms, there must be international wars'. Therefore it is obvious that the economic system should no longer be governed by the question : 'What is good for the growth of the system?', but should be guided by the question : 'What is good for man?'. Very significantly he points out further that 'A new society is possible only if, in the process of developing it a new human being also develops.' This is exactly a repetition of Vivekananda's views quoted earlier. In this light, Socialism has been given a new meaning and a new dimension by Gorbachov who sees Socialism as 'a system of true and tangible ... humanism in which man is really the measure of all things'. Gorbachov shows concern for all humanity when he talks of world peace and the common danger to humanity. Here he goes not on the Marxian path, but on the path treaded once by emperor Aśoka after the Kalinga War and the path shown by Ramakrishna and Vivekananda in the modern era.

The present turmoil in China also is indicative of the modifications of Socialism that are inevitably developing in the country. A new kind of Socialism based on democracy and humanism is coming on the board everywhere rejecting the ideology of dictatorship of the proletariat and totalitarianism.

VIVEKANANDA'S CONCEPT OF A DEMOCRATIC SOCIALISM

Thus we find that Vivekananda's concept of a democratic socialism is gradually taking practical shape in the various socialist countries. Long ago Vivekananda said the same thing which is being said today by men like Eric Fromn— that systems are not important, it is the human beings who are all important. As we have seen already, Vivekananda said, 'Everything goes to show that Socialism or some form of rule by the people, call it what you will, is coming on the boards. The people will certainly want the satisfaction of their material needs, less work, no oppression, no war, more food. What guarantee have we that this or any civilization will last unless it is based on religion, on the goodness of man? Depend on it, religion goes to the root of the matter. If it is right, all is right.'[53]

What is needed is the development of a new kind of human being—honest, conscientious, intelligent, dynamic, bold and courageous, creative, and a human being with a heart. Man-making was therefore given topmost priority in his programme of activities by Vivekananda. And in this matter religion is perhaps the most efficient instrument not only according to Vivekananda but also according to Sorokin and many other thinkers. This is being realized by the Socialist countries now. Moreover, strong individuals honest to the backbone and with courage of conviction can grow only under a system which grants utmost liberty to the individuals. Hence a democratic form of government is very important. Long ago Vivekananda declared emphatically, 'Those social rules which stand in the way of unfoldment of this freedom are injurious and steps should be taken to destroy them speedily. Those institutions should be encouraged by which men advance in the path of freedom.'[54]

Thus the measures that are now being devised and implemented by the Soviet leaders today were long ago

---

53. *C. W.*, V, p. 202.

54. *Letters of Swami Vivekananda*, p. 419.

envisaged and suggested by Vivekananda. Maybe that for this reason Vivekananda is being recently hailed in the Soviet Union as 'the prophet of human emancipation' and of 'peace and progress'.

XI

CONTRIBUTIONS OF VIVEKANANDA TO THE DEVELOPMENT OF THE SOCIALIST IDEAL

In the beginning of this chapter we have stated that Vivekananda considered that true Democracy was possible only under Socialism. In the end of this chapter we find that he considered that it was possible to realize aims of Socialism only under Democracy. Thus, we find that in his system of thought each of these two great ideals is indispensable for the other, for the realization of their respective goals, they are complementary and not contradictory.

So long these two ideals were held as incompatible by the western Socialists. But Vivekananda long ago showed their complementarity. This is one of the greatest contributions of Swami Vivekananda to the political concepts of the world. With the realization of their complementarity in the socialist countries today, the importance of Vivekananda's thought in this respect has become evident. By showing this complementarity he made the ideals of Socialism and Democracy more acceptable to the thinking men all over the world.

CHAPTER 17

Law, Liberty, Equality and Rights

I

LAW

The Concept : According to Harold Laski, the eminent writer on Political Science in the present century, 'The law of any given society is the expression of the push of the social forces in that society and we cannot explain its substance without regard to these forces.'[1] According to Vivekananda also, a law enacted by the State reflects the pull of the existing social forces. He does not hesitate to point out that in a society divided between the rich and the poor, law often seeks to safeguard the vested interests of the rich to the detriment of the interest of the poor. While writing about a shipping law he made his ideas on this point very clear. 'It was the rich', he said, 'and influential men of the country ... who would appropriate the benefits of commerce, or ravage, or conquest of different countries, and the poor people were simply to shed their blood and sacrifice their lives—as has been the rule throughout the world's history!'[2] This is in conformity with Laski's statement running as follows : 'Law is those rules of behaviour which secures the purposes of the society's class structure and will be, if necessary, enforced by the coercive power of the state.'[3] This conformity indicates how advanced and scientific was Vivekananda's concept of law.

Obedience to Law : As regards the question of obedience to law, Vivekananda's view sounds totally revolutionary. Talking about obedience to laws of nature he says, 'I disagree with the idea that freedom is obedience to the laws of nature. . . . According to the history of human progress, it is disobedience to

---

1. Harold Laski—*Grammar of Politics*, p. vi.
2. *C. W.*, VII, pp. 314-15.
3. *Grammar of Politics*, p. vii.

nature that has constituted that progress. . . . I never saw a cow steal. An oyster never told a lie. Yet these are not greater than man.'[4] 'This life', he adds, 'is a tremendous assertion of freedom; excess of laws means death.'[5] This obedience to law carried far enough, would make of us simply matter—either in society or in politics or in religion. Thus he points out clearly that obedience to political and social laws also, just as in the case of natural laws, cannot be carried too far, it cannot be unconditional and absolute. The purpose of social and political laws are to safeguard the freedom of the individual. If instead they infringe freedom then they are not justified. Disobedience under such circumstance, is rather justified. Vivekananda laid down this revolutionary thesis when the idealist thinkers were claiming unconditional and absolute obedience to the State and its laws.

The Abstract Idea of Law : The abstract idea of law, very popular in the West at one time, was rejected by Professor Harold Laski. Presenting that concept of abstract law in an explanatory note he says—'Law is regarded binding because it is useful, or because it embodies reason, or because it expresses the general ends of society in particular rules or because it is a search for such canons of behaviour, the observance of which will maximize the satisfaction of demand.' Denying the validity of this view Swamiji says that the object of the State is to maintain some given system of class-relations in society. Law, ultimately therefore, is a body of rules which seeks to fulfil the object of the State. These rules are maintained because, normally, those who dissent from the rules are not in a position to challenge the authority which lies behind them.

The concept of absolute obedience, therefore, is not accepted by the modern thinkers in view of the fact that in the present-day society based on class divisions it is more or less agreed today that law represents the interest of the ruling class only and not of the people as a whole. Vivekananda did not make any particular reference to the laws of the State but considered social laws in general with regard to the question of obedience. And since the social laws are often the basis of the laws of the State, his view with regard to social laws in this respect would apply also to the

4. *C. W.*, VIII, pp. 257-58. 5. ibid., p. 258.

laws of the State. First of all, he explodes the dogma of 'eternal law' so far as society is concerned. 'Our Vedanta', he says, 'is the assertion of freedom always. . . . If there is to be an eternal law binding him [man] all the time, where is the difference between him and a blade of grass? We do not believe in that abstract idea of law.'[6] Thus it is clear that Vivekananda also had no faith in the abstract idea of law.

What more he utters on this point sounds revolutionary : 'It is freedom in every way, i.e., advance towards *mukti* is the worthiest gain of man. Those social laws which stand in the way of unfolding of this freedom are injurious and steps should be taken to destroy them speedily and those institutions should be encouraged by which men advance in the path of freedom.'[7] Freedom—physical freedom and spiritual freedom is the watchword of man according to Vivekananda. No social or State laws should go against this watchword. Freedom is the birth-right of man and State and social laws should seek to safeguard it and not to limit it or deny it.

II

LIBERTY : A SOCIALISTIC CONCEPT

It is evident from the above that Vivekananda was perhaps the greatest champion of individual liberty in recent history. At the same time, it is to be particularly noted, that his concept of 'liberty' is socialistic in character. By 'liberty' he did not mean absence of restraint like some of the champions of 'Individualism' in the nineteenth century West. J. S. Mill's essay *On Liberty* is the most famous vindication of Individualism in the nineteenth century, his main thesis being that the State can further the happiness of the individuals by interfering in their personal affairs as little as possible. Mill's concept of 'liberty' was a reaction against the absolutist view that individual enjoys their fulfilment in the State. Revolting against this concept of absolutism of the State he insists that it is the business of the State to provide for the happiness of the individuals and it has the right to exist only when it fulfils this condition. Karl Marx also

6. ibid., V, p. 288. 7. *Letters of Swami Vivekananda*, p. 388.

supported the absolutism of the State at the stage of proletariat dictatorship after a revolution. In his opinion, the proletariat enjoys liberty in such a State since it is their dictatorship which controls it. It seems not true since the proletariat voters have ousted their own party government in many socialist states today and at present, as we have seen in the previous chapter, there is a clamour for political democracy in all the socialist countries. This shows that they do not think that they enjoy freedom under the dictatorship of the proletariat or of the Communist Party which is said to be their own party. Hence absolute State authority, it is evident, cannot guarantee happiness to the individual. Liberty is the first condition for happiness.

III

LIBERTY AND RIGHTS

By 'liberty' Vivekananda definitely means a system of positive opportunities and rights. This is clear from his definition of liberty which runs as follows : 'Liberty does not certainly mean the absence of obstacles in the path of mis-appropriation of wealth etc., by you and me, but it is our natural right to be allowed to use our own body, intelligence or wealth according to our will, without doing any harm to others, and all the members of the society ought to have the same opportunity for obtaining wealth, education or knowledge.'[8] Liberty, therefore, means in concrete terms certain positive rights—'right to use our own body, intelligence or wealth'. 'Right to use one's own body' includes right to life, right to freedom of movement; 'right to use one's own intelligence' includes right to education, freedom of thought and expression; and 'freedom to use one's own wealth' includes right to property.

Rights : *No Exclusive Rights for Exceptional Persons*: Rights are, therefore, positive opportunities for the development of the individual's potential capacities. According to Vivekananda, all individuals should enjoy the same rights without any exception whatsoever. In a sharp rejoinder to the supporters of exclusive rights for the specially gifted persons he says, 'Those who say

---

8. ibid., p. 387.

that if the ignorant and the poor be given liberty, i.e., full rights to their body, wealth, etc., and if their children have the same opportunities to better their condition and acquire knowledge as that of the rich and the highly situated they would be perverse—do they say this for the good of the society or blinded by their selfishness?' Referring to this exclusive claims he vehemently denies their justification. 'In England too', he says, 'I have heard, "Who will serve us, if the lower classes get education?" ' Condemning their selfish motive Vivekananda says, 'For the luxury of the handful of the rich, let millions of men and women remain submerged in the hell of want and abysmal depth of ignorance, if they get wealth and education, society will be upset!'

'Who is Society', asked Vivekananda, 'the millions or you, I and a few others of the upper classes?'[9]

Here we get a glimpse of Vivekananda, the uncompromising champion of the rights of the poor and the dispossessed. He criticized vehemently the Nietzschean ideas that the types of individuals we conceive to be the best ought to be 'bettered'. Nietzsche failed to realize that in a society where the greater number cannot develop their real capacities, no one, even the best, can effectively develop his own since the development of one is determined by the development of the others. Who would understand the art and philosophy of Nietzsche if the vast majority are next to brutes?[10]

Liberty is a product of Rights : Here we may note that Vivekananda's thought is unique. As observed above, his concept of 'liberty' is Vedantic, hence it is not purely individualistic, it is socialistic in content. At the same time, he wants the individuals to retain their identity. Every individual is unique in his opinion and that uniqueness must be preserved for the benefit of the society. Hence the individual must develop freely apart from the 'society' or any other abstract concept of the whole, e.g., the 'General Will'. At the same time, Vivekananda is not a pure and simple individualist like J. S. Mill, in whose opinion we have seen, least interference from society or absence of restraint whatsoever is the essence of liberty. In Vivekananda's opinion,

9. ibid., p. 388.

10. Dr D. Burns—*Political Ideals*, Chapter X.

while society should not interfere with individual freedom by putting unnecessary restraints, it would be the duty of the society at the same time, to provide positive opportunities equally for all individuals so that they can advance fully to unfold their latent capacity or divinity and ultimately attain *mukti* or spiritual liberation. Professor Laski's definition given much later, is to some extent similar to Vivekananda's definition. 'By liberty I mean', says Professor Laski, 'the eager maintenance of that atmosphere in which men have the opportunity to be their best selves. Liberty, therefore, is a product of rights.'[11] This is a realistic and positive concept of liberty emphasized long ago by Vivekananda who added a new meaning to the concept by expanding it to reconcile both the individualistic and the socialist stand points. The reconciliation was made on the basis of Vedanta which propounds 'individuality in universality'.

SAFEGUARDS TO LIBERTY : RIGHT TO DISOBEDIENCE AND REVOLUTION

According to Professor Laski, 'Nothing is so likely to maintain a condition of liberty as the knowledge that the invasion of rights will result in protest, and if need be resisted.'[12] 'Liberty is nothing', he emphatically adds, 'if it is not the organized and conscious power to resist in the last resort. The implied contingent anarchy is a safeguard against the abuse of government.'[13] Earlier Rousseau pleaded for the right to revolution among other human rights. Since the days of Rousseau and more recently since the Russian revolution one of the most engaging pre-occupation of the political-scientists has been this important right, right to revolution. Communism is essentially a theory of the method of revolution, as we have noticed earlier. It seeks to lay down the principles on the basis of which the transition from capitalism to socialism is to be worked out. The two essential doctrines of Communism are, as we have seen already, (1) the doctrine of class war, and (2) the doctrine of revolution. To be brief, it is a theory of application of force and violence for the capture of power by the proletariat.

According to Vivekananda, 'Everything is conscious which

---

11. *Grammar of Politics*, p. 142. 12. ibid., p. 144. 13. ibid.,

rebels against nature. . . . Where there is struggle, where there is rebellion, there is sign of life, there consciousness is manifested.'[14] Thus in his opinion, the right to rebellion is an inherent natural right of man. When questioned whether this applies to society and nations also, he answered : 'Just read the history of the world and see whether it applies or not.'[15] Right to rebellion was considered by him a matter of natural right which applies equally to men and societies. He did not believe in eternal laws even when they were laid down by 'Rishis' or by the wise men.[16]

He believed in an ideal of a perpetual revolution for a perpetual progress. But it does not mean that he supported armed revolution engineered to capture State power. Vivekananda believed, as it appears from his above statement just quoted, in 'some inherent principle of revolution in human history'.[17]

IV

EQUALITY : THE VEDANTIC CONCEPT

In the same manner as in the case of the concept of 'liberty', the conept of 'equality', so important in political science, underwent a mould at the hands of Vivekananda, resulting in an addition of new strength and new meaning to it. According to Vivekananda, 'The whole universe is a play of unity in variety' and that 'differentiation is the sign of life'. Hence he emphasizes : 'Absolute sameness as to external forms and positions can never be attained.' 'But', he points out, 'what can be attained is elimination of privilege.'[18] On the basis of this argument he shows that equality does not mean stopping variation or differentiation, but wiping out the privileges that are claimed on the basis of this differentiation.

Equality means absence of privileges : Elaborating the idea he emphatically says, 'Let all these variations remain eternally… . You wil be wealthy, and I shall be poor; you will be strong, and I shall be weak; you will be learned and I ignorant;

14. *C. W.*, VI, p. 453.
15. ibid., p. 454.
16. R. K. DasGupta—*Revolutionary Ideas of Swami Vivekananda.*
17. ibid.
18. *C. W.*, I, p. 435.

you will be very spiritual, and I, less so. But what of that? Let us remain so, but because you are physically and intellectually stronger, you must not have more privilege than I, and that you have more wealth is no reason why you should be considered greater than I, for that sameness is here, in spite of the different conditions.'[19] The sameness referred to here is the divine substratrum underlying every being. Equality as interpreted by Vivekananda, does not mean sameness in externalities but sameness in inner soul. 'Equality', therefore, 'means absence of privileges and not sameness of external conditions.' It implies the same rights and opportunities for all. With regard to rights and positive opportunities there should be no discrimination.

Professor Laski uses the very language of Vivekananda when he says, 'Equality, therefore, means first of all the absence of special privilege.'[20] This shows that Vivekananda spoke of vital truths which were subsequently realized by other thinkers also. This perhaps proves also that Vivekananda's ideas worked as a fertilizing force on the world texture of thought imperceptibly.

This is now universally accepted that differences cannot be totally obliterated, but what can be demolished are the privileges and this demolition constitutes the essence of equality. Absence of privileges guarantee everybody the same opportunities for development of his or her potentialities.

V

LIBERTY AND EQUALITY : COMPLEMENTARY CONCEPTS

According to Vivekananda, the two concepts, of liberty and equality, are complementary. Replying to the Maharaja of Kshetri's address of welcome sent to him when he was still in the West in 1895 he said, 'Above all, follow this great doctrine of sameness in all things, through all beings, seeing the same God in all.' And he added that : 'This is the way to freedom, inequality, the way to bondage. No man and no nation can attempt to gain physical freedom without physical equality, nor mental freedom without mental equality.'

The complementary relationship between the two concepts

19. ibid., pp. 435-36.

20. *Grammar of Politics*, p. 153.

'liberty' and 'equality' is based on the Vedantic doctrine of the equality of all beings. On the realization of this equality or sameness depends attainment of *mukti* or liberation. When we realize that everything is the same, identical, One reality, we attain freedom. This ideal, he emphasizes, is the ideal for the householder, this ideal is for the *sannyāsin* (monk) also. In his opinion : 'the ideal of all societies, of all mankind, all animals, and all nature', is to attain to this sameness. And he asserts that 'This is the bane of human nature, the curse upon mankind, the root of all misery—this inequality. This is the source of all bondage, physical, mental and spiritual.'[21] If the two ideas of liberty and equality are complementary, it is clear, that we cannot attain liberty without equality and vice versa. Both must be attained simultaneously if the life of the individual is to be enriched by them. Every state, every society, must guarantee them both at the same time. That liberty without equality is no liberty, is proved in the capitalist countries with formal democracy, that equality without liberty is no equality, is proved today in the socialist states, where there is a cry for liberty and democracy as discussed in the previous chapter in detail.

21. *C. W.*, IV, p. 329.

CHAPTER 18

The Revolutionary Theory of Revolutions

I

CONCEPT OF REVOLUTION

Revolutions are well-known phenomena in history. According to Sorokin[1], just as 'Tension and relaxation, sickness and health, crisis and repose, incessantly alternate in the life process of an individual', a 'similar pulsation seems to occur in the life process of a society', it has also 'its periods of tension and relaxation, stormy crisis and quiet order'. Revolutions have taken place throughout history, in ancient Greece and Rome, in India and China, France, Germany (Central Europe), England, Italy, Spain, Netherlands, Byzantium, Poland, Lithuania, Russia and in almost all the other countries of the world.

Sorokin has spoken of five different kinds of revolutions :

A. predominantly political, the main objective of which is a change in the existing political regime;

B. predominantly socio-economic, the main objective—a modification of the existing social and economic order;

C. national and separatist—the main objective—national indepedence or autonomy;

D. religious upheavals, the main objective—creation of a new kind of men and socio-religious transformations in the end;

E. upheavals with a specific objective—e.g., resistance to a specific law or tax.

The main and the indispensable condition for an eruption of

1. P. A. Sorokin, *Social and Cultural Dynamics* (abridged), Chapter 35.

revolution, i.e., of internal disturbance according to Professor Sorokin, is that the social system or the cultural system or both shall be unsettled.

Marxian theory of Revolution : Marxism, as we have seen already, has been resuscitated as a philosophy of revolution by Lenin in his 'State and Revolution'. The main points of his theory of revolution are : (a) class wars which are perpetual characteristics of society so long as it is based on class divisions; (b) the overthrowing of the existing regime with a violent uprising of the people. The main factor working behind a revolution is technological changes which create contradictions in social relationships leading to a class war. Lenin's context is the capitalist society, its contradictions, fierce class-struggle that ensues as a result, and his main concern is overthrowing of the capitalistic system through a violent revolution and insatallation of a proletariat dictatorship. Lenin championed more a political revolution than a social revolution.

II

VIVEKANANDA'S THEORY : CLASS-WAR

Vivekananda's concept of revolution has a wider context. He has also spoken of class-struggles in history, as we have seen already. His historical studies revealed class-struggle as a historical force. As far as India is concerned, as stated by him, history reveals class-struggle even in very early days—the struggle for supremacy between the two major classes at the time—priests and the kings—Brahmins and Kshatriyas.

Vivekananda has made it a point to show that the same struggle characterized the history of other countries of the world also. Among the Chinese, the Sumerians, the Babylonians, the Egyptians, Chaldeans, Iranians, the Jews and Arabs—among all these ancient nations, the supreme power of guiding society in the first period was in the hands of the Brahmin or the priest. In the next period out of the struggle that went on between the priests and the kings (Kshatriyas), the latter came victorious. Regarding the class-struggle that was waged between the Kings (Kshatriyas) and the Vaishyas in the next period, he said that before the vailant blow of newly risen Vaishya power, many a kingly crown has to kiss the ground, many a sceptre is for ever broken to pieces.[2] In his historical studies he made all this very clear.

Vivekananda recognized class-struggle as a reality not only in the past but also in the contemporary period. This is clear from his following statement : 'But times have changed. The lower classes are gradually awakening to this fact and making a united front against this, determined to exact their legitimate dues. The masses of Europe and America have been the first to awaken and have already begun the fight. Signs of this awakening have shown themselves in India, too, as is evident from the number of strikes among the lower classes nowadays. The upper classes will no longer be able to repress the lower, try they ever so much.'[3]

While speaking about the last phase of the class-struggle in the contemporary period he dwells on its inevitability : 'Yet, a time will come when there will be the rising of the Shudra class, with their Shudra-hood . . . a time will come, when the Shudras of every country, with their inborn Shudra nature and habits . . . will gain absolute supremacy in every society. The first glow of the dawn of this new power has already begun to break slowly upon the Western world. . . . Socialism, Anarchism, Nihilism, and other like sects are the vanguard of the social revolution that is to follow.'[4] Analysing the nature of the struggle he further states—'Those uncared-for lower classes of India—the peasants and weavers and the rest . . . it is they who from time immemorial have been working silently, without even getting the remuneration of their labours! But what great changes are taking place slowly, all over the world, in pursuance of nature's laws! Countries, civilizations, and supremacy are undergoing revolutions.'[5] Like Marx, here he points out that the labourers under Vaishya or capitalistic regime do not get the full value of their own labour.

It is apparent from the above that Vivekananda definitely and clearly recognizes class-struggle as a historical reality. But at the same time he states that mere class-struggles and violent

---

2. *Selections from Swami Vivekananda.*
3. *C. W.*, VII, p. 149.
4. ibid., IV, p. 468.
5. ibid., VII, p. 358.

uprisings are not sufficient to attain the goals of revolution—i.e., progress and prosperity. He speaks therefore, of 'Jaina Revolution', of 'Buddha revolution', which were religious upheavals but at the same time brought in far-reaching social changes conferring on the people their legitimate rights and demolishing the exclusive privileges of the priests. 'With the deluge', he says, 'which swept the land at the advent of Buddhism, the priestly power fell into decay and the royal power was in the ascendant. . . . For Buddhism has shaken the thrones of all the oblation-eating gods and brought them down from their heavenly positions. . . . And to this Buddhahood, every man has the privilege to attain... .'[6] These religious upheavels were, according to Vivekananda, in effect true revolutions since they caused far-reaching social changes as well as all round prosperity and progress.

In spite of recognizing the inevitability of the class-struggle, Vivekananda rejects firmly the political method as an instrument of social revolution, as we shall see below.

III

REFORM, REVOLUTION AND GROWTH

Vivekananda also rejects the policy of reforming society through the social reform movements as they were in vogue at the time. He told the reformers point blank that mere reforms were no solution to the Indian problem. 'To the reformers I would point out', he said curtly, 'I am a greater reformer than any one of them. They want to reform little bits, I want root and branch reform.' His aim was thus a thorough overhauling, not tit bit mending.

Meaning of True Revolutions : He criticized the reformers not because he thought reforms to be unnecessary but because he considered the reform measures suggested by them were superficial and inadequate. Explaining he said, 'The fate of a nation does not depend on the number of husbands their widows get but upon the condition of the masses.'[7] 'The whole defect is here', he added sharply, 'the real nation who lives in the cottages

6. ibid., IV, p. 443.

7. *Letters of Swami Vivekananda*, p. 78.

have forgotten their manhood, their individuality.'[8] To restore this manhood was the essence of revolutions according to him. Hence what was needed was the uplift of the masses but the reformers had hardly any such programme. Only Vivekananda in those days had a concrete programme for the uplift of the masses—a programme for educating them, for giving them back their lost individuality, their manhood, so that ultimately they could attain supremacy in society.

IV

VIVEKANANDA'S PROGRAMME FOR MASS UPLIFT

In a letter to a brother disciple, Vivekananda declared, 'Our mission is for the destitute, the poor, the illiterate peasantry and the labouring classes . . . among these very men teachers will spring.'[9] It is said that in the early days of his Indian itinerary he attempted to engineer an armed revolution by the native princes against the British, hoping that the princes would then work to ameliorate the conditions of the masses. He was soon disillusioned, since they showed little or no concern for the oppressed masses and then he realized that so long as the princes had their own vested interests safe, they were not least bothered by the problems of the masses or of the nation at large. Being thus disillusioned by the upper classes he realized that India's only hope lies in the masses. He cautioned his followers—'Trust not the so-called rich, they are more dead than alive.'[10] Sharply criticizing the upper classes he said, 'They know nothing beyond, happy little souls! Their nice little brown studies of lives never rudely shocked by the wail of woe, of misery, of degradation, of poverty, that has filled the Indian atmosphere—the results of centuries of oppression.'[11]

Elaborating his programme for the masses he wrote to Swami Akhandananda, 'Teach some boys and girls of the peasant classes the rudiments of learning and infuse a number of ideas into their brains. Afterwards, the peasants of each village will collect funds and have one of these in their own village. We help them to help themselves. That they are supplying you with your daily bread, is

8. ibid., p. 98. 9. ibid., p. 402. 10. ibid., p. 137. 11. ibid.

a rare bit of work done. . . . The peasants and the labouring classes are in a moribund condition, so what is needed is that the moneyed people will only help them to regain their vitality and nothing more. Then leave the peasants and labourers to look to their own problems to grapple with and solve it.'[12]

Elevation of the masses without injuring their religion : His motto in this matter was, 'elevation of the masses without injuring their religion'. In a clarion call given to his followers he said : 'A hundred thousand men and women, fired with the zeal of holiness, fortified with the eternal faith in the Lord, nerved to lion's courage by their sympathy for the poor and the fallen and the downtrodden, will go over the length and breadth of the country, preaching the gospel of equality.'[13] Instructing his young followers he said : 'Go and preach to all— Arise, awake, sleep no more; within each of you there is the power to remove all wants and all miseries. Believe this, and that power will be manifested.'[14] 'Teach this to all, and with that spread among the masses in plain language the central truths of science, philosophy, history and geography.'[15] This is a call for awakening manhood, to recreate their being. And finally he said, 'Only one idea was burning in my mind—to start the machine for elevating the Indian masses.'[16] This is the crux of his programme, to set in motion a machine which will bring ideas to the door of the masses, which would work to awaken their manhood, and help the leadership to grow from within the masses, and then leave them to work out their own salvation. Thus it was a plan for a social revolution through social action.

V

THE ESSENCE OF POLITICAL REVOLUTIONS

Now, no revolution is successful without mass participation, particularly if it is a revolution for their liberation. The masses must be made to imbibe the revolutionary gospel through teaching or preaching. And therefore every successful revolution in history was preceded by a period of mass

12. ibid., p. 403. 13. ibid., p. 80. 14. ibid., p. 80.
15. ibid., p. 64. 16. Romain Rolland—*Life of Vivekananda*, p. 134.

preaching. From that point of view Vivekananda's programme of mass education and uplift was a right revolutionary programme. It differed from other revolutionary programmes only in this that this programme is completely dissociated from politics and is based on religious ideas. It did not aim at capturing power with the help of violent mass-uprising and bloodshed, murders and killings on a mass-scale. It did not aim at installing in power this or that revolutionary party preaching this or that 'ism'. He saw it clearly through his deep historical insight that the essence of 'political revolutions' was capturing state-power using violence as its chief instrument throwing all the healthy moral values to the winds whenever necessary and that the revolutionaries of today turn into worshippers of naked power tomorrow.

Hence Vivekananda drew a sword between himself and politics and the violent method of capturing state-power. He had the courage to declare his hatred for politics without caring for the sneering of the world. 'I will have nothing to do with politics', he announced with all the forces that he commanded. He did not care for the sneers of the protagonists of 'isms'. He believed in 'social action for social progress' and not in political action which was inefficient and demoralizing in his opinion.

The Concept of a Total Revolution : Vivekananda's concept of revolution was again a concept of total revolution affecting the fundamental or the root of man's social existence. It is based therefore on moral and spiritual growth which changes men themselves and not the institutions only. He said, '. . . religion is of deeper importance than politics, since it goes to the root, and deals with the essential of conduct.'[17]

Class strifes which occur inevitably in history secure nothing more than overthrowing the existing regime of a particular class and installing another one to power. This act of overthrowing of one class by another does not necessarily mean that the conditions of the masses improve or there results greater justice or that there is social progress automatically and immediately.

---

17. *C. W.*, V, p. 200.

VI

POLITICAL METHOD : A FAILURE ; POLITICS : AN INSTRUMENT OF THE UPPER CLASS TO RETAIN POWER

Vivekananda rejected politics for several reasons. First of all, his distrust of the upper classes led him to reject politics as an instrument of social progress. He knew that political leadership was a monopoly of the upper classes since they had education and control over the media. He had no faith in their liberator's garb. He knew it too well that they would only utilize the ignorant masses to grapple power for themselves. He, therefore, insisted that leadership should grow from the masses. With a view to this he planned to educate them first so that they could work out their own salvation. Emancipation, he was convinced, could never come as a gift from the upper classes, since they were the oppressors and the exploiters, and for that reason they were interested only in safeguarding their own vested interest. They might shed crocodile tears for the appalling conditions of the masses in order to grab power with their help but they would never cease to oppress and exploit them. They would only exploit the situation to further their gains but they would never grant the masses their legitimate rights. He wanted, therefore, of masses to pay for their own education even.

He, of course, advised his followers 'not to set up class strifes between the peasants, the labouring people and the wealthy classes'.[18] Obviously it was a matter of policy to him, not to waste energy on feuds and strifes before the masses were educated and fit to take up the struggle standing on their own feet, i.e., till the leadership grows from within them.

Class Reconciliation : *An Utopian Attempt* ? : On account of this attitude the critics have criticized him for attempting at class-reconciliation, which according to them was an utopian idea. And for this attitude he has been called also a 'reactionary'. According to the Soviet scholar E. P. Chelyshev, '. . . the utopian striving to reconcile class-contradictions stemmed from a fervent desire to unite all the forces of the people for struggle against colonialism.'[19]

---

18. *Letters of Swami Vivekananda*, p. 403.
19. *Vivekananda Centenary Memorial Volume*, p. 511.

But this must be clearly understood that since he did not have any faith in the political method, he did not think in terms of accentuating and intensifying the class-struggle. And he was the greatest of the revolutionaries, since only he in the whole history of revolutionary thinking specially thought in terms of building up revolutionary leadership from among the masses.

He had never the intention of leading the ignorant masses like a horde of cattle to capture power and be involved in an orgy of violence since such an attempt could only install some upper class leader to power. He was the last person to give the upper classes this opportunity to thrive capitalizing on the misery of the masses since he knew that it would only open a new avenue to the upper classes for exploiting the masses. Recently, as we have come to know, in China and Romania some political leaders have made enormous fortunes. Even within the framework of communism this has been possible! Power has given these politicians the opportunity to make wealth creating a wide gulf between the ordinary people and themselves. This has been admitted in a press statement by the new Secretary of the Communist Party in China who succeeded Xao-Xi-Yang, the former party Secretary. The same has been the case in Romania. It amply proves that Vivekananda's distrust of the upper class leadership was justified.

Hence Vivekananda insisted that 'Everyone must work out his own salvation.' With a view to building up leadership from the masses he instructed his followers : 'Let us put some ideas into their heads, and they will do the rest.'[20] Thus it is clear that he decided to shun the political method, the use of which would have thrown the leadership on the upper classes leading to the perpetuation of their domination and thus defeating the purpose of the revolution.

Secondly, he rejected politics since from his historical studies he was convinced that it had definitely proved a failure as an instrument of human welfare. His first disillusionment in this matter came from his own futile attempt to make the native princes to rise in an armed revolution against the British. He saw also what middle class moderate politics at home amounted to; he

---

20. *Letters of Swami Vivekananda*, p. 403.

simply loathed their beggar's policy of stooping down on their knees for having tit bit favours from their imperialistic rulers. He also saw the horrors of imperialism at home and abroad. He was disillusioned of the formal democracy of the West as well, when he had the opportunity to watch their working directly in the West. 'All these things', he said bitterly, 'that you hear about constitutional government, freedom, liberty and Parliament—are but jokes.'

It was clear to him that politics meant corruption, moral bankruptcy, hypocrisy, violence and strifes. 'If you ever saw, my friend,' he went on with his critical analysis, 'that shocking sight behind the scene of acting of these politicians—that revelry of bribery, that robbery in broad daylight, that dance of the Devil in man, which are practised on such occasions—you would be hopeless about man!'[21] It is clear from this that he was convinced that politics debased man. He did not believe, and he was absolutely right, that it is ever possible to do any good to any one, any society, by degrading man.

LESSONS OF POLITICAL REVOLUTIONS OF THE PAST

He studied revolutions that have happened in past history. From his study of the French Revolution particularly, he saw clearly how the revolutionary slogans of 'liberty', 'equality' and 'fraternity' became void and how the revolution was succeeded by a worst form of tyranny, viz., absolute monarchy under Napoleon Bonaparte. Proceeding with his analysis, he observes, 'The whole French nation became mad in the name of liberty and equality—France became a Republic. . . . Not only so, they called all the nations of the world to rise— "Awake, kill the kings who are all tyrants, let all be free and have equal rights." Then all the kings of Europe began to tremble in fear . . . they attacked France from all directions. On the other side, the leaders of the French Republic proclaimed, "Our native land is in peril, come one and all", and the proclamation soon spread like the flames of a conflagration throughout the length and breadth of France. . . . crowds of the poor French people, in rags . . . came out with guns on their shoulders . . . —and boldly faced the vast united force of

21. *C. W.*, VII, p. 158.

Europe. . . . At the head and front of the French army, stood a hero. . . . He was Napoleon. With the edge of the sword and at the point of the bayonet, he thrust "Liberty, Equality and Fraternity" into the very bone and marrow of Europe—and thus the victory of the tri-coloured *Cocarde* was achieved. Later, Napoleon became the Emperor of France and successfully accomplished the consolidation of the French Empire.'[22]

Vivekananda's sarcastic remarks show clearly the fact that the purpose of the French Revolution was defeated. According to Carlyle, 'the open violent Rebellion' was 'a victory of disimprisoned anarchy against corrupt worn out authority'. According to Cabban, the French Revolution was 'primarily a political revolution, a struggle for the possession of power. Essentially the revolution was the overthrow of the old political system of the monarchy and the creation of a new one in the shape of the Napoleonic State'.[23] When it is taken into account that in the orgy of violence, of the total number of people guillotined, only 10 p.c. belonged to the upper class and 90 p.c. to the ordinary people, it becomes difficult to appreciate this revolution. Hence what Vivekananda said in his assessment of the French Revolution is borne out by facts and by the historians who undertook to assess the French Revolution by its results and outcome.

Thus reviewing all the different aspects about politics, its ideal, its methods, its institutions, its working in history—reviewing Democracy, Imperialism, and Revolutions, he arrived at the conclusion that 'The political system that we are struggling for in India, have been in Europe for ages, have been tried for centuries and have been found wanting.' 'One after another,' he points out, 'the institutions, systems, and everything connected with political government have been condemned as useless; and Europe is restless, does not know where to turn.'[24] Thus he was totally convinced that it had proved a total failure.

---

22. ibid., V, pp. 517-18.
23. Quoted by Professor Amalesh Tripathi in his Bengali book on *History and Historian*, p. 69.
24. *C. W.*, III p. 158.

POLITICAL METHOD DECRIED IN THE WEST

That Politics as an instrument of social progress and human welfare was found wanting in the West, as claimed by Vivekananda, is evident also from the writings of Emerson, Romain Rolland, Arnold Toynbee, Bertrand Russell and a host of other thinkers, philosophers and leaders of human affairs. Emerson, dwelling on 'Politics' in his essays *Second Series* (1844), observed : 'Politics is a deleterious profession, like some poisonous handicrafts.'[25] Bertrand Russell argues that 'An unprincipled quest of power transforms all power, first, into a revolutionary power and then, by inevitable gradations, into naked power.'[26] Regarding the consequences of a violent political revolution George Bernard Shaw observed, 'They have never lightened the burden of tyranny : they have only shifted it to another shoulder.'[27] Romain Rolland opined—'Our civilization in its dire peril has vainly invoked the spell of great words : Right, Liberty, Cooperation, the Peace of Geneva or Washington —but such words are void or filled with poisonous gas. Nobody believes in them. People mistrust explosives.'[28]

Toynbee observed : 'In the present age, the world has been united on the material plane by western technology. But this western skill has not only "annihilated distance", it has armed the peoples of the world with weapons of devastating power at a time when they have been brought to point-blank range of each other without yet having learnt to know and love each other. At this supremely dangerous moment in human history, the only way for salvation of mankind is an Indian way.'[29] When we remember that the Indian way is the way of the spirit and the way of the West is 'politics', we find clearly that Toynbee has pinpointed the drastic failure of politics to preserve peace and amity of the world.

Same is the report of the Soviet scholar E. P. Chelishev's remarks on Ramakrishna-Vivekananda: 'The message of Ramakrishna and Vivekânanda is the message of peace, amity

---

25. *Revolutionary Ideas of Swami Vivekananda* by Dr R. K. DasGupta.
26. ibid. 27. ibid. 28. *Life of Vivekananda*, p. 296.
29. Nanda Mukherjee—*Sri Ramakrishna in the Eyes of the Brahmo and Christian Admirers*, p. 112.

and world-brotherhood. That message can indicate the path of survival in the fear-stricken world of today. I personally feel that in the context of the present nuclear menace which is gradually engulfing the earth, it is very much essential to disseminate the message of Ramakrishna-Vivekananda all over the world.'[30] The nuclear threat is the result of the predominance of politics in the West. The sum and substance of what Chelishev says amounts to pleading for supersession of the political method by other methods for serving the interests of the people in different lands.

Professor Sorokin's criticism of political revolutions mercilessly exposes their nature : 'These revolutionary schemes are but utopias of a disintegrated mind, of demoralized man, and come as a by-product of the disintegrated culture of the transitionary period . . . periods of the disintegration of social and cultural systems are regularly marked by the emergence of such schemes, and by revolts of the masses of humanity with unintegrated minds led by groups of intellectuals with a disintegrated mentality. . . . These mobs and their leaders are the vultures that appear when the social and cultural body is decomposing. Their eternal historical function is to pull it to pieces, and thus, though involuntarily, to clear the ground for a new life. Creation is not given to them. Both their 'constructive' plans and they themselves are flesh of the last phase of the disintegrating culture. . . .'[31]

In view of all these shortcomings of the political instrument as an agency of human welfare, Karl Jaspers, the well-known existentialist philosopher, has spoken in favour of a suprapolitical agency for solving the modern political problems so that the looming threat of a total annihilation could be avoided.[32]

THE ALTERNATIVE REVEALED IN HISTORY

Through his independent historical studies and deep insight Vivekananda discovered that politics was never an active agent of social change in India, it was a contribution of the Graeco-Roman civilization. 'The voice of Asia', he says, 'has been the voice of

---

30. *Prabuddha Bhārata*, January 1989, p. 70.
31. *Social and Cultural Dynamics*, p. 627.
32. R. K. DasGupta—*Revolutionary Ideas of Swami Vivekananda.*

religion. The voice of Europe is the voice of politics. ... The voice of Europe is the voice of ancient Greece.'[33] His deep historical insight enabled him to discover also that in India changes revolutionizing the society, its institutions, conventions and laws, have always taken place following religious upheavels. For example, Buddhistic and Jaina religious movements altered social arrangements and class-relations overthrowing the priests and their scriptures along with their caste divisions and all that. 'What could have saved Indian society', points out Vivekananda, 'from the ponderous burden of omniferious ritualistic ceremonialism, with its animal and other sacrifices, which all but crushed the very life out of it, except the Jaina Revolution, which took its strong stand exclusively on chaste morals and philosophical truth? Or without the Buddhist revolution what would have delivered the suffering millions of the lower classes from the violent tyrannies of the influential higher castes?'[34]

Citing examples from history he concludes : 'Such changes revolutionizing society have been happening in India again and again, only in this country they have been effected in the name of religion, for religion is the life of India, religion is the language of this country, the symbol of all its movements. The Chārvāka, the Jaina, the Buddhist, Śaṅkara, Rāmānuja, Kabīr, Nānak, Chaitanya, the Brāhmo Samāj, the Ārya Samāj—of all these and similar other sects, the wave of religion, foaming, thundering, surging, breaks in the front, while in the rear follows the filling-up of social wants.'[35] It is to be noted that Vivekananda uses the words, 'foaming, thundering and surging' to describe the tremendous impact of the revolutionary gospel of the new religious movements on society, causing far-reaching changes in class-relations, institutions and social arrangements. Thus Indian history unfolded to him the revolutionary role of religion, not yet seriously noted by any other social revolutionary thinker of the world.

Religion to form the basis of Communism : Having discovered that while the political instrument had failed in the West, religion had proved a success in India as an instrument of social change and human welfare, he boldly subscribed to the

33. *C. W.*, IV, p. 142. 34. ibid., p. 462. 35. ibid.

latter rejecting the other. And he offered what he had discovered in history to the whole world as an alternative to politics. He said emphatically that the only *ism* that we require now is this wonderful idea of the soul—its eternal might ... purity, and its eternal perfection.[36] It appears that Vivekananda was implicitly referring to the 'isms' he has mentioned at different places of his works, viz., Socialism, Anarchism and Nihilism—all political doctrines. He did not totally deny the great ideal of Socialism but has spoken of the necessity of bedrocking it on the sound foundation of Religion. Vedanta being the universal-science-religion, he wanted to found Socialism on its strong foundation, as we have seen already. We have already quoted also the following revealing statement made by him in 1897 : 'All the social upheavalists, at least the leaders of them, are trying to find that all their communistic or equalizing theories must have a spiritual basis, and that spiritual basis is in the Vedanta only. I have been told by several leaders, who used to attend my lectures, that they required the Vedanta as the basis of the new order of things.'[37]

It is really a revolutionary idea—the idea of placing communism, a gospel of revolution, on the basis of the revolutionary Vedantic doctrine of the Divinity of Man. The doctrine of Divinity of Man, suggesting equality of all, itself suggests a society free from privileges, as we have seen already. When communism comes to be based on Vedanta, its instrument would automatically change, its instrument, political revolution, would be replaced by the instrument of neo-Vedanta.

Vivekananda's firm conviction was, as we have seen, that only religion goes to the root, i.e., can cause a root and branch change which means not only change of the externals, change of the institutions, systems, but a thorough change of the primary elements making a society, viz., the human beings. And he was convinced, also seen already, that the permanence of a social order depends on the quality of men only. And from the recent trends in the socialist countries it is evident that they are coming to realize this that the men composing the socialist state are of supreme importance. Everything depends on their character, their

36. ibid., III, pp. 242-43.

37. ibid., V, pp. 212-13.

strength, their goodness—to be very precise. And Vivekananda was also convinced, we repeat, that religion was the most important factor in the making of men. 'What can religion accomplish?' To this self-imposed question he answers emphatically, 'It brings to man eternal life. It has made man what he is, and will make this human animal a god. That is what religion can do. Take religion from human society and what will remain? Nothing but a forest of brutes.'[38] Obviously a society made of the brutes is not a good society, however good may be the institutions and the system, it is bound to decline, it is bound to fail to attain its avowed objects.

VIII

NEO-VEDANTA : THE ALTERNATIVE INSTRUMENT FOR THE MODERN WORLD

Professor Arnold Toynbee and Romain Rolland made it specifically clear that neo-Vedanta as preached by Ramakrishna and Vivekananda may well serve as the alternative to the political instrument in the present-day world. While speaking about Ramakrishna, Toynbee observes : '. . . here we have attitude and spirit that can make it possible for the human race to grow together into a single family—and in the atomic age, this is the only alternative to destroying ourselves.'[39] Romain Rolland speaking in the same trend observes : '. . . the westerner made the wrong choice. He listened to the tempter, who offered him the empire of the world spread out beneath him. The result is that today the European "Apprentice Sorcerer" sees himself overwhelmed by the elemental powers he has blindly unloosed. For he has nothing but the letter of the formula to control them. He has not been concerned with the spirit. Our civilization in dire peril has vainly invoked the spell of great words : Right, Liberty, Cooperation, the Peace of Geneva or Washington—but such words are void or filled with poisonous gas. Nobody believes in them. People mistrust explosives.'[40] 'Among the spiritual ruins',

38. ibid., III, p. 4.
39. Nanda Mukherjee—*Sri Ramakrishna in the Eyes of the Brahmo and Christian Admirers*, p. 112.
40. *Life of Vivekananda*, pp. 295-96.

he adds, 'strewn all over Europe our "Mother India" will teach you to excavate the unshakable foundations in your capitol. She possesses the conclusions and the plans of the "Master Craftsman".'[41]

Thus it is evident that the doctrine of Divinity of Man is basically a revolutionary doctrine which guarantees equal human rights to every man, every community and nation. This doctrine preaching the unity of the universe is key to world amity and peace.

IX

EXPERIMENT OF THE POLITICAL METHOD IN THE PRESENT-DAY INDIA : A FAILURE

It is an irony of fate that India in its bid to attain independence through the quick process turned its back to the plans of the 'Master Craftsman' and leaned towards politics.What has been the result? We are today virtually ruled by a pack of wolves who call themselves politicians and they have thrown national interest to the air in order to have their own personal ambitions fulfilled. The result? Even our national integration is threatened today. The sky is filled with highsounding socialistic slogans, while actually the upper class politicians are thriving at the cost of the lower classes who form the vast masses. The trade union movement is still under the leadership and domination of the upper classes. Even now, long after the movement had reached its matured stage, leadership has not grown from amongst the masses. The result is that we find more political rivalries and intra-class strifes than genuine class struggle. Not only in the trade union movement, in the political arena in general, there is also predominance of the upper class. Vivekananda did not believe, as we have observed earlier, in their liberator's garb. He knew only too well that these people will thrive capitalizing on the misery of the people, who will remain as they were for centuries, divested of their right to have a say in the affairs of the State.

Today we find the ignorant masses are being driven like

41. ibid.

hordes of cattle to support this or that party leaders who belong to the upper class elites, whose profession is politics, whose livelihood is earned from politics. Their economic interest is guiding them to fan all sorts of divisive forces, even the anti-national forces.

Vivekananda had the foresight to see all these and warned us against all these. His definite instruction was : 'Before flooding India with the political or the socialistic ideas, deluge the country with religious ideals.' But this instruction was thrown to the air by our leaders who had in the meantime chosen to make politics their chief instrument.

It should be borne in mind that as a keen student of history with a unique insight he knew all about not only the great revolutions of the past but of the incoming one also. And with cool judgement he chose to reject the idea of political revolutions, its psychology, its execution and all its auxiliaries. The atrocities in the Stalinist era was of the same nature as those of the French Revolution. The cause was defeated in France, does it not seem that the cause has been defeated in the countries which have chosen this instrument to install socialism? The answer seems to be in the affirmative. And that is why that the need for a second revolution has been felt and this is sought to be implemented in the socialist countries today with a priority on improving the human quality.

Knowing all these facts Vivekananda turned to 'history and reason' only in search of his instrument, rejecting all high-sounding doctrines of revolutions. He declared : 'I am no preacher of any momentary social reform. I am not trying to remedy evils, I only ask you to go forward and complete the practical realization of the scheme of human progress that has been laid out in the most perfect order of our ancestors. I only ask you to work to realize more and more the Vedantic ideal of solidarity of man and his inborn divine nature.'

X

A REVOLUTIONARY THEORY OF REVOLUTIONS

As mentioned already, Vivekananda noticed two phases of

every revolution that took place in Indian history. In the first phase, there occurred a religious upheaval which led to remaking of man through a moral revolution. Then the second phase of revolution followed which led to demolishing of exclusive privileges and transformations of social institutions and customs. As a result of all these transformations at the spiritual and social level, creative capacities latent in the individuals found scope to flower in various directions. And this led to material prosperity, artistic creations, scientific advancement—progress in every sense of the term. That is how the Buddhist period came to be one of the most glorious period in Indian history in terms of creative achievements and all-round prosperity.

Obviously such a revolution grows gradually and does not happen all of a sudden sporadically. Vivekananda, therefore, declared, 'I believe in growth and not in reform.' Spiritual and moral revolution takes time to develop, to spread, to envelop vast masses of people, to recreate their being. It is in the nature of things a time-consuming process. Unless this is granted, the orgy of violence that takes place in the name of a 'revolution' installs a regime of tyranny. Tyranny replaces tyranny—only there is change in the authority who perpetrates it. Such has been the lesson of history, lesson of all the revolutions, major or minor, the lesson of the two latest revolutions of major type, viz., the French revolution and the Russian revolution. After the French revolution Napoleon succeeded to grab absolute power, after the Russian Revolution, the Stalinist regime of oppression succeeded.

Gramschi, who attempted to remould Marxist doctrines to make it free from its shortcomings and contradictions, has therefore spoken of a 'passive revolution'. Solzhenitsyn has also re-examined the theory of revolutions, particularly the Marxist doctrine and given his verdict against it.[42]

Thus it is clear—no revolution can achieve its goals unless there precedes a moral and spiritual revolution, re-making of man, as suggested by Vivekananda. And this is the most important phase of a revolution, since the achievement of the goals of a social revolution depends on it.

---

42. *Solzhenitsyn—A Biography*, published by Medical Scrammel (1985), pp. 235-36, 666-68, 792-93.

It is clear from the above that Vivekananda's contribution to the philosophy of revolutions is an outstanding one, as outstanding as his contribution to the realm of religion and philosophy. He has successfully shown that the doctrine of 'Divinity of Man', the central doctrine of Vedanta, is really a doctrine of perpetual revolution. Man must have all those rights which would help him to unfold his infinite latent capacities. This means that there must not be any privilege granted to any one since everyone has the same latent capacity and therefore everyone should enjoy the same opportunities as the others. This doctrine, as we have seen already, strikes at the very root of privileges. It also denies authority, tradition, and the doctrine of eternal law.

The message of Vedanta is *Charaiveti* (move on), hence it is a theory of perpetual progress, which means perpetual revolution. Hence it has been aptly observed by Dr R. K. DasGupta, an eminent Indian scholar : 'The Vedantic foundation of Vivekananda's revolution gives it a universal significance, it presents to the world at large an ideal of perpetual revolution or a perpetual revolution for a perpetual progress.'[43] Bringing out the tremendous significance of Vivekananda's concept of total revolution Dr DasGupta has further observed, 'No revolution, political or religious, in the history of the world, was so rooted in such a comprehensive philosophy.'[44] Herein it far surpasses the doctrines of Voltaire, Rousseau and Marx. Truly the doctrine of 'Divinity of Man' is potent with much more revolutionary significance than the vague concepts of 'Natural Right', 'Liberty', 'Equality' and even of 'Socialism'. All these concepts have no root unless they are grounded on the doctrine of 'Divinity of Man', since natural right, liberty, equality even socialism emanate from the concept of divinity of man.

Socialism grounded on materialism refuses to see the real nature of man and therefore fails to secure for him freedom from every kind of servitude, it only seeks to arrange equal distribution of creature comforts, that too unsuccessfully.

Thus socialism only touches the fringe of the problem. What

---

43. *Revolutionary Ideas of Swami Vivekananda*, p. 39.
44. ibid., p. 36.

about the privileges claimed by the intellectuals, by the physically strong and the spiritually advanced over the ordinary people, not having much intellect, physical strength and spiritual attainments? Their claims have no justification since potentially every one has the same latent capacity. Since the western doctrines of socialism relies on political revolution as their instrument, one kind of servitude is substituted by the other. They have not succeeded so far in liquidating servitude totally, there is no such prospect in the near future.

But Vivekananda's concept of revolution aims at destroying every kind of servitude. 'In the universal melody', he emphasized, 'three ideas stand out—freedom, strength and sameness.'[45] Vedanta aims at freedom from every kind of servitude, not only political, social or economic, but also from the servitude of man to nature, ignorance, to other men, misery, institutions and dogmatism.

By now it is clear that since political revolutions debases man, the revolutionary leaders become one of these day worshippers of naked power. Thus ultimately the purpose of the revolution is defeated. Vivekananda's concept of Vedantic revolution seeks to uplift man and that is why it has the potentiality for success. We have seen such successful revolutions in history, the effects of which disappeared when men were debased again through the intervention of forces which are anti-spiritual, i.e., materialistic. Very often as revealed in history, this intervening force is political.

Thus there is only one method of man's progress. That is the method of making a man a man. Man must be helped to grow to his full stature, made to manifest his infinite possibilities, his creativity, his divinity. Until then he is ensnared by ignorance, his emancipation cannot be secured, no amount of social and institutional change is of any consequence.

As Vivekananda points out, progress does not 'consist in the amount of money in your pocket, or the dress you wear or the house you live in, but in the wealth of spiritual thought in your brain'. 'That looking upward', he says explaining, 'and going upward and seeking perfection are what is called salvation.' 'It is

45. *C. W.*, VII, p. 20.

religion', he adds, 'this enquiry into the beyond, that makes the difference between a man and an animal.' 'That is what makes for human progress', he asserts, 'that is the source of all material and intellectual progress, the motive power behind, the enthusiasm that pushes mankind forward.'[46]

Thus man must be in a perpetual process of 'being and becoming', realizing in the process freedom from fear, from prejudices and superstitions. Man must grow and work out his own salvation, being guided by 'reason'. He is the maker of his own destiny. Institutional changes they will work out to suit the need for his growth. They are of secondary importance.

Socialism is one such important institution but it must be based on Vedanta, or on the theory of a perpetual revolution, not on a theory of revolution which takes place once for all. It must be based on democracy and individual liberty as Vedanta implies that.

THE REVOLUTIONARY SLOGAN—'BE AND MAKE'

Vivekananda's concept of revolution has a global aspect as it is obvious from our discussion so far. As shown by Romain Rolland the aim of Vivekananda was to build a 'City of Mankind' since that is the inevitable result of Advaita Vedanta and its doctrine of 'Universal Unity' made practical. 'But', as pointed out by Rolland, 'he had not only built the city, but the souls of its inhabitants as well.' This was the crux of the strategy of Vivekananda's revolution—'to build the souls of individuals' or 'to re-make our beings'. 'Be and make' was therefore a revolutionary slogan handed down by him to the future generations—'Be man and help others to be men.' 'Be divine and help others to be divine.'

---

46. ibid., IV, p. 208.

CHAPTER 19

Nationalism, Internationalism, and Universalism

I

THE CONCEPT OF UNIVERSAL RELIGION AND NATIONALISM

In terms of his philosophy of Universal Religion Vivekananda envisages national unity within international unity. He envisages also the unity of the diverse races and heterogeneous linguistic, religious and ethnic groups within a particular nation. He envisages, ultimately, unity of mankind. His call was also for 'unity of action, reason, love and work and unity within the vast ocean of all religious thought and all rivers past and present', as pointed out by Romain Rolland.[1] With unity of all these and 'unity of thousand sects of Hinduism', and unity of every man and woman, Vivekananda sought to bring national awakening in India.

Obviously, his call of national awakening was not a call of narrow nationalism. Yet it was thoroughly national since unity of man or universal brotherhood was typically an Indian ideal. '*Svadeśaḥ Bhuvanatrayam*' in Sanskrit meaning 'three worlds are my country' was uttered long ago in India by its seers and saints. 'Hinduism', Arnold Toynbee says, 'is unique among the historic higher religions in holding that neither Hinduism nor any other religion is unique representation of the truth or a unique way of salvation. In the Hindu view, each of the higher religion is a true vision and a right way and all of them alike indispensable to mankind because each gives a different glimpse of the same truth, and each leads by a different route to the same goal of human

1. Romain Rolland, *Life of Vivekananda*, p. 287.

endeavour.' And Toynbee adds significantly, 'In Sri Ramakrishna's testimony to the harmony of religions we have the attitude and the spirit that can make it possible for the human race to grow together into a single family.'[2]

CONCEPT OF WORLD UNITY AS ENVISAGED BY VIVEKANANDA

This concept of religion which is synonymous with universalism integrates nationalism and internationalism. On the one hand, Vivekananda defended India's distinctive cultural heritage, which became the basis of the upsurge of India's nationalistic spirit, at the same time, he desired the world to be benefited by this spiritual culture of India and India to be benefited by the fruits of western civilization. This implies unity of the East and the West. According to Romain Rolland, Vivekananda held that 'The time is past for the pre-eminence of one incomplete and partial civilization. Asia and Europe, the two giants, are standing face to face as equals for the first time. If they are wise, they will work together and the fruit of their labour will benefit all.'[3] This concept of world unity was a valuable contribution to political thought in those days when narrow nationalism was having its heyday.

National Unity : Vivekananda in his call of national unity showed that heterogeneity of the people to an unlimited extent even, is no bar for national unity. All of them can be harmonized to a common pattern as is found in the case of India, India is a case in point of 'unity in diversity'—its unity lies in its faith in the spiritual unity of all living beings. All the heterogeneous groups within the borders of India share this faith.

Narrow Nationalism decried by Vivekananda : Emphasizing that narrow nationalism is a fruitless pursuit for solving human problems and that only internationalism holds the key to this solution Vivekananda observes, '. . . in politics and sociology, problems that were only national twenty years ago can no more be solved on national grounds only. They are assuming huge

2. Nanda Mukherjee—*Ramakrishna in the Eyes of Brahmo and Christian Admirers*, p. 112.
3. ibid.

proportions, gigantic shapes. They can only be solved when looked at in the broader light of international grounds. International organizations, international combinations, international laws are the cry of the day.'[4]

Pointing out that narrow nationalism leads to war and other disastrous effects, Vivekananda says in a critical tone, 'In the present times a huge wave of nationalism is sweeping over Europe, where people speaking the same tongue, professing the same religion, and belonging to the same race want to unite together. Wherever such union is being effectively accomplished, there is great power being manifested; and where this is impossible, death is inevitable. After the death of the present Austrian Emperor, Germany will surely try to absorb the German-speaking portion of the Austrian Empire—and Russia and others are sure to oppose her; so there is the possibility of a dreadful war.'[5]

While he did oppose such narrow nationalism, nevertheless he upheld the rights of nationalities to self-determination. Since 'A nationality, in the Swamiji's eyes', writes Sister Nivedita, 'had all the sacredness of a Church—a Church whose inmost striving was to express its own conception of the ideal manhood.'[6] He wanted the nationalities to retain their distinctiveness, their uniqueness and enjoy freedom and independence.

II

HUMANISTIC NATIONALISM AND NARROW NATIONALISM

Nationalism has been, since the history of French Revolution, the most important driving force of domestic, imperial, and international politics. From the late eighteenth century to the first half of the nineteenth century—nationalism was essentially inspired by humanistic and democratic ideas. For example, Giuseppe Mazzini, the apostle of nationalism in the modern West, says, 'Every people has its special mission, which will cooperate towards the fulfilment of the general mission of humanity. That mission constitutes its nationality. Nationality is

4. *C. W.*, III, p. 241.
5. ibid., VII, p. 389.
6. Sister Nivedita, *The Master As I Saw Him*, p. 209.

sacred.'[7] This concept of nationality is democratic and humanitarian. This is evident in the following utterance of Mazzini again, 'All unjust rule, all violence, every act of egotism exercised to the injury of the people, is a violation of the liberty, equality and fraternity of the peoples. All the peoples should aid and assist each other in putting an end to it.' This concept of humanistic nationalism ultimately merges into internationalism. This is also evident from still another statement of Mazzini which runs as follows : 'Humanity will only be truly constituted when all the people, of which it is composed, have acquired the free exercise of their sovereignty, and shall be associated in a Republican Confederation, governed and directed by a common Declaration of Principles and a common pact, towards the common aim—the discovery and fulfilment of the Universal Moral Law.'[8]

From the late eighteenth century to the early nineteenth century nationalism as an ideal was upheld in this sense in countries like France, America, Czechoslovakia, Italy, Ireland and Poland. In the second half of the nineteenth century nationalism took a different course, it became an ally of parochialism, intolerance, bigotry, persecution of minorities, racialism, imperialism and aggression. This is evident from 'the record of pan-Germanism, Tsarist imperialism, Japanese militarism, Fascism, and finally, Communist imperialism', as has been pointed out by Ebenstein.[9]

Vivekananda was an exponent of the democratic humanistic type of nationalism and vehemently opposed the narrow nationalism of the second type. It is evident from his statements quoted above.

III

RIGHTS OF ABORIGINES AND OTHER TRIBES WITHIN A NATION

Not only the nationalities, in Vivekananda's opinion, every distinct group, ethnic, linguistic, cultural, religious, etc., within a

7. Quoted in *Modern Political Thought—The Great Issues*, William Ebenstein, Oxford Publishing Co., 1960, p. 753.
8. ibid.
9. ibid., p. 741.

particular nation has a right to preserve their distinctiveness. He condemned the European policy which led to the destruction of such distinctive groups. 'And may I ask you, Europeans', he said in mood of sharp criticism, 'what country you have ever raised to better conditions? Wherever you have found weaker races, you have exterminated them by the roots, as it were. ... What is the history of your America, your Australia, and New Zealand, your Pacific Islands and South Africa?'[10] In this connection he points out the significance of the Aryan convention of integrating each weaker racial group into the nation body through the institution of *Varṇa* as is found in India. 'In Europe', he says, 'it is everywhere victory to the strong, and death to the weak. In the land of Bhārata, every social rule is for the protection of the weak.'[11] He protested against the European policy at the Paris Congress held in 1900.

IV

ONE WORLD : THE DREAM OF VIVEKANANDA

Now each single group, each nationality small or big, according to Vivekananda, has distinctive contribution to make to human civilization, each has a place in the confederation of nations. What Vivekananda dreamt of was 'one world' with a multiplicity of nations, small and large, enjoying equal rights and each working out in its own way the betterment of human life. This concept of Vivekananda was brought to light by Romain Rolland who observed : 'That which emerges (from his message of spiritual oneness of the universe) is his universal sense. He had hopes of democratic America, he was enthusiastic over the Italy of Art, Culture and Liberty—the great mother of Mazzini. He spoke of China as the treasury of the world. He fraternized with martyred Babists of Persia. He embraced in equal love the India of the Hindus, the Mohammedans, and the Buddhists. He was fired by the Moghul Empire; when he spoke of Akbar the Great, tears came flowing into his eyes. He could comprehend and defend the grandeur of Chenghis Khan and his dream of Asiatic Unity. He made Buddha the subject of magnificent eulogy : "I am the servant of the servants of Buddha".'

10. *C. W.*, V, pp. 536-37.

11. ibid., p. 537.

With this universal sympathy, this lively acceptance of all that is great and good in every nationality, his nationalism was in fact a great ideal of unity of mankind, it is a nationalism which merges into internationalism, nay, into universalism in the end. A distinctive characteristic of his ideas is the comprehensiveness of his vision, he looks upon mankind as a manifestation of the Universal Soul. In each particular nationality is this Universal Soul manifested and nothing else. All the varieties, therefore, are manifestations of the Universal Soul, all the varieties exist in that Universal Unity. Vivekananda thus perceived spiritual unity as the ultimate ground of all diversity.

As shown by him unity is the one goal of all human knowledge. It underlies all religious doctrines and mystic experiences, all philosophical conceptions, all ethical ideals and scientific discoveries. And according to him further, it unites all forms of existence, penetrates all phases of life. He perceived that the forms differ but the substance is the same. A particular nationality differs from another in form but at bottom the same human nature is to be found lurking in the peoples belonging to that nationality as in the case of other different nationalities. And he who has a vision of this One Self pervading all, abhors none, shuns none, loves all, accepts one and all. Hence he says, 'If you go below the surface, you find that Unity between man and man, between races and races, high and low, rich and poor, gods and men, and men and animals. If you go deep enough, all will be seen as only variations of the One, and he who has attained to this conception of Oneness has no more delusion. . . . He knows the reality of everything, the secret of everything. . . . He has traced the reality of everything to the Lord, the Centre, the Unity of everything, and that is Eternal Existence, Eternal Knowledge, Eternal Bliss.'[12] It seems as if Vivekananda has been speaking of his own experiences in the above statement.

Hence to him every nationality had the same worth as the other and through the different nationalities the human race as a whole was struggling for the fulfilment of its highest goal. Hence Romain Rolland observes, 'Far from feeling that there was a fundamental natural difference between Europe and Asia, he was convinced that deep contact between Europe and Asia would

12. ibid., II, pp. 153-54.

inevitably lead to a renaissance of Europe; for she would renew her vital stock of spiritual ideas from the East.'[13] But not only was Europe to benefit from Asia, Asiatic countries were also to benefit from Europe. 'India has to learn from Europe', says Vivekananda emphatically, 'the conquest of external nature, and Europe has to learn from India the conquest of internal nature. Then there will be neither Hindus [Indians] nor Europeans—there will be the ideal humanity which has conquered both the natures, the external and the internal. We have developed one phase of humanity, and they another. It is the union of the two that is wanted. The word freedom which is the watchword of our religion really means freedom physically, mentally, and spiritually.'[14] Thus diversity of nationalities, according to Vivekananda, points out towards unification of humanity. Nationalism here becomes a gospel of humanism of a unique type.

Thus Vivekananda's concept of nationalism is an integral part of internationalism gradually converging into universalism. This is an unique idea of nationalism fed on the ideal of universal brotherhood, peace and amity that he preached rising above all parochialism, narrow ideas of nationalism. As has been aptly stated by one writer : 'A distinctive characteristic of Swami Vivekananda is the comprehensiveness of his vision. He is remarkably universal, his message universal, his life and work universal. He stands up for mankind in general, without distinction of race or nationality, creed or age. He has in his view all types and grades of human beings, takes into account the various aspects of human life, and dwells on the basic problems of human existence. He sees the divine self of man and looks upon the human form as the very symbol of the divinity. In Vivekananda the universal spirit has found a loving, dynamic, and all-encompassing expression, which is rarely to be found elsewhere.'[15]

Thus the keynote of Vivekananda's nationalism is universalism. Hence those who criticize Vivekananda for having preached spiritualistic imperialism of India in the name of nationalism, is miles away from the truth.

---

13. *Life of Vivekananda*, p. 154.
14. *C. W.*, V, p. 216.
15. Swami Satprakashananda—'Swami Vivekananda's Universality' in *Swami Vivekananda in the East and the West*, Ramakrishna Vedanta Centre, London, 1968, p. 183.

Part V

The Economic Ideas

CHAPTER 20

Indian Economic Thinking in the Nineteenth Century

I

THE PIONEERS

The history of Indian economic thought has been rather a neglected branch of study in this country for long. Only recently, it is gratifying to note, that two eminent economists of our country have come forward to deal with it. They are Dr Bhabatosh Dutta of Calcutta University[1] and Dr B. N. Ganguly of Delhi University.[2] Here and there may be a few other authors dealing with the subject, but their works are not so well known.

According to them, the pioneers in the field of economic thinking in India are Dadabhai Naoroji (1825-1917), Mahadev Govinda Ranade (1842-1901) and Ramesh Chandra Dutta (1848-1909).

Dadabhai in those days had vast knowledge of the economic problems of India. He is well known today for his 'Drain Theory' and his book *Poverty and Un-British Rule in India*. This book was the first study of the poverty of India. In his studies he exposed the exploitative colonial fiscal policy of the British which was according to him at the root of the spreading poverty of the country. He made also the first ever estimate of the national income of India. Ramesh Chandra Dutta is well known for his treatise *Indian Economic History*. Mahadev Govinda Ranade is well known for his philosophy of economic nationalism and his

1. Dr Bhabatosh Dutta—(1) *Evolution of Economic Thinking in India*, (2) *Indian Economic Thought*, Twentieth Century Perspective.
2. Dr B. N. Ganguly—*Indian Economic Thought* (*1976*), Nineteenth Century Perspective, Tata Mcgraw-Hill.

'Poona Sarbojanic Sabhā' which was set up by him for carrying on field survey of the economic conditions of some of the districts of Maharashtra.

Another person, an associate of Ranade, J. V. Joshi, drew notice on account of his remarkable essay on the financial condition of India and sectoral imbalances.[3] Gopal Krishna Gokhale the well-known nationalist leader received attention as a constructive thinker on 'Welfare and Development'.[4]

II

ECONOMIC THINKING OF THE RENAISSANCE LEADERS

Besides the above mentioned thinkers, nineteenth century economic thinking in India was enriched by the three most prominent leaders of the renaissance, viz., Rammohan, Bankim-chandra and Vivekananda. But Dr Dutta has chosen to give recognition to Rammohan only, while Dr Ganguly has chosen to recognize Bankim as well, as a constructive economic thinker. Dr Dutta surprisingly expressed surprise at the lack of economic thinking among those leaders who came following Rammohan, when actually there was no dearth of it among them. He observed that while the intellectuals of the nineteenth century were acquainted with the works of J. S. Mill and the economic thinkers of the West, no one came following the foot-steps of Rammohan to devote their attention to the economic problems of the country, although they left their mark of impress on other branches of knowledge, e.g., philosophy and history.[5]

Dr Dutta and Dr Ganguly both sought to ignore Vivekananda in this respect even without a word of apology. The exclusion of Bankim by Dr Dutta is really surprising since Bankim wrote a number of articles on economic problems under the title 'Sāmya'.

Vivekananda's Knowledge of Economics : The exclusion of Vivekananda is a pointer to the fact that the garb of the monk in his case led to the general misconception among the intellectuals that he cannot have anything to do with a mundane subject like

3. ibid., pp. 103-25.
4. ibid., pp. 217-35.
5. Dr B. Dutta—*Evolution of Economic Thinking in India*, p. 16.

economics. We have already referred to the fact that Vivekananda was well-versed in economics and he mastered economic theories and problems so much so that he addressed the annual convention of the American Social Science Association on 6 September 1893 before he addressed the Parliament of Religions on September 11, 1893, which brought him world-wide fame. As mentioned by Marie Louise Burke, the *Daily Saratogian* reported on September 7 under the heading 'Money was the Subject' that on the second day's session of the American Social Science Association held at Saratoga, 'the addresses and papers all pertained to finance', and Col. Jacob L. Greene of Hartford read a paper on 'Bimetalism', 'A paper by Dr Charles B. Spahr of New York followed on the state of silver', 'A paper by President E. Benjamin Andrews of Brown University on "The Monetary Experiment in India" was a masterpiece for thought and intellectual ability'. 'At the conclusion of the reading', the report continues, 'Vivekananda, the Hindu monk, addressed the audiences in an intelligent and interesting manner, taking for his subject. "The Use of Silver in India".'[6] Obviously, unless a person was well conversant with monetary economics he could not have participated in the deliberations on such a technical subject as 'Money' at an august assembly like the annual convention of the American Social Science Association in an intelligent and interesting manner. The incident speakes volumes about Vivekananda's knowledge of economics.

Vivekananda's Knowledge of Economic Problems : Vivekananda had not only the theoratical knowledge of economics, but also first-hand knowledge of the economic problems of India and other countries more than any other nineteenth century Indian economic thinker. As noted already, he traversed through the length and breadth of the sub-continent on the soles of his feet for seven long years (1886-1893) and acquired this first-hand knowledge. This sub-continent was at the time in the grip of terribly devastating famines in which millions died and millions turned paupers. Sharing their hunger, their privations and misery, he tried to find out the causes responsible

6. *Swami Vivekananda In America—New Discoveries* (2nd edition), pp. 47-48.

for this economic distress and was convinced that the colonial economic policy of the British and the exploitation of the masses by the aristocracy were responsible for the situation.

When he arrived at Bombay in July 1892, the Bombay Millhands' Association had already seen the light of the day, and the first Factory Act passed in 1881 had been just amended in 1891. The conditions of the emerging proletariat were at the time simply appalling. A keen observer always, he could not have missed also the significance of the labour strikes that took place since 1875. He in fact mentioned them while once talking to his disciples, pointing out that these were indicative of the day when the proletariat will win power. 'The masses of Europe and America', he said, 'have been the first to awaken and have already begun the fight. Signs of this awakening have shown themselves in India, too, as is evident from the number of strikes among the lower classes nowadays.'[7] He could not also have overlooked the message of the two labour journals that came out at the time, viz., Lokhande's *Dīnabandhu* from Bombay and Shashipada Banerjee's *Śramajībī* from Calcutta.

Throwing light on Vivekananda's knowledge of the practical economic problems of India, Romain Rolland has significantly pointed out that 'He (Vivekananda) was conversant with the problems of industrial and rural economy whereby the life of the common man was controlled.'[8] Sister Nivedita, while referring to the conversations of Swamiji during their travels together through Northern India in 1899, has also thrown light on the matter. 'Nowhere does his love seem more intense than as we passed across the long stretches of the plains covered with fields and farms and villages. Here his thought was free to brood over the land as a whole and he would spend hours explaining the communal system of agriculture, or describing the daily life of the farm housewife.'[9] Pointing out that his knowledge was first hand, acquired during the days of his roaming over India, Nivedita further observes, 'It was the memory doubtless, of his own days as a wanderer, that so brightened his eyes and thrilled in his voice, as he told us these things.'[10]

---

7. *C. W.*, VII, p. 149. 8. Romain Rolland—*Life of Vivekananda*, p. 22.
9. Sister Nivedita, *The Master As I Saw Him*, pp. 88-89. 10. ibid.

Vivekananda's Knowledge of the Problems of the Labour Classes : His knowledge of the problems of the labour classes in India is evident from his following observation : 'Those uncared-for lower classes of India—the peasants and weavers and the rest, who have been conquered by foreigners and are looked down upon by their own people—it is they who from time immemorial have been working silently, without even getting the remuneration of their labours! But what great changes are taking place slowly, all over the world, in pursuance of nature's laws! Countries, civilizations, and supremacy are undergoing revolutions.'[11] Here it is evident that he knew of 'surplus value', of which the labourers were being deprived; and he knew also of the revolutionary upsurges that were taking shape at the time in the different countries of the world for the redemption of their birthrights.

Referring to this aspect of his thought E. P. Chelishev observes :'His voice keenly attuned to the voice of the epoch, Vivekananda was able to discern in it the still indirect grumble of the toiling masses rising to the fight for their rights.'[12] In support of his view Chelishev quotes the following passage from Vivekananda : 'The lower classes are gradually awakening to this fact and making a united front against this, determined to exact their legitimate dues.' We may quote again the following statement of Viekananda which reveals that he was well versed with the problems of labourers and their struggles for the redemption of their rights : 'The masses of Europe and America have been the first to awaken and have already begun the fight. Signs of this awakening have shown themselves in India, too, as is evident from the number of strikes among the lower classes nowadays.'[13] Buchanan mentions a cessation of work by some workers in the Empress Mills, Nagpur, in the 1890's and since then cessation of work by the workers began to assume a deliberate character. The strikes in Bombay cotton mills in 1892 and jute workers strike in Budge Budge near Calcutta in 1895 were of such types.[14] That none of these events escaped

11. *C. W.*, VII, p. 358.
12. *Vivekananda Centenary Memorial Volume*, p. 510.
13. *C. W.*,•VII, p. 149.
14. Dhiresh Bhattacharya—*The Concise Economic History of India*, p. 187 (1st edition).

Vivekananda's notice is only apparent from his just quoted statement.

Vivekananda's role in bringing political, social and economic consciousness among the people : In modern India one notices a dynamic upsurge of new political and social consciousness. It was brought forth by Vivekananda. Vivekananda's vital role in this matter has been brought out with ample support of evidences by Professor Sankari Prasad Basu in the seven volumes of his monumental work in Bengali, viz., *Vivekananda O Samakālīn Bhāratvarṣa* ('Vivekananda and the Contemporary India').[15] It must be remembered that political consciousness is always accompanied by economic awareness since the aims of political movements cannot be fulfilled without the realization of the economic goals. Actually, state power is needed by a people to solve their economic problems. Thus it is an absurd proposition that Vivekananda, who brought national awakening, political consciousness and kindled the desire for fighting out the way to independence among the people of this country, had no idea of its pressing economic problems. Only he, among the stalwarts of the nineteenth century, had the opportunity to dive deep into the ocean of the life of the toiling masses and acquire first hand knowledge about them since he was a roaming monk, living on the charity of the poorest of the poor, often lying with them in their humble cottages. This opportunity was not available to Rammohan, a member of the landed aristocracy, Bankim, a civil servant, Dadabhai, an upper class elite; Ranade, a member of the highest judiciary in the country, R. C. Datta, a topmost civil service holder. Their knowledge was only second hand. And Vivekananda, who had a heart of the Buddha felt deeply concerned with the problems of the toiling masses — their poverty, their misery, their privations. Vivekananda's heart and soul was involved in finding out a solution of the burning economic problems of the masses in India.

---

15. Sankari Prasad Basu, *Vivekananda O Samakālīn Bhāratvarṣa*, Mondal Book House.

III

CONTEMPORARY ECONOMIC HISTORY

Besides, it must also be borne in mind that Vivekananda was always a keen student of history and had acquired vast knowledge of world history. Such a person could never be indifferent to the contemporary economic situation as revealed through the contemporary economic history of his own country and of the world, which was strikingly eventful and dramatic. It is an absurd proposition that he did not learn anything from this history to enrich his own thought. His very sensitive mind must have felt very much involved when he read the account of the revolt of the peasants against the indigo planters that took place almost in the contemporary period. Of the Deccan riots he must have learnt during his days of travelling through the Deccan region in the early 1890's. The Indigo Revolt started in the wake of the Sepoy Mutiny of 1857 and the Deccan riots in 1875 in the wake of a devastating famine in the region. Similar other violent revolts broke out in the post-Plassy-war period in Bengal, e.g., the struggles of the weavers and Malangis, the peasants' revolt against Devi Singh, the rent collector of the East India Co., the peasants' revolt in Bankura, the Chuar Revolt in Medinipur and the Sannyasi Revolt in Northern Bengal, all against the economic exploitation of the peasants and artisans by the British.[16] That all these did not escape his attention is evident from his statement quoted by Chelishev, mentioned above. He was thoroughly conversant about the Indian economic crisis of the period and gave a concrete shape to the economic aspirations of the renascent nation with a special emphasis on the solution of the problems of the exploited masses.

The Indian newspapers of the period : The Indian newspapers (*patrikā*) of the period played a vital role in focussing the economic problems and the colonial economic policy of the British. *Hindu Patriot* of Harish Chandra Mukherjee, *Amritabazar Patrika* of Sisir Ghose, *Tattvabodhinī* of Akshay Kumar Dutta, *Saṁvād Prabhākar* of Ishvar Gupta,

---

16. Nemai Sadhan Bose—*The Indian Awakening and Bengal* (2nd Edition), p. 202.

Baṅgadarṣan of Bankim Chandra, *Bengali* of Surendra Nath Banerjee and *Śramajībī* of Shashipada Banerjee—provided abundant materials for provoking thoughts in a person like Vivekananda for solving the economic problems of the country. Always a voracious reader, always a dynamic personality, always ready to learn from all available sources, always deeply concerned with the problems of the masses who formed the nation, Vivekananda could never have missed the import of the materials supplied to him by the newspapers of the period.

The role of voluntary associations : Besides these newspapers, there were various associations, e.g., British Indian Association (1837), Indian Association (1875), Śilpa-Vidyotsāhinī Sabhā (1854), Baṅgīya Samāj-Vijñān Sabhā (1867), formed during this period which held meetings, seminars, and discourses regularly, functioned to throw light on the burning economic and social problems of the day, particularly on the land revenue policy of the British, the conditions of the factory and plantation labourers and the condition of the peasantry.

Moreover, between 1867 and 1880, regular exhibitions of the traditional Indian handicrafts were organized by the Hindu-Melā Committee. The National Society of Navagopal Mitra also played an important role in the efforts made for the revival of the Indian traditional handicrafts. Vivekananda was a member of the gymnasium started by 'National' Navagopal (as he came to be known) and was therefore well acquainted with his role in the matter.

Born and brought up in this atmosphere, Vivekananda had some positive thinking on all these vital economic questions focussed by the newspapers, associations and exhibitions.

The best evidence of his thorough knowledge of the economic problems of India is to be found in the account mentioned above of his discourse on the 'Use of Silver in India' at the annual convention of the American Social Science Association on 6 September 1893, before he became famous on 11 September 1893 by delivering his historic speech at the inaugural session of the Parliament of Religions. The British rulers in India at the time, were experimenting with Bimetalism in India and both gold and silver were in use as the currency basis. It is clear that Vivekananda was quite conversant with the experiment and the controversy that centred round the question of Bimetalism as the currency basis at the time. Otherwise how could a layman dare to speak on such a technical subject as monetary economics before the august assembly of distinguished economists and social scientists of America. And as we have noted earlier he won a word of appreciation from the press for his speech.

IV

WORLD BACKGROUND OF HIS ECONOMIC THOUGHT

Vivekananda's economic thinking, which we will presently analyse, was positivistic in character and had a world background. This positivistic and realistic traits of his economic thought were the result of his direct contact with the masses—the result of his studies of the economic problems of the masses direct from the pages of the book of life. We are told by his biographers that Vivekananda discussed these practical economic problems of the masses with the native princes. The problems of the landless peasantry, the declining handicrafts, the famines, the appalling poverty of the masses—everything came up in his conversations with them. Actually his main object of visiting the royal courts was to awaken them to their duties towards the masses.

Similarly, in the West also he availed every opportunity to make direct contact with the masses and took every opportunity to be conversant with the economic problems of the region he went to visit. Focussing light on the matter Mary Louise Burke points out, 'As was said of him he acquired the "greatest familiarity with the institutions of this country— religious, political and social". Nor was this familiarity acquired through contact with the intellectuals alone; rather, as he said, he spoke during the course of his mid-western tour also with the labourers and farmers, his finger was, as it were, on the pulse of the nation.'[17] His predictions about the proletariat revolution taking place either in China or Russia, mentioned earlier, speak volumes

17. *Swami Vivekananda In America—New Discoveries* (Part II), p. 368.

of his knowledge of the economic conditions of the masses in these countries. He visited China, but never had the opportunity to visit Russia, nevertheless he had full information of the economic conditions of the masses in Russia also. Through his historical studies he knew that the masses there were oppressed—oppressed under the dual tyranny of feudalism and the imperial power.

On his way to Chicago in 1893 he visited China and Japan and noted the contrast between the two countries as regards their economic conditions. He saw that China, engrossed in extreme poverty, had become totally static, whereas Japan was well ahead on the way to prosperity through her self-efforts to adopt modernization of industries.

The child-labour in China shocked him. 'The Chinese child', he commented, 'is quite a philosopher and calmly goes to work at an age when your Indian boy can hardly crawl on all fours.'[18] That extreme poverty was behind this misuse and tyrannyzing of childhood was apparent to him. 'Their extreme poverty', he went on to observe further, 'is one of the causes why the Chinese and the Indians have remained in a state of mummified civilization. To an ordinary Hindu (Indian) or Chinese, everyday necessity is too hideous to allow him to think of anything else.'[19] In a country where there is extreme poverty there must be extensive unemployment also. As a result, in such a country people fall heavily on petty-trading for their livelihood. Revealing this Vivekananda further observed : 'Every house is a shop, people living on the top-floor.'[20] China's economic conditions at the time become vivid from this description. Regarding the Japanese self-effort at industrialization he observed : 'The match factories are simply a sight to see, and they are bent upon doing everything they want.'[21] Japan's economic prosperity attained through self-effort fired him and he wrote to his followers to engage themselves in making the same kind of efforts.

His reflections on the various European countries in his *Memoirs of European Travel* give us a glimpse of their economic conditions. His observation on Serbia and Bulgaria is an

---

18. *Letters of Swami Vivekananda*, pp. 56-57.
19. ibid., p. 57.
20. ibid.
21. ibid.

example. Unveiling the conditions of these two countries he pointed out that 'Throughout Serbia and Bulgaria you find the same mud houses, and people dressed in tattered rags, and heaps of filth—and I was almost inclined to think I was back to India! . . . Living in a mud house with mud roof, with tattered rags on his person, and surrounded by hogs—there you have your Serb or Bulgarian!'[22] Herein he has brought out in full the extreme poverty of the masses in the two European countries, pointing out that economically they were not better-off than the Indians.

Thus it is evident that he had direct knowledge of the economic conditions of many different countries, eastern and western.

Finally, as we shall see presently, Vivekananda had full knowledge of the phenomena of capitalism and imperialism which were responsible for the underdevelopment and poverty of the country like India. All these show that he had full knowledge of the world economic conditions of the time. This served as the background of his economic thinking, as we shall see in the next few chapters.

---

22. *C. W.*, VII, p. 391.

CHAPTER 21

The Role of Labour and Socialist Economic Thinking

I

ROLE OF LABOUR

Since Vivekananda learnt economic problems directly from the book of life—his attention was drawn, from the very beginning, to the problems of the labour class. In his opinion labour was the basic class in society on which depended prosperity of nations and flourishing of civilizations. Regarding this concept of labour being the chief instrument of production it might be that like Karl Marx he was influenced by Ricardo. Since he considered the labour class as the foundation of society, no problem regarding them could ever escape his notice.

II

DIVISION OF LABOUR AND MECHANIZATION

As we all know, division of labour in large-scale industries makes mechanization of the minutest process of production possible. Dwelling on how this development affects labour he observes : 'Machinery in a small proportion is good, but too much of it kills man's initiative and makes a lifeless machine of him. The men in factories are doing the same monotonous work, day after day, night after night, year after year, each batch of men doing one special bit of work—such as fashioning the heads of pins, or uniting the ends of threads, or moving backwards or forwards with the loom—for a whole life. And the result is that the loss of that special job means death to them—they find no other means of living and starve. Doing routine work like a machine, one becomes a lifeless machine[1].' The example he has given here reminds us of Adam Smith's famous example on this matter, viz., that of eighteen different stages of producing a small pin.

Consequences of Mechanization : Here he brings to light two consequences of the modern technology—of mechanization—which are not conducive to the interests of the labourer. Firstly, mechanization leads to specialization at every minute stage of production which may lead to difficulty in getting another job in case a labourer loses the one he has been presently holding due to technological changes, since his specialized knowledge would not suit any and every job. In such a case he has no alternative but to remain unemployed. Secondly, since his initiative is killed for repeating the same minutest part of the total productive work mechanically, he declines in capacity and gradually becomes unable to acquire new skill. This is surely detrimental to his interest. This is the same as the Marxian view on division of labour. Dwelling on it Adam Ferguson, whom Marx follows in this matter, says, 'Whilst the division of labour raises the productive power of labour and increases the wealth and refinement of society, it impoverishes the worker and reduces him to a machine.'[2] This is also the essence of Vivekananda's statement quoted above.

III

THE IMPORTANCE OF THE ORDINARY WORKERS

Vivekananda in his statements on labour points to the extreme importance of the ordinary unskilled labourers and this is his original contribution to labour economics since no other thinker prior to him has revealed this. 'Who invented ship?' Vivekananda asks. To this self-imposed question he replies, 'No one in particular. That is to say, like all machinery indispensable to men—without which they cannot do for a single moment, and

1. *C. W.*, VII, p. 317.
2. Adam Ferguson—*Principles of Moral and Political Science*, p. 1/24, quoted by W. G. Runsiman in his *Social Science and Political Theory*, Cambridge, p. 49.

by the combination and adjustment of which all kinds of factory plants have been constructed— the ship also is the outcome of joint labour.'[3] 'Take for instance', he adds by way of elucidating the point further, 'the wheels; how absolutely indispensable they are! From the creaking bullock-cart to the car of Jagannath, from the spinning wheel to the stupendous machinery of factories, everywhere there is use for the wheel. Who invented the wheel? No one in particular, that is to say, all jointly.'[4] Thus, according to him, the most important inventions of common and indispensable use are to be credited to the joint effort of the ordinary unskilled labourers. Hence their importance in productive activities should never be forgotten.

IV

WAGES AND SURPLUS VALUE

We have already referred to Vivekananda's view regarding wages—that wages received by the labourers do not equal the value of their labour. While dwelling on the role of Indian labourers in the economic life of the world as a whole he gave his views on this matter. 'The uncared for labour classes of India', he says, 'the peasants and the weavers and the rest . . . it is they who from time immemorial have been working silently, without even getting the remuneration of their labour.' Thus he points out that a part of the value produced by the labourers is taken away by the non-productive classes—that they do not get the full value of their produce. This is also the essence of the theory of 'Surplus Value' propounded by Karl Marx.

V

EXPLOITATION OF THE LABOURERS

In his various observations Vivekananda pointed out that the labourers of the colonial countries were exploited not only by the upper non-producing classes, i.e., the aristocratic elites at home, but also by the imperialist ruling class from foreign countries belonging to the class of merchant-capitalists. He showed also

---

3. *C. W.*, VII, p. 310. 4. ibid.

that the exploitation of the labourers of the colonies like India was the basis of the economic prosperity of the imperialist and capitalist countries, who ruled the colonies. Referring to this exploitation he observed, 'Ye labouring classes of India, as a result of your silent, constant labours Babylon, Persia, Alexandria, Greece, Rome, Venice, Genoa ... Denmark, Holland, and England have successively attained supremacy and eminence! And you?— Well, who cares to think of you!'[5] Here he shows clearly that from time immemorial the labourers of India have been exploited by all the imperialist countries known in history in spite of the fact that the prosperity of these countries was in a sense created by these labourers who produced various commodities for the exploiters. In a sense therefore, they were the makers of civilization. And Vivekananda warned us that the makers of civilizations could also destroy civilizations if the exploitation was allowed to go on unabated.

According to Vivekananda, the toiling masses in the imperial countries were also exploited by the same ruling class at home who sent them to the colonies as soldiers to conquer their territories in the interest of themselves. 'They that have money', he revealed, 'have kept the government of the land under their thumb, are robbing the people and sending them as soldiers to fight and be slain on foreign shores, so that in case of victory, their coffers may be full of gold by the blood of the subject-people on the field of battle.'

VI

SOCIALISTIC THINKING IN THE NINETEENTH CENTURY INDIA

We have referred already to the fact that Vivekananda hailed Socialism although he did not consider it in its present form an ideal or a perfect system. He hailed it since it held out a promise for the labourers, exploited so long, to regain their legitimate dues, viz., the full value of their labour and their just human rights. None among the other nineteenth century thinkers in India seems to have such a clear vision of the impending advent of

5. ibid., p. 358.

some sort of a socialistic system. No one, beginning from Rammohan to Ramesh Chandra Dutta, made any reference to the necessity of any radical change in property relations in Indian society. Vivekananda is the sole exception in this matter. He spoke clearly and boldly in favour of a root and branch change in the social arrangements.

Rammohan : Rammohan spoke of the necessity of a rent-freeze to ameliorate the conditions of the peasantry while appearing before a Selection Committee of the British Parliament, but never did he say a word in favour of abolition of the *zamindari* system or of any other measure for bringing about a radical change in the land system so as to confer ownership of land to the tillers of the soil.

Bankim : Bankim in his essays on *sāmya* (equality) discussed the philosophical aspects of the utopian socialism as known at the time, but he never showed any awareness of the impending revolutionary event— of Shudras ascending to supremacy in society. While protesting against the oppression of the *zamindar*s on the tenants in the past, he at the same time hailed the Tenancy Reform Act of 1885 with the comment that the oppression of the peasantry by the landlord has ceased, rather it is the landlord who is now weak and the tenant is a tyrant.[6] To say this about the Tenancy Reform Act of 1885 is to manifest a sentiment which is definitely pro-feudalistic and not pro-revolutionary or socialistic by any means.

Dadabhai, Ramesh Dutta and Ranade : Dadabhai never paid any attention to the question of socialism as such, while Ramesh Chandra Dutta's attempt to eulogize Permanent Settlement reveals the fact that he was miles away from any type of socialistic thinking. Ranade's thought also is characterized by the absence of socialistic thinking. According to him, the Tenancy Act of 1885 was a 'communistic measure'![7] As argued by him if the tenants were to be granted any sort of right in land, then they must buy it 'on payment of a fair price'.[8] He never thought it over that the poor tenants living on subsistence level could not have

6. *Bankim Rachanāvalī*, Vol. II, Sāhitya Saṁsad, p. 287.
7. Dr Bhabatosh Dutta—*The Evolution of Economic Thinking in India*, p. 16.
8. ibid.

the means to purchase their ownership rights. He did not also realize that it was the height of injustice to deprive the tillers of the soil the right to ownership on land and to confer it on a parasitic class playing no role in productive activities in the agricultural sector.

Vivekananda : Vivekananda, on the otherhand, clearly and emphatically denied the rights of the parasites to exist. He upheld the rights of the peasants and toilers since they, in his opinion, played the most crucial role in the system of production. 'But they are', he said forcefully, 'the backbone of the nation in all countries. If these lower classes stop work, from where will you get your food and clothing?' Continuing on the same topic he further said, 'Engrossed in the struggle for existence, they had not the opportunity for the awakening of knowledge. They have worked so long uniformly like machines ... and the clever educated section have taken the substantial part of the fruits of their labour. . . . The lower classes are gradually awakening to this fact and making a united front against this, determined to exact their legitimate dues.'[9] Pointing out unerringly to the incoming future events he said, 'You will be destroyed by internecine quarrels and fights—which you have been having so long. When the masses will wake up, they will come to understand your oppression of them, and by a puff of their mouth you will be entirely blown away.' When one reads between these lines it strikes him or her as if something inevitable is being related by a person who is an eye-witness to the future great event.

Vivekananda's vision of the Shudras coming to power : Finally, Vivekananda had that great vision, related in the same vivid manner, of the event of the masses, exploited and oppressed from time immemorial, ascending to power and 'the upper classes who were already dead' according to him, disappearing in the void. His prophetic vision was expressed in his inimitable language thus : '... you, the upper classes of India! . . . Fleshless and bloodless skeleton of the deadbody of Past India that you are. . . . You merge yourselves in the void and disappear, and let New India arise in your place. Let her arise —out of the peasants'

9. *C. W.*, VII, pp. 148-49.

cottage . . . out of the huts of the fisherman, the cobbler, and the sweeper. Let her spring from the grocer's shop, from beside the oven of the fritter-seller. Let her emanate from the factory, from marts, and from markets. Let her emerge from groves and forests, from hills and mountains.'[10] In this vision it is clear that Vivekananda envisaged a thorough change in the economic arrangements and social relations. In this future stage of society with the toiling classes rising to power and gaining upperhand in society, capital will be owned by them, the upper classes disappearing in the void, the productive system will be under their control and there will be no exploitation. He speaks therefore of total extinction of the exploiters not by force but in the natural course of evolution. Describing this natural course he states : 'The peasant, the shoemaker, the sweeper, and such other lower classes of India have much greater capacity for work and self-reliance than you. They have been silently working through long ages and producing the entire wealth of the land, without a word of complaint. Very soon they will get above you in position. Gradually capital is drifting into their hands, and they are not so much troubled with wants as you are. Modern education has changed your fashion, but new avenues of wealth lie yet undiscovered for want of the inventive genius. You have so long oppressed these forbearing masses; now is the time for their retribution. And you will become extinct in your vain search for employment, making it the be-all and end-all of your life.'[11]

From this account it appears clearly that his economic thinking has totally a socialistic bias.

---

10. ibid., pp. 326-27.
11. ibid., p. 148.

CHAPTER 22

Capitalist Development and Underdevelopment

I

EXPLOITATION, TRADE AND CAPITALIST DEVELOPMENT

As mentioned in the preceding chapter Vivekananda in his writings and speeches has brought out very ably the fact that the exploitation of the colonies was the source of the prosperity and growth of the imperialist countries. Pointing out that many of the prosperous nations since the very ancient days attained their prosperity through exploiting India, he observes, 'Most people are ignorant of the extent to which the opulence of ancient countries like Babylon, Persia, Greece, and Rome depended on Indian commerce. After the downfall of Rome, Baghdad in Mohammedan territory, and Venice and Genoa in Italy, became the chief western marts of Indian commerce. And when the Turks made themselves masters of the Roman Empire and closed the trade-route to India for the Italians, then Christopher Columbus (Christobal Colon), a Spaniard or Genoese, tried to explore a new route to India across the Atlantic, which resulted in the discovery of the American continent.'[1] Continuing he points out further, 'The Portuguese, in the meantime, discovered a new route to India, doubling Africa. The fortune of India smiled on Portugal—then came the turn of the French, the Dutch, the Danes, and the English. Indian commerce, Indian revenue and all are now in the possession of the English; it is therefore that they are the foremost of all nations now. . . . This the Europeans are unwilling to admit. That India, the India of "natives", is the chief means and resources of their wealth and civilization, is a fact

1. *C. W.*, VII, 357.

which they refuse to admit, or even understand.'[2] What he states here is in essence the theory of capitalist development as propounded by the modern economists, according to whom capitalist development takes place utilizing the resources squeezed out from the colonies.

Vivekananda, however, pointed out that exploitation by some of the nations by the others was no unique phenomenon specific to the capitalist age. In ancient days also, in his opinion, there was exploitation of some countries by the others and the exploiting countries thrived at the cost of the exploited ones. Unfortunately India was always a happy hunting ground of invaders and traders who exploited her to the utmost extent. Since she was known for her rich economic resources even in ancient days, invaders and traders flocked to this land. For example, we get a reference of her riches in Dante's writing *The Riches that were India*. Vivekananda mentions, as quoted above, a number of countries in ancient days, which thrived squeezing Indian resources. He mentions that 'After his conquest of Persia, Alexandar the great despatched a general named Niarchus to explore a sea-route, passing by the mouth of the Indus, across the ocean, and through the Red Sea.'[3] Thus it is a historical fact that since ancient days many countries were in search of finding a route to India so as to exploit her resources for their own development.

In later days also we find that England fought other countries to attain supremacy over India and England's development, her industrialization were all attained by squeezing the resources of India. This has been clearly brought out by Vivekananda in the passage quoted above.

This line of thinking was far in advance compared to that of Rammohan, Bankim Chandra, Ramesh Chandra Dutta, Ranade and even of Dadabhai, the most eminent economic thinker of the period. They also criticized the British for their misrule but none went so far as to expose the true nature of imperialistic exploitation and capitalist development and their interrelation, as was done by Vivekananda.

Dadabhai Naoroji's exposition of British exploitation of

2. ibid., p. 358.

3. ibid., p. 357.

India runs as follows; 'In reality there are two Indias—the one prosperous, the other poverty-stricken. The prosperous India is the India of the British and other foreigners. They exploit India as officials, capitalists in a variety of ways, and carry away enormous wealth to their country. To them, of course, India is rich and prosperous. The more they can carry away, the richer and more prosperous India is. The second India is the India of the Indians—the poverty-stricken India.'[4]

Rammohan argued in favour of economic modernization and the revolutionary measure of freezing of rent. As pointed out by Dr B. N. Ganguly, 'Rammohan was perhaps the only Indian at the time who formulated the objection to the salt monopoly system in a rational manner.' But Rammohan said nothing against imperialism; in fact, he was a great admirer of British rule in India, he said nothing against draining out India's wealth by the foreign rulers, and it seems he had no idea about the process of capitalist development.

Ramesh Chandra Dutta wrote on the theme of 'imperialism'. But at the same time he eulogized 'liberal imperialism', as if such a thing is possible. His sharp criticism of 'aggressive imperialism' runs as follows : 'Never perhaps since the death of Castlereagh in 1822, has imperialism been so rampant; never have the purely animal instincts of self-love and self-aggrandizement been stronger or more violent, never have the higher instincts of humanity and justice, of respect towards rival nations and fairness towards subject nations, been at such a lower ebb.'[5]

Ranade's prescription for the Indian ailment, viz., poverty, was industrialization and urbanization. In this connection he lamented over 'the complete absence of a landed gentry or a wealthy middle class' (viz., the bourgeoisie) which could perform the economic function of capital accumulation and also over the fact that 'the laws and institutions favoured a low standard of life, and not concentration of wealth'. He regretted of course, 'the economic drain of wealth and talents, which foreign subjections had entailed on the country'.[6] None of these

4. Quoted by Dr B. N. Ganguly in his *Indian Economic Thought*, p. 148.
5. ibid., p. 187.

protestations against British exploitation of India amounted to revealing the intricate nature of capitalist development with all its ramifications manifested in the highly developed countries of the time.

In contrast what Vivekananda succeeded in unveiling about imperialism and capitalist development is in essence the same as that has been revealed by the modern economists dealing with economic development and growth. For example, Oscar Lange, the renowned economist, in reply to his self-imposed question 'What was the essential feature of capitalist development?', writes, 'The essential feature was capital accumulation and productive investment by the urban middle class.' 'Where did resources for such investment come from?' is another self-imposed question to which his answer is '. . . profits from trade and production . . . became the basis of the investment which led to capitalist development. . . . In addition, there were the other sources; one, and an important one in the emergence of capitalist development was the exploitation of the colonies.'[7]

Referring to Vivekananda's reflections over capitalist exploitation, Chelishev observes, 'In his public statements Vivekananda relentlessly exposed bourgeoisie chauvinism, capitalist competition, the quest for profit, the fabulous luxury of the handful of exploiters and disastrous impoverishment and rightlessness of millions of toilers.'[8] Vivekananda specifically mentioned also that this capitalist exploitation was the basis of capitalist development.

II

CHARACTERISTICS OF A COLONIAL ECONOMY: UNDERDEVELOPMENT

Vivekananda, while describing the state of the Indian economy in his speeches and writings, has clearly brought out the characteristics of a colonial economy. He succeeded in establishing in his analysis the fact that colonies were not only

6. ibid., p. 172.
7. Oscar Lange—*Essays In Economic Planning*, 1961.
8. *Vivekananda Centenary Memorial Volume.*

the source of capital accumulation of the imperialist countries, but also the supplier of raw materials as well as the market for the finished goods of the imperialist countries. Thus the exploitation of the colonies were the countries. Thus the exploitation of the colonies were the foundation of their prosperity and industrial growth.

How the once industrially advanced economy of India exporting manufactured goods, was gradually transformed by the British ruler to conform to the pattern of a colonial economy is depicted beautifully by Vivekananda in the following statement : 'Uptill a century ago, the whole of the world's demand for cotton cloth, cotton, jute, indigo, lac, rice, diamonds, and pearls, etc., used to be supplied from India. Moreover, no other country could produce such excellent silk and woollen fabrics, like the kinkob, etc., as India.'[9] 'But now', he proceeds with depicting the transformation, 'Indian products are being grown in countries like America and elsewhere, even better than in India, and she has therefore lost something of her prestige.'[10] Elaborating the same point he proceeds to observe further, 'In this country of abundance, the produce of which has been the cause of the spread of civilization in other countries, you are reduced to such straits! Your condition is even worse than that of a dog. . . . People of foreign countries are turning out such golden results from the raw materials produced in your country, and you, like asses of burden, are only carrying their load. The people of foreign countries import Indian raw goods, manufacture various commodities by bringing their intelligence to bear upon them, and become great.'[11]

THE BASIC CAUSES OF UNDERDEVELOPMENT

From the above statement it is crystal clear that the imperial countries attained development and prosperity by squeezing the resources of the colonies. The result was that the latter remained underdeveloped, as merely raw material producing countries. They then inevitably became dependent on the imperial country for the supply of the manufactured goods that they needed. Thus the most important characteristics of capitalist development was

9. *C. W.*, VII, p. 357. 10. ibid., p. 358. 11. ibid., p. 145.

manifested—the perpetual cleavage between the developed and the underdeveloped nations, a few countries developing at the cost of others. The underdeveloped countries remained underdeveloped for good, the developed countries developed further, the divergence between the two became more and more pronounced as time passed off. This feature of capitalist development became one of the main point of analysis in Development Economics long after Vivekananda. His thoughts were much in advance of his time, since he anticipated all the main points. At the time when he dealt with the matter, the only other person who also dwelt on it was Karl Marx. But his impact was not felt at the time on the economists and other social thinkers. Economic analysis at the time centred round the Equilibrium Theory. Growth Economics was yet to develop and underdevelopment of certain countries were considered racial deficiency. In recent years M. Todaro dealing with the subject of development observes, 'The principal benefits of world trade have accrued disproportionately to rich nations and within poor nations disproportionately to both foreign nationals and wealthy nationals.'[12] This was also the essence of Vivekananda's observations quoted above.

The Widening Gap between the Developed and the Underdeveloped Countries : In the statement of Vivekananda quoted above, which shows the gradual transformation of India from a manufacturing country to a raw material producing country, a very important feature of capitalist development has come out, viz., the ever widening gap between the developed and the underdeveloped countries, the former attaining higher and higher growth rates by utilizing the resources of the colonies, the latter remaining stagnant or experiencing declining growth rates.

Colonial Trade Pattern : The pattern of international trade is the channel of squeezing the colonies by the imperial countries. Vivekananda has accurately read this trade pattern, viz., that a colony is an exporter of raw materials and importer of manufactured goods. This trade pattern shows that a colony is mainly an agricultural country, producing primary raw materials only, lacking development of manufacturing industries. Thus the

---

12. M.Todaro—*Economics for a Developing World*, p. 314.

fact of unbalanced growth of these countries has been revealed here.

III

BALANCED DEVELOPMENT AND MODERNIZATION

Vivekananda advocated thorough modernization of India in the matter of application of technology and of science so that India could enter into an era of economic growth and development. 'We talk foolishly against material civilization', he said. 'Material civilization, nay, even luxury is necessary to create work for the poor.'[13] Thus he pleaded strongly for an era of economic development for India and creation of employment for the unemployed.

He emphasized the need for balanced development of the underdeveloped countries—they must be developed both materially and spiritually. And he wanted balanced development as between different nations. Never should a few of the nations, in his opinion, be allowed to grow at the cost of others. Flaying the claim for exclusive privileges put forward by the advanced nations he said very sharply, 'They think that God Almighty has given them a charter to rule all over the world, to advance His plans, to do anything they like to turn the world upside down. They have a charter to rob, murder and kill.'[14] According to Vivekananda, unequal development which leads to this sort of claims being made by the developed nations leads ultimately to war and destruction. Having a look at the depth of the past world history he points out, 'So empire after empire has arisen—glorious, resplendent, now vanished away—gone, nobody knew where; it may have been stupendous in its ruin.'[15]

He was convinced that this cannot go on for long in the modern era when the underdeveloped nations were equally forcefully demanding their legitimate rights to have development and prosperity. Looking at the depth of the future he said

13. *Letters of Swami Vivekananda*, p. 141.
14. Marie Louise Burke—*Swami Vivekananda* : *His Second Visit To The West*, p. 332.
15. ibid.

slashingly : 'But imperial babes could have no place in the centuries ahead when mutual understanding and exchange of service between the peoples of the world constitute their only hope for survival.'[16] Mutual cooperation for development of the backward nations was the only solution, he envisaged, for the problem of unbalanced development. Pointing out this solution Marie Louise Burke observes, 'One of Swamiji's dreams of which he often spoke was of an exchange of ideas and achievements between the East and the West.'[17]

He saw clearly that the East, which was economically underdeveloped needed technological aid and the West which was spiritually starved at the time needed spiritual sustenance from the East. 'Send us mechanics', he said addressing the western developed nations, 'to teach us how to use our own hands and we will send you missionaries to teach you spirituality.' In this way with mutual cooperation and exchange of achievements both were to develop more fully and attain greater prosperity, stable progress and peace. As rightly observed by Marie Louise Burke, 'It was a dream that not only reached far into the future, but was itself, perhaps, the seed of future fact.'[18]

Indian Economy on the background of the World Economy : Neither Rammohan nor Bankim, Ranade, R. C. Dutta, not even the most astute economic thinker of the nineteenth century India, viz., Dadabhai Naoroji, did place India's economic problem on the background of the entire world economic situation as Vivekananda did. None of them had that breadth of vision, that depth of historical insight which Vivekananda had. None of them at the time could think in terms of world cooperation for the development of the underdeveloped countries. Neither did any of them think that India had any world mission—that India was capable of giving aid or guidance to the developed nations of the world in any matter. A sense of inferiority complex covered their minds, they thought that India was only to imitate the West and get sustenance thereby. It was Vivekananda who for the first time harped on India's world mission—a very significant one. Only he did point out that India was to receive aid from the West not as a

16. ibid. 17. ibid. 18. ibid., p. 333.

supplicant but as an equal partner of a mutual cooperation, as a participant in a fair 'give and take' deal on a footing of equality.

None of the other nineteenth century stalwarts seems to have realized the extreme importance of balanced or equal development of nations. Either equal development or ruin, there was no other choice in between for the nations developed at the cost of the nations underdeveloped. Only Vivekananda realized and emphasized this just like the development economists of more recent days.

Here again we may compare the views of Vivekananda with those of Oscar Lange who says, 'This is what we can realistically aspire for : a situation where by means of international cooperation necessary political and economic adjustments, national emancipation and economic and social progress are achieved in a peaceful manner. To be workable, it must be a situation in which progress goes on, and in which the people of the world improve their economic, social and cultural position.'[19] International cooperation for mutual development is a twentieth century idea, mostly a post Second World War idea. But we find that it was thought out and emphasized by Vivekananda as early as in the late nineteenth century.

19. Oscar Lange—*Essays In Economic Planning*, p. 31.

CHAPTER 23

The Problem of Poverty in India and Its Solutions

I

THE PROBLEM OF POVERTY IN INDIA

As mentioned earlier, it was the problem of poverty in India which was the chief concern of Vivekananda all through his life. According to him, poverty and ignorance were the two main problems of India. He said before his departure for U.S.A. for the first time : 'I have now travelled all over India. But alas! it was agony to me, my brothers, to see with my own eyes the terrible poverty and misery of the masses, and I could not restrain my tears. It is now my firm conviction that it is futile to preach religion amongst them without first trying to remove their poverty and their suffering. It is for this reason—to find more means for the salvation of the poor of India that I am going to America.'[1] Finding solution of the problem of Indian poverty was so much a concern for him that he decided to go to America to find some way out. It must be borne in mind by all concerned with Vivekananda studies that Swamiji did not visit America primarily to preach religion.

II

ESTIMATE OF POVERTY AND NATIONAL INCOME

Estimate of per capita income : What actually seems surprising to us in this connection is that just like an expert economist he attempted to estimate poverty in terms of per capita national income. According to Dadabhai Naoroji, who made first

---

1. Romain Rolland—*Life of Vivekananda*, pp. 30-31.

ever estimate of India's national income, India's per capita income was Rs 20/- per annum, total national income being Rs 300 million in 1872.[2] More than half a century later Professor V.K.R.V. Rao estimated the per capita income in India in 1967-68 to be in the region of Rs 23/- or Rs 24/- per annum, thus revising Dadabhai's estimate by 15 p.c.[3] According to Vivekananda[4], the average monthly income of an Indian was at the time near about Rs 2/- only. Vivekananda has given monthly estimate, while others have given yearly estimates. However, Vivekananda's estimate is near Dadabhai's estimate and exactly the same as that of the revised estimate of V.K.R.V. Rao. Obviously Vivekananda must have been conversant with the literature published in those days dealing with the subject.

Dollar estimate of India's National Income : The appalling poverty of India was often referred to by Vivekananda in his public lectures in U.S.A. In a lecture delivered at Salem, U.S.A., on August 28, 1893, he said, 'India with an area smaller than the United States contains twenty-three hundred millions of people, and of these three hundred millions earn wages, averaging less than fifty cents per month. In some instances the people in the whole district of the country subsist for months and even years, wholly upon flowers, produced by a certain tree which when boiled is edible.'[5] Further proceeding with the same subject he stated : 'In other districts the men eat rice only, the women and children must satisfy their hunger with the water in which the rice is cooked. A failure of the rice crop means famine. Half the people live upon *one meal a day*, other half know not from where the next, whence the next meal will come.'[6]

Thus he gives an estimate of poverty in India in terms of per capita both in rupee and in dollar value which is the accepted scientific method of estimating poverty today. He gives also a vivid description of the appalling poverty in non-monetary terms based on his personal experiences during the days of his Indian

2. Dantwalla—*Poverty Now and Then*, p. 2.
3. Rao, V. K. R. V.—*An Essay on India's National Income*, p. 22.
4. *Swami Vivekanander Vāṇī O Rachanā*, Vol. III, p. 383.
5. Marie Louise Burke—*Swami Vivekananda in America* : *New Discoveries*, Part I, pp. 47-48.
6. ibid., p. 48.

itinerary when he had the opportunity to make a direct study of the mass poverty of India as he often lived with the poorest of the poor, the toilers who struggled hard for a morsel of food. The description that he has given makes vivid the very depth of the appalling poverty prevailing in India at the time.

III

CAUSES OF INDIAN POVERTY

According to Vivekananda, the causes of this appalling poverty of India were two :

1. Exploitation of the country by the British imperialistic rulers.
2. Exploitation of the masses by the aristocracy and the priests.

Exploitation by the British : Describing the nature of exploitation by the British he says : 'No good can be done when the main idea is blood-sucking. . . . In spite of the centuries of anarchy that reigned during the struggles of the English to conquer, the terrible massacre the English perpetrated in 1857 and 1858 and the still more terrible famines that have become the inevitable consequence of British rule (there never is a famine in a native state) and that take off millions, there has been a good increase of population. . . . Indian labour and produce can support five times as many people as there are now in India with comfort, if the whole thing is not taken off from them.'[7]

Elaborating further the horrors of British exploitation he observes : 'There has been a reign of terror in India for some years. English soldiers are killing our men and outraging our women—only to be sent home with passage and pension at our expense.'[8] Giving an idea about the extent of exploitation he states, 'All property and lands granted by the previous governments for supporting education have been swallowed up, and the present Government spends even less than Russia in education.'[9]

All these statements quoted above make it sufficiently clear that :

---

7. *C. W.*, VIII, pp. 475-76. 8. ibid., p. 476. 9. ibid., p. 477.

(1) we were impoverished by the terrible famines that took place at the time, these being the inevitable consequence of the British economic policy in India;
(2) that these famines took heavy toll of life every year;
(3) that the extent of impoverishment was enormous. It can be guessed from the fact that unless Indian wealth and income were squeezed away, India could support five times a larger population;
(4) even the resources earmarked for education previously were diverted to satisfy the greed of the imperialistic rulers.

The Economic Drain : From the above it is clear that the 'economic drain', of which so much was written by Dadabhai Naoroji, was emphasized by Vivekananda also as one of the major factors responsible for the mass poverty in India. That the drain was not in material forms only but also in non-material forms, has been made very clear by Vivekananda. For example, he mentions that the decline of education was due to the squeezing of the resources earmarked for education. Decline of education means decline in economic efficiency, decline in turn in productivity which means ultimately enhancing of poverty.

Exploitation by the Aristocracy : Besides the exploitation by the British, according to Vivekananda, the other cause responsible for the impoverishment and degradation of the masses in India was the exploitation by the aristrocracy—*zamindārs*, elites and the priests. The masses were not only economically squeezed, being deprived of their due share of the national income, but also were denied the right to education and culture. Total degradation and abject poverty were their only lot.

Thus Vivekananda makes both imperialism and feudalism responsible for the mass poverty in India.

Exploitation by the Priests : Speaking of the exploitation and oppression perpetrated by the priests he sharply observes, 'A country where millions of people live on flowers of the *mahua* plant, and a million or two of the *sādhus* (monks) and a hundred million or so of Brahmins suck the blood out of these poor people without even the least effort for their amelioration—is that a country or a hell?'[10] Speaking of the exploitation by the aristocracy he says, 'Their nice little brown studies of lives never rudely shocked by the wail or woe, of misery, of degradation and poverty, that has filled the Indian atmosphere—the result of oppression. They little dream of the ages of tyranny, mental, moral and physical, that has reduced the image of God to a mere beast and burden.'[11] Speaking of the *zamindārs* he says, 'Why among the poor in India are so many Muhammedans? It is nonsense to say that they were converted by the sword. It was to gain their liberty from the *zamindārs* and the priests. And as a consequence, you find in Bengal that there are more Mohammedans than Hindus among the cultivators, because there were so many *zamindārs* there.'[12] Of course, all *zamindārs* were not Hindus and all the *zamindārs* of whether they were Hindus, Mohammedans or Christians were equally oppressive, equally exploitative so far as their tenants were concerned. Pointing to this he says, 'Trodden under the foot of the Hindus, Moslems or Christians, they (masses) have come to think that they are born to be trodden under the foot of everybody who has money enough in his pocket.'[13]

On the whole, it is clear from the above, that Vivekananda held both feudalism and imperialism responsible for the appalling mass-poverty in India.

IV

SOLUTION OF THE PROBLEM OF POVERTY

The measures that were recommended by Vivekananda for the solution of the poverty in India are :

(1) social and institutional, and (2) economic.

The measures are also both short term and long term, to be worked out within a short period, and those which would require a longer time to be fruitful.

THE SOCIAL AND INSTITUTIONAL MEASURES

Among the social and institutional measures, the following

10. *Letters of Swami Vivekananda*, p. 9.
11. ibid., p. 65. 12. ibid., p. 137. 13. ibid., p. 98.

are significant because of the similarity these have with the measures suggested by the modern development economists.

1. *Attitudinal changes* : First of all, Vivekananda suggested a thorough change of attitudes and outlook. 'The present Hindu Society', he observers, 'is organized only for the spiritual men and hopelessly crushes out everybody else. Why? Where shall they go who want to enjoy the world a little with its frivolities? Just as our religion takes in all so should our society. This is to be worked out by understanding the true principles of our religion, and applying them to society. This is slow but sure to be done.' Here he makes it clear that our society deviated from the religious injunctions which preach equality of all beings and it should be made to be based on these injunctions. He suggests also that the process of these changes are time-consuming because attitudes cannot change in a day, it takes a long time to change through gradual stages.

The religious injunctions in relation to economic activities have been misinterpreted and misunderstood by the Hindus themselves and it is naturally therefore that the western elites and the English-educated modern Indians are very critical of them. According to these elites, our religion has always been a hindrance to economic development since it breeds an other-worldly attitude. But history speaks otherwise, in spite of its religion India was at one time economically a very prosperous country because of which foreigners were allured to flock to this country. Religion did not actually prove a hindrance, rather it was conducive to economic prosperity as we shall presently see.

There are certain doctrines in our religious philosophy which are generally believed to be other-worldly, e.g., (1) the doctrine of asceticism, (2) the view that the world is all *māyā* or an illusion, (3) the view that the human desires are the source of misery, (4) and finally the law of *karma* relating present rewards with past actions and present actions with future life. But, it must be noted here that (1) asceticism was never recommended for all, it was always meant for a select few only; (2) *māyā* does not mean that the world is an illusion, it is a statement of fact. It is positivism. It means only that the universe is not what it seems to be, it is not unreal, passing, full of misery and death, it is divine, it is Existence Absolute, Knowledge Absolute, Bliss Absolute; it is not 'matter', it is consciousness. (3) The essence of the law of *karma*, boldly preached in the *Gītā*, was that by doing *karma* without a selfish motive one could attain the highest goal. The *Gītā* advises one to do his work selflessly, boldly, and fearlessly. According to it, fighting is a virtue, one must fight against the evil-doers, even defying death. Death is unreal, soul being immortal. According to Swami Vivekananda, the doctrine of *karma* is characterized by optimism, since it encourages everyone to do good work so that they could have a happy future life. Hence it is absolutely wrong to say that these philosophical and religious doctrines bred other-worldliness among the Indian people. Besides, there are the scriptures like the *Śukranītisāra*—a book which is also considered a part of our religious literature, which lauds wealth as a means to happiness and favours its accumulation by 'legitimate ways', e.g., by learning, service, valour, agriculture, commerce, etc.[14] *Mahābhārata* denounces poverty as a sin and emphatically asserts that 'he that has no wealth has neither this world nor the next'.[15] In the same book we find that after the Kurukṣetra War was won, Yudhiṣṭhira, the Pāṇdava prince, being horrified by the devastation caused wanted to renounce the world but he was prevented by the great sage Vedavyāsa and Śrī Krishna, the god incarnate— they prevailed upon him by telling him that his only duty was under the prevailing circumstances to the subjects, to maintain law and order so that they could undertake their daily activities properly, that renouncing the world on the part of a king under a situation of chaos after a war was not a virtue but a vice.[16]

People naturally felt confused being confronted by the misinterpretations of our central religious ideas. Singer, however, is of the opinion that 'this worldly' and 'other worldly' elements in Hinduism are not incompatible. It is possible for an Indian to believe in meditation and the law of *karma* and yet possess all the traits (frugality, rationality, hard work and spirit of adventure, etc.) essential to economic development.[17]

---

14. *India's Economic Problems,* edited by Uppal, p. 73.
15. *Mahābhārata*, Part XII, Chapter 8.
16. ibid. 17. M. Singer—*Religion and Social Change*, p. 501.

Vivekananda points out that the Vedic Religion laid down rules for the fourfold attainments of life, viz., *dharma*, *artha*, *kāma* and *mokṣa*. '*Dharma* is that', he says, 'which makes man seek for happiness in this world or the next. *Dharma* is established on work; *dharma* is impelling man day and night to run after and work for happiness.'[18] And according to him, *mokṣa* is that which teaches that even the happiness of this life is slavery, and same is the happiness of the life to come, because neither this world nor the next is beyond the laws of nature.[19] 'However', he continues, 'the central fact is that the fall of our country, of which we hear so much spoken, is due to the utter want of this *dharma*.' 'The householder', he adds, 'must earn money with great effort and enthusiasm, and by that must support and bring comforts to his own family and to others, and perfrom good works as far as possible. . . . The nature of the *dhārmika* is constant performance of action with efficiency.'[20] Thus it is not true that Hinduism preached inaction. He rightly points out also that 'without enjoyment renunciation can never come'. 'For this reason', he points out, 'find out, first of all, the ways and means by which men may get enough to eat and have enough luxuries to enable them to enjoy life... .'[21] Buddhism eulogizes *mokṣa* only. According to Vivekananda, over-emphasis on *mokṣa* in our attitude, is a product of the Buddhistic period.

Vivekananda suggested a thorough change of attitudes. A nation as a whole, the entire population, cannot follow the path of *mokṣa*, which is the path meant for the chosen few only—those who have enjoyed life and are now prepared to renounce. In view of this he emphatically said, 'We talk foolishly against material civilization . . . in all India there are, say, a hundred thousand really spiritual men and women. Now for the spiritualization of these, must three hundred millions be sunk in savagery and starvation? Why should any one starve. . . . Material civilization, nay, even luxury is necessary to create work for the poor.'

Institutional changes : Next to change of attitude Vivekananda emphasized the need for some institutional changes. The nature of change that he wanted centres round

18. *C. W.*, V, p. 446.
19. ibid., pp. 447-49.
20. ibid., pp. 448-49.
21. ibid., p. 353.

eradication of priestcraft and social tyranny. 'No priestcraft', he said, 'no social tyranny. More opportunity for everybody.'[22]

Political freedom and the emancipation of the masses : In this connection he made it clear also that political liberty would only mean subjugation of the masses and the supremacy of the upper classes unless steps were taken simultaneously to make the society free from the grip of the latter. 'Our young fools', he observes, 'make meetings to get more power from the English. ... Suppose the English gives over to you all the power. Why the powers that be, then will hold the people down, and let them not have it. Slaves want power to make slaves.'[23] Among all the thinkers of the nineteenth century, Vivekananda was the only person who thought of emancipation of the masses as a necessary condition of the emancipation of the country.

Eradication of Priesthood : He was certain that unless the emancipation of the masses from the grip of the upper classes were secured, there could not be any economic development. 'Kick out the priests', he said, 'who are always against progress. Because they would never mend, their hearts would never become big. They are the offspring of centuries of superstition and tyranny. Root out priestcraft first. Come, be men. Come out of your narrow holes and have a look abroad. See how nations are on the march.'[24] He said this in connection with his appreciation of Japan's march of progress on the path of industrialization. According to him, this institutional change is to be brought along gradually and through India's own method, viz., through religion. 'Now, this is to be brought about', he makes a clear statement, 'slowly and by only insisting on our religion and giving liberty to society. Root out priestcraft from the old religion and you get the best religion of the world. . . . Can you make a European society with India's religion?' 'Start only on religious grounds', he adds emphatically, 'and do not preach any violent social reform at present; only do not countenance foolish superstitions. Try to revive society on the old grounds of universal salvation and equality as laid down by the old masters, such as Śaṅkarāchārya, Rāmānuja, and Chaitanya.'[25]

---

22. *Letters of Swami Vivekananda*, p. 141.
23. ibid.
24. ibid., p. 60.
25. *C. W.*, IV, p. 369.

V

THE ROLE OF RELIGION IN ECONOMIC DEVELOPMENT

This is surely a new idea that a social reform or institutional change which is to be conducive to generate material prosperity and economic development for the purpose of eradicating poverty is to be brought in through the preaching of religious ideal. Vivekananda in one of his lectures has clearly said, 'Whenever any religion succeeds, it must have economic value. Thousands of similar sects will be struggling for power, but only those who meet the real economic problem will have it.' Here he makes it clear that religion has an important role to play in the economic development of a country. This is not Vivekananda's idea alone since the relation between religion and economic development are recognized by some modern writers also. We may particularly mention the names of Max Weber and M. Singer. According to them, the relation between religion and economic development and their interaction follow the following pattern :

Religious Teachings and Interpretations→Changes in Values and Attitudes→Actions→Changes in Institutions →Economic Development.[26]

The basic links are clearly laid down in this behavioural model. Vivekananda actually suggested it when he said that the dynamic philosophy of universal equality as laid down by Śaṅkara, Chaitanya, Rāmānuja, Dādu, Nānak and Kabīr, was to revive our society.[27] This philosophy, particularly the philosophy of the *Gītā* would infuse the people with a value sense for dynamic action—dynamic action for a thorough-going development. When the non-economic factors, viz., social institutions, values and attitudes do change, economic development proceeds with the help of the economic factors, viz., accumulation of capital, acceleration of investment and technological revolutions. All these economic factors, viz., accumulation of capital, acceleration of investment and technological revolution depend to a large extent on values and attitudes.

---

26. Uppal—*India's Economic Problems*, p. 29.
27. *C. W.*, III, p. 219.

VI

TECHNOLOGICAL REVOLUTION FOR ECONOMIC DEVELOPMENT

Vivekananda emphasized the necessity of introducing western technology and science for the development of industries so as to secure eradication of poverty. In this connection, he talked of borrowing technological know-how from the West. Addressing the western people he often said, 'Teach us how to use our hands, we will teach you spirituality.'

Agricultural technology : labour-saving not suitable for India : So far as technology in respect of agriculture is concerned, we find a difference between Vivekananda and Ranade. Ranade favoured introduction of large-scale farming under state ownership in India.[28] In this connection he supported the 'Culture System' as introduced in Java by the Government of Netherlands. Explaining the system he said in an article entitled *Netherlands, India, and the Culture System*, 'The theory of the system was that all Government lands not required for rice cultivation which afforded subsistence to the cultivator, were to be planted with commercial crops, and sell the produce to government at fixed rates, and liquidate any advance made to them by instalments in a fixed number of years. . . .'[29] According to Ranade, in this system the agricultural worker was to receive good wages and employment. Referring to the working of the system in Java, Ranade further stated : 'There was profit for the contractor as well as for the government who sold the commodities in the European market at specially remunerative prices.'[30] It is clear that it was not only a large-scale but also a mechanized system of production that has been insisted by Ranade. And the government was to arrange 'duty-free importation of machinery'.[31]

Capitalistic farming : But this is capitalistic farming operated on a large-scale and using mechanized process, in which the agriculturists are converted into mere wage-earners, the profits

28. Dr B. Dutta—*Evolution of Economic Thinking in India*, p. 16.
29. Quoted by Dr B. N. Ganguly in his book *Indian Economic Thought*, p. 175.
30. ibid. 31. ibid.

being appropriated by the rich contractors, mostly foreign nationals, and imperialist Dutch Government. 'The Culture System' advocated by Ranade was thus only a new method of imperialistic exploitation which did not benefit the cultivators much, excepting that they could earn 'good wages'. But were these 'good wages' in conformity with the real value of their labour? Most probably not, since profit-earners in a capitalistic system misappropriate the lion's share of the total income produced.

Importance of small-scale farming and small-scale operations : Vivekananda, in contrast, insisted on small-scale farming and revival of small-scale industries in India. Sister Nivedita writes throwing light on the matter : '. . . in everything including the problem of distribution, he listened with suspicion to all arguments that would work for the elimination of small interests.'[32]

Actually Vivekananda saw in the large-scale capitalistic system of production an instrument of exploitation. Throwing light on the matter Nivedita again writes, 'At the end of his last visit to America he told me that on first seeing western civilization he had been greatly attracted by it, but now he saw mainly its greed and power.'[33] America was a capitalist country and the nature of capitalism in all its different aspects was like an open book to him. Always a keen observer, he had also a full knowledge of the differences in factor-endowments in India and America. This is clear from the following statement of Nivedita : 'Like others he had accepted without thought the assumption that machinery would be a boon to agriculture, but he could now see that while the American farmer with his several square miles of farm might be the better for machines, they are likely to do little but harm on the tiny farmlands of the Indian peasantry. The problem was quite different in the two cases.'[34] In India since the population is large and the pressure of population on land quite heavy, the farm-holdings are small in size. Hence, mechanization, which is suitable for large-scale operation, is not suitable for Indian farming.

---

32. Sister Nivedita, *The Master As I Saw Him.*
33. ibid., pp. 221-22.
34. ibid., p. 222.

It is apparent, therefore, that Vivekananda's views were based on a realistic understanding of the Indian situation. Writing long after Vivekananda, Gunnar Myrdal, the famous economist, expressed the same view. 'Most important reason', he says, 'why modern western techniques cannot be simply appropriated for use in South Asia is the very different factor proportions. Almost from the very beginning agricultural technology in the advanced countries was geared to a situation where the agricultural labour force was declining rapidly . . . the situation in South Asian countries is radically different. Their huge, even now largely underutilized agricultural labour force will be increasing rapidly for decades to come.'[35] Thus it is clear that in a labour-surplus economy, Vivekananda's stand in this matter was justified, that the agricultural technology should be for a country like India, labour-absorbing.

Myrdal has further shown that small farming is not necessarily less efficient. From the results of the farm-management studies available to him he was convinced that 'yields per acre are inversely related to farm size'.[36] A study of the rice-growing methods in Japan, as stated by Myrdal, supports this conclusion. And it is not that a small-scale farming method cannot adopt modern technological devices. According to Myrdal, it is quite feasible, but these devices will, of course, not be 'labour-saving' but will instead call for a bigger 'labour input'.[37]

VII

THE SCOPE OF LARGE-SCALE OPERATION WITH MODERN TECHNOLOGY IN INDIA

Although Vivekananda did not think that large-scale mechanized farming was suitable for the conditions of India, he was not against applying modern large-scale mechanized technology in the fields of production other than agriculture. This is apparent from his support given to the efforts of Jamshedji Tata, the pioneer of Indian Iron and Steel Industry. Vivekananda was, in

35. Gunnar Myrdal—*Asian Drama*, Vol. II, Part V, p. 1254.
36. ibid.
37. ibid.

fact, keen to adopt any modern technique which was suitable to the Indian conditions. And he was very much in favour of application of science to agriculture and other fields. Addressing a disciple he once said, 'With the help of western science set yourselves to dig the earth and produce foodstuff—not by means of mean servitude to others but by discovering new avenues to production, by your own exertions aided by western science.'[38]

VIII

PLAN FOR TECHNICAL TRAINING AND WORKSHOPS

Vivekananda advocated and planned to establish training institutes-cum-workshops for imparting knowledge of agriculture and industry to the people of this country. Obviously, his purpose was to impart knowlege of modern technology—both farm technology and industrial for training at every capital city in each Presidency, i.e., at Calcutta, Bombay, Madras and Delhi. 'Gradually', he said explaining his plan, 'In these main centres will be taught agriculture, industry, etc., and workshops will be started like those already in existence.'[39] Vivekananda planned to include in the Mission a full-grown technical Institute along with making it a centre for studying philosophy and religion. He wanted to create a band of monk-teachers for imparting technical education to the country. And for this purpose he wanted to establish a colony in central India and at places such as Hazaribagh district in Bihar where abundant fertile land was available for establishing a big institute for imparting technical education and workshops, etc.[40]

In the resolutions that were passed at the meeting held on 1 May 1897 at Balaram Babu's House to form the Ramakrishna Mission, it is stated that among the Mission's methods of action which will be undertaken to fulfil its objectives, will be (i) methods 'to train men so as to make them competent to teach such knowledge of sciences as are conducive to the material and

38. *Diary of a Disciple*—Sarat Chandra Chakravarty.
39. *Letters of Swami Vivekananda*, p. 337.
40. Sankari Prasad Basu—*Vivekananda O Samakālīn Bhāratvarṣa*, Vol. V, p. 253.

spiritual welfare of the masses; (ii) to promote and encourage arts and industries'.[41]

Vivekananda's support given to Tata's plan of Post-graduate Institute of Research : Swami Vivekananda met Jamshedji Tata in 1893. They were travelling in the same ship when both were on the way to U. S. A.—Swamiji to attend the Parliament of Religions at Chicago, Tata on business purpose. Swamiji at the very beginning of their acquaintance told Tata 'Why not establish match factory yourself, why do you sell Japanese product in this country? If you could do this your country will be benefited.' Five years later, Jamshedji Tata announced his desire to establish in this country a Post-graduate Research Institute for imparting training in science and technology at the highest level by making a donation of rupees 30 lakhs. Remembering what Vivekananda told him at their first meeting, Jamshedji Tata wrote a letter to him on 23 November 1899, requesting him to support his scheme for the proposed Post-graduate Research Institute (Government accepting the scheme sought to rename it as the Indian Institute of Science). And in response, support was given to his appeal in an editorial written in *Prabuddha Bhārata* (April 1899), an official organ of the newly established Ramakrishna Order. It was mentioned in the said editorial that if India was to survive and advance, if India was to take a place among all the nations, then the first thing she must do was to solve the problem of food and in these days of competition the only solution to the problem was to found the two branches of the economy—agriculture and industry—on science, since these two were the sources of making living for mankind.[42] According to Sankari Prasad Basu, the renowned scholar, most probably the editorial was written at the direction of Vivekananda.[43]

IX

EXPORT PROMOTION

That Vivekananda planned also for export promotion is

41. Romain Rolland—*Life of Vivekananda*, p. 121.
42. Sankari Prasad Basu—*Vivekananda O Samakālīn Bhāratvarṣa*, Vol. V, pp. 239-50.
43. ibid.

revealed in his statement just quoted above in which he stated that to sell the manufactures of those workshops in Europe and America associations will be started. In this respect, it must particularly be noted, that he planned to eliminate the middleman, who is an exploiter. And this reveals a very modern way of thinking. 'The simplest method to be worked upon at present', he observed, 'is to induce Indians to use their own produce and get markets for Indian artwares, etc., in other countries. This should be done by persons who are not middlemen themselves, but will devote the entire proceeds of this branch to the benefit of the workers.'[44] By eliminating the middlemen he wanted to give the workers the full value of their labour. Thus he never forgot his socialistic aim—doing away with the exploitation of the masses.

X

SELF-RELIANCE AND THE ELIMINATION OF THE MIDDLEMAN

Vivekananda's whole attitude in respect of economic development being anti-capitalistic, he wanted self-reliance to grow among the peasants and workers. He wanted to educate them in such a way that they would be able to solve their own problems.[45] Obviously he wanted them to put an end to the heyday of the landed aristocracy, middlemen and money-lenders. This is evident from his following advice given to Swami Akhandananda, who was at the time working according to the programme of Vivekananda for the uplift of the masses, 'Teach some boys and girls of the peasant classes the rudiments of learning and infuse a number of ideas into their brains. . . . The moment they will come to understand their condition, and feel the necessity of help and improvement, know that your work is taking effect.'[46] Thus he emphasized the necessity of imparting education, training and knowledge to the masses as well as giving them essential values like self-reliance more than preaching political slogans for the solution of their problems.

---

44. *Letters of Swami Vivekananda*, p. 337.
45. ibid., p. 360.
46. ibid., p. 403.

XI

ECONOMIC DEVELOPMENT THROUGH MASS PARTICIPATION AND GROWTH OF A NEW SOCIAL ORDER

Vivekananda was convinced, as already stated, that the peasants, workers and toilers in every variety of work will be coming to control the economic system and the upper classes will be following the path of self-destruction until they were totally extinct. In a significant statement he observes, (we quote it again) 'The peasant, the shoemaker, the sweeper and other lower classes of India have much greater capacity for work and self-reliance than you. They have been silently working through long ages and producing the entire wealth of the land, without a word of complaint. Very soon they will get above you in position. Gradually capital is drifting into their hands and they are not so much troubled with wants as you are. Modern education has changed your fashion, but new avenues of wealth lie yet undiscovered for the inventive genius. You have so long oppressed these forbearing masses; now is the time for their retribution. And you will become extinct in your vain search for employment, making it the be all and end all.'

A BOLD PROGRAMME

At the end of this discussion on poverty and its solution, as viewed by Vivekananda, we find he suggested very bold programme of self-reliance for the solution of the problem of poverty, a programme which in the process of being worked out was also to establish a new economic order eliminating the capitalist, the middlemen, and the money lender, with the workers and toilers at the helm of affairs to gear the productive and the distributive system of the economy. For this, education and vocational and technical training measures were to be launched. And he has given a definite plan in this regard as we shall see in a chapter following.

CHAPTER—24

The Meaning of Development

I

MODERN CONCEPT OF DEVELOPMENT

According to the modern economists, 'While economic progress is an essential component of development, it is not the only one. This is because development is not purely an economic phenomenon. Ultimately, it must encompass more than the material and financial side of peoples' lives.' Today development is conceived as a multi-dimensional process involving re-organization and re-orientation of the entire economic and the social system.[1] It definitely means improvement of incomes and output, level of employment, improvements in distribution of income and wealth, but it also involves 'radical changes in institutions, social and political, as well as radical changes in attitudes and values'.

As Goulet has pointed out, 'It matters little how much information we posses about development if we have not grasped its inner meaning.'[2] What is this inner meaning of development? This is obviously a question of prime importance. And this is particularly important for our present purpose since Vivekananda also has made attempts to probe into the inner meaning of 'development'.

INNER MEANING OF DEVELOPMENT

Traditional economic measure of development has been per capita growth of gross national product (GNP) at a rate faster than the growth rate of population. But this concept which was upheld between 1950's and 1960's came to be modified in the

1. M. Todaro—*Economics for a Developing World*, p. 87.
2. ibid.

1970's. The questions that were raised in relation to development on the basis of actual experience has been best put by Professor Dudley Seers thus : 'The questions to ask about a country's development are. . . . What has been happening to poverty? What has been happening to unemployment? What has been happening to inequality? If all three of these have declined from high levels, then beyond doubt this has been a period of development. If one or two of these central problems have been growing worse, especially if all three have, it would be strange to call the result "development" even if per capita income doubled.'[3]

Thus the concept of development came to include not only GNP growth in relation to growth of population but also reduction or elimination of poverty, inequality and unemployment within the context of a growing economy. This modification was based on actual experiences in some countries in which in spite of 6 p.c. GNP growth there was decline in employment and in the real incomes of bottom 40 per cent of their population.

The concept of development came to be further modified today when it cannot be measured by simple measurements of incomes, unemployment and inequality or in the economic sense of the term any longer. Today underdevelopment refers to a state of mind as well as a state of national poverty.

It is agreed everywhere today that development means a sustained 'elevation of the entire society and social system towards a better or more humane life'.

According to Todaro, in conformity with Goulet, there are three components of development corresponding to three universal core-values of good life, viz., (1) Life-sustenance, (2) Self-esteem, and (3) Freedom. These relate to fundamental needs of human beings as manifested in all societies and cultures of all time.

1. *Life-sustenance* : Life-sustaining needs are food, shelter, health and protection. Without these basic amenities, life would be impossible. The basic function of the economic system is to provide all these to every member of the community. Thus elimination of absolute poverty, rise in per capita income, a decent standard of living, job opportunities for all, minimum

---

3. Dudley Seers—*The Meaning of Development* : *Eleventh World Conference of the Society for International Development*, New Delhi, 1969, p. 3.

medical facilities and security of life and property constitute the necessary conditions of development. Without these there cannot be any development at all.

2. *Self-esteem* : Self-esteem refers to a sense of distinctive worth of an individual, of a society, of a particular culture to oneself, to others, to the world. All people, individuals and societies, seek some sort of self-esteem all the time. The care for self-esteem is universal at all times in all societies. In the past often this was derived from the distinctive cultural wealth of a nation. But today in the estimation of economically advanced nations material prosperity is the only criterion of worth of a nation. This has created a lot of confusion in the minds of the underdeveloped nations. In order to gain esteem in the eyes of the first-world countries they have devoted their whole attention to gaining material prosperity since material prosperity has become today an universal measure of worth. Even countries like India, the birth-place of Buddha and with a glorious civilization, and China, the birth-place of Confucius and with similar high civilization, are looked down on by the first-world and the second-world countries because of their economic poverty and backwardness.

3. *Freedom* : Freedom is considered similarly as a universal core-value of development. For without freedom material prosperity is meaningless and self-esteem impossible. 'Freedom here is not to be understood', says Todaro, 'in the political or ideological sense (e.g., 'free world') but in the more fundamental sense of freedom or emancipation from alienating material conditions of life and freedom from the social servitude of men to nature, ignorance, other men, misery, institutions and dogmatic beliefs.'[4] The social goals of development can be attained through 'freedom' only. W. Arther Lewis says in this connection, 'The advantage of economic growth is not that wealth increases happiness, but that it increases the range of human choice.'[5] Wealth enables a man to have greater control over his leisure, freedom to have more material prosperity or to live a life of spiritual contemplation.

---

4. M. Todaro—*Economics for a Developing World,* p. 97.
5. W. Arther Lewis, *Theory of Economic Growth*, p. 420.

In terms of these three core values, as pointed out by Todaro, the development in all societies must have at least the following three objectives:

1. to increase the availability of basic life-sustaining goods, e.g., food, shelter, health and protection to all members of society;
2. to raise the levels of living, providing higher income, more jobs, better education and greater attainment of cultural and humanistic values. These will not only enhance material well-being but also give greater self-esteem to individuals and nations;
3. to give people freedom from all kinds of servitude and dependence on other peoples and nations and freedom from ignorance and misery, giving them greater freedom of choice.

In terms of these goals three questions can be formulated to bring out the meaning of development :

1. have general levels of living improved so much in a society as to eradicate absolute poverty, i.e., whether life-sustenance is guaranteed?
2. has economic progress advanced so far as to enhance self-esteem of individuals and nations to oneself and others?
3. has economic progress advanced so far as to guarantee freedom from every kind of servitude and give men widest range of choice?

According to Professor Dudley Seers, 'If the second and third of these central questions for all societies are not positive, e.g., their freedom to choose has been constrained, then even if the provision of life-sustaining goods and improvements in levels of living are occurring, it would be misleading to call the result development.'[6]

Hence there are three primary components of under-development—1. low level of income (life-sustenance), 2. low self-esteem, and 3. lack of freedom.

---

6. M. Todaro—*Economics for a Developing World*, p. 98.

II

VIVEKANANDA'S CONCEPT OF DEVELOPMENT

To any serious research student the striking similarity between the modern concept of development and Vivekananda's concept is an astonishing revelation. Vivekananda emphasized in his speeches and writings the very same three core-values as components of development or progress of our national life long before Todaro, Seers and Goulet. In those days development economics has not yet grown.

1. As to the first core-value, viz., life-sustenance, Vivekananda was perhaps the only nineteenth century Renaissance leader who emphatically spoke of the urgent necessity of liquidating poverty and providing life-sustaining amenities to the masses on a basis of equality with the other classes. And with a view to attaining this goal he emphasized the great need for rapid economic growth through modernization of industrial and agricultural technology. With the application of science he wanted to revolutionize the productive processes so that income and employment generation may be accelerated. He had plans to open workshops and training centres all over the country for the purpose. And he included training and employment generating activities to be carried on for the benefit of the masses in the constitution of the Ramakrishna Mission. We have seen all these in the previous chapter. We have also seen that he envisaged a revolutionizing of attitudes and values and radical transformations of social institutions for the purpose.

2. While today some people consider economic development as the only criterion of attaining self-esteem, Vivekananda considered that in addition to attaining economic prosperity, retention of national cultural distinctive achievements was one of the major steps towards attaining self-esteem. The economic and non-economic criteria in this respect was considered by him as complementary. Todaro also argues that wholesale imitation of the life-patterns and norms of the developed nations, are not conducive to economic growth and all-round development of a nation. Vivekananda puts all the emphasis that he commanded on this point. 'My ideal is', he says, 'growth, expansion,

development on national lines.'[7] In an oft-quoted passage in *Modern India* he reminds us that the tendency of imitating others is a sign of lost self-esteem and a sure way to national degradation and not conducive to progress.[8] 'India! With this mere echoing of others,' he says, 'with this base imitation of others, with this dependence on others, this slavish weakness, this vile detestable cruelty—wouldst thou, with these provisions only, scale the highest pinnacle of civilization and greatness? Wouldst thou attain, by means of thy disgraceful cowardice, that freedom deserved only by the brave and the heroic?'[9]

Vivekananda disliked not only imitation of life-styles but also wholesale imitation of technology as we have seen in the previous chapter. In the nineteenth century he alone warned us against the unscrupulous tendency of wholesale imitation of the West which is indicative of lack of self-esteem and growth of inferiority complex. Long after him Michel Todaro speaking in the same tune observes, 'A subtle but very significant factor contributing to the possibilities of underdevelopment has been the transfer of first and second world values, attitudes, institutions and standards of behaviour to the third world nations.' 'Such attitudes', he adds, 'can breed corruption and economic plunder by a privileged minority.'[10]

Vivekananda's reflections on the matter is a pointer to the fact that it would lead to a worst form of cleavage between the privileged minority and the rest of the population. 'When I see', he says, 'Indians dressed in European apparel and costumes, the thought comes to my mind, perhaps they feel ashamed to own their nationality and kinship with the ignorant, poor, illiterate, downtrodden people of India!'[11]

Vivekananda, however, never said that we have nothing to learn from the West. He said, 'Yes, learn we must many things from the West, but there are fears as well.' He wanted application of judgement, discrimination and reason in deciding what is to be adopted and imbibed to enrich the main course of our national development.

---

7. *C. W.*, III, p. 195. 8. ibid., IV, p. 479. 9. ibid.
10. M. Todaro—*Economics for a Developing World.*
11. *C. W.*, IV, p. 479.

To be a Man : To be a Person : Important Criterion of Development : Not only the nations must have self-esteem, but the individuals composing the nation must also have this sense of self-esteem so as to promote development. Vivekananda laid great emphasis on it. He said, 'We must have life-building, man-making, character-making assimilation of ideas.'[12] 'Men, men, these are wanted : everything else will be ready, but strong vigorous, believing young men, sincere to the backbone, are wanted.'[13] To the masses also he wanted to give back their lost individuality. 'The only service', he said, 'to be done for our lower classes is to give them education, to develop their lost individuality. . . . They are to be given ideas. . . . Every nation, every man, and every woman must work out their own salvation. Give them ideas—that is the only help they require, and then the rest must follow as the effect.'[14] Todaro also points out that every individual must have 'a sense of worth and self-respect; of not being used as a tool by others for their own ends' for development to be realized this sense of individuality or 'to be a person' in Todaro's own language, is essential.

3. *Freedom* : Regarding the third core-value, viz., freedom, Vivekananda considers it as the 'first condition of growth' and as we have seen in Part III, it includes, according to him, 'political, social and spiritual liberty'. 'To care only', he observes, 'for spiritual liberty and not for social liberty is a defect, but the opposite is still a greater defect. Liberty of both soul and body is to be striven for.'[15] Thus Vivekananda gave us a concept of complete freedom and not a partial one like that of the Marxian view, according to which liberty or freedom has meaning only in the economic sense of the term. That the modern thinkers are coming gradually nearer to Vivekananda's concept in this respect is evident from Todaro's definition of freedom, quoted above. Vivekananda's concept was the broadest possible. 'Liberty of thought and action', he asserts, 'is the only condition of life, of growth and well-being. Where it does not exist, the man, the race, the nation must go down.' 'Just as a man', he adds, 'must have liberty to think and speak, so he must have liberty in food, dress,

12. ibid., III, p. 302.
13. ibid., pp. 223-24.
14. ibid., IV, p. 362.
15. ibid., VI, p. 86.

and marriage and in every other thing, so long as he does not injure others.' It is obvious, here he implies that man must be free from every kind of servitude, to nature, society, other men, misery, ignorance, he means this when he adds 'liberty in every other thing' in addition to the matters mentioned specifically.

It must be noted specially that Vivekananda uses the term development and growth in the broadest possible sense. 'The notion of development', declares the First Congress of the World Social Prospects Study Association, 'as synonymous with mere economic growth should be denounced and abandoned and replaced by the concept of an all-embracing endogenous development covering the economic, social, political and cultural fields permitting the full development of the individuals and the mankind.'[16] Vivekananda has given this very concept long ago.

Thus Vivekananda's programme for the development of the country was a three-pronged scheme based on the three core-values, viz., (1) Life-sustenance, (2) Self-esteem, and (3) Freedom. This is evident also from the three objectives of the Ramakrishna Mission formulated by Vivekananda himself, viz., (I) 'to train men so as to make them competent to teach such knowledge of sciences as are conducive to the material and spiritual welfare of the masses', (II) 'to promote and encourage arts and industries' and (III) 'to introduce and spread among the people in general Vedantic and other religious ideals as elucidated in the life of Ramakrishna'.[17]

---

16. *Life of Vivekananda* by Romain Rolland, pp. 120-21.
17. ibid.

Part VI

Impact of Ramakrishna-Vivekananda on the Socialist Countries

CHAPTER 25

The Prophets of Human Emancipation

I

SOCIALIST COUNTRIES' INTERESTS IN RAMAKRISHNA AND VIVEKANANDA AS PROPHETS OF HUMAN EMANCIPATION

We have already mentioned that Ramakrishna and Vivekananda are today hailed in the Soviet Union as the prophets of human emancipation, of progress, amity and peace. Apparently the Ramakrishna-Vivekananda ideal, professing faith in spirituality, stands poles asunder from the Marxist ideal of dialectical materialism in which the Soviet Union places its faith. Where lies the common ground between the two? It is a matter of very interesting and exciting investigation no doubt. And we will venture to undertake the challenging task in this chapter.

Not only in the Soviet Union, recently we find that China also is trying to probe into the Ramakrishna-Vivekananda philosophy. It has already shown its interest in an appreciative note. We shall also have a look into it at the end of this part.

II

RUSSIA : PRE-REVOLUTIONARY PERIOD

The names of Ramakrishna and Vivekananda are nothing new to Russia since she had her first acquaintance with their names in the late nineteenth century, i.e., in the pre-revolutionary days.

In 1893 Prince Volkenski attended the Parliament of Religions at Chicago and was acquainted with Vivekananda.[1]

1. *Swami Vivekananda : Studies in Soviet Union*—Ramakrishna Mission Institute of Culture (1987), p. 5.

That he was deeply impressed by Vivekananda is evident from the record of his speech delivered on October 31, 1893 at St Louise, in which he paid tribute to Vivekananda in the following terms : 'There was only one man there who was the epitome of spirituality.'[2] However, Vivekananda's name appeared for the first time in Russia in the *Church Chronicle*, 1894. And this was the only time that his name was published in the Russian Press in the nineteenth century.[3]

Nevertheless his world-moving ideas reached the Russian intellectuals towards the close of the nineteenth century. In a letter to one Anendra Kumar Datta, who had sent a copy of *Rāja-Yoga* by Vivekananda to Tolstoi, the latter observed : 'So far humanity has frequently gone backwards from the true and lofty and clear conception of the principle of life, but never surpassed it.'[4]

A. P. Gnatyuk-Danil'chuck commenting on this letter writes : 'We see that Vivekananda's very first work read by Tolstoi left on him an indelible impression and forever became one of the favourite books of the writer.'[5]

Ramakrishna's name reached Russia sometimes later in 1898 when *Ramakrishna* : *His Life and Sayings* by Max Müller came out in German. At once it drew the attention of the Russian orientalists as is evident from the fact that in 1899 at the Convention of the Orientalists, Academician Ol'denberg presented a report of the book in which was quoted a number of Ramakrishna's sayings.[6] Max Müller's *Life of Ramakrishna* was translated into Russian by I. F. Nazivin in 1913. A compilation of Ramakrishna's sayings under the title *The Holy Man from Dakshineshwar*, was published in Russian several times prior to the revolution. Another, the most voluminous collection (300 pages), in the pre-revolutionary days, with a preface by Swami Abhedananda, a brother monk of Vivekananda, was published in 1914.[7]

Long before these publications in 1903, Tolstoi read the sayings of Ramakrishna in a German journal. The name of the

2. Marie Louise Burke—*New Discoveries*, Part I, p. 99.
3. *Swami Vivekànanda* : *Studies in Soviet Union*, p. 5.
4. ibid. 5. ibid., p. 163. 6. ibid. 7. ibid., p. 6.

journal was *Theosophischer Wegweiser* (Theosophical Guide). Tolstoi wrote in his diary : 'These ideas are very much similar to my ideas', and in 1906 he told his physician that Ramakrishna who died about fifty years back was uncommonly a wise person. In 1903 and again in 1909 Tolstoi included some of the sayings of Ramakrishna and Vivekananda in his publications[8] and curricular prepared by him for mass-education.[9]

First Russian translations of Vivekananda's Works ('My Master') came out in 1907 and between 1907 and 1917 more were published and Russians could read Vivekananda's four Yogas in Russian. In 1908 came out the *Voices of the People* by I. F. Nazivin, which included Vivekananda's 'Hymn of the People' and 'God and Man'. After going through these two writings in a letter to Nazivin, Tolstoi wrote : 'I have just finished reading your wonderful book *Voices of the People*. ... The Hindu's article has left a great impression on me. This is unusually good.'[10] And in an article (1908) entitled 'Religion and Science' he virtually said that mankind must assimilate the heritage of Vivekananda along with that of the other sages.[11]

From Vivekananda's biographies we come to know that he met the great Russian revolutionary and leader of thought, Prince Kropotkin, in 1900 on the eve of the Paris Congress. It is a matter of great regret that no one recorded this all-important encounter between the two master-minds. According to Chelishev, 'This meeting exercised a definite influence on Vivekananda. This enabled Vivekananda to assess the development of events properly and observe that "The next great upheaval which is to bring about a new epoch will come from Russia or China".'[12] Of course we differ from E. P. Chelishev in this matter; Vivekananda made similar utterances before he met Kropotkin, actually when he was sailing for the West for a second visit. From his *Memoirs of European Travel* we have already quoted similar utterances in the previous chapters.

---

8. ibid.
9. *Vishva-Chetanāy Sri Ramakrishna* (Bengali), Udbodhan (1987), pp. 818-19.
10. *Vishva-Viveka*—edited by Sankari Prasad Basu and others.
11. *Swami Vivekananda* : *Studies in Soviet Union*, p. 9.
12. ibid., p. 69.

But is it possible that the great anarchist leader was not himself influenced by Vivekananda's fiery utterances, when they came live from his lips? Romain Rolland after thirty years of their utterances felt as if he had an electric shock when he read them. Even Chelishev writes that Vivekananda's words struck him like electric charges. Kropotkin must also have been similarly struck but it is a thousand times pity that the conversations between the two great leaders of thought were not recorded. It was an historical error on the part of those who arranged the meeting.

Vivekananda's biographies give us another very tacit information that it was proposed at one stage during his stay in the West that he should visit Russia but it was subsequently dropped. Who made the proposal? Why was it dropped? In one of his letters Vivekananda commented, 'Can Indians be Russianized?'[13] Why did he make such a comment? It indicates that behind the scenes certain events took place into which we are debarred from having a peep. Any research worker working on Vivekananda would legitimately feel discontented over the silence of the biographers on this matter.

In the travel diary of Sri Dilip Kumar Roy, the noted singer, entitled *Tīrthaṅkar*, it is recorded that Romain Rolland told him that there were many Russian writers who repeated the name of Vivekananda constantly in the manner of telling the beads. This is a very significant piece of information since it reveals the behind-the-scene fact that in the fiery days preceding the revolution Russian intellectuals and writers were imbued with the ideas of Vivekananda. Historians may give a serious thought on the significance of this matter.

III

RUSSIA : POST-REVOLUTIONARY ERA

It is evident from the above that Russia has a long association with the names of Ramakrishna and Vivekananda and the great ideals they stand for. But all that happened in the pre-revolutionary period. What seems really astonishing is the keen interest of the

---

13. *Vivekananda Centenary Memorial Volume* (1963), p. 514.

Russians in the teachings of Ramakrishna and Vivekananda in the post-revolutionary era. They hold them in very high esteem as would be evident from our subsequent discussions.

According to E. P. Chelishev, the foremost among the scholars involved in the Ramakrishna-Vivekananda studies in the Soviet Union today, a band of research workers are today engaged in these studies and that they all got inspiration from the works of Tolstoi.[14] And as further stated by him a new urge to study came during the centenary celebrations of Vivekananda. As we all know the celebrations were observed in different parts of the world with great enthusiasm. In Russia also keen enthusiasm was visible. Particularly the celebrations that were held in Moscow and Leningrad deserve special mentioning.[15] In Moscow a seminar was organized jointly by the three foremost associations, viz., 'Institute of the Peoples of Asia', 'Institute of Philosophy', 'Academy of Science' under the presidentship of Academician P. N. Fredosiev and papers entitled 'Vivekananda—the Humanist', 'Vivekananda, the Great Fighter for Social Progress', 'Philosophical Ideas of Swami Vivekananda', 'Vivekananda and Indian Literature', 'The Illuminating Ideas of Swami Vivekananda' were presented and deliberated upon. At Leningrad, the Leningrad University in collaboration with the Leningrad branch of Soviet-Indian Cultural Society held meetings in which following topics were discussed—'The International Relations of India and Swami Vivekananda's Activities', 'Humanism of Swami Vivekananda', 'Swami Vivekananda, the Great Son of India'. From the headings of the papers read it is clear that Russian intellectuals were keenly interested in the various different aspects of Vivekananda's thought and they were carrying on systematic studies of the same.

IV

THE GREAT INDIAN HUMANIST : E. P. CHELISHEV

In 1963 in a notable article entitled 'Swami Vivekananda—

14. *Swami Vivekananda : Studies in Soviet Union*, 'Preface', p. XIII.
15. *World-Wide Celebrations of Swami Vivekananda Centenary*—published by the Centenary Committee, Calcutta, p. 128.

the Great Indian Humanist, Democrat and Patriot', E. P. Chelishev observed, 'Together with the Indian people the Soviet People who already know some of the works of Vivekananda, published in the U.S.S.R., highly revere the memory of the great Indian patriot, humanist and democrat, impassioned fighter for a better future for his people and all mankind.'[16]

From this observation we get a few valuable informations : (1) in the Soviet Union today many of the works of Vivekananda have been published in Russian, (2) the Russian people are acquainted with them, (3) the Soviet people hold Vivekananda in a very high esteem.

How deep is this respect of the Russian people for Vivekananda is evident from the fact that during his first visit to India while he was at Kanyakumari, Chelishev swam through the shark-infested sea to visit the Vivekananda rock and there he sat to meditate on one who showed a new way of life to his people. 'I thought of his life', writes Chelishev, 'brief but dazzlingly bright, full of indefatigable activity and an impassioned desire to make his compatriots aware of their greatness and lead them into the road to a new life.'[17]

Vivekananda's greatest contribution : *Development of the lofty ideal of Humanism* : In Chelishev's estimate Vivekananda's greatest contribution is the development in his teaching of the lofty ideals of humanism which incorporate 'the finest feature of Indian culture'. And in the light of Vivekananda he was able to realize that 'Since ancient times lofty life-asserting ideas have formed the foundation of India's world outlook. These ideas have been expressed in religious-philosophical forms which as they developed paved their way in constant struggle against the scholastic, ascetic and passive contemplation of the world. It is these ideas that infuse many of the works of Vedic literature, the ancient Indian epics, the greatest writings of Kālidāsa and the democratic poetry of *Bhakti*.'[18]

Modification of Vedanta to enable it to tackle with the problems of the common people : Chelishev is of the opinion that Vedanta philosophy was modified by Vivekananda to suit the

---

16. *Vivekananda Centenary Memorial Volume*, p. 518.
17. ibid.
18. ibid.

conditions of new life and tackle the problem of the common man. Vivekananda made use of the Vedantic doctrine of equality in the divinity of man for protecting the human rights from being trampled by the privileged class in society and by the colonialists.[19]

Vivekananda's doctrine of Active Humanism : According to Chelishev, 'Vivekananda's concept of humanism has nothing in common with the Christian ideology which dooms man to passivity and to begging God for favours.'[20] In order to elevate man Vivekananda put forward the idea that 'The highest divine substance—Brahman is personified in millions of ordinary living people and therefore the worship of God is tantamount to serving man.'[21] And Vivekananda called for positive human qualities to develop in every man, a sense of human dignity in all on the basis of their divinity. According to Chelishev, Vivekananda's assertion of ordinary man's right to happiness in this world is a notable element of his humanism.

Contradiction in Chelishev : Although as a Marxist Chelishev could not accept the idealistic basis of Vivekananda's humanism (viz., 'every living being is Brahman'), yet he considers that Vivekananda's humanism 'possesses many features of active humanism manifested above all in a fervent desire to elevate man, to instil in him a sense of responsibility for his own destiny and the destiny of all people, to make him strive for the ideals of good, truth, and justice, to foster in man abhorrence for any suffering'.[22] Herein all the practical aspects of Vivekananda's revolutionary active humanism has been beautifully brought out. We find that the Vedantic interpretation of the essence of man has been designated by Chelishev as the humanistic interpretation. And this Vedantic interpretation, viz., the doctrine of divinity of man determines the democratic nature of Vivekananda's world outlook and his great concern for the masses.

Vivekananda and other liberal reformers : In India, as Chelishev points out, the cause of the oppressed masses attracted the notice of some other liberal thinkers of the period also. But they talked of partial reforms only and Vivekananda showed the

---

19. ibid. 20. ibid. 21. ibid. 22. ibid.

inadequacies of their reform measures. The former wanted to ease their conditions, while Vivekananda wanted to root out the causes of their oppression. And therefore Vivekananda declared : 'The one problem you have is to give the masses their rights.'

A revolutionary and not a mere reformer : It is clear from the above statements that Vivekananda was talking not of reform but of a revolutionary change. Hence he told the reformers that he was a greater reformer compared to them. Realizing the true import of Vivekananda's attitude in the matter Chelishev says that 'Vivekananda was rather a revolutionary than a reformer.'

Chelishev further points out that Vivekananda 'instinctively' understood the active role of the masses in the historical development of the country. Actually he did not realize this 'instinctively' but his deep historical insight led him to this conclusion. He observed in his historical studies that the influence of the Brahmins, the power of the Kshatriyas and the wealth of the Vaishyas were possible because of the physical labour of the Shudras, i.e., of the proletariat. Thus he saw clearly that the Shudras were the foundation of the society. Chelishev raises two points in this connection which are interesting : (1) Vivekananda was a revolutionary only so far as his ideas were concerned; (2) that he knew historical realities 'instinctively'.

Vivekananda—a Utopian thinker? : Thus according to Chelishev, Vivekananda was an active humanist but not an active revolutionary, he was revolutionary only so far as his ideas were concerned. By revolutionary activism Chelishev means accentuating class-struggle. But according to him, Vivekananda wanted to rely on class reconciliation in order to put an united front in the national revolutionary struggle against the British. Hence in his opinion, Vivekananda was a utopian thinker and not a revolutionary activist so far as social changes were concerned.

But Vivekananda talks of the total extinction of the upper classes in a clear-cut statement : '... the upper classes of India!... Fleshless and bloodless skeletons of the dead body of Past India that you are... . You merge yourselves in the void and disappear, and let New India arise in your place. Let her arise—out of the peasants' cottage, grasping the plough; out of the huts of the fisherman, the cobbler, and the sweeper. Let her spring from the grocer's shop, from beside the oven of the fritter-seller. Let her emanate from the factory, from marts, and from markets. Let her emerge from groves and forests, from hills and mountains.'[23]

Strangely enough this well-known and oft-quoted utterance of Vivekananda was not taken note of by Chelishev or any other Soviet scholar working on Vivekananda.

In his *Conversations and Dialogues* Vivekananda makes it clear that 'When the masses will wake up, they will come to understand your oppression of them, and by a puff of their mouth you will be entirely blown away!' To Sister Nivedita also he once said, 'We will solve the problems of the Shudras but after what tumults, what tumults!'[24] All these indicate that he pointed towards the days of struggles for the establishment of the rights of the masses.

Of course to Swami Akhandananda he wrote : 'But then you must take care not to set-up class-strife between the poor peasants, the labouring people and wealthy classes. Make it a point not to abuse the moneyed classes . . . the wise men should achieve their own objects.'[25] From this last sentence it is clear that Vivekananda spoke of avoiding class-strifes as a matter of policy, only in order to make the upper classes to pay for the education of the masses.

Chelishev himself refers to Vivekananda's lack of faith in the upper classes in his article. 'While at first', says Chelishev, 'he thought that the British domination would be overthrown through an uprising of the princes, subsequently he arrived at the conclusion that India's only hope was her masses. The higher classes were dead physically and morally.'[26] Thus Vivekananda considered that the class battles were inevitable.

Of course, Vivekananda did not consider class-battles were revolutions at any stage or in other words, capturing power with violent means constitutes a revolution. We have seen already that such violent outbursts result in the defeat of the aims of

23. *C. W.*, VII, p. 327.
24. Sister Nivedita—*The Master As I Saw Him*, Udbodhan (1939), p. 296.
25. *Letters of Swami Vivekananda*.
26. *Vivekananda Centenary Memorial Volume*, p. 510.

revolutions. Hence he had no plan for engineering class battles or violent revolutions of the Marxian type. His view was that social action was necessary for a thorough-going social change. Hence he laid down plans for social actions to achieve his goal of a 'root and branch' social change. The implementation of the plan was started by him as we all know through the social service activities of the Ramakrishna Mission founded by him.

Thus we find that only a misconception of his ideas led Chelishev to hold that Vivekananda's socialism was of a utopian brand. Actually it is not utopain, it is intensely practical, only it is not of the Marxian brand.

Chelishev contradicts himself : It is interesting to note that whenever Chelishev is critical of Vivekananda, he at once contradicts himself. Here also in the same breath Chelishev says, 'His ear keenly attuned to the voice of the epoch, Vivekananda was able to discern in it the still indistinct grumbles of the toiling masses rising to fight for their rights.'[27] Chelishev quotes Vivekananda : 'The lower classes are gradually awakening to this fact and making a united front against this [oppression], determined to exact their legitimate dues.'[28] Vivekananda made this clear also that the signs of this awakening was visible in India also in the labour strikes that occurred at the time in the country. Making reference to this statement Chelishev opines that Vivekananda had flayed social injustice and felt that justice will be secured when the oppressed workers will attain supremacy in society and declared that it was inevitable.

Failing to understand properly the plan for social action of Vivekananda, Chelishev opines that Vivekananda had shown a split mind, he had spoken of the inevitability of the class battles and at the same time has thought of class-reconciliation. Actually Vivekananda wanted the youth of the country to implement his plan of mass education and mass awakening and then to leave the masses alone to determine their own course. This is apparent from his following instruction to Swami Akhandananda : 'Teach some boys and girls of the present classes the rudiments of learning and infuse a number of ideas into their brains. . . . Then leave peasants and labourers to look to their own problem to

27. ibid., p. 510.

28. *C. W.*, VII, p. 149.

grapple with and solve it.'[29] Vivekananda was convinced that true emancipation can never be secured unless it is self-won. As we have seen in an earlier chapter, Vivekananda was the only nineteenth century thinker who thought of leadership emerging from the masses. He relied on the penniless youth in this matter for they are the real revolutionary in every country who make supreme sacrifice for making the revolutions successful. Vivekananda definitely did not rely on the rich people whom he wanted of course to make retribution of their sins for exploiting the masses by paying for their education. How can a person who had such a practical programme of action be a utopian?

Actually the Soviet scholars jumped to the conclusion that Vivekananda's socialism was a utopia since as Marxists they were committed to the idea that Vedanta which was the basis of Vivekananda's socialism was an idealistic philosophy.

The voice of a revolutionary : Instead, Chelishev admits that Vivekananda's voice was essentially the voice of a revolutionary, who had with his deep historical insight accurately made predictions about the inevitability of Socialism and the toiling masses attaining supremacy in society and that his humanism was really a gospel of activism.

Industrialization, Capitalism, and the Working Class : According to Chelishev, another great merit of Vivekananda was that although the proletariat class was just emerging at the time since industrialization also had just started in India, he was convinced about the decisive role that it was to play in the course of future social development.

Chelishev believes that Vivekananda acclaimed industrialization through the process of capitalist development since it was to bring India's deliverance from backwardness and feudalism. He, however, shows that 'Vivekananda was aware of the many contradictions of capitalist society which turns the worker into a mere appendage of the machine.'[30]

Vivekananda's world-outlook : In spite of this advanced view of Vivekananda, Chelishev considers arbitrarily that there was some 'haziness' about his social ideals and his world- outlook

29. *Letters of Swami Vivekananda.*
30. *Vivekananda Centenary Memorial Volume*, p. 511.

was somewhat abstract. Chelishev at once concedes that in spite of this, Vivekananda firmly believed that only the ordinary people, the toiling masses, as they become their own masters of destiny, could be builders of a new society[31] and hence it was the bounden duty of every upright man to give them education and raise their cultural level.

The question is, how could the ideas of a man who could clearly visualize the vital role of the proletariat in the future social development of a country be 'hazy' and abstract? Vivekananda does not show any haziness of thinking and his ideas are clearly concrete. His background philosophy, viz., Vedanta is a comprehensive philosophy combining science and mysticism. Actually his commitment to the Marxist standpoint led Chelishev to make althrough contradictory statements in the same breath.

Chelishev holds that notwithstanding 'utopian striving for class reconciliation', Vivekananda boldly protested against the colonial rule and boldly stood in defence of his own oppressed people.

Vivekananda's war against superstition and fanaticism : Chelishev shows that while struggling against colonialism, Vivekananda sought support in the ancient tradition, particularly religious ideology. He interpreted Hinduism in such a way as to bring religion in defence of India's interests, to unite the people to fight for independence. Although he gave his call in the name of religion, Chelishev makes it a point to assert that religious fanaticism was unknown to Vivekananda, that Vivekananda was dead against superstitions and declared war against it, saying that it was thousand times better to be an atheist than be superstitious. Faith in supernaturalism was, according to Vivekananda, a sign of weakness. Here Chelishev was able to grasp the true spirit of Vivekananda's religion.

Call to end colonial slavery : Chelishev shows clearly that Vivekananda's call was to the people for awakening their inner strength so as to fight against 'the legacy of colonial slavery'. And Chelishev rightly points out that this call of Vivekananda has not lost significance even today. Indian people has to get

31. ibid.

sustenance from this message of calling forth inner strength in their fight against the legacy of colonial slavery, viz., poverty and ignorance. As stated by Chelishev there is a contemporary ring in his message that 'We want infinite energy, infinite zeal, infinite courage, infinite patience, then will great things be achieved.'[32] Actually he reminds man that he is an infinite storehouse of strength and energy and that must be manifested in his life, through all his activities.

Crusader against colonialism : According to Chelishev, however, all these calls were to inspire his people to fight against colonialism. In the estimate of the Soviet people today Vivekananda is held in high esteem since he was a fervent fighter against colonialism.[33] Herein we find that Chelishev is full of praise for Vivekananda's contribution. To quote Chelishev's own words : 'This indefatigable sower of truth and flayer of every injustice walked thousand kilometres along the roads of India. He beheld tears and grief, the starvation and death of his disinherited brothers and sisters.'[34]

Chelishev believes that Vivekananda's love for his motherland and the people was greater than his faith in divinity since he wrote that the only God that existed was his people, 'their hands, feet, eyes, ears everywhere they covered everything'.[35] Chelishev's conception in this respect is rather hazy since to Vivekananda not only his people was God but the people of every country, every man, every living being was God and this is in terms of his Vedantic teaching that 'everything is Brahman'. His love for people was again the result of his faith in divinity.

Not a narrow nationalist : Chelishev rightly points out that although Vivekananda was an ardent nationalist, 'sentiments of national narrow-mindedness was alien to him'.[36] Vivekananda, in fact, was dead against national isolation and he wanted the Indian people to assimilate the best of every other nation's culture. He was convinced that isolation from other peoples was one of the reasons for India's stagnation.

Though not a narrow nationalist, always in favour of

32. ibid., p. 512.
33. ibid., p. 513.
34. ibid.
35. ibid.
36. ibid.

assimilation of good things from other nations, Vivekananda was not influenced by the outward glitter of western civilization. In the words of Chelishev, 'Vivekananda relentlessly exposed bourgeois chauvinism, capitalist competition, the quest for profit, the fabulous luxury of the handful of exploiters and disastrous impoverishment and rightlessness of the millions of toilers, religious and racial discrimination, intrigue and violence.'[37] Herein lies the difference between Vivekananda and the other nineteenth century Indian leaders who, in the words of Chelishev, 'naively believed in the miracles of western civilization'.

His second visit, as we have seen, made him disillusioned about America which he thought at first 'a land of freedom'. He did not visit Russia but met the revolutionaries in exile like Prince Kropotkin who, Chelishev believes, influenced Vivekananda in making his utterances about the inevitability of proletariat uprising. But they must also have been influenced by Vivekananda as is revealed in the following utterance of Vivekananda himself : 'All the social upheavalists, at least the leaders of them, are trying to find that all their communistic or equalizing theories must have a spiritual basis, and that spiritual basis is in Vedanta only. I have been told by several leaders, who used to attend my lectures, that they required the Vedanta as the basis of the new order of things.' Moreover, as noted by us already, studying the conditions in the two countries Vivekananda predicted that the next upheaval would usher in either Russia or China. The Soviet writers have failed to take note of the significant statemetns made by Vivekananda quoted just now.

Creator of Modern India : Chelishev repeats that one aspect of Vivekananda's world-outlook is idealistic and this is reflected in his attempt to unite the people on the basis of the doctrine of spiritual unity of the people. Nevertheless in Chelishev's estimation this does not minimize the role Vivekananda played in creating the present day's 'united, monolithic and peace-loving state'.

Initiator of World-peace Movement : While calling his people to fight against the darker forces, Vivekananda called them at the

---

37. ibid., p. 514.

same time for the establishment of friendly relations with other nations on the basis of 'love of men for each other'. Chelishev points out that for this reason Vivekananda is to be accepted as one of the initiator in India of 'one of the most humane movement of our time, viz., peace movement'.

Merit of Chelishev's *assessment* : Here it may be mentioned that Chelishev did not think, like other foreigners or like Marx himself, that India was a country ruled only by caste-divisions and communal discords. His eyes were not fixed on only the priest-ridden society of India, they penetrated through it to have a look at the true India which sang all through the ages the songs of unity of mankind, and preached peace, love and amity. Chelishev has mentioned very aptly in this connection the soul-stirring message of Vivekananda that the 'world is not ruled by the arms, it is ruled by love'.

Contradictory interpretations of Vivekananda : In trying to assess Vivekananda, Chelishev rightly rejects the two views that hold ground at present in this respect : (1) the first view considers Vivekananda to be merely a religious preacher and a mystic, imposing supernatural traits on him; and (2) the other view which considers him a thinker of the Marxist school. While rejecting both the above views Chelishev maintains that Vivekananda's world-outlook was inseparably connected with the entire economic, social and political life of India in his time and hence it reflects 'contradictions inherent in the ideologies of the advanced Indian intelligentsia who took the road to struggle for India's national liberation but at the same time still had no clear-cut definite ideological foundation and philosophical basis'.

Concept of ideology—early Marxian and modified versions : Herein we find that Chelishev shows strict adherence to the early Marxian formulation of the concept of 'ideology', according to which ideology always reflects the contradictions in society.[38] But later on the concept has been modified by Gramschi and Lukacs—Marxian formulation to which an 'ideology' is a reflection of distorted consciousness. Rejecting this negative concept Gramschi develops a positive concept, according to which 'ideology' is a specific system of ideas or 'a conception of

38. *Marxism and Ideology* by Jorge Larrain, pp. 82-83.

the world that implicitly manifest in art, in law, in economic activity and in all manifestations of individual, and collective life'. Thus 'ideology' is conceived by Gramschi as a positive world-view.

The leaders of thought in India had definite and positive ideological foundation and philosophical basis. In the case of Vivekananda, Vedanta was this philosophical foundation which is based on a positive world-view and thus there is no contradiction in his philosophical basis. In the age-old philosophy of Vedanta is not reflected the contradictions of socio-economic life of the present day. Vivekananda's social philosophy is a logical development of Vedanta philosophy as interpreted by him in the light of modern science.

As is pointed out rightly by Chelishev, definitely for a proper understanding of Vivekananda, it is necessary to ascertain the intricate interconnection of traditions and modern scientific outlook in his thought and activities. But while doing so it must be remembered that his thought successfully synthesized the two—ancient traditions and modern outlook and that there is no contradiction in his thought. Failure to realize this has led Chelishev to make such wrong assessment that 'His [Vivekananda's] idealistic outlook prevented him from properly understanding and appraising life around.' This is in contradiction to Chelishev's own earlier statement made in the same article that Vivekananda has seen life in all its aspects, shared the misery and privations of the masses, and that he correctly read the situation and the pivotal role of the masses in future social development.

Chelishev very aptly points out towards the end of the article that 'The attempt to revive the ancient religious philosophical traditions and adopt religion to the requirements of the present age, Vivekananda objectively helped to popularize among the masses the ideas of liberation and imparted to these ideas the nature of a sacred religious duty.' And Chelishev never forgets to mention 'the spontaneous rebellious spirit' of Vivekananda 'against social injustice'. In his opinion further, in spite of the fact that Vivekananda had a combination of 'reformism and revolutionary protests', and in spite of 'the historical conditioning and class-limitations' of his philosophical and sociological views, his world-outlook as a whole played a constructive part in the development of the national liberation movement in India, in rallying the Indian people to struggle against colonialism.

A pertinent question arises here. How can an idealistic outlook without a realistic basis can play a constructive role in history? Chelishev has not made that clear. Reflecting his own contradiction in thought he observes again that Vivekananda's historical merit was that 'He was the first ideologist of the epoch of national awakening who openly and resolutely called for active struggle to remake society and to win independence.'

Chelishev ends with the words of highest praise for Vivekananda. 'We can safely say', he observes in his concluding remark, '. . . many years will pass, many generations will come and go. Vivekananda and his time will become the distant past, but never will there fade the memory of the man who all his life dreamed of a better future for his people, who did so much to awaken his compatriots and move India forward, to defend his much suffering people from injustice and brutality. Like a rocky cliff protecting a coastal valley from storm and bad weather, from the blows of ill winds and waves Vivekananda fought courageously and selflessly against the enemy of his motherland.'[39]

NEO-VEDANTIC ETHICS OF VIVEKANANDA

In another article entitled 'Neo-Vedantic Ethics and Swami Vivekananda',[40] Chelishev points out that at the time when Vivekananda was preaching, India was passing through a thorough-going socio-economic transformation—from a feudalistic society a bourgeois society was emerging and that Vivekananda's moralistic sermons were inseparably related to the social and political problems and 'reflected the new traits of moral consciousness developed in the process of gradual transformations of the feudal moral relations into the bourgeois'.[41]

In the opinion of Chelishev, Vivekananda was 'a zealous,

39. *Vivekananda Centenary Memorial Volume*, p. 531.
40. *Swami Vivekananda* : *Studies in Soviet Union*, p. 31.
41. ibid., p. 31.

aim-oriented reformer of democratically-nationalistic type who wanted attainment of independence and democratic social emancipation of the masses', and who criticized orthodox Hinduism but did not come out of the confines of religion. 'Vivekananda, however', Chelishev points out, 'concentrated not on the outer aspects of religion, i.e., rituals and all that but on the inner aspect which in his opinion form the vital basis of the activities of the Indians.'[42] Here the critical ring in Chelishev's statement seems subdued.

Only Advaita : the basis of morality : According to Vivekananda, 'Only Advaita is in a position to give a satisfactory explanation of the principles of morality and reveal its true nature.' *Bhagavad-Gītā* also deals with the inner world of man but in the opinion of Chelishev, more than the *Bhagavad-Gītā*, Vivekananda asserts human personality as a source of initiative, choice and action, with assertion of its role and significance in society. According to Vivekananda, all morality is based on the Vedantic concept of Ātman-Brahman identity. He emphatically says, '. . . each individual soul is a part and parcel of that Universal Soul, which is infinite. Therefore in injuring his neighbour, the individual actually injures himself. This is the basic metaphysical truth underlying all ethical codes.'

Definition of morality : Defining morality Vivekananda says, 'That which is selfish is immoral, and that which is unselfish is moral.' The source of this interpretation is Vedanta. As shown by him selflessness is an outcome of the realization of identity with the universal soul, 'while egotism is a reflection of the loss of this identity'.

Selflessness as an ethical value in the socio-political context : Vivekananda introduced new, non-traditional features. The problem of egoism was treated by him not only in its metaphysical aspect, but also in its practical socio-political context. According to Chelishev, Vivekananda considers contradiction between personality and society merely as 'an evil of the material bourgeois West' and that it could be overcome by 'Indian spirituality' only. Chelishev's critical tone in this respect emerges from the Marxist doctrine that contradictions of

---

42. ibid., p. 32.

personality and society, having their origin in the material conditions or in the economic situation, could be overcome only with the overcoming of contradiction in the economic field.

Karma-Yoga : In order to eradicate egoism Vivekananda recommended Karma-Yoga, performance of self-less activities, which would ultimately efface egoism and bring liberation. These activities, as laid down by Vivekananda, includes social-political activities.

Greedlessness : 'Selflessness' and 'greedlessness' are the two key-words to Vivekananda which everyone performing his own duty will have to acquire. Chelishev points out that according to Vivekananda, the future of India depends on the performance of such selfless and greedless activities in order to secure independence and to secure the institution of Shudra-rāj in Society.

Real and Apparent Man : *Misconception of Chelishev* : According to Chelishev, Vivekananda has shown that a morally perfect man is a 'real man' and an 'apparent man' is he who has not achieved moral perfection. This interpretation by Chelishev of Vivekananda's two notable lectures 'The Real Nature of Man' and 'The Real and the Apparent Man' in his *Jñāna-Yoga* has missed the point. What Vivekananda propounds is that when a man realizes identity of Ātman and Brahman becomes one with the universe, then he sees everybody as his own self and loves everybody. He bears no longer any ill-feeling against anybody, he cannot injure anybody and tries to do good to the whole world. Hence realization of Ātman-Brahman identity makes a man morally perfect. A 'real man' is one who attains this state of identification of Ātman-Brahman. He becomes a morally perfect man also on account of this identification. He looks upon the world as his own self, hence he is unable to do injury to anybody. This should not be put other way round as has been done by Chelishev that a morally perfect man is a real man. It may suggest that self-realization is not a necessary condition of attaining the state of 'real manhood' and moral perfection. It is not exactly that Vivekananda considers every man 'apparent' who has not attained moral perfection, what he means is that a man who has not attained the realization of Ātman-Brahman identity has no knowledge of his real nature. He is an apparent man, who has not realized his true self.

Gradual self-sacrifice : Chelishev points out that self-sacrifice was recommended by Vivekananda for demolishing the 'apparent' in an individual and his gradual elevation to his real nature. These gradual steps include love for the family, for the community, for the society, for the nation, for the world, for the whole universe.

Concept of 'Renunciation for Service' : In this connection Chelishev rightly points out that the idea of renunciation for service is a new moral code sought to be introduced by Vivekananda and this was not included in the ancient Hindu injunctions. Renunciation of this type is the crux of the Karma-Yoga as conceived by Vivekananda.

Superiority of the Sannyāsa : Self-sacrifice is to be practised by the householder as well as by the sannyasi, according to Vivekananda. However, a sannyasi is superior to a householder since he cuts off all family ties and dedicates himself solely to the service of humanity, which has been made by him a stepping stone towards self-knowledge and attainment of liberation. This concept of superiority of the sannyasi is criticized by Chelishev since, according to him, this leads to the creation of a new social hierarchy. But it should be borne in mind that the basis of social hierarchy is always privilege. The basis of the supposed superiority of the *sannyāsin* is renunciation. Hence no new social hierarchy is to result from Vivekananda's treatment of morality.

New concept of Sannyāsa : Herein lies, according to Chelishev, the difference between the old concept of *sannyāsa* and Vivekananda's new concept. The old idea was, as described by Vivekananda, that a sannyasi makes complete renunciation of all worldly position and wanders forth into the world to live a life of self-sacrifice and to persistently seek self-knowledge.[43] Vivekananda's new concept is that a band of young sannyasi would play a very dynamic and pivotal role in awakening the masses and to make them strive for their own better future and material and spiritual revival of India. Their main aim for their striving would not be merely attaining personal liberation, which

43. *C. W.*, V, p. 186.

would of course automatically result from their utterly selfless action.

Demolition of the boundary line between the secular and the religious : This new concept, Chelishev notes, 'helped in removing the boundary line between the secular and the religious activities'.[44] In the opinion of Chelishev by doing so Vivekananda has given priority to a new type of activities, directed to the development of national consciousness of the masses, to the awakening of enthusiasm for national liberation[45] and thereby a new type of hierarchy of activities was created. But actually Vivekananda attempted to make Vedantic teachings practical when he tried to spiritualize the secular activities. Chelishev has unfortunately missed the illuminating comments of Sister Nivedita on the matter, which runs as follows : 'If the many and the One be indeed the same Reality [which neo-Vedanta preaches], then it is not all modes of worship alone, but equally all modes of work, all modes of struggle, all modes of creation, which are paths of realization. ... To labour is to pray. To conquer is to renounce. Life is itself religion. . . . To him, the workshop, the study, the farmyard, and the field are as true and fit scenes for the meeting of God with man as the cell of the monk or the door of the temple.'[46] Nevertheless, according to Chelishev, the nationalistic spirit was roused by this new message, new definition of activities of a sannyasi. Chelishev points out also that Tilak and Aurobindo were deeply impressed by the idea of self-sacrifice for a nationalistic cause amounting to the practice of religion.

Concepts of Mokṣa and Dharma : Dwelling on Vivekananda's concept of *mokṣa*, Chelishev points out that by *mokṣa* Vivekananda means complete freedom, attaining which a man becomes perfectly moral. In Vivekananda's own words : 'The man who is perfectly moral cannot possibly hurt anything or anybody. . . . No one is more powerful than he who has attained perfect non-injuring. No one could fight, no one could quarrel, in his presence. Yes, his very presence, and nothing else, means peace, means love wherever he may be. . . . Even the animals,

44. *Swami Vivekananda : Studies in Soviet Union*, p. 42. 45. ibid.
46. *C. W.*, I, 'Introduction' to Vivekananda's *Complete Works*, p. xv.

ferocious animals, would be peaceful before him.'[47] Criticizing him on this explanation, Chelishev says that these considerations are some of the weakest points in Vivekananda's ethical views since he loses here touch with the actual problems of the contemporary situation. Chelishev, it seems, considers such moral values as non-injury, non-violence, love as irrelevant to the contemporary issues. But Vivekananda considered them essential for man-making which was in turn the pivotal point of his plan for the regeneration of India and the world.

Dharma : Regarding *dharma*, the code of duty, Vivekananda classifies them under *Jāti-dharma* and *Swadharma*. *Jāti-dharma* means different caste-duties, while *Swadharma* refers to personal code of conduct. According to Vivekananda, the present downfall of India was due to the fact that 'the basis of *Jāti-dharma* has been tampered with', Vivekananda vehemently protested against the monopolization of all privileges by the higher castes as well as rigidity and lack of flexibility in the hereditary caste system. He opined that re-establishment of *Jāti-dharma*, that is to say, allocation of caste-duties, according to qualities, would improve the situation since that would bring forth flexibility in the system and equality in the status and position of the different castes.

Caste-System : Rules and Obligations : According to Chelishev, this non-acceptance of the present position of the caste-system was the result of a change in the moral consciousness of the individual due to breaking up of the feudal relations and formation of bourgeois relations and to the general intensification of the national liberation movement. All these, according to him, made the moral choice more complicated.

The three guṇas : Analysing Vivekananda's concept of the structure of *dharma*, Chelishev points out that *sattva*, *rajas* and *tamas* are the three qualities that characterize every man. A man with predominance of *sattva* is a Brahmin, with *rajas* a Kshatriya. And according to Vivekananda, in the existing situation of India priority of *rajas* was required since good deal of intense activities were required for the regeneration of the country. And he believed that change of caste was possible according to change in quality.

---

47. ibid., VI, p. 126.

According to Chelishev, this justification of the relativity of caste limits and caste obligations was an attempt to meet the new social conditions. 'Affirming the relativity of caste obligations', Chelishev observes, 'Vivekananda . . . firmly approached the social historical necessity of the individualized, relatively independent moral choice, which was for the bourgeois relations under making.'[48] But, Chelishev forgets that the caste rigour was relaxed in India for the first time two thousand five hundred years ago at the time of Buddha when there was no question of a bourgeois society emerging at the time. The difficulty with Chelishev is that he does not take into consideration the fact that the Vedantic concept of equality goes straight against caste-hierarchy and privileges. What Vivekananda was trying all the time was to make the society to be based on Vedanta or to make Vedanta real in social life.

Chelishev considers, 'Vivekananda's views on the duty of a Kshatriya, on the need for the dominance of the spirit of *rajas*, had behind them essentially the necessity to present the individual as the centre of socio-political activity.' 'What we want now', said Vivekananda, 'is an immense awakening of *rājasika* energy, for the whole country is wrapped in the shroud of *tamas*. The people of this land must be fed and clothed, must be awakened, must be made more fully active.'[49]

Concept of good and evil : According to Vivekananda's Vedantic doctrine, good and evil are the two sides of the same coin. Chelishev points out that in Vivekananda's view, the good and evil are 'conventional expression of the soul' of each individual at a stage where the 'man has still not realized his divine essence'. As a Vedantist Vivekananda points out that good for him who strives for *mokṣa* is one; and good for him who possesses *dharma* is another. According to Chelishev, 'Vivekananda's views on the duties of a sannyasi and of the householder give grounds to assume that he discerns the objective criteria of good and evil as dictated by contemporary reality.'[50]

In the opinion of Vivekananda, good and evil are realtive in

---

48. *Swami Vivekananda : Studies in Soviet Union*, p. 45.
49. *C. W.*, V, p. 403.
50. *Swami Vivekananda : Studies in Soviet Union*, p. 47.

essence. It is relative to time and circumstances and state of the mind of the individual who makes the judgement. But of one thing he was certain that 'the sumtotal of the good in the world has been the same all through in relation to man's need and greed'. This concept of a static ratio between good and evil, according to Chelishev, contradicts Vivekananda's own call for selfless service for the good of the country. But that there is no contradiction in Vivekananda is explained by his own statement which has been quoted by Chelishev himself : 'There is no good work that has not a touch of evil in it.'[51] So we must do what brings the maximum amount of good and the least evil.

Chelishev thinks that here in his approach to the problem of good and evil Vivekananda shows elements of dialectical approach. 'Both good as well as evil', says Chelishev, 'from Vivekananda's viewpoint, are realtive, it is only their mutual relation which is absolute.'[52]

According to Chelishev, Vivekananda's treatment of good and evil, is marked by a whole range of original characteristics, e.g., Vivekananda considers that good is affirmed just by its contrast to evil. Following the teaching of Vedanta one should make an attempt to remove this contrast but for doing so one must do good to other, 'actively involving himself in the affairs of the world, displaying his strength and not weakness'.

Strength and Weakness : Vivekananda's View : Arising from the Vedantic concept of the divine essence of man, strength is considered by Vivekananda a virtue, and weakness a sin. And as stated by him, 'Strength is the medicine for the world's disease. Strength is the medicine which the poor must have when tyrannized over by the rich. Strength is the medicine that the ignorant must have when oppressed by the learned; and it is the medicine that the sinners must have when tyrannized over by other sinners... .'[53] And to Vivekananda 'All sins and all evils can be united in one word—weakness. Weakness is the cause of all sinful actions.'[54]

---

51. *C. W.*, V, p. 248.
52. *Swami Vivekananda* : *Studies in Soviet Union*, p. 49.
53. *C. W.*, II, p. 201.
54. Quoted by Chelishev—*Swami Vivekananda* : *Studies in Soviet Union.*, p. 51.

Chelishev aptly points out that 'strength' for Vivekananda is a complex formation, a peculiar identity of the inner and the outer, the spiritual and the physical. But to him 'spiritual strength is the determining factor of strength', 'strengthening of the body is required because it is inseparably linked with the spiritual substance and by perfecting it, man helps the development of this divine essence'.[55]

In this connection, Chelishev points out, Vivekananda condemns the weakning role of religion. 'If we sit with folding hands', Vivekananda says, 'and pondering over the imperfections of our body and spirit, we shall understand nothing.' And Chelishev thinks Vivekananda was not consistent in his criticism of religion since he thought that it was only because of the ignorance of the people about the true principles of religion that they behaved in the above manner. But Chelishev fails to see what Vivekananda criticized was aberrations of religion and not religion itself. He emphatically maintained the position always that religion was not at fault, but the aberrations were responsible for the evils that we find in our society today. Religion was the central point of Vivekananda's life and thought, he was essentially a preacher of religion. His entire socio-political thought emerged as a result of his attempt to make religion practical in life. And as we have pointed out earlier, religion springs from fearlessness and not from fear.

Strength and Weakness in the socio-political context : Chelishev points out that Vivekananda's view on 'strength' and 'weakness' as motives of actions are linked with his socio-political views. This is evident in the following statement of Vivekananda : 'Our country needs at present muscles of iron, nerves of steel, gigantic will of which nothing can withstand', and again, 'We have already bowed our heads enough, there is no need to cry any more, rise on your own feet and become men.'[56] Chelishev fails to see that 'strength' and 'fearlessness' are the two values which were propounded by Upanishads and held high by Vivekananda. These values were not therefore products of the socio-economic situation, but they were sought to be used to meet the socio-economic situation.

55. ibid.

56. *Letters of Swami Vivekananda.*

Self-help as moral value for individual and for the nations : Chelishev further points out that from the concept of strength as the leading motive for moral actions Vivekananda deduced self-help for both the individual and the nations as great moral values. The individual is to help himself in his path of spiritual struggle and the nation also in its path of progress and prosperity. Since he saw that colonialism was retarding growth and development of the country he emphasized manifestation of strength in the people so that they could engage themselves in tireless work on development. He said, one 'must not depend on any foreign help'. 'Nations', he added, 'like individuals, must help themselves. . . . If a nation cannot do that, its time has not yet come. It must wait. . . . the new light must spread all over India. With this end you must work.'[57] In the opinion of Chelishev, 'The general humanist pathos of Vivekananda's ethical views consisting in the assertion of the value of human personality, human dignity, strength and possibilities of man as an active member of the society, was determined by specific conditions of social development in the environment of colonial dependence.'[58] But were not these virtues held high during the age of the *Mahābhārata*, in the *Gītā*? They are eternal values for any kind of society for progress and prosperity.

The problem of ends and means : Vivekananda urged the necessity of securing national emancipation. As regards the means that were to be adopted for securing it, the question of violent and non-violent means assumed importance.

First of all, according to Vivekananda, 'means are as important as the ends'. He asserted that 'whenever failure comes, if we analyse it critically, in ninety-nine per cent of cases we shall find that it was because we did not pay attention to the means'.[59]

Resistance vs Non-resistance as moral values : Next, Vivekananda makes it clear that resistance is a virtue for the householder while non-resistance for the sannyasis. He is of the opinion that before one reaches the highest ideal, man's duty is to resist evil; let him work, let him fight, let him strike straight from

57. *C. W.*, V, p. 108.
58. *Swami Vivekananda : Studies in Soviet Union.*, p. 54.
59. *C. W.*, II, p. 1.

the shoulder. Then only, when he has gained the power to resist, will non-resistance be a virtue.[60] Making his position further explicit he says, 'The one who from weakness resists not, commits a sin ... while the other would commit a sin by offering resistance. ... Then, having the power, if we renounce it and do not resist, we are doing a grand act of love... .'[61]

Was Vivekananda in favour of social compromise?: Since Vivekananda does not advocate violence always, Chelishev concludes : 'Admitting in principle the possibility of resisting evil by violence, Vivekananda also at the same time adhered to the positions of reformation and strove to secure social compromise.'[62] We differ from Chelishev on this point. He forgets for the moment, although he mentions in another place in his article that Vivekananda supported killing of Bhīṣma by Arjuna in the *Mahābhārata* since otherwise the evil-doing king Duryodhana could not be brought down. Vivekananda never talked of social compromise, his attitude for example, regarding the elimination of the priests and the upper-classes, as we have seen already, was totally uncompromising.

Social needs and a balance between activism and contemplation : Formulation of ethical principles by Vivekananda is considered by Chelishev 'clever' and 'confusional-metaphysical formulations'. Here it is evident that Chelishev has not probed deep into the basic philosophy of Advaita-Vedanta from which emerge all the moral formulations of Vivekananda. They were not just 'clever' inventions and there is no metaphysical confusion in the clear and bold theories of Vedanta. However, he considers that 'Vivekananda's sermon of resisting evil was "first and foremost a call for effective actions for the good of the country".' The social needs, the needs of *Swarāj*, sought expression. Vivekananda gave that expression and he reminded his countrymen that *Bhagavad- Gītā* had preached the gospel of activism, the philosophy of fighting the evil, which they must now emulate. Vivekananda points out that India secured a balance between activism and contemplation which has to be re-established for the solution of the problems of India.

---

60. ibid., I, p. 39. 61. ibid., pp. 38-39.
62. *Swami Vivekananda : Studies in Soviet Union*, p. 58.

Criticism of Vivekananda's View of Activism by Chelishev : Here again Chelishev is critical about Vivekananda, since the latter did not follow the Marxist analysis of the situation and did not accept the Marxist solution . Chelishev says, 'In the quests of the lost harmony between activity and contemplation Vivekananda builds up a utopia in which materialize on the one hand his progressive-democratic aspirations and dreams of emancipation of the masses, and appears on the other a wrong understanding typical of bourgeois theoreticians, of the class character of society and of the class-struggle proceeding from it, and its radical non-acceptance.'[63] Chelishev forgets to note the fact that Vivekananda arrived at his conclusion making a thorough study of the historical developments in India and elsewhere, that he was fully aware of the class contradictions and class-struggles that took place in history, but he arrived at different conclusions regarding the means that were to be used as compared to Marx. To label all intellectuals who differ from the Marxian line of thought as 'bourgeois theoretician', is the weak point of the Soviet thinkers. We have already discussed elaborately about Vivekananda's independent historical investigations, his independent view of class struggle, his views about the means to be used, which are logically established. The two structures of thought—that of Marx and that of Vivekananda are so different that it confuses the Soviet thinkers every now and then. Vivekananda preached activism, the spirit of fighting the evil, for attaining national emancipation as well as for achieving social emancipation of the masses. These two objectives were considered complementary by Vivekananda. Herein it differs basically from the thinking of bourgeois theoreticians. His plans and programmes, his instrument for implementation of them differed from those of Marx and the bourgeois theoreticians both.

Utilitarianism in ethics and bourgeois moral values : Vivekananda sharply criticized utilitarianism and hedonism which formed the basis of bourgeois morality. Chelishev approves of Vivekananda's criticism in this respect and points out, 'Despite the traditional reference that all troubles have their source in the human body, the thinker in these judgements rightly

63. ibid., p. 59.

criticizes utilitarianists for their lack of concern for the lofty spiritual aspirations of man.' 'Observing at the time of his foreign travels', adds Chelishev, 'an unrestrained egoistic pursuit of profit, open individualism receiving legal sanction in bourgeois society, Vivekananda rightly points to the spiritual poverty of the peoples concentrating all their attention on material needs and becoming, in the ultimate count, slaves of their desires. These desires ultimately devour the man, there is no end to them, a man can never fully satisfy his desires.'[64]

Chelishev himself points out that Vivekananda does not accept the utilitarian criteria of usefulness as the criterion of the vital activity of man. In Vivekananda's own words, 'In these days, we have to measure everything by utility—by how many pounds, shillings, and pence it represents.' According to Chelishev, here 'Vivekananda shows in his judgements the definite dependence of utilitarian principles of morality on capitalist reality.'[65] Chelishev points out that Vivekananda clearly shows that 'All the current social norms and methods are derived from society as it exists', i.e., the bourgeois society. But the basic moral values like love of man and equality cannot be derived from them. He, however criticizes Vivekananda for attempting to show that they can be derived from 'Indian spirituality' which he thinks played a great part in Vivekananda's nationalistic utopia, in the 'building up of a factually bourgeois society short of its contradictions'.

Chelishev admits that the basis of this 'spirituality' for Vivekananda was in the religious-moral principles of Vedanta—Vedantic morality being considered by him eternal and unchangeable, 'adaptable for all peoples, at all times and society'. Chelishev does not see the points that according to Vivekananda, Vedantic truth underlies, every religion, hence it is the universal truth. And as we have seen already, the exponents of modern physics assert that Vedantic truth underlies the conception of Reality as perceived by modern science. It proves that Vedanta is universal and eternal. Hence in the opinion of Vivekananda the basis of all morality is the universal and eternal truth that underlies all religions and even science and not what Chelishev thinks to be 'Indian spirituality'.

---

64. ibid., p. 61.

65. ibid.

Chelishev, however, admits that Vivekananda's thesis that religion forms the basis of all morality, was not formulated to prove the superiority of religious moral principles of Vedanta but to save his country from the injurious ideas of utilitarianism and hedonism. In this connection Chelishev further points out that 'The moral indignation which Vivekananda expressed with regard to contemporary bourgeois norms of morality was extremely significant.'[66] Vivekananda's criticism of capitalism, according to him, 'played a progressive role, for it helped in the growth of national liberal aspirations'.

Vedantic ethics of Vivekananda——any contradiction in it?: Coming to assess the Vedantic ethical principles as laid down by Vivekananda, once again Chelishev's tone becomes sharply critical. 'The ethical views of Vivekananda', observes Chelishev, 'like that social soil on which these developed, are contradictory.' To support his view Chelishev points out that objectively helping in the affirmation of the principles of early bourgeois individualism, which consisted in the protest against strictly regulated moral norms and precepts, Vivekananda proclaimed the ideas of free development of personality; at the same time 'he criticized bourgeois individualism in that form of it in which it came before him in the developed capitalist society'.[67] Here Chelishev mistakenly thinks that Vivekananda supported free development of individual personality by being influenced by early bourgeois individualism, while actually Vivekananda stood firmly on the Vedantic concept of the freedom of the individual.

All Chelishev's criticisms emanate from one single source, viz., his misconceptions about Vedanta, on the basis of which Vivekananda formulated his social philosophy and the interrelated ethical norms. Chelishev denying what he considers 'the idealistic basis' of Vivekananda could not comprehend the latter's standpoint fully.

However, Chelishev praises Vivekananda's anti-colonial stand, his criticism of capitalism, his active humanism, his protest against moral principles, his criticism of utilitarianism and hedonism and in spite of his misconceived criticisms to the effect that all the criticisms and protests of Vivekananda against 'the

66. ibid., p. 62.

67. ibid., p. 65.

bourgeois structure and particularly of the morality of bourgeois ready money was of a purely limited moralistic nature', he considers that 'the name of Vivekananda is associated with a very important page in the history of Indian ethical thought'.[68] In the words of Chelishev—'Reflecting spirit of those tasks and transformations which the country was facing in the socio-political conditions of that time, the thinker provided an impetus of its own kind to a fresh understanding of many problems, including also the ethical, having created a relatively whole ethical teaching—the ethics of neo-Vedantism. The eminent political leaders and thinkers of Indian national liberation movement—M. K. Gandhi, J. Nehru, Rabindranath Tagore, B. G. Tilak, Aurobindo Ghose—constantly turned to the creative heritage of Vivekananda.'[69]

We find therefore Chelishev's inevitable conclusion is that Vivekananda's utopia was creative in nature and it played a dynamic role in bringing forth national liberation! If we turn to the pages of history of freedom movement in India we will find that the national revolutionary upsurge, which ultimately brought the freedom of the country, was created by Vivekananda. And those who are untiringly continuing with the struggle for the social emancipation of the masses outside the arena of political field today are also inspired by his spirit. We remember what Professor Benoy Kumar Sarkar, an eminent Indian Sociologist, observed, viz., that 'We should never forget that today we could accept socialistic and communistic ideas because of Vivekananda. He was the father of socialism in India just as he was the father of nationalism in India.' Hence Vivekananda's ideas were not utopian, were no dreams, impractical good wishes, they were practically realizable guidelines.

THE PROPHETS OF HUMAN EMANCIPATION

'Arise and Awake'—a call to the poor and the Shudras : Chelishev's critical tone is totally subdued in his two interviews that he gave to two periodicals in India in 1984 and 1986 regarding Ramakrishna-Vivekananda. To the fortnightly journal *Paribartan*, published in Bengali from Calcutta, he said, 'To my

---

68. ibid., pp. 65-66

69. ibid.

mind, there is close similarity between Dialectical Materialism and Vedantic Humanism of Ramakrishna-Vivekananda. There is a good deal of common grounds between the two. When we probe deep we find that the message of Vivekananda is in essence a glorification of Communism.' Vivekananda has used the call of the Upanishads—'Arise, awake and attain greatness' to awaken the Shudras. He has given the call to the poor and Shudras to breakdown the chain of servitude. From this point of view the message 'Arise and Awake' is the message of Socialism.[70]

Epitome of manliness, courage, strength and warring spirit : In another interview given to Swami Purnatmananda for *Prabuddha Bhārata*, an official organ of the Ramakrishna Mission, Chelishev said in great admiration of Vivekananda, 'Whenever I see his photograph, I see his eyes, I feel inspired, I feel great power working within me, I become bolder, I become stronger. He is a full man, a valiant warrior, a real hero. And when I go through his work, his speeches, his letters, I get electrified, I get charged and re-charged. To me Vivekananda stands for manliness, for strength, for courage, and for warring spirit.'[71]

Positive vs Negative religion : When the interviewer asked him—'Being a Marxist don't you find it difficult to appreciate Vivekananda, a monk and a religious leader?', Chelishev answered : 'A communist should well understand and then analyse the real situation in a country. If there is a natural religious sentiment in the vast population of a given country, it should be given due consideration.' 'A true communist should understand', he continued, 'that just as religion can be an instrument of communal dissension in the hands of the reactionaries, a proper religious consciousness, on the other hand, can also inspire people to strive for doing good. Really speaking, religion has two aspects, one positive and the other negative. Vivekananda chose the positive aspect of religion and tried to apply it in the process of uplifting his country and his people.'[72] It is evident here that Marxist viewpoint has undergone modification since Marx never distinguished between negative

70. *Paribartan*, February 1, 1984, translated by the author.

71. *Prabuddha Bhārata*, January 1989, p. 68.

72. ibid., p. 70.

and positive religions, his condemnation of religion was total. As exponents of this positive religion, Vivekananda has won the admiration of the Soviet scholars today.

The prophets of human emancipation : Chelishev then added a few very significant words in the course of this interview, which shows Vivekananda in true light and his pivotal role in world history. These words are : '. . . we do not consider Vivekananda and his mentor Ramakrishna Paramahansa to be mere religious leaders as they are commonly looked upon. They are the prophets of human emancipation, of equality, and human progress.'[73]

The message of peace and amity : To the straight question of the interviewer as to whether he thinks that the philosophy and message of Vivekananda has got anything to contribute to the present world-predicament, Chelishev answered : 'The message of Ramakrishna and Vivekananda, is the messge of peace, amity and world brotherhood. That message can indicate the path of survival in the fear-stricken world of today. I personally feel that in the context of the present nuclear menace which is gradually engulfing the earth, it is very essential to disseminate the message of Ramakrishna-Vivekananda all over the world.'[74] The interview came to a close with the further significant remark from Chelishev, significant for the future of India as well as of the world, that 'There is no doubt that their message was necessary and relevant in India and the world of their times; but it is still more necessary and relevant in the present Indian context and in the context of the contemporary world.'[75]

---

73. ibid 74. ibid. 75. ibid.

CHAPTER 26

A Crusader for the Rights of the Downtrodden

I

CHAMPION OF THE RIGHTS OF THE DOWNTRODDEN

Here in this chapter we continue with the same topic—the impact of Vivekananda in the socialist countries. In the previous chapter we have devoted our entire attention to E. P. Chelishev, the most well-known among the Soviet scholars on Ramakrishna-Vivekananda. He received the prestigious Vivekananda Award for his contribution to Vivekananda studies. In this chapter we deal with the views of others. All of them agree that Vivekananda's socialism is a utopia with its base on idealism, but he was nevertheless 'a Crusader for the rights of the downtrodden' and that his doctrines inspired the national revolutionary movement for the emancipation of India from the imperialistic domination of Great Britain.

II

E. N. KOMAROV

Growth of anti-bourgeois thinking in India : According to E. N. Komarov, in the history of the social thought in India up to the 70's of the nineteenth century we find an acceptance of bourgeois relations as an absolute bliss. This was the period when bourgeois relations were gradually growing in India, manifesting the contradictions inherent in them and the feudal relations were on the process of liquidation. While Rammohan supported, Bankim and Vivekananda criticized the contradictions. According to Komarov, this criticism was still subjective 'sentimental' (to use Lenin's words), 'moralist' resulting in 'utopian social formulations'. Komarov, however, admits that their criticism of bourgeois society, despite its subjective and utopian character, helped in asserting the cause of 'national liberation and democratic ideas'. And he observes that here was a development of Indian social thought towards a definite anti-bourgeois tradition.

Condemnation of the influence of money : Ramakrishna's preaching : In his opinion Ramakrishna's preaching against *kāminī* and *kāñchana*—particularly against the last one—was representative of an unconscious social protest against the domination of money in a bourgeois society.[1] But Komarov forgets that this preaching against lust and wealth was age-old in India; from time immemorial, abolition of these two constituted the most essential vows of the monks. Hence Komarov's thesis in this matter is definitely wrong. Ramakrishna's preaching against *kāma* and *kāñchana* was not a protest against bourgeois society, but it became meaningful to those who protested against the bourgeois society.

Vivekananda, in the opinion of Komarov, reflected the attitude of growing democratism and along with it the criticism of bourgeois relations combined with religious moralist preaching.

Vivekananda's contributions to the development of Indian social thought : Komarov is of the definite opinion that 'The socio-political views of Vivekananda played an extremely important role in the development of Indian social thought and growth of national liberation movement.'[2]

According to Komarov, Vivekananda rejected more forcefully than everybody else the thesis that the British domination was a blessing to India. He saw in the colonial domination the source of national oppression, and main obstacle to material and cultural development of the country and a cause of the monstrous poverty of the country.

Most important and progressive feature of the socio-political views of Vivekananda : Further, in the opinion of Komarov, 'The most important, progressive feature of social-political views of Vivekananda was that he envisaged the national liberation of

1. *Swami Vivekananda : Studies in Soviet Union*, p. 100.
2. ibid., p. 116.

India and the democratic social emancipation of the masses as mutually related and the two-fold goal.'[3] For making the masses conscious of their rights he wanted to go to the masses and give them education and open their eyes and he called upon the youth to undertake the task. Vivekananda's ideas in this respect were concrete and not just a dream or utopia.

More than anybody else, Komarov points out, Vivekananda realized the class-character of the propertied classes in relation to the national liberation movement. While Bankimchandra had some hopes about the *zamindars*, Vivekananda had none. As Komarov points out, in Vivekananda there was intensification of the criticism of bourgeois society.

Vivekananda knew scientific socialism : Komarov's most significant discovery about Vivekananda is that he knew about the idea of scientific socialism since he was the first among the Indians to expound the ideas of systematic change in social formations and declare that feudalism and capitalism was inevitably to give way to the power of the Shudras—the working people, i.e., to socialism.[4] But Komarov considers that it was a naive idea for Vivekananda to hold that under the regime of the working people there will be some decline of culture. But today we find that it is being feared in certain quarters that the worship of materialism and ruthless dictatorship is causing decline of rationalism in the socialist countries, which is also one of the causes of the introduction in Russia of Gorbachov's policy of *Perestroika* and *Glasnost*. At least Gorbachov has presented this view in his policy declaration about *Perestroika*.

Komarov also reveals the important fact that compared to his predecessors, Vivekananda took a step forward to understanding the real nature of class conflicts in India. He alone could read the true significance of the labour strikes in India at the time and that he was the first to realize that the class-struggle of the working people was peculiar to the modern age.

But Komarov misjudging Vivekananda on the matter like all the other Soviet scholars, observes that 'sympathizing with the idea of establishment of the power of the working people and even considering it inevitable in all countries of the world,

3. ibid.

4. ibid.

Vivekananda, like Bankimchandra, regarded socialism as an extremely remote perspective'.[5] Actually, Vivekananda never gave that impression that socialism was only a remote possibility. In his *Modern India* he clearly stated : 'The first glow of the dawn of this new power has already begun to break slowly upon the Western world. . . . Socialism, Anarchism, Nihilism, and other like sects are the vanguard of the social revolution that is to follow.'[6] He was convinced, therefore, that socialism was to come not at a distant date, but soon. Komarov opines further that 'Fighting for the awakening of the masses and welcoming its first signs in India, he (Vivekananda), however, did not any more raise the question of organization of the working people on a class basis.'[7] According to Komarov, Vivekananda lacked understanding of the objective laws of bourgeois relations and this and the tendency of class unification for securing national liberation prevented Vivekananda from organizing the working classes and 'led him to utopian endeavours to eliminate social and class conflicts without liquidating the material basis of society'.[8] Here Komarov forgets that he had himself stated, as we have seen above, that unlike Bankimchandra, Vivekananda had no faith in the upper classes playing any role in the struggle for national liberation. Actually Vivekananda pinned his faith only on the masses in the matter of attaining national liberation, as we have seen earlier. And his strivings were concentrated on one point only : in awakening the masses, and giving them their lost individuality so that leadership might grow from among them and thereby they could attain supremacy in society.

Vivekananda and foreign capital : *Was he an ally of Indian capitalism*? However, Vivekananda saw, Komarov admits, like a few other predecessors that the British dominance was obstructing the economic, particularly the industrial development of India, condemning the country to backwardness. The cause of the evil, he saw, was in the pre-dominance of foreign capital. And as a solution he did not see any other way but to encourage native private capitalist enterprise. Since socialist enterprise under

5. ibid., p. 123.
6. *C. W.*, IV, pp. 468-69.
7. *Swami Vivekananda* : *Studies in Soviet Union*, p. 123.
8. ibid.

foreign rule was inconceivable, this was the only alternative left. He encouraged men like Jamshedji Tata who later on built up the first Iron and Steel factory in India. But not understanding the situation Komarov following Chelishev criticizes Vivekananda for encouraging private capitalism in the country.

Komarov points out that though Vivekananda's criticism of the bourgeois relations amounts to giving only moralistic sermons, yet 'in Vivekananda this moralistic sermons acquire a great socio-political trend, as a completely conscious attempt, on the one hand, to make the propertied (upper) classes to yield concessions to the working people (lower classes), and on the other, to restrict within definite limits further development of class-struggle of the working people'.[9] Komarov is of the opinion that while welcoming the class struggle and the impossibility of stopping it Vivekananda does not yet want it to reach the level of a revolutionary struggle. According to him, Vivekananda, like Bankim, wanted the matter to be amicably settled between the two classes; Vivekananda thunders that the well-being of the higher classes now lies in helping the lowers to get their legitimate dues. But Komarov fails to see that Vivekananda did not believe that class-battles were necessarily speaking a 'revolutionary' phenomena. Vivekananda was engaged in preparing the masses for a more fundamental revolution, as we have seen already.

Religion : *Instrument of social compromise or social revolution* : Komarov points out also that Vivekananda more consciously than other ntionalists sought in religion not only a national banner in general, not only a means of unification of the people, but also 'a weapon of social compromise and of the creation of an ideal society, which would, remaining a class society, still be free from exploitation and oppression'. This is the same wrong thesis as was propounded by Chelishev discussed above to which we have objected by pointing out that the Soviet scholars have developed this thesis of social compromise by choosing to neglect Vivekananda's vision of a new India, depicted in his *Memoirs of European Travel* in which the great thinker makes it clear that the upper classes were destined to

9. ibid., p. 127.

'disappear in the void', clearly indicating that in the future society there will remain only one class, viz., the toiling class.

Vedantic Socialism : Komarov observes in this connection that created by Vivekananda the idea of a religious version of socialism became popular among the nationalists and came to express fully the aspirations of the radical nationalists of the period. The conception of the Vedantic Socialism is thus described by Komarov as a utopia of the nationalists.

Views of religion and the concept of Ideology : At this stage Komarov attempts to discuss the religious views of Vivekananda. Adhering strictly to the Marxist doctrine of Ideology as reflection of class-contradictions and not caring to consider the reinterpretation of the doctrine made by Gramschi and Lukacs, Komarov gave his verdict that 'Vivekananda's religious views reflected the tendency peculiar to capitalism of fulfilling the religious ideology with the norms of morality which the bourgeois ideologists call universally human.'[10] 'Of such ethical norms', he further points out, 'some reflect class interests of the exploiters (particularly holding right to private property as sacred) and others are positive norms of human relations.' The ethical norms as propounded by Vivekananda emanated from his Vedanta philosophy, which originated in the hoary past, when there was no sign of the bourgeois society. Komarov's thesis in this respect seems based entirely on wrong premises.

Quite oblivious of the fact that Vivekananda never held any brief for private property (he never said that right to private property was a sacred right), Komarov further observes, 'being incapable, due to social and historical reasons, of actually rising against the first cause of evil, viz., private property, Vivekananda attacked its consequences'.[11] Here Komarov forgets completely that Vivekananda gave whole-hearted support to socialism in spite of some misgivings in his mind regarding some of its consequences. That these misgivings were true is evident from the recent turn of events in the socialist countries, as we have noticed earlier.

It is definitely wrong to suggest that Vivekananda's support to the cause of the poor ended with moralistic sermons in

10. ibid., p. 128. 11. ibid.

accordance with a number of traditional Indian religious philosophical thought. Actually Vivekananda's programme for the masses were not merely moralistic or religious sermons, they were positivistic and realistic measures, the machinery for the implementation of which was geared by Vivekananda himself and it is still in operation with full swing as we shall see in the next part of the book.

Meaning of realization of God : Komarov's interpretation of the meaning of 'realization of God as attainment of moral perfection' is based on thorough misunderstanding of realization. Realization means direct experience or direct perception of God or Brahman, it means attaining a state of super-sensory and super-rational state of consciousness in which there is identification of *ātman* with Brahman. That it is possible to attain such a state has been admitted by scientists like Professor F. Capra, Professor Schrödinger, Charles Townes, as we have already seen. Besides, we have pointed out in the previous chapter that moral perfection is a consequence of the 'realization' and not identical with it.

Vedanta in the eyes of the Soviet scholars : Similar naive interpretation has been given to Vedanta by almost all the Soviet scholars as reflected in the following comment by Komarov—'As the starting point, Vivekananda took the positions of Vedanta about the top hierarchy of the Brāhmaṇas and of soul as manifestation of Brahman in man.' Vedanta has no relation with the top hierarchy of the Brahmins. Upanishads, forming the basis of Vedanta, was developed by the Kshatriyas (the military power). Its main tenets are that the ultimate Reality is One and the Reality is not matter but consciousness with which, according to Professor Capra and Schrödinger, modern physics is in full agreement. This One Reality permeates through all beings and everything in the universe.

Komarov's exposition of Vedanta is totally wrong since he states that, according to Vedanta, the divine soul which is a manifestation of Brahman was originally pure but that purity was destroyed later on coming into contact with the material world. Vedanta never propounded any duality, any distinction between the divine soul, the Brahman and the material world. Brahman appears as the material world due to ignorance, the Absolute, seen through time, space and causation, is the universe. The ever pure Reality always is the same, always purity itself. Renunciation is recommended not to recover purity but to dispel *māyā* or ignorance.

New orientation to the concept of renunciation : Komarov rightly points out that Vedanta is the foundation of Vivekananda's social philosophy. As noted by him the concept of 'renunciation' has been given a new orientation by Vivekananda who recommends selfless service to near ones and those who need his care for the householder and complete dedication to self-less service to the humanity for the monks. According to Komarov, this is a typical concept of a peasant society to which 'some elements of contemporary trivial bourgeois notions' have been added by Vivekananda. But many topmost thinkers of the modern industrialized society have accepted this moral principle as one of the highest. And there is no reason why it cannot be pursued even in an industrialized society. Actually the concept of selfless service is not peculiar to an agricultural society as is supposed by Komarov.

But, Komarov admits that the purpose of Vivekananda's religious moralistic sermons of selfless-work for near ones were 'a call for working for the welfare of the country and for the well-being of the poor'.[12] And here it is very interesting to note that Komarov thinks that in propounding his gospel of service to the poor Vivekananda has used the expression of Engels—'turning to the poor as select deities' while actually Vivekananda has used, as we all know, Ramakrishna's message '*Jīva* is Shiva', 'Every living being is God' as the basis of his gospel.

Is Vivekananda's stress on religion against historical development? Komarov is of the opinion that in over-emphasizing the role of religion in modern society Vivekananda has shown lack of knowledge of historical development and that for that matter he has considered the decline of the role of religion in the West as an exclusive feature of the 'materialistic West' and predominance of medieval religiosity of India and the backward eastern countries as a special merit, forgetting that

12. ibid., p. 130.

similar situation prevailed in the medieval West. But Komarov neglects the fact that today many scientists in the West thinks that the eastern religious concepts are very much similar to the concepts of modern physics and this certainly implies that religion of the East was not merely a 'medieval' affair, it is scientific and very much relevant today, to this age of Science. And the fact that there is a revival of religious spirit in the Soviet union today shows that historical development in modern time has not rejected religion as a mere primitive affair. Hence, Vivekananda was right in emphasizing the religiosity of the East and 'the need for recovering religion for solving the human problems of the West'.

Without probing deep into Vivekananda's thought and the context of his utterances Komarov unjustifiably gives the verdict that 'return to religion sharply deepened the contradictoriness of Vivekananda's social position'. He criticizes Vivekananda for condemning on the one hand the social laws sanctioned by religion as oppressive and on the other hand for stating : 'In the land of Bhārata, every social rule is for the protection of the weak.' That the social laws in India never attempted to exterminate anybody is a historical fact, in the hierarchy of castes everybody had a place, lower or higher. It is also true historically that the original idea of caste formation was misused in later days by the priests for claiming exclusive privileges for themselves. When Vivekananda praised the Indian social rules he referred to the original ideas behind them, when he condemned them he referred to their misuse by the priests. According to Vivekananda, religion is not responsible for the oppressive social laws but priestcraft is responsible for them.

Averting class-struggle : Vivekananda did not give a call for class-struggle, he advised his colleagues to avert it. Komarov thinks that it is wrong to give a call of awakening to the masses and then restrict and avert class-struggle by preserving religiosity of the masses. Komarov believes that religiosity generates humiliation and shame. But Vivekananda believed that religion generates fearlessness, manliness, and great courage and determination to fight out every injustice. Vivekananda did not want to lead the blind masses to commit acts of senseless violence to install some upper class leaders to power.

India's historical mission of carrying spirituality to the West : Regarding India's historical mission of carrying spirituality to the West, Komarov thinks that Vivekananda has expressed 'even utilitarian considerations of their own kind, while putting forward the idea of exchange of spiritual values of India for scientific technological attainments of the West'. And in his opinion, a section of the western intelligentsia accepted the idea without giving consideration to the socio-political reality behind it. This western intelligentsia itself, according to him, was in its own way conditioned by the socio-political reality in the West which aroused moralistic protest to capitalism among many of them particularly among the representatives of the middle-strata in the West.

Despite this, Komarov grants one credit to Vivekananda and other radical nationalist thinkers of the period : that their purely subjective 'sentimental' protest against capitalism played a progressive role in heralding the beginning of the anti-capitalist tradition of advanced India's social thought. At the same time he denies that Vivekananda had knowledge of the objective law of capitalism and therefore while protesting in a moralistic manner he had to subscribe to capitalistic process of 'Industrialization'.

Utopia of overcoming capitalist contradictions without a class-struggle : Komarov's misconception about Vivekananda's ideas :

According to Komarov, finally the emergence of mass national liberation movement and the already started democratic upsurge led to the emergence of a peculiar radically nationalistic utopia. That utopia consisted in the belief that after the British colonial dominance is overcome, it would be possible to overcome social contradictions in Indian society emerging out of the capitalistic development and to create a society free from exploitation, without a class-struggle.

But Komarov forgets that Vivekananda has spoken of the inevitability of class-struggle, and that he had shown that class-struggle has a long history in India beginning from the earliest period. Vivekananda, however, did not consider that the solution of the problem, i.e., securing emancipation of the masses could be attained unless, we repeat once more, the masses were awakened, educated and unless leadership emerged from amongst them. Till that was attained he did not think that it was wise to accentuate class-struggle, which would, in his opinion, result in installing to power leaders coming from upper strata of society, who being politically ambitious, would attempt to thrive at any cost. That would not secure the emancipation of the masses from oppression. Since he had a true revolutionary spirit, Vivekananda wanted a thorough revolutionizing of the society, with mass leadership at the helm of affairs.

III

V. S. KOSTYUCHENKO

Vedanta and the problem of correlation of Indian and European Culture : V. S. Kostyuchenko has dealt with the topic 'Vedanta and the problem of correlation of Indian and European culture', in which he has tried to make an assessment of the social ideas of Swami Vivekananda.

Religiosity of Indian Culture challenged : First of all, he has criticized the religiosity of Vedantic character of Indian culture, and the doctrine of harmony of 'spirit' and 'reason' in Indian philosophical standpoint. He had accepted the interpretation by the Marxist writer D. Chattopadhyay who has tried to write the history of Indian philosophy according to the strict Marxist formula which has been questioned, as we have seen earlier, by Dr Nihar Ranjan Roy, the eminent Indian historian.[13] According to Chattopadhyay, the main trend of philosophical thought in India has been althrough history atheistic and materialistic and not spiritualistic. Dr S. Radhakrishnan, the world-renowned Indian philosopher of the modern age, says, 'The country has had a tradition in religion that it is not a matter of doctrine or dogma or rites, it is a matter of man's encounter with the ultimate Mystery of the world. All these doctrines and dogmas, rites and ceremonies, are instruments which help the human individual to see his God face to face.'[14] According to Vivekananda, India has

13. *Religion and Society in Ancient India,* edited by Pranabananda Jash, p.31.
14. S. Radhakrishnan, *Our Heritage*, Orient Paperbacks, p. 8 (1973).

all through its history predominance of this religious and spiritualistic tradition. But he does not deny that towards the end of the Vedic period due to decline of spirituality and predominance of the priests who claimed exclusive privileges, the masses in order to have relief from the oppressive ritualism, joined the group of the materialists, the Chārvākas. According to him further, the clash between spirituality and materialism has been going on from the beginning yet the question has remained unsettled till today.[15]

Kostyuchenko, however, praises the humanistic trend of poet Rabindranath's thought, which, he says, was a development of Vivekananda's spiritualistic thought. His concluding words in this respect are very significant. 'These values', claims Kostyuchenko, 'belongs not only to the Indian people but also to their friends, that is also to our people for whom Tagore ever had the kindest, most friendly feelings. These values belong to the whole of mankind.'[16] Actually, the basis of these values are the Upanishads, regarded as the pinnacle of the spiritualistic Vedantic philosophical texts. And Vivekananda, basically an exponent of these values, explicitly, pointed out to the world that they were the treasures of mankind as a whole, not the treasures of any particular nation.

Socio-Economic background of neo-Vedanta : In a second article entitled 'Conception of neo-Vedanta', while emphasizing in the Marxist way the socio-economic background of the development of the neo-Vedantic thought, Kostyuchenko points out that it was an ideology suitable to the contradictions of the period, viz., the necessity of getting rid of feudalistic values and giving expression to the democratic values and opposing the evils of foreign capitalism; according to him, in India the language of this expression was religion and there took place what he describes as a 'philosophical renaissance'.

According to Kostyuchenko, certain modifications were introduced into the old Indian philosophical systems in the nineteenth century to suit the conditions of the idea of social hierarchy, the idea of freedom in subjection to caste rules, the idea of social activity in contrast to quietism, and the idea of

15. *C. W.*, III. 16. *Swami Vivekananda* : *Studies in Soviet Union*, p. 86.

importance of worldly comforts to the ascetic ideal, were introduced. All these ideas, according to him, appeared in a religious garb. The author makes a serious mistake here, nowhere in the old Indian philosophical thought or religious ideas the idea of inequality or social hierarchy has been preached or supported. The social rules were the working of the priests. Equality and freedom was the keynote of the Vedas and the Upanishads, religion has nothing to do with the priestly injunctions. As Vivekananda points out, priestcraft is the denial of religion. Hence the concept of equality and freedom were inherent in the Vedantic philosophical thought in India from the beginning, only they have been emphasized by the nineteenth century Renaissance leaders.

According to Kostyuchenko, in addition to 'equality and freedom', the following elements were also emphasized in the nineteenth century Indian thought : (1) faith in the great 'cleansing' and 'liberating' role of 'reason' and 'science'; (2) faith in the dissemination of knowledge as the radical means of struggle against hunger, diseases, prejudices, and 'barbarian customs' inherited from the medieval time; (3) faith in the rationalized religion as compatible with enlightenment. According to Kostyuchenko, these main trends of thought came to the fore with greatest force in the period.

Relation between philosophical thoughts and the socio-economic forces : According to Kostyuchenko, these trends of thought manifested variously at different stages of development of philosophical thought in the nineteenth century India and these thoughts were related to socio-economic development of the country—crisis of feudalism in the first half of the century and the growth of capitalism in the second half. In the early period of development of bourgeois ideology, according to Kostyuchenko, when the opposition to feudal ideas was mounting up they turned to European ideas and sought the help of colonial power for the removal of the social evils. This is manifested in Rammohan. In the second phase, a sharply expressed anti-English orientation characterizes Dayananda and his Ārya Samāj. Rammohan and Dayananda had one point in common, both of them opposed polytheism.

The third stage in the evolution of Indian philosophical thought is characterized by Vivekananda's exposition of Vedanta. His views, according to Kostyuchenko, has an affinity to the *Gītā*. 'With the help of its set aphorisms and images', Kostyuchenko observes, 'which have become a part of universal culture, it was possible to appeal not only to reason but also to the hearts of the millions.'

Finally, Kostyuchenko derives the conclusion that in Rammohan was reflected the rejection of the majority of the features of Hinduism, in Dayananda the emergence of militant Hinduism, and in Vivekananda there was an attempt to identify common bases of religions, preserving (but at the same time relativising) the concrete forms of religious worship.[17]

Karma-Yoga and Practical Vedanta : Kostyuchenko finds Vivekananda's new orientation of *Karma*-yoga highly interesting and his conception of 'Practical Vedanta' as a 'change-over' to the development of ethical-psychological and social aspects of Vedanta associated with historical requirements.

Ramakrishna's new-orientation of Vedanta : Dwelling on Ramakrishna's teachings of Vedanta, Kostyuchenko points out that Ramakrishna reveals a number of substantial differences from Advaita :

(1) the Brahman endowed with form is here declared as much real and true as also without it; (2) the sphere of variably-diverse, born of 'divine' play (*līlā*), is by no means illusory, *līlā* is as real as *nitya* (invariable, absolute); (3) the 'non-reality' of the world is spoken of in the sense of its dependence on the absolute and variability, *māyā* is just what obscures this aspect.

Thus, Kostyuchenko derives the conclusion that in the nineteenth century, progressive Vedantic thinkers is to be noticed the tendency of acceptance of the reality of the world. Of course, in his opinion, denial of illusionism does not imply a denial of idealism. In his opinion the main tendency of deviation from *Māyāvāda* (and orthodoxy) was very significant in the then socio-economic context. He thinks that Vivekananda gave *Karma*-yoga first and foremost position among all the yogas. He forgets that balance between the four yogas was the essence of the teachings of Ramakrishna-Vivekananda.

17. ibid., p. 191.

Radical unorthodoxy of Vivekanadna : According to Kostyuchenko, the attitude of Vivekananda was radical unorthodoxy, since he had an extremely ironical attitude to the traditional notions of paradise, hell, miracles, etc., and denied the 'eternalness' of the Vedas.

Characteristics of neo-Vedanta :

(1) Kostyuchenko points out that neo-Vedanta synthesizes between the Dvaita, Viśiṣṭādvaita and Advaita, and Ramakrishna describes the three standpoints as the three main stages of Yogic experience. This synthesization was important in his views, since this opened up the further possibilities of synthesization and solved the problem of communal clashes.

(2) Next, characteristics of neo-Vedanta, according to Kostyuchenko, is that it pays attention to ethical-psychological and social implications of Vedantic theories. And Vivekananda strives to bring it down from the heights of scholastic theorization to the earth and democratize them.

In this connection he points out further that Vivekananda denies the hierarchy implied in the formulation of the theory of *pāramārthika* and *vyavahārika*, from his point of view the acceptance of the spiritual universal oneness leads first to a denial of all privileges. The concept of spiritual oneness is also brought by him to support individual freedom and fraternity. And here Kostyuchenko makes a very significant statement by way of assessment : 'Thus the great slogans born in the course of anti-feudal revolutions in Europe are essentially rendered in the language of Vedanta.'[18] But Kostyuchenko mistakenly thinks that all the radical ideas that were spelt by Vivekananda have a foreign source, viz., antifeudal revolutionary thoughts of Europe. Actually they were all inherent in the Vedantic doctrines and they were brought out by Vivekananda.

Reformation, Enlightenment, and Restoration in Modern Indian philosophical thoughts as reflected in Vivekananda : In a third article written by Kostyuchenko entitled 'Philosophical Teachings of Vivekananda', Kostyuchenko points out beautifully that 'three motifs constantly resound in Vivekananda's works'.[19] And these are the principal motifs of the whole of the modern

18. ibid., p. 221.

19. ibid.

Indian philosophical thought. These motifs are : (1) 'the motif of reformation' is 'universal religion', 'putting an end to religious discords, superstitions and fanaticism'; (2) 'the motif of enlightenment' is reason, science, education, shaking off the stagnant forms of social existence; and lastly, (3) 'the motif of restoration' is the humanist idea of 'free man on free earth', of man who has thrown away the burden of outlived notions which undermined his dignity and checked his development.

Non-orthodox attitude : Kostyuchenko points out rightly that 'Vivekananda is against blind obeisance to authority, against acceptance of traditions only on the strength of their centuries-old existence' and points out that Vivekananda perferred a thinking atheist to a person blindly accepting a faith only on the basis of authority.

Criticism of utilitarianism and religion as the panacea of capitalism : Vivekananda's justified criticism against utilitarianism, a bourgeois ideology, has been appreciated by Kostyuchenko who, however, considers that Vivekananda mistakenly 'sees in religion the panacea for the misfortunes of capitalism'. Actually Vivekananda saw in religion the most effective man-making instrument but the problems of capitalism, according to him, were to be fought by such men who have been properly brought up, trained and educated at the socio-economic level. Kostyuchenko thus misunderstands Vivekananda on this point. Not only Kestyuchenko, but all the Soviet scholars misunderstood Vivekananda on this point, their common misconception arising from the standpoint of Marxism. First of all, Kostyuchenko himself forgets to mention the line of demarcation between the two varieties of materialism mentioned by him. Secondly, the author forgets that Vivekananda was the greatest champion of social and economic freedom. Only he believed that a society based on the Vedanta philosophy will make that possible. He believed in the Vedantic concept of equality and freedom and wanted to translate them into practice in life.

Precariousness of Modern Civilization : Vivekananda, Kostyuchenko further points out, sees the precariousness of the position of modern civilization in two circumstances : (1) rivalry and mutual denial of existing religions; (2) the positions of religions in relation to science. To solve the first problem his recommendation was universal religion and to solve the second he showed the agreement between science and religion.

Universal Religion : To Kostyuchenko Vivekananda's statements in defence of tolerance, against fanaticism and communal feeling were historically progressive.

Revealing contradiction typical of Soviet line of thought, in the same breath Kostyuchenko observes, 'Despite all its positive points, this theory (of Universal Religion)' was in many ways a simplification, and the attempt to create harmonious relations between religions—utopian.'[20] According to him, the utopianness of this concept of conciliation between religions conceived by Vivekananda is revealed in the fact that these differences are being actively used by the dominant class in class societies to deviate the attention of the masses from the dominant economic issues. As an example, he points out that despite Ramakrishna-Vivekananda's efforts, communal discords today continue even in Bengal, their home state. These differences can only be obliterated by taking active steps against these forces.

But the question is why in a part of the Soviet Union (in Georgia) where reactionary forces are said to have been eliminated long ago through the implementation of socialism, there is racial battles today? Why Ramakrishna-Vivekananda's message of amity and brotherhood is being welcomed by persons like E. P. Chelishev, if they are of no avail? Are not these pertinent questions to be answered? Surely the concept of Universal Religion is a positive concept and not a mere device to distract the masses from their economic struggle. The concept is relevant even in a socialist state.

Vivekananda's opposition to superstitions and miracles : Kostyuchenko himself welcomes Vivekananda's opposition to superstitions and miracles. And he admits also that Vivekananda's exposition of India's contribution to the world contains a great deal of truth, since some of the ancient Indian theories of cosmos, evolution of living beings, etc., anticipated some features of modern scientific views.

Asia-centrism in Vivekananda: Kostyuchenko is critical of

---

20. ibid.

the trend of Asia-centrism in Vivekananda though he admits that some influence of Indian philosophical tradition on Pythagorianism and Platonism is quite probable, thus confirming Vivekananda's thesis that from Asia civilization spread to the West.

Conformity of Science and Vedanta : Dwelling on Vivekananda's arguments showing conformity of science and Vedanta, Kostyuchenko agrees that 'The concept of universe, eternal in time and infinite in space, in which everything is in motion, occurring according to laws which are immanent and not dictated by interference of any external force indeed correspond to the notion of modern science.' But in his opinion there is nothing specifically Vedantic in these ideas. Vedantic ideas are introduced when it is stated that the true essence of this universe is spiritual. We have already discussed what the eminent scientists think about it today—that according to some of them 'matter originated in consciousness', which means that this universe is a spiritual and not a material entity. We have also seen how scientists like Schrödinger and Capra have endorsed the mystic experience of the Indian Yogis; they have also pointed out that the ultimate Reality, of which the universe is a manifestation, is spiritual in nature.

Scientificness of the concept of Brahman : Kostyuchenko states that Vivekananda's attempts to establish scientificness of the concept of Brahman on two arguments, viz., (1) that the concept is based on direct experience and may be verified, and that, (2) it corresponds to the urge of science for unity, has not succeeded.

According to him, there is a radical difference between Vedantic experience and the scientific understanding of experience. Since one is direct perception without the interference of the mind and the other is perception through the mind. But as we have seen already, Sorokin has shown that modern science recognizes the super-rational, super-sensory instrument of knowledge today. And Capra makes it a point to show that sub-microscopic physics points out to a Reality which can be experienced through such an instrument of knowledge only.

Regarding the second proof, i.e., unity urge of science, the author is of the opinion that science propounds material unity. But as we have seen already it has been shown by Sorokin that materiality of Reality has been exploded with the development of modern physics and hence the unity that is implied in the modern scientific theories is actually spiritual unity.

Theory of Involution as propounded by Vivekananda : Kostyuchenko does not show any argument against the following views of Vivekananda : (1) that nothing can be created out of nothing; (2) and that for that matter if consciousness is manifested in the later stage of evolution it must have been in an involved stage in the beginning also; (3) that evolution is preceded by a process of involution. But after mentioning these views of Vivekananda, he sarcastically quotes Vivekananda saying, 'Buddha is already involved in the protoplasm' as if it was a preposterous argument. But logically is it so? Can Kostyuchenko prove that something can be created out of nothing in this universe?

Vivekananda's theory of evolution has been ascribed by Kostyuchenko as not only idealistic but 'metaphysical'. Since Kostyuchenko does not produce any convincing argument in favour of his views, his assertion appears like a dogmatic statement without any logical foundation.

Attitude towards materialism : Kostyuchenko is impressed by Vivekananda's attitude towards materialism. 'With all his theoretical opposition', Kostyuchenko observes, 'to ideas of materialism and atheism he had a more than tolerant attitude towards atheists.' He also admires the skill with which Vivekananda builds up a bridge, the link between the inner transformation of man leading to the attainment of spiritual liberation and attainment of social liberty on the outer plane through radical transformation in the existing social system with the new interpretation of the traditional concept of *mokṣa* (liberation).

Vivekananda's plan for social transformation :

Kostyuchenko has fallen to the grip of the same misconceived ideas common to all the Soviet scholars regarding Vivekananda's plan for securing social transformations, *rapprochement* between the reformists and rejection of the political instrument since they believe that the only instrument of securing social transformation is politics and that there is no alternative to a political revolution. To repeat once again what has been stated umpteen times in this book that Vivekananda wanted social action, and not political action, for a social cause and that he criticized the reformists who attempted tit bit reforms confined to upper strata of society, since he wanted a 'root and branch reform' or radical transformations to take place in the social life so as to eliminate privileges. He criticized them also for seeking the help of the British rulers for their social reforms, considering that humiliating for the nation.

Vivekananda was not conservative and indifferent to social reform : Kostyuchenko at this stage supports Vivekananda's stand *vis-à-vis* the liberal reformers and moderates in Indian politics and points out that he was not a conservative and was not indifferent to social reforms. The author shows also that Vivekananda wanted radical change to be carried out with the participation of the masses and for the sake of improving their lives.

'*Self-help*' : Taking a stand for 'self-help' Vivekananda ridiculed the liberals and observed, 'The fools hold meetings to gain greater power from the hands of the British. The slaves desire power to subjugate other slaves.' Kostyuchenko notes this in a tone of appreciation and points out that as regards the question of winning independence from the British, Vivekananda was in favour of complete independence as against the claim of the liberals for limited powers within the British Empire. He quotes here a revolutionary from Bengal who stated that Vivekananda emphasized, 'the need to pay the foreign usurpers back in their own coin' and to 'liberate the citadel of eastern culture from the palpus of foreign Octopus'.

Politicization of Vedanta : Referring to Vivekananda's attitude towards using violent means, Kostyuchenko observes that the politicization of Vedanta, so characteristic of the extremist leaders like B. G. Tilak and Aurobindo Ghose, was thus essentially done by Vivekananda, despite all his outworldly proclaimed indifference to politics.

Stages of history : Criticism of ancient Hindu idea : To Kostyuchenko the ancient Hindu view of rotation of history through *Satya, Tretā, Dvāpara,* and *Kali yuga* is a pessimistic one since the course is from 'light to darkness' although the cycle begins again 'the trend remains the same'. Here the influence of Marxian linear theory of progress on Kostyuchenko is apparently clear but the theory of linear progress has been rejected by the modern sociologists as unscientific, as seen earlier. Nevertheless Kostyuchenko admits that 'Vivekananda affirms the possibilities of social progress on global scale.'

Vivekananda's theory of the four stages of class-domination : Kostyuchenko has given his views on Vivekananda's theory of the succession of the four stages of class-domination in society. Since from the early stage of domination of the Brahmins in India there comes in succession, periods of domination of the Kshatriya, Vaishya and Shudra, the author thinks that history thus turns out to be a process of constant rise upwards of those who earlier occupied the lower rungs. He thinks that this concept deviates from the earlier cyclical concept and implies an ascent to the higher stages of the social order. 'History is not so much an aggregate of circles as an "ascent" towards something higher dialectically "removing" the previous stage to social state', says Kostyuchenko. Hence he suggests that Vivekananda does not ultimately subscribe to the cyclical concept but to the concept of linear progress. But Kostyuchenko has missed the important statement of Vivekananda that after the rule of the Shudras when all will enjoy the same status they will be elevated to Brahminhood and ultimately the cycle will start again with the ascendency of Brahmins to power. He has also missed another equally important statement of Vivekananda, viz., 'No progress is in a straight line.'

Vivekananda's concept of the varṇas : Kostyuchenko then takes account of Vivekananda's concept of struggle between the *varṇa*s as the decisive factor in historical process, his view that masses play the all important role in placing one or the other class in power and finally the view that the masses are the real base of the society. These judgements, according to Kostyuchenko, 'are nothing but vague enigmas'. Since he considers that Vivekananda's concept of *varṇa*s are not the same as the known concept of 'class'.

Vivekananda's depiction of *varṇa*s as something eternal and universal is naturally objected to by Kostyuchenko who thinks that the struggle between the classes, according to Vivekananda, is not on economic issues but on spiritual issues like monopolization of knowledge. Monopolization of knowledge is a matter of the priests and therefore this issue is not at all spiritual. That their interests in monopolizing knowledge is purely economic has been made amply clear by Vivekananda in *Modern India* in which he states that Brahmins fight to preserve ceremonialism, etc., purely in the economic interest, since it is means of their livelihood. Here Vivekananda has been misunderstood thoroughly by Kostyuchenko and other Soviet scholars, since they did not take note of the significance of the line of demarcation between 'religion' and 'priestcraft' as drawn by Vivekananda. Thus it is clear that according to Vivekananda the struggle between the *varṇa*s is based on economic interests and as such they are eternal and universal. *Varṇa*s classified on the basis of occupations are classes based on differences of economic interests. Here Kostyuchenko has missed the point.

East and the West : *Necessity of a synthesis between the two* : To Vivekananda, the rule of the Vaishyas was equivalent to the bourgeois society of the West in the contemporary period. Speaking of the future he thinks a synthesis between the two—East and the West was necessary.

In this connection Kostyuchenko raises questions about Vivekananda's findings. These questions are : Why did the development of bourgeois and its successes appear so novel to India? Why in India over thousands of years only two stages of development, viz., Brahmin-rule and Kshatriya-rule were realized, why the third, viz., Vaishya-rule had to be imported?

The differences between the East and the West : According to Kostyuchenko, for the answers to these questions Vivekananda had recourse to identifying the difference between the eastern and the western civilizations originating in Greece. The differences, according to Vivekananda, as summarized by Kostyuchenko, are : (1) the West values the physical strength the most, India values spiritual sublimity; (2) the first cultivates gratification of the senses, the latter self-renunciation; (3) the former studies the outer world, the latter the inner; (4) the goal of the former is political freedom, of the latter—spiritual; (5) the most valued to the former are earthly joys, to the latter—eternal bliss. Besides, the sense of religious tolerance is characteristic of India, which also lacks the tendency of grabbing other nations' territories. Further if the West has demonstrated how much it can 'blow up' the man's needs, India has shown how much these can be restricted.

According to Kostyuchenko, it is on the strength of these differences that Vivekananda thinks that an 'empire of the Vaishyas' has become possible in the West—a bourgeois society with characteristic development of technology.

Superiority of Indian Civilization : According to Kostyuchenko, all this analysis of the differences of the East and the West by Vivekananda constantly reveals the superiority of Indian civilization. He thinks that this tendency was natural, in the background of 'Europe-centrist furies' and apologies for colonialism in the period, but it at times led to Asia-centrism.

In this connection the author points out that the European culture was by no means always secular and oriented towards natural science. And he thinks also that 'the actual correlation between the ideas and social existence giving rise to them is, in Vivekananda, turned upside down'—a view which is based on strict Marxist formulae. And in this analysis he depends on the book of D. Chattopadhyaya, a book in which the conclusions were known even before data collections began. He raises the question why in spite of so much Indian influence over the Greek—the Greeks followed a different path? Komarov may take note of the fact that this is just the same with India today—in spite of so much European influence, she has not given up religion, it is still the mainstay of our national life. The fact is that the main trend of a nation is not easily overturned to give place to a new one and this is the lesson of history.

Stagnation of Indian Civilization : He points out that to the European, India of Vivekananda's time was 'a dismal picture of mass poverty, disease, hunger, ignorance and lawlessness' and

Vivekananda admitted it to be true and affirmed that this was the result of colonialism. According to Vivekananda further, the colonizers could make ground in the Indian soil due to 'mummifying' of Indian civilization. This stagnation in his opinion, was due to two causes : (1) one-sidedness of Indian civilization—laying overstress on *mokṣa* since the Buddhist period, although prior to that period there was an attempt to strike a balance between the four goals of life, viz., *dharma*, *artha*, *kāma*, and *mokṣa*. And in this connection Vivekananda points out that the irony of history is that although in the *Gītā* in India the need for physical force was stressed, and in Christianity the need for non-violence was stressed, the people of both the countries have followed just the opposite path. According to Kostyuchenko, this interesting anti-thesis essentially leads Vivekananda to believe that not ideas, but social existence determined the conduct of the people.

As to the second reason for the mummification of Indian civilization, Vivekananda, according to Kostyuchenko, touches upon the quite real social roots of this phenomenon and this is the avidity of the upper caste members and corruption of the initial ideal of *varṇa* and *dharma*. And the author appreciates Vivekananda's condemnation of castes and privileges in this connection.

Both the Civilizations—One-sided : Vivekananda pointed out that both the civilizations of the East and the West were one-sided and they would gain by mutually exchanging their achievements—India by adopting from the West technological knowledge and the West adopting from the East spirituality. Yet, Vivekananda warned India and advised that she must avoid both 'the Scylla of old orthodoxy and the Charybdis of modern European civilization', since the old orthodoxy has brought stagnation and degradation and since the latter has lost control over inner self and also since the corrupting influence of the privileges of wealth was eating up the vitals of the European nations.

The lucid exposition of the bourgeois society by Vivekananda (discussed earlier in the previous chapters) is considered by Kostyuchenko as being directly related to 'utopian-socialistic' tendency. However, Kostyuchenko appreciates that Vivekananda realized the synthesis of the positive achievements of Indian and European civilizations desired by him, could not be achieved either by the classes ruling in India who were 'morally and physically dead' or by the top hierarchy of the West European society called by him a 'pack of wolves' and pinned all hopes for better future of India and of mankind on the working massses, on the lowest Shudra *varṇa*.

Socialism of Vivekananda : Referring to the socialism of Vivekananda, Kostyuchenko says, 'Of course, he is far from scientific socialism, his socialism on the whole has a petty bourgeois romantic, utopian character.' First, reason for this view is that the *varṇa* in Vivekananda is not at all the proletariat but the 'oppressed' or the 'unprovided' ones, in the conditions of India the reference was largely to peasants and partly to craftsmen. According to the author, therefore, the victory of the Shudra *varṇa* means not a radical change in the class structure. This conclusion is arbitrary since peasants and craftsmen are also the working people. Though Vivekananda also spoke of the industrial proletariat class and their strikes, yet Shudras or the working people included not only the industrial proletariat but also the peasants, craftsmen, petty traders—the entire mass of the have-nots. When this composite group comes to power superseding the upper classes, there is definitely radical change in the class structure of the society and change in the property relations since the upper classes then disappear in the void, according to Vivekananda. Hence the analysis of Kostyuchenko in this respect does not seem convincing.

Then Kostyuchenko refers to Vivekananda's concept of peaceful transformation of the society from capitalism to socialism and the role of religion in such a society and the concept of the society of the *jīvanmuktas* of which the empire of the Shudras proper is the prologue. In this connection he observes, 'But such a society without Hinduism and Vedanta is unthinkable.' Socialism has to have its firm ground on Vedanta or on the spiritual concept of the universe if it is to survive. It cannot survive long on the sandstone of materialism. It does not imply by any means the superiority of Hinduism or of

Vedanta, since the essence of every religion, according to Vivekananda, is the same, in its essence every religion is Vedantic.

Kostyuchenko, in spite of his criticisms of Vivekananda on several points, thinks that 'Vivekananda's services as one of the first to express his support for non-capitalist development of India are nevertheless indisputable. And his final remarks are interesting : 'Through the haze of romantic illusions and utopain desires Vivekananda was nonetheless able to discern the contours of the future with adequate clarity—and at times, even simply with striking precision.' The statement clearly manifest the contradictions in the judgement of the Soviet scholars. How can one whose vision is hazy with romantic illusions and utopian desires can correctly read the future? Is it not an impossibility? In future we expect an answer from the Soviet scholars on this point.

CHAPTER 27

The Harbinger of a New Revolution

I

A. D. LITMAN

Vivekananda : An Outstanding Historical Personality: According to A. D. Litman, the determining traits of Vivekananda as an outstanding historical personality lies not in his religious mystical ideas but in his democratic convictions, ardent patriotism and enlightenment. He did not pass his days in seclusion of the monastic order meditating on God. 'He unified the whole of India and kept a close and direct contact with the lives of the millions', 'he penetrated deep into their needs and aspirations, and strove to find real and effective ways and means of fulfilling their countries' old aspirations'.[1] This is a correct assessment of Vivekananda's contribution to the regeneration of national life.

As depicted by Litman, Vivekananda attended the Parliament of Religions at Chicago in 1893 to draw the attention of the world not only to the spiritual grandeur of India, but also to the poverty of the people and seek the aid of the West for its mitigation. He, however, soon discovered the anti-people, anti-democratic essence of imperialism of the West, its exploiting nature, and 'the hypocrisy and falsehood of the bourgeois democracy in the West'. According to Litman, 'Vivekananda then irrevocably and resolutely removed all illusions of assistance from the West and pinned all his hopes and aspirations on the awakening of his own people, on the growth of their own spiritual and physical powers, on the revival of their ancient distinctive culture.'[2]

As rightly understood by Litman, Vivekananda had recourse

1. *Swami Vivekananda : Studies in Soviet Union*, p. 148.
2. ibid., p. 150.

to Vedantic concept of man/God identity in order to instil a sense of self-confidence in the people.

Vivekananda's Concept of Equality : Vivekananda's concept of equality has been best understood by Litman among all the Soviet scholars. 'If the man himself is God', says Litman, 'it means . . . that all people are equal, that there are then no high or low. . . . Since all men are equal, all nations, all peoples are also equal.'[3] And this means that 'colonial oppression is a contradiction, a phenomenon contrary to natural laws'. These humanistic ideas inspired the people to rise against colonialism and demand their just right to self-government.

Regarding the struggle for independence, Litman points out that although Vivekananda did not put forward any concrete plan of struggle but emphasized that whatever may be the way the 'Indians must display courage, a sense of self-sacrifice, stability and heroism in the struggle.'[4] And he mentions also that the thinker was against the ideas of non-resistance to evil.

Here we note a difference between Kostyuchenko and Litman, while Kostyuchenko holds that Vivekananda on the whole preferred non-resistance, Litman holds that he preferred resistance.[5]

Vivekananda's Call to the Have-Nots : According to Litman, Vivekananda was against all vestiges of the past, which in some way or other were undermining the dignity of some and exalting others and in this connection he quotes Vivekananda's wonderful statement : 'Oh! How I would wish to destroy the boundaries of "untouchability", and uniting everybody, and go on exclaiming : "Come all poor and have-nots, come all of you who can walk on your feet. We are united in the name of Ramakrishna." '[6]

Education : As an Instrument for fighting the problems of the masses : Litman appreciates Vivekananda's role as a true enlightener, who was an ardent champion of the education of the people, of wide propagation of knowledge among the masses. According to Vivekananda, there was no problem, however intricate it might be, which could not be solved by the magic word 'education'. Litman brings to light that Vivekananda subjected the existing system of education to sharp criticism as

3. ibid. 4. ibid., p. 152. 5. ibid. 6. ibid., p. 153.

one for the upbringing of slaves. Vivekananda brings out also that the clergy (the priests) 'simply cheated the people, thereby amassing great wealth and stifling the working people both spiritually and physically'. 'The power of the priests and foreign dominance', said Vivekananda, 'have been supressing the poor people of India for centuries together and at long last they have forgotten what it is to be human beings.'[7] As pointed out by Litman further, 'Swami Vivekananda saw the source of all suffering, poverty, and oppression of the Indian people only in darkness, obscurity and illiteracy of the working masses.'[8] Vivekananda was very angry with the moneyed class who had an extremly 'despicable and arrogant attitude' towards the education of the working people. He quotes Vivekananda's statement of bold protest in this matter : 'It matters nothing if the working people, unlike you, have not read books. . . . They are instead the shame of nations in all countries . . . absorbed in the struggle for existence, they have no possibility of acquiring knowledge. . . . But with the passage of time many men of genius will come out of them.'[9] It shows that Vivekananda had great faith in the intellectual capacity of the working people.

Vivekananda's attitude towards Religion : Litman appreciates Vivekananda's attitude towards limiting the sphere of religion. He quotes Vivekananda : 'We insist that religion has no right to be law-giver of the public. . . . Keep your hands off! Keep yourself within your limits, and all will be well.'

Litman mentions also Vivekananda's vehement opposition to fanaticism and his sharp criticism of asceticism.

He admires Vivekananda's steadfast faith in the people though according to him, 'The Indian thinker was not able to bring himself to a differential approach to various classes in the general masses of the working peoples.'

Role of Religion : *Misconception of the Soviet thinkers* : But Litman, like all other Soviet thinkers, considers 'Vivekananda's ideas on enlightenment retaining the stamp of contradictions and inconsistency, inherent in his world outlook'.[10] This view is upheld by the Soviet scholars because Vivekananda rejected political struggle as an instrument of social transformation. And

---

7. ibid. 8. ibid. 9. ibid., p. 154. 10. ibid., p. 155.

Litman thinks that it is contradictory on the part of Vivekananda to seek to restrict the sphere of religion from the social field and then again to say that 'political and social reforms must always be carried out in India, proceeding from her religious life'. To this criticism we would point out that when the thinker talked of restricting religion from the social field he has been speaking of religion of the priests, and in the second statement he means religion in the spiritual sense which elevates man. In his opinion, as we have seen earlier, elevation of man is a precondition of the success of a struggle, social or political.

Role of the masses and the role of the individuals : Litman objects to also Vivekananda's attitude of placing faith in the masses yet exaggerating the role of the individual in the historical process, which is reflected in his following statement : 'The history of the world is the history of a few men having confidence in themselves.' But is not the truth of this statement borne out by the twentieth century history of Soviet Russia itself? Is it not a making of Lenin, Stalin, and of Gorbachov? What Vivekananda wanted to emphasize was this : that the persons in the leadership must be men of convictions and self-confidence.

Shudra-rule : Litman thinks that due to the idealistic understanding of social life Vivekananda was sceptical about the 'rule of the Shudras'.[11] In one place he said with enlightenment, men of genius will come from amongst the masses, at another place speaking of the advantages and disadvantages of the stage of Shudra-rule he said, 'Its advantages will be the distribution of physical comforts, its disadvantages (perhaps) the lowering of culture. There will be a great distribution of ordinary education, but extraordinary geniuses will be far less and less.' It is possible to have geniuses from among the working class but that does not mean that there may not take place a decline of culture among the multitude. There is complaint in Soviet Russia today about a decline of rationality and work-sense—two important components of culture—among the Soviet people. We have referred to it in detail in a preceding chapter.

Litman is of the opinion that : 'Applying all his efforts to the work of enlightenment, Swami Vivekananda did not go beyond

11. ibid., p. 157.

awakening within the masses a consciousness of their own strength' and that 'he did not put forward any concrete programmes of masses' actions against colonial dominance, or suggest any cardinal measure for liquidating the system, of social inequality and oppression.'[12]

But as we have pointed out so many times in this book that his plan was to awaken the masses and then the enlightened masses were to decide what course they will adopt for winning their emancipation. He did not want them to install leaders coming from the upper class elites to power, he wanted the masses to produce their own leader who would ultimately be installed in power in due course of time. Hence he did not organize the masses for political actions.

Vivekananda's ideas were progressive : But at the same time Litman is of the opinion that in the specific conditions of the late nineteenth century India, Vivekananda's ideas of enlightenment, as well as his entire outlook, was progressive.[13] Thus like all other Soviet scholars, Litman also makes contradictory statements in assessing Vivekananda. Vivekananda is to him utopian and progressive at the same time. 'His teaching', in his opinion, 'had an effective influence on the formation in India of democratic ideas.'[14] How can an utopia have an effective influence? If it is effective then it must be real and not an utopia, a mere dream. Litman's further remarks in this matter make it clear that the ideas of Vivekananda was not an utopia. 'His social-political and especially enlightening ideas', says Litman, 'objectively helped in the awakening of the masses of India and prepared them for the subsequent growth of national liberation movement, which, as a result of the heroic efforts of the Indian people, culminated in the historic victory, in the creation of the independent Republic of India.'[15] He adds in conclusion significantly that 'This is just why we, along with the friendly Indian people, greatly respect the name of her glorious son, the ardent patriot, humanist, thinker and enlightener, Swami Vivekananda.'[16]

---

12. ibid.
13. ibid.
14. ibid., pp. 157-58.
15. ibid., pp. 13-30 and 294-438.
16. *Asia and Africa Today*, No. 3, 1989.

II

A. A. TAKACHEVA AND R. B. RYBAKOV

Soviet writers have also discussed the 'Reformation of Hinduism' in two different articles, viz., 'Role of Swami Vivekananda in Reformation of Religious Organization of Hinduism' (by A. A. Takacheva) and 'Bourgeois Reformation of Hinduism' (by R. B. Rybakov) in which Vivekananda's ideas of reorientation of Hinduism stressing on Karma-Yoga and universal religion have been discussed.[17] According to Rybakov, the orientation was given to suit the democratic aspirations of bourgeois society. Actually, we think, it was reoriented to form the basis of a socialistic order of society. We have discussed the matter at length elsewhere in the book.

III

RYBAKOV'S ASSESSMENT OF RAMAKRISHNA

Rybakov's assessment of Ramakrishna[18] is characterized by deep reverence for the great Indian saint of the modern era and a surprisingly correct understanding of the Indian ideas.

He begins with the moving comment—'By right, Ramakrishna (1836-1886) may be placed on a par with such religious teachers as Buddha, Jesus Christ, Mohammad, and yet, he is not altogether cast in the same divine mould.' The differences between Ramakrishna and the older generations of luminous personalities—Buddha, Christ and Mohammad, according to him, lies in the fact that Ramakrishna was born in the modern era and is therefore a historical and not a legendary figure. Secondly, Rybakov points out that the great difference between Ramakrishna and his predecessors lies in the fact that he did not found a new sect. What Ramakrishna did was to systematize and harmonize Hindu philosophy—'... by spanning with his whole life and his distinctive method the seemingly clashing and opposite dogmas, doctrines, traditions, the chaotic

17. The matter was made available by the Ramakrishna Mission Institute of Culture, Calcutta.
18. ibid.

mix-up of precepts, rules and ideas, that have accumulated in Hinduism over the centuries.'

A Key-figure in Indian Culture : Penetrating into the depth of Indian culture Rybakov observes, 'Ramakrishna is a key-figure in Indian culture.' Dwelling on this point he further writes : 'If one comprehends his lore, one gains an insight into the very soul of India that no longer appears the mysterious far-away oriental country of the days beyond recall, with its semi-legendary wise men, Rishis, the shining host of many-armed heavenly beings and gods, its worship of the animate and the inanimate, phantasmagoria of mystics, rites and cosmic perception of existence.' According to Rybakov, 'The great contribution of Ramakrishna lies in his ability to propitiate the conflict of contravarieties and reach unity through multiformity.'

Larger-than-Life Personality : Among all the Soviet scholars, only Rybakov has discovered Ramakrishna in his true light, i.e., in his depth of spiritual attainment. Revealing his great discovery he says, 'Ramakrishna's larger-than-life personality captivates not only those who seek to fathom the mystifying magnetism of India. The life and doing of the humble priest from the Dakshineshwar temple will inspire everyone who thirsts to break the bounds and open up new ranges of self-improvement.' These words sound like those uttered by an Indian with a spiritual outlook and not a scholar from a Marxist country with a materialistic outlook.

Ramakrishna's Life : *A Turbulent Fight of a Stormy Spirit* : 'Ramakrishna's life', observes Rybakov in another revealing comment, 'far from abounding in actual events was a turbulent fight of a stormy spirit whose manifestations were unorthodox, inexplicable and arcane to such a degree that any evidence from his contemporaries bears the impress of a legend. An ever present nervous exaltation of a high-strung soul, spells of trance recurring several times a day, and the faculty of clairvoyance went far beyond the commonplace, familiar and mundane.' Rybakov here raises the question of questions—'Is it all impossible, only becaue it is unlikely?' Ramakrishna's life holds out the answer : though it seems unlikely, it is not impossible.

Referring to Ramakrishna's uncommon experiences he raises

another significant question direct to the sceptics : 'Have we, indeed, established what exactly is or is not the norm in the human psyche?' Certainly we have not, Rybakov firmly upholds that. Until we succeed in establishing such a norm it would be unreasonable to reject the experiences of Ramakrishna only because they were uncommon.

Finally, Rybakov raises the all-important question in this respect : 'But if we were to window out everything that fails to fit in with worldliness, what will be left of Ramakrishna?' Of course like a typical westerner Rybakov thinks that 'some of the hagiographic details are in all probability a latter-day add-on supplemented by Ramakrishna's disciples'. Those who know something about Ramakrishna's disciples, know also the fact that it was impossible on their part to make any 'add-on' in later days since they were, like their master, worshipper of truth only. It was rather easier for them to give up Ramakrishna than to give up the truth.

In the opinion of Rybakov scepticism is the first obstacle to understand Ramakrishna. Several other obstacles are, in his opinion, due to the typical Christian and Moslem conceptions—conceptions of irreconciliable contrarieties—God and Satan vying with each other.

Hinduism is Essentially a World-Outlook :

As rightly pointed out by Rybakov, Hinduism as a whole, as well as Ramakrishna's religion, is essentially a world-outlook rather than a religion in the western sense of the term. 'Hinduism', says Rybakov, 'is an illuminating statement in the path travelled by the cosmic evolution and at the same time, a social organization, a mode of living, and philosophy fused together into an indissoluble whole.' As Rybakov shows, to Hinduism 'religion becomes life, and life religion'.

In view of this, Rybakov emphasizes that 'Ramakrishna's heritage will remain a sealed book to us unless we overcome our stereotyped understanding of religion. It is not only that a new outlook on religion is necessary, but also shaking off of certain prejudices and preconceived ideas before a westerner or a modern man can grasp Ramakrishna. As for example, Rybakov points out that it is very common among the so-called modern man to label the word 'mystic', as a visionary with his head in the clouds, 'impractical to the point of deliberate utopianizing escapism'. Ramakrishna was a mystic and he is likely to be rejected as an impractical visionary, his teachings having no value in our practical life. Rybakov warns us against such prejudices which may prevent us from properly understanding Ramakrishna.

Rybakov points out that 'The flaming core of Ramakrishna's teaching is an impassioned call to serve humanity, that was later picked up by his favourite disciple and spiritual successor, Swami Vivekananda, who spread Ramakrishna's message far and wide after his teacher's death.' Hence, it is not abstract humanism that Ramakrishna-Vivekananda have preached. 'Serving humanity to them implies', according to Rybakov, 'an active involvement in the life of the temporal world, unremmitting work toward shaping a new virtuous, strong, daring, spiritually lofty person.' 'Serving humanity means also', says Rybakov, 'championing the cause of the poor—the corner-stone article of faith for Swami Vivekananda and guiding principle for the Ramakrishna Mission Order he instituted.'

The Awakeners : Rybakov points out also that 'Ramakrishna and Vivekananda awakened India and their teachings gave birth to a revolutionary spirit, a sense of unity, tolerance, self-less service to humanity.' All these wholesome values given by this mystic still serve as the guidelines to the socially conscious India in its march towards the goal of a new society. As stated by Rybakov, Ramakrishna's role in reawakening of India is unique. 'Ramakrishna', says Rybakov, 'spearheaded the spiritual revival of the country by reviewing ancient Hindu principles and putting a new construction on religious philosophy.'

In this connection Rybakov mentions how English education in India at first brought the reform movements which in fact heralded a cleavage between the old and the new. Ramakrishna offered the solution to the problem of discords in national life. He showed that the reformist's version of religion was a growth of the ever flexible Hindu thought and that there was no real contradiction between the old and the new interpretations of religion in India.

In this period of predominance of Ramakrishna-Vivekananda, India awoke also against colonialism. Ramakrishna's interpretation of Religion enabled the ideologists of national liberation to make full use of the traditional Indian culture for inspiring an upsurge of the nationalistic spirit. Thus Ramakrishna saved India from a split and worked out the unity of the nation. This was in Rybakov's opinion, Ramakrishna's most significant historical contribution.

According to Rybakov, it would be a bad judgement to view Ramakrishna as a late nineteenth-century relic, best relegated to the past, for Ramakrishna is as relevant today as he was in the nineteenth century. 'His influence', shows Rybakov, 'did not burn itself out after he had played so decisive a role in India's revival, for his preaching of the fundamental unity of all religions elevated philosophy to a new level of comprehension of the place of religion in history.'

Finally, Rybakov brings to light the point that 'Ramakrishna did not indulge in abstract philosophizing or castle-building. He helped to release the latent forces in all those who sought his advice, "bringing out the most sublime in the human heart".' He cites several examples : 'Narendranath (Vivekananda), a man endowed with exceptional talents, Sarada Devi, a simple-hearted peasant woman, Lata (Latu), a page who did not learn to read or write. After Sri Ramakrishna's departure from this world', Rybakov goes on to observe, 'Sarada Devi and Lata (Latu) won over many a contemporary's heart by their wisdom, perception and the greatness and magnanimity of their soul.' Hence, this was Ramakrishna's another great contribution that 'through patience, consideration and persistence he had himself modelled ordinary young people into a shining host of apostles of good and spirituality, not preter-human prodigies, but men of wisdom who carried on and augmented their traditions of their great land'.

IV

CONCLUSIONS REGARDING THE ASSESSMENT OF VIVEKANANDA MADE BY THE SOVIET SCHOLARS

It is apparent from what we have analysed above that

Vivekananda's ideas were progressive on the whole according to the Soviet reviewers. Of course, they differed from the Indian standpoint. This is due to the cultural differences between the two countries. They have not been able to understand Vivekananda entirely. Particularly his spiritual ideas have been thoroughly misunderstood.

Despite the misunderstanding in certain matters, despite their criticism of Vivekananda and Ramakrishna in certain respects, admiration for them appears to be immense, and it is still increasing. Their deep reverence for Ramakrishna-Vivekananda and their great ideals is unquestionable.

In January 1987 a Peace Conference and a seminar on Ramakrishna were held under the joint sponsorship of India and Russia at the Ramakrishna Mission Institute of Culture, Calcutta. At this conference the Soviet scholars pointed out that they felt highest admiration for the Ramakrishna's unique message—*ananta mat ananta path* (as many opinions, so many paths) since in this message highest respect has been shown to the opinion of every individual, high or low and since it reflects that each individual was held in highest esteem by the giver of this message. This message in their opinion was very much significant for the present-day society facing the danger of a third world war. There can not be a greater message of peace and amity than this. This message held out the prospect of the survival of human civilization, and of a bright future for mankind as a whole. They agreed that this message contained the essence of humanism.

Besides, they stated that they highly appreciated Ramakrishna's capacity for man-making. They cited two very appropriate examples, (1) how Latu, born of low class, without any education, serving as a domestic hand, became a great preceptor, a vast store-house of spiritual knowledge and power; (2) next, how with Ramakrishna's touch, Sarada Devi, a simple village girl, turned to be one of the greatest women of the modern world. In a letter written to a senior monk of the Ramakrishna Order on 30 November, 1986, one of them wrote, 'I have now an idea about my future book on Ramakrishna. The idea is to start with Sarada Devi whom I consider to be one of the greatest, nay, the GREATEST (if you permit me to say) achievements of Sri Ramakrishna in this world. She was an ordinary Indian village girl and he made her into an absolutely outstanding personality which for me is a symbol of India herself. Divine, yet human, a real woman, but saintly, the Mother has an irresistible appeal to me. She was so modest that only few could fathom her greatness while she was alive. But in my view she was the force and inspiration behind the whole Mission and behind Swami Vivekananda as well.'[19]

This is really surprising, a scholar of a Marxist country, thus came to appreciate not only Ramakrishna and Vivekananda, but also Sarada Devi, the story of whose simple life is purely a manifestation of spiritual power and nothing else.

V

CHINA

In China also studies on Swami Vivekananda started very recently towards the end of the seventies of this century. Here is the sum and substance of a book written on Ramakrishna and Vivekananda by Professor Huang Xin Chuan of the Institute of South Asian Studies, and of the Chinese Academy of Social Sciences, Peking University:[20]

'Vivekananda stands out as the most renowned philosopher and social figure of modern India. His philosophical and social thought and epic patriotism not only inspired the growth of nationalist movement in India, bus also made a great impact abroad in 1893. Vivekananda visited Canton and its neighbourhood. He noted his impressions of the visit in a letter addressed to the citizens of Madras. He had some knowledge and understanding of Chinese history and culture. He often cited and spoke highly of China in his writings and speeches. He made a prophecy that the Chinese culture will surely be resurrected one day like the "phoenix" and undertake the responsibility of the great mission of integrating the western and the oriental cultures. His biographer, Romain Rolland, has narrated the evolution of Vivekananda's idea on this aspect. When Vivekananda went to

19. ibid.

20. ibid.

America for the first time, he hoped that country would achieve this mission. But during his second visit abroad, he realized that he was deceived by dollar imperialism. He, therefore, came to the conclusion that America could not be an instrument of accomplishing this task, but it was China which could do it.'

Vivekananda had infinite sympathy for the Chinese people living under the oppression of feudalism and imperialism and he pinned much hope on them. After his visit to China, he made a very interesting comment. He said, 'The Chinese child is quite a philosopher and calmly goes to work when your Indian boy can hardly crawl on all fours. He has learnt the philosophy of necessity too well.' This shows Vivekananda's enormous sympathy towards the miseries of the children of China in the old society.

'While explaining his visionary socialism Vivekananda made an interesting gospel. He said that the future society would be ruled by the labouring people and that this would first take place in China*. In *Modern India* he said, "But there is hope. In the mighty course of time, the Brahmin and the other higher castes, too, are being brought down to the lower status of the Shudras, and the Shudras are being raised to higher ranks. . . . Even before our eyes, powerful China, with fast strides, is going down to Shudra-hood, . . . Yet, a time will come when there will be the rising of the Shudra class, with their Shudra-hood . . . a time will come, when the Shudras of every country . . . will gain absolute supremacy in every society. . . . Socialism, Anarchism, Nihilism, and other like sects are the vanguards of the social revolution that is to follow." '

'From the materials cited above and his life and works, we can see at least that Vivekananda felt very much concerned and sympathized with the people of China who were living under the rule of feudalism and imperialism and placed great hopes on them. But we do not agree with B. N. Dutta that the success of the Chinese and Russian Revolutions coming into being at concrete historical movements should be credited to the "gospel" of Vivekananda. This would make him a divine mystic personality.

---

* Actually Vivekananda said that this was to take place either in China or in Russia.

We have seen that Vivekananda's approach to the laws of social developments was unscientific. However, it is not possible for any advanced thinker to make a correct prediction of the phases and events of history in minute details. We should, therefore, appraise Vivekananda in the light of seeking truth from facts.'

'In conclusion, Vivekananda was the most eminent figure among the democratic patriots. He paid high tributes to our glorious ancient culture and loved the Chinese labouring people. We pay our homage to him.'

Although like a typical Marxist thinker Huang thinks that Vivekananda's conception of socialism was a visionary one and that the Indian thinkers' ideas on social development was not scientific, yet the note all through in the appraisal is of highest admiration. Vivekananda to this Chinese man of letters is 'a great democratic patriot' whose social and philosophical thought and epic patriotism made a great impact in India and all over the contemporary world.

In a letter written to Swami Lokeswaranandaji, the then Secretary, Ramakrishna Mission Institute of Culture, Calcutta, on May 5, 1984, Huang Xin Chuan added, 'In the past years, Swami Vivekananda gave a strong support and deep sympathy for Chinese people when they struggled for freedom, and encouraged them to unite with the people all over the world. Chinese people cannot forget such a person and pay high reverence to him.' He further added in the same letter, 'I will make further efforts to spread the thoughts of Sri Ramakrishna and Swami Vivekananda in China and outside.' These remarks shows the depth of the impression made by the thoughts of Vivekananda on the Chinese people.

VI

SCIENTIFICNESS OF COMMUNISM

The difficulties with all the thinkers excepting Rybakov in the Socialist countries is their firm faith in the theory that only the philosophy of Marxism or Communism is scientific, all other philosophical standpoints are idealistic. Recently, Stanley Kober of the Cato Institute of U. S. A. has examined this claim of scientificness of communism and observed, 'Communism partakes of the Enlightenment and the rise of scientific thinking in that period. The problem was that communism took a "very primitive definition of Science".' 'Science', Mr Kober explains, 'is an investigative process. Its end product is not an immutable law or a definite truth but a conjecture which can be disproved tomorrow. Hence Newtonian physics seemed unassailable for a few centuries but was overthrown by Einstein.' Communism, according to Kober, began by believing that science was a way to certain truths. By definition these truths were inviolable and once this practice became applied to history and the social sciences the road was open to Stalinism. Mr Kober quotes a contemporary Soviet leader who makes explicit the connexion between science as a dogma and the Gulag society. Under Marxism science is a dogma and therefore it leads to the dogmatic assertion that only Marxism is scientific and not other standpoints. Hence Vedanta is idealism according to them. And therefore what Vivekananda states is idealistic and utopian. They should be aware of the fact that nineteenth century science on which Marxism was based has been exploded by the twentieth century science. Today Vedanta, as we have seen in the early part of the book, is much nearer to science than Marxism.[21] Hence Vedantic Socialism is today scientific and not idealistic as is claimed by the scholars dealing with Swami Vivekananda and his Vedantic Socialism in the Soviet Union.

CONCLUDING REMARKS

From our discussions in this part of the book it came out clearly that Vivekananda as well as Ramakrishna and Sarada Devi, in fact, are held in high esteem by the Soviet and the Chinese men of letters in spite of some hesitation in respect of accepting some of their views, and in spite of some misunderstanding of them due to the great cultural difference between India and the two prominent socialist countries. They revere Ramakrishna-Vivekananda as 'the prophet of human emancipation, of amity, peace and progress'.

---

21. For Kober's views mentioned here, see *The Statesman*, dated 6th December 1990.

However, what the intellectuals failed to realize was realized by a poet, Valentine Sidorov, who writes about Vivekananda :

'It has been rightly said of him,
He was like a naked sword,
His thought was ringing like a steel blade,
Glistening, sparkling, fluttering
A stroke, another stroke.'

Regarding the essence of his message the poet says :

'Thus spake
Vivekananda to his followers :
We are not weak.
And if you are weak
It is because you love your own weakness.'

As regard Vivekananda's message to the youth the poet says :

'Perhaps, because I am poor myself
I carry in my heart all sorrows of poor man
I can bequeth you nothing but my love,
My struggles for better life for hungry ones'
and poor ones'
I will call a person a Mahātmā,
The one who realized the light in him,
Whose light was born out of inner silence,
Whose heart is beating for other's sake,
Bleeding for all the suffering humanity,
For poor and the oppressed of all the lands.'

And the poet sounds a note of unification of the two worlds, of Russia and India, in spite of their great cultural differences, because in his poetic vision it was clear that all divisions are unreal, there exists only One (of which Vedanta speaks):

'Two worlds. Two Poles. Two outlooks.
But the division lies between them—
As all things that divide—are an illusion.
The time is ripe for somebody to come
And collect the scattered grains of truth.'

The poet realizing the great unity, speaks of the great moment when this unification will take place and the world will be revolutionized. And who will take the initiative? The poet quite convincingly asserts :

> 'So who will undertake this necessary work?
> I'll speak out loud of what is in my heart,
> I'll speak without doubt—it is Russia.'[22]

Perhaps the poet is right, the great country which had gone through the fire of a revolution, is the most suitable soil for the second great revolution of much greater dimension and impact to take place. Ramakrishna-Vivekananda with their message of unity and peace are the harbingers of this new revolution.

---

22. *Vedanta Keshari*—July 1986, p. 268.

Part - VII

Role of Vivekananda in the Socio-Economic and Cultural Transformationn in India

CHAPTER 28

The Great Question : Emancipation of Women and the People

I

THE PRIME CONCERN OF VIVEKANANDA : THE CAUSE OF THE WOMEN AND THE PEOPLE

To Swami Vivekananda the great question was the emancipation of woman and the people. 'Our Master', writes Sister Nivedita, '. . . regarded the Order to which he belonged as one whose lot was cast for all time with the cause of woman and the people.' 'This was the cry', she adds, 'that rose to his lips instinctively, when he dictated to the phonogram in America, the message that he was to send to the Raja of Kshetri. It was the one thought too, with which he would turn to the disciple at his side, whenever he felt himself nearer than usual to death in a foreign country, alone; "Never forget", he would then say, "the word is, woman and the people".'[1]

II

EMANCIPATION OF THE PEOPLE : VIVEKANANDA'S IDEAS

That his chief concern was the people, their emancipation from social oppression, poverty and degradation have been noticed by almost all who met him and even long after his departure from this world by the research workers who are working on his social ideas today. For example, the noted Soviet scholar, E. N. Komarov, as we have noted earlier in this book, has observed in a recent article, 'The most important, progressive feature of social-political views of Vivekananda was that he considered national liberation of India

1. Sister Nivedita, *The Master As I Saw Him*, p. 280.

and democratic social emancipation of the masses as mutually related and the twofold goal.'[2]

Vivekananda's plan : As stated by Komarov further, 'He (Vivekananda) regarded the education of the working people as the first step on the way to this goal, called upon the youth to go to the people, and try to work in this direction.' Describing his plan for the regeneration of the masses Vivekananda wrote—'. . . our mission is for the destitute, the poor, and the illiterate peasantry and labouring classes.'[3] 'Teach some boys and girls of the peasant classes,' he advised Swami Akhandananda, a brother disciple and a great constructive worker, 'the rudiments of learning and infuse a number of ideas into their brains. Afterwards the peasant of each village will collect funds, and have one of these boys in their village.'[4] He thus wanted leadership to grow from within the masses with spread of education. He firmly pointed out with a quotation from the *Gītā* that 'One must raise oneself by one's own exertions. We help them to help themselves.' Explaining his plan further he says, 'The peasant and labouring classes are in a moribund condition, so what is needed is that the moneyed people will only help them to regain their vitality, and nothing more. Then leave the peasants and labourers to look to their own problem to grapple with and solve it.' Thus the emancipation of the masses was to be won by the masses themselves. The course of action for winning emancipation was also to be decided by them. He wanted no interference and involvement of the upper classes in this matter.

The Struggle for Emancipation of the masses may not be wholly peaceful : But he was aware that this struggle may not be wholly peaceful. Sister Nivedita writes—'We are to solve the problems of the Shudras', he said one day, 'but oh! through what tumults! through what tumults?' Nivedita then adds the comment, a very significant one—'He spoke like one gazing direct into the future, and his voice had the ring of prophecy; but, though the listener waited, hoping eagerly for more, he only became silent lapsing into deeper thought.'[5]

Uplifting the masses—first thing to be done : He wanted

2. E. N. Komarov, *Swami Vivekananda: Studies in the West*, p. 116.
3. *Letters of Swami Vivekananda*, p. 402.
4. ibid., p. 403.
5. *The Master As I Saw Him*, p. 292.

education to be imparted to the masses by the wandering monks and the youth, 'who would carry the magic lantern, the camera, and some means of simple chemical experiments'.[6]

The Instrument of Regeneration—Education : Education that was to be provided would be both religious and secular according to Vivekananda. Laying down his plan he said, '... my plans are . . . to reach these masses of India.'[7] 'We have to follow the plan laid down by our ancestors, i.e., to bring all ideals slowly down among the masses. Raise them slowly up, raise them to equality. Impart even secular knowledge through religion.'[8] Elaborating his plan to his followers he says, 'Get every evening a crowd of the poor and the low, even the Pariahs, and lecture to them about religion first, and then teach them through the magic-lantern and other things, astronomy, geography, etc., in the dialect of the people.'[9]

He wanted the teachers to go to the villages and since the working people cannot afford to come to schools he wanted to go door to door. 'If a ploughman's boy', he said, 'cannot come to education, why not meet him at the plough, at the factory, just wherever he is? Go along with him, like his shadow.'[10]

Addressing his followers he said further, 'Your duty at present is to go from one part of the country to another, from village to village, and make the people understand that mere sitting idly won't do any more. Make them understand their real condition and say, "O ye brothers, arise! Awake! How much longer would you remain asleep!" Go and advise them how to improve their own condition, and make them comprehend the sublime truths of the Śāstras [scriptures], by presenting them in a lucid and popular way. . . . Impress upon their minds that they have the same right to religion as the Brahmins. Initiate all, even down to the Chaṇḍālas, in these fiery Mantras. Also instruct them, in simple words, about the necessities of life, and in trade, commerce, agriculture, etc.'[11]

Continuing on the same theme he added : 'It would be better if the people got a little technical education so that they might find work and earn their bread, instead of dawdling about and

---

6. ibid. 7. *C.W.*, VIII, p. 88. 8. ibid., V., p. 213.
9. ibid., p. 35. 10. ibid., VIII, pp. 88-89. 11. ibid., V, p. 381.

crying for service.'[12] Education for the masses, according to Vivekananda, must be all-round, character-building, man-making and at the same time practical for bread-earning. He said therefore, 'The education which does not help the common mass of people to equip themselves for the struggle for life, which does not bring out strength of character, a spirit of philanthropy, and the courage of a lion—is it worth the name?'[13] Summarizing his whole plan of education for the masses he observed, 'We want that education by which character is formed, strength of mind is increased, the intellect is expanded, and by which one can stand on one's own feet'.

These are very practical ideas and revolutionary too. His plan is a total plan for the regeneration of the masses for their uplifting to a higher level. His idea was to give them back their lost individuality so that they could work out their own emancipation. This is thoroughly revolutionary since he wanted the leadership to grow from the masses and he wanted them to win their freedom themselves.

The detailed programme : For regeneration of the masses, we have already seen that he included in the 'Aims and Objects' of the Ramakrishna Mission such programmes as (1) to train men as to make them competent to teach such knowledge or sciences as are conducive to the material and spiritual welfare of the masses; (2) to promote and encourage arts and industries; (3) to introduce and spread among the people in general Vedantic and other religious ideas as elucidated in the life of Sri Ramakrishna.[14]

Spreading of Vedantic ideas was a very important part of his programme since these ideas were to awaken the masses, make them stand on their own feet to fight fearlessly for their human rights. In fact Vedanta was his only revolutionary weapon.

The future India that was to emerge according to this great revolutionary would be a thoroughly revolutionized one. He said addressing the upper classes—'You merge yourselves in the void and disappear, and let New India arise in your place. Let her arise—out of the peasant's cottage, grasping the plough, out of the huts of the fisherman, the cobbler, and the sweeper. Let her

12. ibid., p. 367. 13. ibid., VII, p. 147.
14. Romain Rolland, *Life of Vivekananda*, p. 121.

spring from the grocer's shop, from the factory, from marts, and from markets. Let her emerge from groves and forests, from hills and mountains.' It is a very clear vision of the revolutionized future India. To make this vision real he undertook the task of awakening the masses by preaching the Vedantic ideas of equality and giving them general education.

III

EMANCIPATION OF WOMEN

Vivekananda fought all his life tooth and nail for the emancipation of women from the letters of a priest-ridden society.

The first step : The first step in this respect was taken by Raja Rammohan who left no stone unturned to stop the heinous practice of burning the 'Satī'. Pandit Ishvar Chandra Vidyasagar, another hallowed name among the nineteenth century stalwarts, worked on the same line, viz., removing certain immediate social evils like child-marriage. He made untiring efforts to introduce re-marriage of the child-widows against all-out opposition of the priest-dominated society. He made also commendable efforts to spread women's education when women were denied the right to education.

Philosophy of Equality : Vivekananda concentrated his efforts to develop a full-fledged philosophy of equality—equality between men and women, between the privileged and the underprivileged of all categories in the society. For securing the complete emancipation of women, this was the need of the hour since for centuries the priests have harped on the doctrine of inequality. They taught the nation to look down upon women as 'despicable worms' and denied them their human rights to freedom, even the right to education. They even preached, 'Women are the gate-ways to the hell!'

Vivekananda, a true Vedantist, and a real revolutionary, never believed in such preposterous theories. At the same time he did not believe in the piece-meal efforts in conceding a little bit of this and that right, as was done by the reformers. He believed in what he called 'root and branch reform'. He talked, therefore, of total emancipation and full freedom.

The essence of Vedanta philosophy, as we know already, was

expressed in three brief words by his Guru, Sri Ramakrishna, viz., '*Jīva* is Shiva'. In these brief words, the genius of Vivekananda discovered the seed of a fiery philosophy of revolution.

If '*Jīva* is Shiva', i.e., if 'every living being is god', then, of course, everyone must be granted the same human rights. No privilege could be granted to any one on ground of sex, creed, birth or wealth or on any other ground since everyone has the same potentiality to become great and good. Obviously, therefore, in a society based on this great Vedantic ideal, women also would enjoy the same rights as men and no discrimination is admissible against them. A Vedantic society is therefore a revolutionized society in the true sense of the term.

In the *Smṛtiśāstras* it is laid down that a woman has no right to freedom and she must remain under the domination of her father in her childhood, of her husband in her youth and of her son in her old age. Vivekananda could not just tolerate such ideas. 'It is very difficult to understand', he said, 'why in this country so much difference is made between men and women, whereas the Vedanta declares that the one and the same conscious Self is present in all beings.'[15]

Attitude of the Reformers—not in conformity with the idea of Total Emancipation : During the nineteenth century the reformers debated on the question of granting freedom to women in the journals. Surprisingly all of them harped on the theme of limitations of women, their disabilities, some even accused them of evil tendencies and all agreed that women were not fit for freedom; they must remain under the control of men, though they might be allowed to have a little bit of education, suitable for their role in domestic life, i.e., they should learn domestic science, cooking, child-care, etc. Even Brahmananda Keshav Chandra Sen, the great Brahmo religious preacher and reformer, objected to teaching women metaphysics and logic.[16]

Vivekananda was the only person at the time to register a protest against such an attitude. 'You always criticize the women', he said sharply, 'but say what have you done for their uplift?

---

15. *C. W.*, VII, p. 214.
16. Article by Dr Chitra Dev in *Udbodhan* (86th year, No. 1, Bengali year : Māgh 1390).

Writing down Smṛtis, etc., and binding them by hard rules, the men have turned the women into mere manufacturing machines!'[17]

Vivekananda was never tired of harping on the theme of absolute equality of the two sexes. 'In the highest reality of the *Parabrahman*', he said, 'there is no distinction of sex. ... Therefore do I say though outwardly there may be difference between men and women, in their real nature there is none. Hence, if a man can be a knower of Brahman, why cannot a woman attain to the same knowledge?'[18] Thus he squarely defends the right of women to the highest truth, denied so long by the priests.

Ramakrishna's *attitude towards the women* : Ramakrishna looked upon every woman as the living embodiment of the Goddess of the Universe.[19] It is significant to note that a low-caste rich woman, Rani Rasmani, built a temple for his spiritual practices. Then he accepted a woman, viz., Yogeśvarī Bhairavī Brāhmaṇī as his teacher for his practices according to Tantric system. She was a nun and a profound scholar in Tantric and Vaishnava literature. It is also significant that his first disciple to receive his unique message was a woman, Sri Sarada Devi, his wife, whom he worshipped as the Divine Mother incarnate. In her life it was proved that a woman was not the 'gateway to hell' but 'an associate in the path-way to the Supreme Truth', since her cooperation and the life she lived was of great help to Ramakrishna, her husband. She became after his departure from this world, the Guru, guide and the unquestioned leader of the spiritual order that came to be founded in his name.

All these were revolutionary events from the points of view of the emancipation of women and so these appeared to Vivekananda. 'Hence', he observes, 'in the Ramakrishna Incarnation, the acceptance of a woman as the Guru, hence His practising in the woman's garb and frame of mind, hence too His preaching the motherhood of women as representations of the Divine Mother.'[20] 'The distinction between man and woman', he added in another place, 'between the rich and the poor, the literate and the illiterate, Brahmins and Chaṇḍālas—He (Ramakrishna) lived to root out all.'[21] He believed that a new era

17. *C. W.*, VII, p. 214.
18. ibid., p. 219.
19. Swami Saradananda, *Śrī Śrī Rāmakṛṣṇa Līlāprasaṅga*.
20. *C. W.*, VI, p. 328.
21. ibid., p. 335.

of complete emancipation for women and the people had dawned with the advent of Sri Ramakrishna.

Vivekananda was convinced that 'Without *śakti* (power) there is no regeneration of the world.'[22] 'Why is it', he asked, 'that our country is the weakest and the most backward of all countries?' His own answer was that 'Because *śakti* is held in dishonour there.'[23] Hence, he pointed out that unless the women are raised, given education and freedom, there was no salvation for India.[24]

The Indian Ideal of Womanhood : He was never tired of eulogizing the Indian ideal of womanhood, of the ideal of self-sacrifice, strength of character, the power of leading an intense spiritual life, all epitomized in the character of Sītā, who was also 'purer than purity itself'. At the same time, he was never tired of praising the freedom that the western women enjoyed their practical efficiency, their share in the cultural life of the society. He wanted the Indian women to enjoy the same freedom without losing their old merits. As pointed out by Nivedita, he wanted that the Indian woman must rise in capacity and not fall.[25]

To the ultra-modern woman, who is a carbon copy of the western woman, who is an extremist on the question of woman's liberation, womanhood is of no consequence. To her imitation of the opposite sex in dress, in modes of life, and even in moral aberrations, is the highest pinnacle of freedom for woman. Such an extremist in the field of feminism will not find a sympathizer in Vivekananda for their cause since he considered womanhood as sacred a possession of woman as manhood to man. Of course to him true womanhood, like true manhood was not a matter of the externals. '... the manhood of man', he said, 'the womanhood of woman, the reality of everything is the Lord... .'[26]

Vivekananda's *Concept of Womanhood* : Vivekananda however, never considered that womanhood was associated with any kind of weakness and hence he was dead against making women weaklings and permanent dependents on men. 'Strength, strength, and strength', writes Sister Nivedita, 'was the only quality, he called for in woman as in man.'[27] In a letter to her

22. ibid., VII, p. 482. 23. ibid. 24. ibid.
25. *The Master As I Saw Him*, p. 240. 26. *C. W.*, VI, p. 378.
27. Nivedita School Publication, *Nivedita Centenary Volume*, p. 62.

Vivekananda wrote : 'What India requires today is a veritable lioness.' Commenting on his concept of womanhood, Nivedita writes : 'The mother's heart in the woman of the dawning age, must be enjoined with the hero's will.'[28] He urged the Indian woman to emulate the Rani of Jhansi who fought from the front in the battlefield with the British army and refused to surrender till death in the first war of India's independence, viz., the Sepoy Mutiny.

As Sister Nivedita writes further : 'He would never tolerate any scheme of life and policy that tended to bind tighter on mind the fetters of the body.'[29] 'The greater the individuality', Nivedita adds in an explanatory note, 'the more would she transcend the limitation of feminity in mind and character, and more was such transcendence to be expected and admired.'[30] He laid down great stress on education and spiritual development which was to give woman that individuality. Evidently, he never wanted the woman to be bound by the limitations of femininity, he wanted them to grow in such a way as to transcend these limitations.

Vivekananda's Concept of Total Freedom : Vivekananda had no fear of freedom. He declared : 'My whole ambition in life is to set in motion a machinery which will bring noble ideas to the door of everybody, and then let men and women settle their own fate.'[31] He believed that 'Liberty of thought and action is the only condition of life, of growth and well-being.'[32] Hence he emphatically said, 'Educate your women first and leave then to themselves; then they will tell you what reforms are necessary for them.'[33]

No meddling by men in women's affairs : Since he held the males responsible for the oppression of women he never liked their meddling into the affairs of the women. Addressing the males he said sternly, 'Who are you to solve women's problems? ... Hands off, they will solve their own problems.'[34]

Surely this is the Magna Carta of woman's right to freedom. Vivekananda was dead against such customs as child marriage and the burning of the *Satī*. 'What expression', he said sternly,

28. *The Master As I Saw Him*, p. 284.
29. ibid., p. 286.
30. ibid.
31. *C. W.*, V, p. 29.
32. ibid.
33. ibid., VI, p. 115.
34. ibid., III, p. 246.

'of devotedness to a husband is there by forcing a widow to commit Sati? Why make people do virtuous deeds by teaching superstitions?'[35] In an anguish he said sarcastically, ' "Oh, what examples of self-denial are our widows! Oh, how sweet is child-marriage! Is another such custom possible! Can there be anything but love between husband and wife in such a marriage!". . . But as to the men, the masters of the situation, there is no need of self-denial for them!'[36] He did not like the idea that the onus of maintaining the ideal should be on women only. It must be an equal responsibility of both men and women.

Although he eulogized Sītā, the epitome of perfect wifehood, he never considered marriage as the only salvation for woman. According to Nivedita, Vivekananda wanted 'a race of women who would have no home save in their work, no ties save religion, no love but that for guru, people and motherland'.[37] He took a revolutionary step when he granted the woman the right to a life of complete renunciation and planned to establish a woman's monastery for the nuns. He made it clear also that they were to be self-governed and never to be under the control of their male counterparts. In this respect he criticized Buddha, who put the Bhikṣuṇī Saṅgha (the order of the nuns) under the control of the Bhikṣu Saṅgha (the order of the monks).

Vivekananda's first and last word was in favour of complete emancipation of women. According to him, *mukti* or liberation from every letter is the watchward for men and women equally. 'I say, liberate', he thundered, 'undo the shackles of people as much as you can.'[38]

IV

In Swami Vivekananda, the world has seen one of the greatest champion of the emancipation of women just as the world has seen in him one of the greatest champion of the liberation of the Shudras (the proletariat or the people). In a true sense of the term he was like Buddha, the great liberator, 'the liberator of women and the Shudras'.

35. ibid., IV, p. 491.
36. ibid.
37. *The Master As I Saw Him.*
38. *C. W.*, IV, p. 491.

CHAPTER 29

The Role of the Ramakrishna Mission in the Social Revolution in Modern India

From the very beginning Ramakrishna Mission is carrying on activities towards fulfilling the great mission of Swami Vivekananda, for securing uplift and emancipation of the masses. The activities that were first intiated by Swami Akhandananda in the famine-stricken district of Murshidabad in the then undivided Bengal, in the year 1897, aimed to provide relief to the famine-stricken people. Gradually there grew a permanent developmental centre at Sargachhi, district Murshidabad, with an orphanage, a basic school, a primary school, a technical education centre, etc., to elevate the masses by giving them religious, general and technical education. At present there are hundreds of such centres, mostly situated in the rural and tribal areas, difficult to approach for want of roads and transport, to provide education and employment to the people. Recently, a mini-jute mill has been established at one of the rural centres, viz., at Kamarpukur in the district of Hooghly, to provide employment to the rural youth.

Actually this one programme may revolutionize the face of rural India. Two other notable centres in this connection deserve special mentioning : the first one is the 'Lokaśikṣā Pariṣad' or the Institute of Social Education and Recreation situated at Narendrapur. According to a report of its director, in 1979, 'The Parishad now has 86 associated centres mostly in the districts of 24 Parganas and Medinipur, and a few centres in the district of Bankura and Purulia. The activities are mainly conducted by the local youth clubs. It is a common experience that the efforts of youth clubs are mostly confined to sports and games and cultural activities, and they generally take little interest in developmental programmes, though they are quite suitable for such work. That is why, the Parishad has, from the very beginning, directed its efforts towards persuading youth clubs to take up economic and social service programmes as a part of their community activities. It is gratifying to note that the Parishad has largely succeeded in doing so. As a result, under the leadership of the Parishad, a network of youth clubs are now engaged in carrying forward a quiet revolution in the rural areas.'[1] This revolution has spread subsequently over 1400 villages. Using local resources, forming capital out of the small savings made by the rural people themselves, the drive has succeeded in liquidating both illiteracy and unemployment in many of the villages.[2] Surely this programme, with little bit of more publicity, may spread like fire to cover the entire rural India, really it should. The lack of publicity is definitely regrettable which actually shows the apathy of the media towards the activities of the non-political agencies excepting the one that is associated with the name of Mother Teresa.

The other institution which we would like to mention is the 'Divyāyan' or the institute for imparting training in modern process of agriculture among the tribals in the tribal area of Ranchi. This institute is directly run by the Ranchi Ramakrishna Mission Centre. According to an account of Swami Atmasthanandaji Maharaj, 'One *Krishi Vijñān Kendra*, recognized by the Indian Council of Agricultural Research, has recently been added to Divyāyan for training village youths, particularly the *ādivāsīs* (tribals) in agriculture, dairy, poultry, horticulture, beekeeping, farm machinery and social service. The training is free of cost. Divyāyan life includes learning the discipline of corporate living as well as accepting others as one's own. Emphasis is given on technical know-how about modern techniques of farming, guidance and demonstration, through

1. *The Ramakrishna Movement—Souvenir 1979-1980 of the Ramakrishna Mission*, New Delhi, p. 52.
2. Unpublished record of a speech delivered by Dr S. S. Chakravarty on 18.2.88 at a seminar held at the Ramakrishna Misssion Institute of Culture under the auspices of the Nivedita Vrati Sangha.

community living and its various activities, in respect of religious harmony, social fellowship and love for the nation. A well-equipped audio-visual unit goes out to villagers for motivated programmes. Under the guidance of the Divyāyan there are many *sevā-kendra*s to follow-up this programme in their own villages at Purulia and Jalpaiguri in West Bengal.'[3] It has also brought perceptible changes in the surrounding tribal areas.

Thus in the difficult hilly areas, in the interior of distant villages in the different parts of India, among the hill people, who are poorest of the poor, among the rural poor, who are totally helpless, constructive developmental work is silently going on to implement the social ideas of Swami Vivekananda to uplift the masses to a position of equality with the upper classes. It is the path that has been chalked out by Swami Vivekananda for transforming the society through social action—socialism through social action—that the Ramakrishna Mission is successfully following.

How far they are succeeding in their great mission would be apparent from an evaluative study of the Ranchi branch by the Department of Social Welfare, Government of India, made as early as in 1972 : '32% of trainees in the first three years were found to have increased their land production significantly, 22% achieved increase between 50% and 300%. For a beginning among backward people, depressed for many centuries, this is a most encouraging achievement. . . . It is clearly seen that as the ex-trainees apply their knowledge of double cropping, use of fertilizer and composts, irrigation techniques, growing new kinds of crops, there is marked awakening of interest and energy. . . . The natural resistance to new ideas prevalent in depressed people is being rapidly broken down as results of the training become observable. . . . Equally important is the awakening of social service interests in the youth. Some of the ex-trainees are running night schools in their villages, many have combined together under an independent organization to fulfil the function of extension and follow up of the training programme.'[4] Since then

3. ibid., p. 85.
4. Quoted in the *Ramakrishna Math and Ramakrishna Mission Convention 1980 Souvenir*, p. 110.

the work has been much extended. According to a comparatively recent report, 'More than 300 villages have been covered by its "Village Adoption Scheme" which focuses on social, economic and cultural development. The ex-trainees of Divyāyan are organized in the villages to start night schools, cottage industries, improved methods of farming, etc., in order to make the villagers self-supporting.'[5] Surely the face of the rural and tribal India is changing fast in this part of the country as is evident from the report of Social Welfare Department of the Government of India, Ranchi branch, quoted above.

Like the Narendrapur and Ranchi branches of the Ramakrishna Mission in West Bengal and Bihar, Perianaickenpalayam branch in Tamil Nadu conducts extensive work in the field of rural development. To help poor villagers whose monthly income is less than Rs 200/-, it opened a 'Help to the Poorest Society' to offset their difficulty in getting bank loans. This branch also provides employment to villagers in small industries like rural textile, basket-making, tractor and automobile servicing, and agricultural equipment repairing. 'Its own workshop produces engineering goods like electric motors, domestic and agricultural pump sets, sugarcane crushers, elevators, grinders, pressers, and flour mills which are designed to meet the needs of the villagers.'[6]

75 p.c. of the activities of the Math and Mission, according to a recent study, are village-based. Coming to its educational and health service activities we find that for the backward communities and the tribals in the north-eastern states, Madhya Pradesh, Tamil Nadu, Kerala, Andhra Pradesh, Gujarat, Bihar and West Bengal, the Math and Mission run one degree college, one intermediatic college, 15 high schools, 97 primary and middle schools, 78 night schools, 10 vocational training industries, 4 technical and industrial schools, 6 hospitals, 23 dispensaries, 8 mobile dispensaries, 54 milk distribution centres, 40 libraries, 3 mobile libraries. 47% of the students at the

---

5. 'The Ramakrishna Math and Mission among common men'—Swami Someshwarananda, *Ramakrishna Mission Convention 1980 Souvenir*, p. 110.
6. ibid.

educational institutions run by the Ramakrishna Math and Mission come from scheduled castes and/scheduled tribes.[7]

The largest tribal concentration next to Africa is in India, tribals constituting about 7% of the total population. In Madhya Pradesh in India there is a large concentration of the tribals in the district of Bastar.

In spite of seven national economic plans, the benefits of development did not trickle down the poorest of the poor tribals. According to a report, 'In reality, increase in GNP was accompanied by increase in the absolute level of poverty for a growing number of people. The benefits of growth achieved so far have mostly siphoned off by dominating class which enjoys power.'[8] The main reason for this failure is that the plans based on grants and subsidies, failed to stimulate self-reliance. The voluntary organizations can play a more effective role in this respect.

The Ramakrishna Mission, with its experience of working among the tribals came out through its Raipur centre, to serve the tribals of Bastar in general and those of Abujhmarh in particular in 1985. It is an integrated tribal development programme known as 'Abujhmarh Rural Development Project' under which the following planned activities started immediately:

1. Out-Patients' Department of a 30-bed hospital;
2. Mobile Dispensary;
3. Residential School for Tribal Boys;
4. Fair Price Shopping Complex;
5. Vivekananda Vanavāsī Yuba Prashikshan Kendra—Residential Training Centre for the tribal youth—to build up a task force of spirited and rightly motivated young tribal boys with patriotic fervour dedicated to the cause of tribal emancipation. It has arranged to give training to the youth in (a) Agriculture, Horticulture, (b) Sericulture, Beekeeping, (c) Bamboo work, (d) Carpentry, (e) Tailoring, (f) Teaching, (g) Nursing and First Aid. It was also proposed to introduce the following trades among the students of the neighbouring area : (a) chalk-stick,

7. ibid.

8. ibid., p. 109.

blackboard paint making, (b) bakery and dairy farming, (c) press job and weaving, (d) terracotta and belmetal work, and (e) incense-making and soap-making. It was also proposed to develop an 'Urja Udayan' in the base-camp as a demonstration centre for all non-conventional sources of energy such as solar energy, etc. The Ramakrishna Mission also runs several service centres inside Abujhmarh.[9]

Programme for implementing the Vedantic Concept of Socialism

This programme shows how the Ramakrishna Mission works to materialize the Vedantic concept of socialism through efforts to elevate the backward and neglected classes. The greatest emphasis in these schemes is on recreating human beings by making him to manifest all his latent capacities. With this elevation automatically privileges do break down, inequalities are also eliminated. With emphasis on religious education the character and potentiality of the youth forces are being built up, they are being made self-reliant, creative, energetic, work-minded, in a word dynamic, who are the main resource for building up a just society free of privileges—a society in which continuous efforts are made to realize economic prosperity and development on an equal basis, and in which nobody is deprived from the benefits of growth and development.

In Swami Vivekananda's scheme we find that there is an attempt to breakdown the dichotomy between urban and rural societies. They are to be equally developed, just as individuals low or high are to be equally elevated and uplifted. Swamiji was convinced that Vedantic socialism could establish a just society by eliminating inequalities through social action based on Vedantic spirit of unity of the universe. And this is being worked out slowly but steadily by the efforts of the Ramakrishna Mission.

Many satellite organizations are also working with the same ideas side by side with the Ramakrishna Mission to make Swamiji's dream real. To mention a few names only : Vivekananda

---

9. 'Ramakrishna Mission's Involvement in Bastar' by S. Chatterjee in *Abujhmarh Rural Development Project Souvenir*—published by the Ramakrishna Mission Vivekananda Ashrama, Raipur, p. 184.

Society, Howrah Ramakrishna-Vivekananda Ashrama; the educational complexes at Itachuna, district Hooghly, West Bengal, under the Prabuddha Bhārat Saṅgha; the Ramakrishna Ashrama at Nimpith, Sundarban, district 24 Parganas, West Bengal. There are thousands of such societies spread all over the country. The Ramakrishna-Sarada Mission also has undertaken similar activities in Shillya, district Burdwan, where the majority population is Muslim; in Thakurpukur, district Medinipur; in Amtala, district South 24 Parganas, for the elevation of the rural poor. We have not here mentioned the relief activities of the Mission, under which also various constructive activities such as 'own your own house' scheme in the rural areas of West Bengal, Gujarat and South India and other areas, have been undertaken. Vivekananda believed that a revolution grows and today it is in the process of growing in the rural and tribal India where in certain parts already the face of the country has radically changed. The process of this growth is steady and sure. Many of the young generation will live to see the full impact of Vivekananda's ideas revolutionizing Indian society after its own fashion, when Vedantic socialism will be a reality.

CHAPTER 30

Education : An Instrument of Social Revolution

The role of education in giving a re-mould to the society must have to be discussed in any treatise on social revolutions since reconstruction of society is impracticable without reconstructing the human beings who constitute the society. As we all know, human society is never static, it is always extremely a dynamic phenomenon. This is so because the components of society, viz., the human beings are themselves extremely dynamic. They are themselves changing, evolving, not of course physically today, but mentally and spiritually all the time. Evolution means radical transformation in human elements and to suit this transformation society must also change radically.

This is one way of looking at things, but there is another way also. According to this second view, the social formation depends on its economic basis, i.e., the mode of production. The mode of production determines the social, political and spiritual processes in the life of the society. When there is a change in the base, there is change in the superstructure standing on it. But the change in the economic base is caused by men. Karl Marx, to whom the credit of formulating this theory goes, himself said, while criticizing Feuerbach : 'The materialist doctrine that men are products of circumstances . . . and therefore changes in men are the products of other circumstances, forgets that it is men who change circumstances.' Obviously therefore upon education depends the way the human beings will mould the economic base of the society.

Social transformation in a desirable way or social reconstruction in a planned manner is the aim of all the social philosophers and active social reformers.

To understand the role of education in social transformation, it is necessary to understand the social change process.

There are two popular theories of social change : (1) revolutionary theory, and (2) evolutionary theory.

(1) Revolution as an instrument of social transformation has become very popular in the modern world. Its chief instrument is violence, i.e., brute force. In order to overthrow a regime of exploitation and injustice, it is considered an indispensable instrument for the have-nots to use. The process is political since the aim of such revolutions is to capture the State power by the revolutionary party or the revolutionary leaders.

(2) Evolutionary theorists advocate the growth of the new social order from within the existing society. It means that the process is a time-consuming one. Since germination it passes through several stages until there is the final culmination in the form of completely a new social order. It is not a political process since the immediate aim is not to capture State power but to change the men who compose the society. Thus in the evolutionary process education is the chief instrument of social revolution. James Mill and his illustrious son John Stuart Mill upheld that the great organ of social change at the modern time was education. Mill wrote to Gustov D'Eich on 14th September 1839, 'No Good seed is lost; it takes root and springs up somewhere.'

Swami Vivekananda, the nineteenth century Indian stalwart, boldly rejected the political method. He firmly believed that politics, the invention of Graeco-Roman civilization, has failed to deliver the goods, it has failed as an agency of human welfare. His study of the western civilization and history made him thoroughly convinced of that. He saw clearly that the pursuit of State even for a noble cause turns out after some time to be a naked pursuit of personal power, when the ambitious politicians place his selfish interest above the interests of the people and the nation. The tragedy of the French Revolution was an eye opener to him. The revolutionary slogans ended in the establishment of worst form of tyranny. He saw also how democracy became a mere myth under imperialism. Hence Swami Vivekananda placed a naked sword between himself and politics and declared that 'I will have nothing to do with the nonsense of politics.'

His chief instrument was neo-Vedanta, a philosophy that was

born in the forests in the hoary past but was remodelled by him to include science and every thought that was noble, positive and creative in the modern world.

He reduced, as we have seen earlier, the abstruse Vedanta philosophy into two basic principles :

I. Divinity of Man;

II. Essential Spirituality of Life.

Two corollaries, as we have seen, follow immediately.

I. That every state, every society, every religion should be based on the recognition of this all-powerful presence latent in man.

II. That in order to be fruitful all human interests must be guided and controlled according to the ultimate idea of spirituality of life.

Truly, if every individual, every living being has the same inherent divinity, then they have the same potentiality to be great and good. Hence it follows logically that the same rights, the same opportunities must be granted to all, it must be a privilege-free society and for that matter a class-less society. The aim is to help every individual in unfolding his divine potentialities. This is therefore a sort of spiritual socialism that Vivekananda speaks of . But in this spiritual socialism secular interest are not to be neglected, since the distinction between spiritual and secular disappears when we come to Vedanta. Thus Vedanta made practical has a social revolutionary impact, since Vedanta strikes at the very root of privileges.

How to make this spiritual socialism work? Is it an utopia? Certainly not. But certainly its method is not the political method, capturing State power. That can never be in the nature of things. This lack of a political programme has made many people in this country and outside, specially in China and Russia, as seen previously, to ascribe Vivekananda's socialism as an utopia. He was, in their estimate, a romantic socialist with no scientific basis. But those who have gone deep into his thoughts know that to Vivekananda anything without workability had no value. He said, 'An ounce of practice is more important than tons of theories.'[1]

Vivekananda was all his life an ardent student of history.

1. Romain Rolland—*Life of Vivekananda*, p. 290.

History—to be precise, Indian history revealed to him an alternative to the political method. He saw that throughout her long and chequered history in India politics was never an active agent of moulding society. In a significant passage in his remarkable sociological treatise *Modern India*, Vivekananda says, we quote it again—'Such changes revolutionizing society have been happening in India again and again, only in this country they have been effected in the name of religion . . . . The Chārvāka, the Jaina, the Buddhist, Śaṅkara, Rāmānuja, Kabīr, Nānak, Chaitanya, the Brāhmo Samāj, the Ārya Samāj—of all these and similar other sects, the wave of religion, foaming, thundering, surging, breaks in the front, while in the rear follows the filling-up of social wants. . . . What could have saved Indian society from the ponderous burden of omnifarious ritualistic ceremonialism, with its animal and other sacrifices, which all but crushed the very life out of it, except the Jaina revolution, which took its strong stand exclusively on chaste morals and philosophical truth? Or without the Buddhist revolution what would have delivered the suffering millions of the lower classes from the violent tyrannies of the influential higher castes?'[2]

Vivekananda uses the term 'revolution' as a suffix to the two great religious movements of India—Jainism and Buddhism—in order to indicate the nature of their impact on our social life. Thus in his system of thought the criterion of a revolution is its 'impact' and not the instrument used to implement it. Violent means does not necessarily make a social change 'revolutionary'. The term industrial revolution was used in this sense. Thus in Vivekananda's thought the popular dichotomy between 'revolution' and 'evolution' breaks down.

The social phenomenon as it has manifested itself in Indian history through the ages, as we known already, has revealed two distinct phases of a revolution taking place :

1. First, a spiritual and moral revolution.
2. Second, social revolutions destroying the system of privileges and class-relations. The second revolution always came behind the first as it was the fruit of the first one.

In this historical process of revolution developing through

2. *C. W.*, IV, p. 462.

two different stages education of the masses was the prime factor. The life-giving, soul-stirring preachings of the religious leaders were spread among the masses. Their preachings mostly sought to impress upon the masses the essential equality of all men. And it is obvious that when privileges were broken, the priests were overthrown with their voluminous scriptures and caste-injunctions. The doors of general education were thrown open to the masses. Knowledge was no longer the exclusive possession of the handful upper castes. Spread of knowledge brought culture to them which helped to form high degree of skill in them and the result was manifestation of creative ability in every field of life, art and craft, music, cultivation of sciences, and even in creation of economic prosperity. That is how the Buddhist period in Indian history became a golden age.

Of course society can never be in a state of static equilibrium, not even in the optimum position. Very soon there happens deviation, the forces of privilege-making always were there trying to gain upperhand and it gains upperhand some day. History proceeds through constant clashes between these two forces—forces of privilege-making and the forces trying to break down privileges. According to Vivekananda, priestcraft is a privilege-making force, while true religion is a privilege-breaking force. Religious education is therefore so much important for privilege-breaking, for eradicading the evil of priestcraft.

Thus Vivekananda's concept of revolution is deeply rooted in a comprehensive philosophy, a sound world view, viz., Vedanta which is in conformity with modern science also. According to Vivekananda, 'Art, science, and religion are but three different ways of expressing a single truth.'[3] Vivekananda's concept of revolution was also deeply rooted in history. While paying his homage to history he has paid homage to 'Reason' also. It is a historical theory as well as a rational one.

We have seen already in the modern world Vivekananda's voice is not a lone voice against politics. Karl Jaspers, the well-known existentialist philosopher, has pleaded for a supra-political approach to the problems of the day as the only way out of the great crisis that the world is facing today. And many other stalwarts

3. ibid., I, 'Introduction', p. xvi.

in the West in this century, e.g., Bertrand Russell, Romain Rolland, Pitirim Sorokin, Arnold Toynbee have joined their voices in the same tune. With the threat of a nuclear war looming large upon us, even the Soviet thinker E. Petrovitch Chelishev has subscribed to the view that the way out is to be found in the teachings of Ramakrishna and Vivekananda. And it is interesting to note that the Soviet poet Valentine Sidorov in a poem on Vivekananda has talked of a more fundamental revolution that is yet to dawn to liberate mankind. From what he has written it appears that he was, talking of a supra-political revolution.

The main reason behind Vivekananda's ruthless censure of the political method was that politics degrades man. He noticed that in the working of the various political system of the contemporary world. Even in a democracy, the manner in which votes are manipulated, was described by him as robbery in day-time.[4] He was convinced that no good could be done to society by degrading man. If the men are degraded, the purpose of a revolution is defeated. Hence he laid supreme importance on man-making which could be accomplished with the help of education based on religion. He said, 'We want a man-making education, a man-making religion.'

He was convinced through his historical studies that the future belonged to the common man, the masses, the labouring people. In a prophetic manner, as we have seen above, he said—'... the upper classes of India, do you think you are alive? ... You merge yourselves in the void and disappear, and let New India arise in your place. Let her arise—out of the peasant's cottage . . . out of the huts of the fisherman, the cobbler, and the sweeper. . . . Let her emanate from the factory, from the marts, and from markets.'[5] He was the only nineteenth century thinker who wanted the leadership to grow from the masses. He had no faith in the upper class elites, 'they are more dead than alive'—he said. He foresaw that they would attempt to thrive on the misery of the people and taking advantage of their ignorance would monopolize power. Hence he laid his faith on the masses only and declared, 'India's only hope lies in the masses.'

And he was quite sure that the solution of the problem of the

---

4. ibid., V, p. 462.

5. ibid., VII, pp. 326-27.

masses was 'education'. '... they have many and grave problems, but none that are not to be solved by that magic word "education".'[6] 'Education, education and education alone', he said emphatically.

Therefore he chalked out a programme of mass education and it was thoroughly a concrete programme. He has not only stated the goals but also the means and the manner of execution of the plan. His chief aim was to awaken the masses. He wanted to accomplish this with the message of the Vedanta, the message that every one has the same potentiality to be great and good. And for this purpose he wanted to organize the youth, the self-sacrificing youth.

Elaborating his plan to Swami Akhandananda, a brother disciple, he wrote, 'Our mission is for the destitute, the poor, and the illiterate peasantry and labouring classes', and again, 'Teach some boys and girls of the peasant classes, the rudiments of learning and infuse a number of ideas into their brains. Afterwards the peasants of each village will collect funds and have one of these in their villages.'

'One must raise oneself by one's own exertion, we help them to help themselves.' He believed that emancipation cannot be achieved as a free-gift from the upper classes, it must be self-won.

Elaborating the plan he again says :

'The only service to be done for our lower classes is to give them education, to give them back their lost individuality.'[7] No other thinker has ever emphasized this— restoring the lost individuality of the masses. It was very important for a scheme of emancipation of the masses by themselves. Next 'My plans are to reach these masses of India. We have to follow the plan laid down by our ancestors, that is to bring all the ideals slowly down among the masses. Raise them slowly up, raise them to equality.'[8]

Vivekananda has for this purpose laid great emphasis on religion, since religion makes a man out of an animal. P. Sorokin emphatically said the same thing to make a man a man and not a bundle of flesh, religion was absolutely necessary. A modernist would look upon this idea with sneer but without knowing that the way they shut out their minds as soon as they hear the word

---

6. ibid., V, p. 231. 7. ibid., p. 149. 8. ibid., III, p. 247.

'Religion' does not reflect scientific attitude. But to Vivekananda religion was the very core of education. He wanted to take education to every door. If a ploughman's boy cannot come to education, why not meet him at the plough, why not meet a labourer at the factory, meet every toiler just wherever he is? Go along with him like a shadow. He wanted to teach them orally through magic lanterns, maps, globes, etc., i.e., audio-visual aids. But religion was to be taught first and then other things, astronomy, geography, etc., and a little technical education. He told his disciples : 'Go and advise them how to improve their own condition, and make them comprehend the sublime truths of the Shastras, by presenting them in a lucid and popular way. Impress upon their minds that they have the same right to religion as the Brahmins. Initiate all, even down to the Chaṇḍālas, in these fiery Mantras.'[9] Here we find he wanted to strike a blow to the privileges of Brahmins as regards monopolization of knowledge.

Above all he emphasized character building. 'The education that does not bring out strength of character, a spirit of philanthropy, and the courage of a lion—is it worth the name', he asked. 'We want that education by which character is framed, strength of mind is increased, the intellect is expanded and by which one can stand on one's own feet.'

He was convinced that the enlightened masses, composed of individuals with strong character, courage and manliness will do the rest to revolutionize the society.

He had no political programme, but that does not mean that he had no workable revolutionary programme. To find whether his programme is workable a visit to Narendrapur and the Lokaśikṣā Pariṣad will make it clear how it is working in 1400 villages. In many of these villages today there is no unemployment, no illiteracy.

The master architect has given us the plan, now it is our responsibility to work it out. To have a revolutionized society, education must be made the weapon and it must be a man-making education.

Vivekananda was a revolutionary par excellence. He has given us a revolutionary idea of revolution itself and finally a revolutionary concept of education.

---

9. ibid., VIII, pp. 307-08.

CHAPTER 31

Vivekananda and the Socio-Economic and Cultural Transformations in Modern India

I

SOCIO-ECONOMIC AND CULTURAL CONDITIONS IN THE NINETEENTH CENTURY

The socio-economic and cultural transformations that we see in present-day India germinated much earlier. In the first chapter we have discussed the cultural shocks that India received as a result of its contact with the West and the consequent chaos in the cultural field. We have also discussed the socio-economic disruptions and political turmoil that took place in the country at the time. We have taken an account of the reform movements of the period as well. The reformers considered British rule as a blessing. As a result their philosophical and socio-economic views could not convince the people about their efficacy in the matter of solving their problems and removing their suffering, much of which was caused by the exploitation of the imperialist foreign rulers.

With the spread of English education in this country there emerged a new intellectual class, who were cut off from the intellectual and cultural traditions of India and was wedded to the new western traditions of intellectualism that was born out of the European revolutions of eighteenth-nieneteenth centuries (1780-1830) in the West, viz., the bourgeois intellectualism bedrocked on materialism. The hollow intellectualism did not appeal to Vivekananda, then a young boy with a searching spirit, since it failed to satisfy his deeper urges. Herein lies the deficiency of this intellectualism—it cannot satisfy the deeper urges of the human spirit since it totally ignores the human soul. This hollow intellectualism in the name of rationalism has once again gained ground in free India. And once again a cultural confusion prevails in the fierd.

Ramakrishna and his fiery message : At this moment appeared Ramakrishna, who brought young Naren face to face with the challenge that old India held out for the modern man. Ramakrishna was aparently ignorant of the burning questions of the day having been brought up in the spiritual traditions of ancient India. But, as described by Rabindranath,[1] 'The diverse course of worship from varied springs of fulfilment mingled into his meditations and the manifold revelation of the joy of the Infinite gave form to a shrine of unity to him.' In this shrine of unity were reconciled, as Naren discovered, all the conflicting ideas of the period—Science and Religion, Reason and Faith, Secularism and Spirituality, Values ancient and modern.

His fiery message '*Jīva* is Shiva' was a bold message with the potentiality to revolutionize the human society for if each soul is potentially divine (or is Shiva) then everyone high or low has the same potentiality to become great and good and hence everyone should be given the same opportunities to manifest his latent capacities. In a society based on this idea, everyone would enjoy the same human rights and for that matter it would be a privilege-free society which is the goal of socialism. Hence, Vivekananda discovered in this fiery message of Vedanta a fiery gospel of a social revolution.

Vivekananda's direct experiences of the economic crisis under foreign rule:

After the passing away of his master Vivekananda traversed through the length and breadth of India. We have also seen that already. This was the time when the country was experiencing the worst economic crisis ever known in history. As a result of the revenue and fiscal policy of the British the country was engulfed by a series of devastating famines since 1770 till 1900. And as a wandering monk he actually lived with the peasants, cobblers, sweepers, factory workers and tribals—with men and women

1. *Prabuddha Bhārata*—February, 1936.

who toil in order to earn a morsel of food. Thus he was an eye-witness to their burning problems—their privations, miseries, oppression and hunger. He saw clearly that those that produce the wealth of the country, and build up civilizations did not get even the fruits of their own labour. 'With a soul on fire' he made a futile bid to awaken the princes and the elites—both of the old and of the new schools, to their duties towards the masses. But very soon he realized that the upper classes were 'more dead than alive'. It dawned upon him that the landed aristrocracy along with the priests were responsible for the ruthless exploitation of the masses. Hence he realized that India's only hope lied in the masses.

Colonial Rule : Its Consequences : A Call for Freedom Struggle: Vivekananda realized also that the colonial dominance was not only responsible for national oppression in general, but that it was also the main obstacle to the material and cultural development of India, it was the main cause for the monstrous poverty of the Indian masses. Hence he gave a call to the people for fighting against the menace of colonial rule and attaining emancipation from its clutches.

Essential Unity of India : His direct contact with the masses led Vivekananda to realize the essential unity of the people of India in the midst of endless varieties. But to Karl Marx as seen earlier, India was a country of disunity and superstition.

So far as the analysis of the socio-economic conditions are concerned, both Marx and Vivekananda uphold that feudalism (aristocracy in Vivekananda's terms) and British imperialism were the root cause of the backwardness and the poverty of India. Marxian analysis of the economic conditions in pre-British days pinpointed the stagnation of the system.[2] Vivekananda's analysis revealed the efficiency of the system in sustaining a flourshing foreign trade that brought wealth and prosperity to the country.[3] But at the same time he was convinced that the wealth went to enrich the aristocracy only and did not benefit the toiling masses. Hence a change in the system was inevitably called for.[4]

As we all know the appalling conditions of the masses led

2. *The Statesman*—25 April 1989, article by A. Bose.

3. *C. W.*, VII, p. 357. 4. ibid., p. 359.

Vivekananda to decide to attend the Parliament of Religions at Chicago in 1893, a world forum, on behalf of the 'poor and the people'[5] to find a way out for their deliverance from poverty.

Meeting with the West : *Challenge of Science* : Setting his foot on the western soil he was face to face with the challenge of science which had exploded many of the religious dogmas and doctrines known in the West. Accepting the challenge he showed their compatibility in Vedanta as we have seen already. He preached that religion and science point to the same thing, viz., the unity of the universe, only the language of science at the time differed from that of religion. And he predicted that the day was not far off when science would speak in the same language—the language of religion.[6] Today his prediction has come true. Science today has come to meet religion.

Amaury de Riencourt, a French scholar, in a recent book writes, 'What concerns us now . . . is the outstanding cultural phenomena of our time—contemporary physics finding a more congenial metaphysical extension in the mystical vision of the orient than in the blurred vision of occidental metaphysics.'[7] And Erwin Schrödinger who is immensely equipped from a scientific view point to formulate the synthesis finds plenty of support for the basic Vedantic vision in modern science.[8]

Religion is an aid to Science : Thus in an age of science today religion has become an indispensable aid for having a true scientific vision of the universe. This was envisaged by Vivekananda long ago. Thus the nineteenth century intellectualism based on mechanistic view of science has lost the support of science today. It is a matter of great regret that Indian intelligentsia still affirms its allegiance to this exploded dogma regarding science.

His second visit to the West completely disillusioned Vivekananda of the glamour of the prosperity of the West, and of its false democracy as he was this time face to face with 'the brutal face' of western imperialism which made him full of 'rapatious hatred'.[9] He saw that the West was virtually sitting on

5. Romain Rolland—*Life of Vivekananda* (fifth edition).
6. *C. W.*, V, p. 53.
7. A. de Riencourt—*The Eye of Shiva*, p. 171.
8. ibid., p. 169.
9. Romain Rolland—*Life of Vivekananda*, p. 149.

a volcano, the eruption could take place any day and felt that the political slogans of the West, viz., Rights, Liberty, Equality, etc., were mere meaningless high-sounding words carrying no convictions. He showed how Vedanta stood as the broad-base for lasting harmony between varieties of peoples and races, culture and religions and ideologies. He emphasized that 'The one essential attitude for all people was the affirmation of their substantive divinity not as background philosophy or theory but as a living, immediately relevant facts.'

Vivekananda gave a call of unity—'Unity of every Indian man and woman, unity of hundred different tongues and the hundred thousand gods springing from the same religious centre. . . . Unity within the vast ocean of all religious thoughts.'[10] This call stirred the depths of India and brought a real awakening of the nation. Opposing the reformers he refused to admit the superiority of the western thought and culture and reprimanded those who were in favour of imitating the West. These calls brought a new awareness of the glories of the cultural heritage of this ancient land and thereby brought a sense of national identity and aroused a keen aspiration to vindicate India's prestige as a free nation.

Socialism in the horizon : During his two visits to the West Vivekananda mixed with the elites as well as the labourers and the farmers, studied carefully the labour-capital strifes in the West, studied the socialist movements and met the social revolutionaries. He realized that socialism was inevitable. Welcoming the inevitable he declared, 'I am a Socialist'.

Deficiencies of Socialism : *Socialism and Religion* :

But at the same time he was aware of the deficiencies of socialism. He said, 'I am a socialist not because I think it is a perfect system, but half a loaf is better than no bread.'[11] As he saw clearly that only strong, fearless men not prone to corruption, selfless persons, real brave heroes, who could make supreme sacrifice for the happiness of many, for the good of many, could ensure stability for socialism. In view of the vital role of religion in man-making, it was necessary, he felt, to bedrock socialism on

---

10. ibid., p. 289.

11. Letters to Mary Hale, *C. W.*, VI, p. 381.

religion. Western socialism wedded to materialism was not, therefore, Vivekananda's watchword. Today in the socialistic countries the leaders of thought are coming to realize this, without man-making socialism, the world would turn out to be a myth.

Vivekananda was convinced, however, that socialism was inevitably to come even to India. In a prophetic manner he revealed his vision of new India in which the men who toil to earn a morsel of food would be at the helm of affairs.[12]

Apostle of Nationalism : *Apostle of Socialism in India* :

Thus Vivekananda was the apostle of nationalism, he was also the apostle of socialism in this country. His socialism was based on religion as well as on democracy and individual liberty. He was against any kind of despotism and totalitarianism. The world is today gradually moving towards such a type of socialism, i.e., democratic socialism as conceived by Vivekananda. This is evident in recent history.

National liberation of India and Social liberation of the masses :

It is especially to be noted that to Vivekananda the nation was not composed of a handful of elites, but of the masses who lived on the fruits of their own toils. Hence he considered that national liberation of India and the social liberation of the masses were mutually related. Without the social liberation of the masses, national liberation would be meaningless. 'No amount of politics', he said, 'would be of any avail unless the masses in India are once more well educated, well fed and well cared for. . . . If we want to regenerate India, we must work for them.'

Father of modern materialism in India :

According to Benoy Kumar Sarkar, 'Vivekananda was the father of modern materialism in India.' It sounds anachronistic no doubt since Vivekananda along with his master Sri Ramakrishna was the greatest preacher of religion in the modern era. But at the same time to them the artificial barrier between the secular and

12. *C. W.*, VII, p. 327.

the spiritual broke down since to them everything was in Brahman and everything was divine. Hence, Vivekananda unhesitatingly championed the common man's right to happiness in this world. And for that matter he whole-heartedly wanted industrialization and modernization of technology, improvement of agriculture with the aid of science.

Adopting appropriate technologies necessary : Of course, he had a very practical insight into the matter and he had therefore never spoken of adopting any and every technological devices. It dawned upon him in no time with his stay in America that the factor—endowments in the two countries were different, hence what was appropriate in the American situation was not so for the Indian. Hence when he talked of technological modernization he never meant blind imitation of the West. What he meant was that India was to adopt only those devices which were suitable for the Indian situation.

Champion of Science :

He talked also of the need for teaching science and developing scientific attitude. In the resolutions adopted at the meeting convened to form the Ramakrishna Mission on May 1, 1897, it was stated that one of the methods of action of the Mission would be to train men so as to make them competent to teach such knowledge or sciences as are conducive to the material and spiritual welfare of the masses.[13]

Vivekananda's Concept of Development : According to Vivekananda, development consists of the following three components :

I. Availability of the basic amenities of life including food, shelter, education, job, protection and health measures, etc.

II. Existence of a sense of self-esteem among the people, i.e., sense among the people of their distinctive worth to themselves, to others, to the world. Only men who are conscious of their own worth can advance. Similarly, only a nation having a sense of its own distinctive worth can advance. Vivekananda laid great emphasis on this in his *Modern India*.[14]

III. Existence in a country of 'freedom' in a comprehensive

13. *Resolutions of the Ramakrishna Mission.*

14. *C. W.*, IV.

sense of the term. In his opinion the term 'freedom' has not only the political, economic or social connotations, but it means also spiritual freedom—liberation or *mukti* from every type of bondage.

Thus Vivekananda spoke of the three core values which are the essence of development. Astonishingly, modern development economists like Todaro, Seers and Goulet have recently spoken of the very same core values as essential components of development. They have spoken of (1) self-sustenance, (2) self-esteem and (3) freedom in a comprehensive sense of the term (not only political, economic, social freedom but also spiritual freedom).

This shows how advanced Vivekananda was in his ideas regarding development and growth.

Solution of the Problem of Poverty :

For the solution of the problem of poverty Vivekananda spoke of both (1) attitudinal changes (i.e., change of attitudes) and (2) institutional changes as well as of strengthening the economic resources.

Change of Attitudes : Regarding the first one he pointed out that our society had deviated from the religious injunctions which laid down fourfold goals of life, viz., *dharma*, *artha*, *kāma* and *mokṣa*, for persons of different inclinations. 'But the present Hindu society', he observed, 'is organized for spiritual men and hopelessly crushes everybody else.' '*Dharma*', he explained, 'is that, which makes man to seek happiness in this world and it is impelling man day and night to turn after and work of happiness.' He was convinced that 'the fall of our country, of which we hear so much spoken is due to the utter want of this *dharma*'. He emphasized that a whole nation cannot follow the goal of *mokṣa* which was meant for a few only who had enjoyed the world and realized its hollowness. '. . . in all India', he said, 'there are say, a hundred thousand really spiritual men and women. Now for the spiritualization of these, must three hundred millions be sunk in savagery and starvation? Why should any one starve? Material civilization, nay, even luxury is necessary to create work for the poor.'

It is evident from the above that Vivekananda suggested a thorough change in our attitude to life. He wanted the existing attitude of apathy to material prosperity to go. This change of attitude, according to Vivekananda, was one of the most important factors promoting economic and other developments.

Institutional changes :

Secondly, Vivekananda considered that some institutional changes in society were imperative for economic development. Uprooting of the priests as well as the landed aristrocracy was considered by him very much necessary. Putting the measures in a package he said in a nutshell—'No priestcraft, no social tyranny, more bread, more opportunities for everybody.' He was convinced that unless privileges were exterminated and economic security guaranteed political liberty would be meaningless. No one excepting Vivekananda thought at the time transfer of power to the upper classes would still mean slavery of the people. Uplift and emancipation of the masses was to him an absolute necessity for the eradication of poverty and for economic development.

Not Religion but Priestcraft—a menace to Economic Development :

Here it must be made clear that he did not regard religion as a menace to economic development but definitely considered priestcraft a menace in this respect. 'Priestcraft', he said, 'is in its nature cruel and heartless. That is why religion goes down where priestcraft arises.' Thus the dichotomy he introduced between religion and priestcraft is very significant for practical sociology. In his opinion religion was a privilege-breaking force while priestcraft was privilege-making. 'All beings', said he, 'great or small, are equally manifestation of God, the difference is only in the manifestation. . . . The work of Advaita is to break down all these privileges.'[15]

Vedanta—Dynamics of Activism : According to Vivekananda, religion is a dynamic force since one of its messages is 'work is worship' or Karma-Yoga. Vedanta particularly as interpreted by Vivekananda is a dynamics of activism. He was convinced that

15. Quoted by Romain Rolland—*Life of Vivekanadna*, p. 111.

the preaching of the philosophy would infuse the people with a valuable activism which would find expression in dynamic actions leading to radical reforms, growth and development.

The Role of Education :

For uplifting the masses he considered education the most effective instrument. For eradication of the social evils, like prejudices and superstitions, to him, no other instrument was more effective. For building up of productive efficiency nothing else again was more effective. Hence in education Vivekananda saw the panacea for all social evils and the most important means of promoting self-reliance for growth, development and prosperity.

The Socio-Economic goals of India were set by Vivekananda :

From what has been discussed above it is clear that in the socio-economic sphere Vivekananda set all the goals that are being pursued by India today—the social emancipation of the masses, emancipation of women, their economic freedom—freedom from poverty and unemployment, and of economic development through industrialization and modernization of agriculture through the application of science.

Vivekananda's Socialism was not an Utopia :

Yet he is criticized today in certain quarters as an utopian socialist, a mere dreamer, a meek humanist with no bold programme for organizing the masses for a revolution.[16]

Here it must be remembered that Vivekananda was not a socialist of the Marxist brand whose instrument is the political instrument of violent revolution for capturing power for a revolutionary leader or a party. Vivekananda had no faith in the political instrument. From his intense study of history, he was convinced that politics, an instrument discovered by the Graeco-Roman civilization, had failed to deliver the goods, it had failed as an agency of human welfare. Always a keen student of history with deep insight he saw the tragedy of the French Revolution and other such violent outbreaks, he saw clearly that the purpose of these revolutions were defeated.

---

16. *Prabuddha Bhārata*, January, 1990.

Political Revolutions : Not the Instrument of Vedantic Socialism :

In view of the above, Vivekananda had no intention to lead the blind masses to rise in a bloody revolution in order that a revolutionary leader or leaders forming a party, belonging to the upper class elites, be installed into power. He wrote to Swami Akhandananda, a brother disciple who was working among the masses to educate a peasant boy in every village and hand over the responsibility of the village under his charge. This is how the leadership was to grow from the masses who were to do the rest under this leadership. He believed that emancipation was something which could only be self-won, it would never come as a free-gift from the upper classes.

His positive plan for the masses :

Hence he had a positive plan for the masses but that was naturally different from the one that was prescribed by the believers in politics. His revolutionary plan was to make the leadership grow from the masses. It was more radical in meaning and implications than the one which would make the masses to be blindly led like hordes of dumb cattles to commit acts of senseless violence so that some upper class persons posing to be revolutionary leaders could be installed in power.

An Alternative Instrument found in Indian History :

Vivekananda had the courage to reject politics without caring for the sneers of the world and also had the genius to discover in history an alternative instrument. His study of history revealed to him the important fact that politics was never an active instrument in fostering social changes in India. Social changes in India always came in the trail of a spiritual upheaval—after a spiritual and moral revolution. Citing examples from history he said—'What could have saved Indian society from the ponderous burden of omnifarious ritualistic ceremonialism with its animal and other sacrifices, which all but crushed the very life out of it, except the Jaina revolution, which took its strong stand exclusively on chaste morals and philosophical truths? Or without the Buddhist revolution what would have delivered the suffering millions of the lower classes from the violent tyrannies of the influential higher castes?'

Vivekananda pays homage to 'History' and 'Reason':

Thus when he talked of moral and spiritual revolutions preceding social revolution he was paying homage to both 'History' and 'Reason'. Violent convulsions, he was convinced, cannot bring a true revolution, a root and branch reform, since violence breeds violence. Hence according to Vivekananda, violence retards revolution. True revolution grow, evolve, its momentum gradually accentuates until it fully manifested. The bloodless revolution that is manifest in the Soviet Union at this very moment bears evidence to this view of Vivekananda. Noticing the vital role of religion in generating such a revolution in India he advised his compatriots—'Before flooding India with socialistic or political ideas deluge the country with religious ideas.' Thus Vivekananda has spoken of a more fundamental revolution than an eruption of violence committed on a mass-scale to capture State power. Capturing of State power does not mean necessarily that the masses get their due rights. Many of the socialistic countries which have overthrown communist regime bears evidence to this fact. In order to have their due rights, they have to work out the revolution themselves with their own leadership.

To give them this strength, their individuality, education is a prior necessity. This education must be based on religion to make them strong, fearless individuals capable of working out their own emancipation. Such was the plan of Vivekananda.

Vivekananda wanted to awaken the masses with the fiery message of Vedanta—'Aye! let every man and woman, without respect of caste or birth, weakness or strength, hear and learn that behind the strong and the weak, behind the high and the low, behind everyone, there is the infinite soul, assuring the infinite possibility and infinite capacity of all to become great and good. . . . Stand up, assert yourself, proclaim the god within you, do not deny him.' He called upon the youth to go from door to door and preach this fiery gospel and awaken the masses.

Thus in a nutshell Vivekananda's aim was to awaken the

masses and educate them and make them stand on their own feet and the masses were to do the rest.

Politics, he knew further, degrades man, and he was absolutely convinced that no good could be done to anyone by degrading man, no society dominated by degraded men could ever make any progress.

Hence he wanted a man-making education, a man-making religion. All his efforts were devoted to serve this single purpose.

A Revolutionary Programme for a Social Revolution :

Thus it is evident he was not a mere dreamer, an utopian thinker, a passive humanist with only pious wishes, he had a bold and a positive programme. It was a revolutionary programme in terms of his concept of a true revolution. And his programme for educating the masses was the only such programme at the time.

The Indian leaders after Vivekananda in their over-zealousness to win freedom through quick process made politics their chief instrument against the warning of Vivekananda and thus showed the poisonous tree which now as a hydraheaded monster has spread its fangs all over our national life and eating up its vitals. All the healthy values have been thrown into the air by the unscrupulous politicians and the goal of uplifting the masses have receded farthest back. The politicians are interested only in grabbing power and to hang on to it at any cost. Politics today have degraded into factionalism and healthy politics based on socio-economic issues seems to have disappeared. Political leaders aiming to grab power are fomenting regionalism, communalism, fundamentalism, so on and so forth all divisive forces.

The Cultural Field in Free India :

In the cultural field the denationalized intellectuals are refusing to be modern by clinging to the nineteenth century mechanistic, materialistic and deterministic view of science and they are dominating over the Indian cultural field today. They hold with disdain the folk expression of culture in India. One of them even dares to say that 'present-day Hinduism is vulgar'. It must be borne in mind that the illiterates are not always culturally blank, since they have their education from the book of life. This dominant intellectuals dare to dictate cultural norms to the masses, often to persons with profound wisdom acquired at the battlefield of life. This attempt to dictate norms by persons who are not themselves above cultural confusions have sometimes created confusion worst confounded. To be brief, this must be realized by all concerned that it is not possible to have progress and development in the true sense of the term when spiritual values are neglected, when the soul of man is totally ignored.

Prophets of Human Emancipation :

Even the Soviet thinkers today value the wholesome messages of Ramakrishna and Vivekananda which elevate man and seek to ensure peace, progress and amity among nations. E. P. Chelishev, for example, said significantly in an interview in Kolkata in 1986—'We do not look upon Vivekananda and his mentor Ramakrishna Paramahamsa to be mere religious leaders that they are the prophets of human emancipation of equality and human progress. ...The message of Ramakrishna and Vivekananda, is the message of peace, amity and world brotherhood. That message can indicate the path of survival in the fear-stricken world of today.' 'There is no doubt', he adds, 'that their message was necessary and relevant in India and the world of their time, but it is still more necessary in the present Indian context and in the context of the contemporary world.'

Concluding Remarks : If we want today to tide over the present Indian crisis—the cultural confusion—the political crisis which is threatening our national integration—the economic crisis in the form of heavy burden of poverty and unemployment—the pressing problem of social liberation of the masses—we would do well to look back to the thoughts of this prophet of human emancipation who showed us the path to a new life at the wake of the present century, yet who is as relevant today as ever. He was truly a modern man who paid homage equally to science, history and reason and to the invaluable spirituality of mankind. His plan of action, his positive programme deserves serious attention today in view of the fact that he gave topmost priority to education of the masses and their social emancipation, on solving the problem of poverty and illiteracy and not on political slogans and dogmas.

Part - VIII
Epilogue

CHAPTER 32

Epilogue :

The Philosophy of a Perpetual Revolution

This book is not claimed to be a complete treatise on Vivekananda's historical, social, political, scientific and economic ideas, although it can be claimed, in my opinion, as a fairly comprehensive study. I believe no complete treatise on this subject-matter is ever possible since Vivekananda has given his views very briefly almost in the form of *Sūtra*s or aphorisms and since the *Sūtra*s may be interpreted and re-interpreted, in the process new light is always to be found. He gave his ideas much in advance and the full significance of these is not yet revealed to us. As we have stated earlier, Vivekananda was not a mere political philosopher or a sociologist or a historian or an economist. He came to us in a new era and in his attempt to do so he has spelled out new ideas, significant for human progress, enriching at the same time the arena of political, economic and sociological thoughts of mankind.

In the process of pouring out his above mentioned ideas he has successfully integrated the conflicting political ideologies of Individualism and Socialism, Socialism and Democracy, Religion and Socialism, Nationalism and Internationalism, National Unity and the Rights of Heterogenous Ethnic and Cultural Groups within the 'nation body', just as he has succeeded in integrating Science and Mysticism, Reason and Faith in the philosophical field. In the economic field also he has integrated successfully (1) the idea of industrialization with modern large-scale technique and small-scale operations, the idea which is accepted today but at the time was considered incompatible, and (2) the idea of capitalistic development with social management by workers, so on and so forth.

All these integrations and harmonizations in different fields of human knowledge have opened up a new vista, a new outlook, a new way of thinking, which paved the way to the emergence of a new era. He has also radically re-interpreted the concepts of 'Society', 'Evolution', 'Liberty', 'Equality', all basic concepts in political science and sociology. And above all, he has revolutionized the concept of 'Revolution' itself giving it a new meaning and new dimension.

Surely when the significance of his integratel philosophy based on science, history and Vedanta will be fully realized by mankind, the world will be revolutionized. Actually, to revolutionize the world, to usher in a new era, to uplift man to a new height, that he invented. From the recent developments in various countries, mostly socialistic, it seems today that a social order based on socialism, individual liberty and religion, in which all human interests will be guided and controlled according to the idea of man's ultimate spiritual destiny, as conceived by Vivekananda, is not impossible. That towards approaching that social order man is struggling hard is apparent from the emergence of the concept of Euro-Communism, struggle for democracy in China, East Germany, Hungary and Poland, the emergence of the concepts of *Glasnost* and *Perestroika* in the Soviet Union, and above all by the appreciation of Vivekananda in the communist countries. The integrated system that man is aspiring for was given a concrete shape in his philosophy by Vivekananda. However may the present-day conflicts and confusion cloud our judgement to-day—this is certain as has been pointed out by Marie Louise Burke that 'When a prophet of the stature of Vivekananda inaugurates a work on the visible level—a tremendous creative current is set in motion at a deeper, more subtle levels, which nothing can stop from becoming a historical force.'[1] And it should be borne in mind that (to use the words of Marie Louise Burke once more) 'The spiritual stature of Swami Vivekananda was such that he could not live among men

---

1. Marie Louise Burke—*Swami Vivekananda : His Second Visit to the West*, p. 671.

without altering, enriching and illuminating the very texture of world thought.'[2] His thoughts are working imperceptibly, as a fertilizing force. This is surely to produce fruits in due time. The world will be revolutionized. The impact of his thought on thinkers like Sorokin, Toynbee, Aldous Huxley, Isherwood and many others in the western world, as well as on the Soviet and Chinese thinkers in the Socialist countries is an indication towards the fact that the world texture of thought is getting revolutionized under his impact.

Before we close, it must be noted also that, as pointed out by Sister Nivedita, 'His prime concern was vindication of Humanity, never abandoned, never weakened, always rising to new heights of defence of the undefended, of the chivalry for the weak.'[3] It is also to be noted that although Vivekananda rejected politics as an instrument of social change, he laid down some of the most healthy political ideas, significant for the redemption of the rights of the oppressed, the weak, the downtrodden. His constructive ideas on organic growth, immanent change, involution, stand out in bold contrast with the mechanical and destructive views of revolutions so popular today with its antecedents of violence, bloodshed and imposed externalistic institutional changes which have proved disastrous in the socialist countries of today.

Vivekananda's view on revolution, a thoroughly revolutionary one, was given boldly to a world which while realizing the failure of their political method and of the method of externalistic institutional changes, was groping in darkness in search of an alternative. He had the genius, vision and boldness to give the world that alternative revealed in Indian history. This historically proved method was actually a method of revolution growing from the root causing a change in the human element and manifesting as a multi-dimensional revolution covering spiritual, mortal, political, social and economic fields. It is a process of growth and development.

Romain Rolland most aptly chose to call Vivekananda a 'living hymn of work'. His philosophy, in truth, is a Dynamics of Action. It is also a rousing call to awaken our souls, 'to recreate

2. ibid., p. 611.
3. Sister Nivedita—*The Master As I Saw Him*, p. 171.

our Beings' and to set on to build the 'City of Mankind' or 'One World' on the basis of his Universal-Science-Religion, or true Scientific Socialism. And we are reminded of Chelishev's statement once again in this respect : 'The message of Ramakrishna and Vivekananda, is the message of peace, amity and world-brotherhood. That message can indicate the path of survival in the fear-striken world of today. I personally feel that in the context of the present nuclear menace which is gradually engulfing the earth, it is very much essential to disseminate the message of Ramakrishna-Vivekananda all over the world. There is no doubt that their message was necessary and relevant in India and the world of their times, but it is still more necessary and relevant in the present-day Indian context of the contemporary world.'[4]

Vivekananda believed : 'What will save Europe (West) is the religion of the Upanishads', i.e., Vedanta. Hence he chastised us for our tendency to imitate blindly the West in which materialism and hollow intellectualism was the order of the day. In an oft-quoted passage in his *Modern India* he reminds us that the tendency of imitation is a symptom of lost self-esteem and a sure way to degradation. 'India!', he says, 'With this mere echoing of others, with these base imitation of others, with this dependence on others, this slavish weakness, . . . wouldst thou, with these provisions only, scale the highest pinnacle of civilization and greatness? Wouldst thou attain, by means of thy disgraceful cowardice, that freedom deserved only by the brave and the heroic? O India! Forget not that the ideal of thy womanhood is Sītā, Sāvitrī, Damayantī; forget not that the God thou worshippest is the great Ascetic of ascetics the all-renouncing Śaṅkara, the Lord of Umā . . . forget not that thou art born as a sacrifice to the mother's altar . . . forget not that the lower classes, the ignorant, the poor, the illiterate, the cobbler, the sweeper, are thy flesh and blood, thy brothers. Thou brave one, be bold, take courage, be proud that you are an Indian. . . .'[5]

This is a reminder of the national worth of India and a rousing call to us to take pride in it and feel self-esteem. This is a reminder of the necessity of freeing ourselves from the shackles

4. *Prabuddha Bhārata*—January 1989.

5. *C. W.*, IV, p. 479.

of slave mentality, poverty and caste rigidity. It also reminds us the fact of our national unity and strength and the necessity of granting human rights to the underprivileged in our society. It is a nationalistic call for unity and a socialistic call to attain equality.

Finally, as we have already seen in the chapter on 'Law, Liberty and Equality' in Part IV, Vivekananda emphasized total freedom and emancipation of man from every kind of servitude. 'All nature is crying', he points out, 'through all the atoms for one thing—its perfect freedom.'[6] 'That is our life:', he adds, 'one universal cry for freedom . . . . Have you marked the eternal cry going on through the ages in every breast?'[7] Pointing out that freedom includes political as well as spiritual freedom, he says, 'The Greek sought political liberty, the Hindu has sought spititual liberty. Both are one-sided. . . . To care only for spiritual liberty and not for social liberty is a defect but the opposite is still a greater defect. Liberty of both soul and body is to be striven for.'[8]

Vivekananda's concept of development, mentioned earlier, is a comprehensive concept of development, based on the three universal core values : (a) self-sustenance, (b) self-esteem, and (c) freedom. Without self-sustenance, no development is conceivable, without self-esteem no development can be sustained and without freedom no development is meaningful.

'It is freedom in every way', says Vivekananda, 'that is, advance towards *mukti* is the worthiest gain of man. To advance oneself towards freedom, physical, mental and spiritual, and help others to do so is the supreme prize of man.' Hence says E. P. Chelishev, speaking about Vivekananda and his master Sri Ramakrishna (as we have noted earlier also), 'That is why we do not consider Vivekananda and his mentor Ramakrishna Paramahamsa to be mere religious leaders as they are commonly looked upon. They are far greater than that, they are prophets of human emncipation, of equality and of human progress.' In the activities of the Ramakrishna Mission today we notice a gradual growth of a Vedantic social revolution as conceived by Vivekananda. These activities have only one single aim—elevation of the masses.

In the end we would like to remind the reader what a group of

---

6. ibid., p. 241. 7. ibid., p. 240. 8. ibid., VI, p. 86.

Vedanta student of Vivekananda said about him after his death : 'Vivekananda has shaken the world with his sublime thoughts and they shall echo through the halls of time until time shall be no more.'[9] And surely for eternal time to come in every society in every country, the weak, the poor, the oppressed, the downtrodden, the backward and outcast will turn to his fiery message for the redemption of their just rights. For who else did put forward their case in a better manner than he when he said— 'Aye, let every man and woman and child, without respect of caste or birth, weakness or strength, hear and learn that behind the strong and the weak, behind the high and the low, behind everyone, there is that Infinite Soul, assuring the infinite possibility and capacity to become great and good. Let us proclaim to every soul : Arise, awake and stop not till the goal is reached. . . . Stand up, assert yourself, proclaim the God within you, do not deny Him.' This is a call to free the sleeping forces of the enslaved spirit of man, a call to reawaken God in man, a call to recreate our beings. Surely it is a message which shall 'echo through the halls of time untill time shall be no more'.

---

9. Marie Louise Burke—*Swami Vivekananda : His Second Visit to the West*, p. 602.